THE ASHKENAZIC JEWS:
A Slavo-Turkic People In Search Of A Jewish Identity

Paul Wexler

Slavica Publishers, Inc.

Slavica publishes a wide variety of scholarly books and textbooks on the languages, peoples, literatures, cultures, history, etc. of the former USSR and Eastern Europe. For a complete catalog of books and journals from Slavica, with prices and ordering information, write to:

Slavica Publishers, Inc.
PO Box 14388
Columbus, Ohio 43214

ISBN: 0-89357-241-1.

Typesetting by WordByte, P.O.B. 3102, Beer-Sheva, Israel.

Printed in the United States of America.

CONTENTS

"A peculiarity of higher cultures is their ability to undergo renaiscence. Either the same people or a people coming later assumes in part a former culture as its own—through a sort of right of inheritance or awe" (Burckhardt 1910:67).

"I will believe the goal of the present lines [establishing the Khazar origins of the Ashkenazic Jews] to have been achieved if I succeed through these studies in drawing attention to the facts and in inspiring new investigations, which ought to find a fruitful field especially in the domain of philology" (von Kutschera 1910:271).

"Cyrus has been dead for two and a half millennia and was forgotten by his own people though remembered with honor by others. The defenders of Masada too were forgotten by their own people, and remembered only by a renegade who wrote for a foreign audience in a foreign language. Yet both have been recovered, reinterpreted and given a new role in the modern history of their respective nations" (Lewis 1975:41).

"The pleasure of discovery in science derives not only from the satisfaction of new explanations but also, if not more so, from fresh (and often more difficult) puzzles that the novel solutions generate" (Gould 1991:27).

ACKNOWLEDGEMENTS

The need for rare materials necessitated research in many farflung libraries; I am grateful to the staffs of the following institutions for their assistance: Brandeis and Harvard Universities, the Universities of Helsinki, Pennsylvania, and Tel-Aviv, the Annenberg Institute and the Academy of Natural History (both in Philadelphia), the Institut des Études Slaves (Paris), and, in London, the School of Slavonic and East European Studies, the Francisk Skaryna Byelorussian Library and the British Library (where Brad Sabin Hill of the Oriental and India Collection called my attention to important materials). I also thank Milica Mihailović (Jevrejski istorijski muzej, Belgrade) for providing otherwise inaccessible materials, Eli Ben-Raphael, Julia Horvath and Yakov Shavit (all of Tel-Aviv University) for their comments on the manuscript at various stages, and Gregory Livshits (also Tel-Aviv University) for his informative discussions of Jewish genetic research.

The Lucius N. Littauer Foundation of New York generously provided a subvention to cover the costs of typesetting; this help is greatly appreciated.

Paul Wexler
Department of Linguistics
Tel-Aviv University
Tel-Aviv, Israel 69978

1

THE CRUX OF THE MATTER: BORROWING OR INHERITANCE?

The student of Jewish history is struck by the extent to which each Jewish diaspora community displays numerous cultural, religious and linguistic similarities with the surrounding non-Jewish majority. In their Palestinian homeland as well Jews shared numerous folkways with neighboring non-Jews. The intriguing question is how the Jews acquired non-Jewish practices both inside and outside of Palestine. Three explanations come to mind:

(a) Practices of non-Jewish origin could have been diffused to the Jews through contact with the non-Jewish donors. In this case we can say that non-Jewish customs have been "*borrowed* by Jews".

(b) Practices of non-Jewish origin could have found their way to the Jewish community when such large numbers of non-Jews converted to Judaism that they came to constitute the majority of the Jewish community. Such customs would be more accurately defined as "*inherited* from the non-Jewish peoples" that came to constitute the bulk of the new "Jewish" populations.

(c) Two societies could develop similar or even identical cultural patterns independently.

While most cases of shared features prove to be the result of drift from one community to another, the possibility of diffusion resulting from incorporation (or perintegration) of peoples, or chance similarities, must always be checked.

The modern-day descendants of the Iberian (or Sephardic) Jews who settled in the Ottoman Empire after their expulsions from the Iberian Peninsula between 1492 and 1498 illustrate the problems in choosing between explanations (a), (b) and (c). The Iberian Jews who settled in the Eastern Mediterranean reveal a penetrating Balkan imprint in their folklore, religious practices and language alongside a diminished Hispanic cultural component (see Armistead and Silverman 1982). Balkanization could be due either to the diffusion of cultural practices from the coterritorial indigenous groups to the Iberian Jewish emigrés, or to the amalgamation of the indigenous Greek- and Slavic-speaking Jews with the Sephardic emigrés who were soon to constitute the majority in most Balkan Jewish communities. Almost all the Greek and Slavic Jews became Spanish-speaking, but prior to losing their original linguistic identity, they could have transmitted a considerable part of their culture to the Iberian Jewish refugees. The perintegration of the three Jewish groups is probably the cause for the dramatic Balkanization of the Spanish Jews.

All students of the Germano-Slavic (or Ashkenazic) Jews identify two major European non-Jewish imprints on this group: a German imprint is allegedly manifested in the very use of Yiddish (which most speakers and non-native observors believe is a form of German), in religious practices and folkways of German origin; a Slavic imprint is manifested in a wealth of basic vocabulary items in Yiddish from Polish, Belorussian and Ukrainian, and to a lesser extent, from Czech, Slovak and Russian, as well as in religious practices and folkways of Slavic origin. Most historians and linguists are convinced that Yiddish is a form of German that was spoken by the Ashkenazic Jews who first took form in the 9th–10th centuries when French and possibly Italian Jewish settlers reached the southwest German lands (and marginally Bavaria); some three hundred years later, the Ashkenazic Jews began migrating eastward across the German lands into monolingual Slavic Europe.

If the Askhenazic Jews are viewed as the direct descendants of Mediterranean Jews who reached the German lands primarily through France, then it is clear why most scholars readily assumed that the German and Slavic practices of the Ashkenazic Jews were due to *borrowing from the non-Jews,* and that the German impact on the Ashkenazic Jews predated the Slavic impact by several centuries.

I find these descriptions of early Jewish settlement history and the genetic classification of Yiddish unconvincing. In the present book I will explore the proposition that the Ashkenazic Jewish community—the largest by far of all the so-called Jewish communities in history—owes its formation mainly to the mergers of majority non-Jewish proselyte populations with tiny ethnic Palestinian Jewish populations; such mergers probably began in various parts of Asia Minor and Europe even before the Christian era. The major component in the Ashkenazic ethnogenesis is Slavic; minor strains came from European Turkic, Germanic, Hungarian, Balkan and possibly heterogeneous Western Asian (Anatolian) ethnic groups. In other words, the numerous non-Jewish practices in Ashkenazic religious and folk culture are best considered as an *inheritance* from the non-Jewish converts to Judaism who constituted the European Jewish communities, rather than as a *borrowing* by Palestinian Jews and their descendants from non-Jews.

In this case, it is not so much the Jews who became "acculturated" to their non-Jewish neighbors, but the latter whose pagan, Christian and even occasionally Muslim traditions became the basis of Jewish culture and religion outside of Palestine. Eventually, at the beginning of the second millennium of our era, these traditions gradually underwent "Judaization"—a conscious search for biblical and talmudic precedents for non-Jewish practices and beliefs and for Hebraisms and Judeo-Aramaisms with which to enrich the Yiddish language.[1] I believe I can show that much of the Palestinian Jewish religion and folkways attested among the Ashkenazic Jews was actually borrowed by the latter as recently as seven or eight hundred years ago from Palestinian Jewish literary sources—the Bible and Talmud—and was not an uninterrupted inheritance brought over from Palestine. The process of Judaization has rarely been documented in the scholarly literature. But the near-total absence of Hebrew documents or tombstone inscriptions from Europe and the ignorance of the Talmud in Europe until the close of the first millennium make the claim of late Judaization very compelling.

Hence, the reader should keep in mind that I will employ the term "Jew" in any historical period other than the Old Palestinian or early diaspora periods to denote an ethnically non-Palestinian Jew who came to identify himself as ultimately of Old Palestinian Jewish origin. This will eliminate the need for quotation marks with the word Jew or a cumbersome unfamiliar terminology.

Three interesting implications emerge from my hypothesis of Ashkenazic Jewish origins: (a) Ashkenazic Jewish customs which have an Old Palestinian Jewish precedent might owe their present existence or popularity to contact with European pagan and Christian cultures, i.e., some customs may originally be of non-Jewish origin. (b) European Jewish folkways and religious practices can enable us to reconstruct, even if only *grosso modo,* pagan and early Christian practices, primarily among the Slavs. (c) Finally, my hypothesis prompts a radical reassessment of Jewish migrational patterns in Europe in the first millennium.

The present book has four purposes: to identify (a) the non-Jewish populations that espoused some form of Judaism in Asia Minor and Europe and (b) Slavic practices among the Ashkenazic Jews; (c) to define the mechanics of Judaization, and (d) to ascertain the carriers of the Jewish literary and religious tradition which served as the basis of the Judaization program in the Germano-Slavic lands in the Middle Ages.

The uniqueness of the Ashkenazic experience emerges in greater clarity if we compare the diffusion of non-Jewish practices and linguistic influences among the Ashkenazic "Jews" and Old Palestinian Jews. The Palestinian Jewish communities absorbed numerous non-Jewish speakers of Indo-European and Afro-Asiatic languages in the course of centuries, but there is no conclusive evidence that non-Jewish ethnic groups ever constituted the majority of the Jewish population in Palestine at any time in history. Hence, non-Jewish religious practices and folkways recorded in the Bible and Talmud which are attested among Jews can be regarded as "borrowings". Even the several thousand Greek words used in Palestinian Mishnaic Hebrew and Judeo-Aramaic (see Lieberman 1942) would not require the assumption of widescale conversion of Greeks or others to Judaism.

In their linguistic behavior, the Ashkenazic Jews differ strikingly from their alleged Palestinian Jewish ancestors. While the Ashkenazic Jews have made use of the Hebrew and Judeo-Aramaic religious literature with its significant Greek imprint only since the 10th or 11th century, they never spoke the two indigenous Jewish languages, Hebrew or Judeo-Aramaic. Hebrew became obsolete as a spoken language in Palestine in about the 3rd century A.D.; Aramaic died out shortly thereafter in Europe, and lingered on in Palestine until the Arab invasion in the 7th century, though it still serves as a spoken language among Jews in Kurdish ethnic territory (split between Azerbajdzhan, Iran, Iraq, Syria and Turkey) and among Christians there and in scattered villages of Arab Syria, southeastern Turkey and Khuzistan (Iran). Instead, the European, Asian and African Jews invented "Judaized" variants of non-Jewish spoken languages, e.g., of Romance (Italian, French, Spanish, etc.), Slavic, Berber, to name a few. Finally, the Jewish languages that developed outside of Palestine have (a) minimal borrowings from Hebrew or Judeo-Aramaic (though Yiddish, in certain periods, dramatically increases this component), and (b) a meager Greek component, most of which is not found in the rich Greek corpus of Hebrew and Judeo-Aramaic.

A variety of linguistic, ethnographic and demographic facts could alert us to the possibility that the Palestinian Jews who emigrated to Europe at the beginning of the Christian era may not have contributed significantly to the ethnogenesis of the European Jewries. I believe that the most convincing evidence for any hypothesis of discontinuity and change in the ethnic identification of the Jews must first and foremost be sought in the Jewish languages, since it is only in the domain of language that we have the tools to distinguish borrowings from nativisms with relative certainty. The linguistic data can also explain some hitherto unresolved demographic mysteries relating to early Ashkenazic settlement in Europe.

But not all linguistic facts are equally persuasive. For example, the massive Greek *lexical* impact on Hebrew and Judeo-Aramaic that I noted above need not be evidence of largescale conversion of Greeks to Judaism. Words travel easily from language to language—and their diffusion certainly does not require the hypothesis of proselytism. No more so than the sharing of pagan art models or religious symbols and practices by Jews and Christians would establish a pagan ethnic component in the two communities, due to the ease of transfer and recalibration of the models (see Bickerman 1986). Furthermore, Turks and Iranians borrowed enormous quantities from Arabic, their liturgical language, without absorbing masses of Arabs; the borrowing process was performed through the Koran and classical Arabic literature—and not by contact with speakers of living Arabic.

In contrast to vocabulary, the grammar and sound system of a language are less amenable to transfer across language boundaries. So it behooves us to determine the origin of the grammars and sound systems of the languages spoken and written by the Ashkenazic Jews. From time immemorial, they spoke Yiddish—while they wrote either Hebrew or Yiddish. In the last century, Hebrew acquired a spoken function and eventually surpassed Yiddish in number of users. As I have demonstrated elsewhere (1990f, 1991b), Yiddish—in contrast to its massive German vocabulary—has a native Slavic syntax and sound system—and thus must be classified as a Slavic language; Yiddish has a Slavic syntax and phonology since it was a form of the West Slavic language Sorbian which became re-lexified to High German. A massive German lexicon cannot make Yiddish German, just as the massive Franco-Latin component of Modern English gives no grounds for declaring that English has ceased to be a Germanic language, and has moved over to the Romance camp.

Since no child learned Hebrew at birth between the 3rd and early 20th century, obviously Yiddish speakers could have had no access to "native" Hebrew syntactic and phonological patterns. They could only have produced a written or spoken Hebrew that used the syntax and phonology of their native language—Yiddish. In other words, the almost exclusively written Hebrew of the Ashkenazic Jews, known to us since the late Middle Ages, and its successor, revived Modern Hebrew in

Israel, is in reality Slavic Yiddish with a borrowed Biblical and Mishnaic Hebrew lexicon inserted in place of the customary Yiddish lexicon. Among non-Ashkenazic Jews, a similar process of creating "Hebrew" took place, so that the written Hebrew of the Arab Jews is best defined as a dialect of Arabic, etc.; all non-Slavic recensions of Hebrew disappeared in the 20th century with the rise of Modern Israeli Hebrew. Thus, Medieval and Modern Hebrew cannot be regarded as an heir to Old Palestinian Hebrew, which was a Semitic language (related to Judeo-Aramaic, Arabic and Akkadian, etc.).

Hence, throughout their long history, the Ashkenazic Jews have made use of three distinctive languages: (a) two lexically distinct variants of Yiddish—one with a predominantly German vocabulary, one with a predominantly Hebrew vocabulary—which are mutually unintelligible (hence, I will regard them as separate "languages") and (b) Judaized (or "Ashkenazic") German. Of the two distinctive languages of the Ashkenazic Jews, Yiddish and Hebrew (i.e., medieval written, modern written and spoken Israeli Hebrew) are Slavic; this fact provides the key to the ethnic origins of the Ashkenazic Jews. Judaized or "Ashkenazic" German was a form of German spoken and/or written by some German Jews intermittently from the Middle Ages to the end of the last century which had a few deviations from Christian German vocabulary and phonology and a borrowed Hebrew lexical component.

As I suggested above, it is not just two of the three languages of the Ashkenazic Jews that are Slavic in origin. The bulk of their religious practices and folkways also prove to be of Slavic origin. The evidence is therefore mounting that the Ashkenazic Jews may be in the main *ethnic Slavs*—who could have swelled the ranks of the tiny Jewish communities in the Caspian-Black Sea area, the Balkans or in the mixed Germano- and Hungaro-Slavic lands. In all these areas, smaller numbers of Turkic groups became submerged within the majority Slavic populations; some linguistic evidence from Yiddish also points to contact between Jews and Turks. Hence, we are entitled to speak of a mainly "Slavo-Turkic" ethnic basis of the Ashkenazic Jews. I will show below that many of the Old Palestinian Jewish religious practices and folkways of the Ashkenazic Jews—as well as a large number of Hebraisms in Yiddish—are the result of later borrowing (i.e., Judaization) rather than uninterrupted inheritance of a colloquial Old Hebrew and an Old Palestinian religion and culture.

There is no point attempting to build my claim exclusively or primarily on historical testimony, no matter how varied, since the latter is speculative and fragmentary. However, against the background of linguistic and ethnographic data, the historical evidence may acquire a new significance; hence, I will reexamine it in some detail (in chapter 6 below).

The reader should keep in mind that this book is making two entirely separate claims:

(a) That it is imperative to try to distinguish between the borrowing and the inheritance of religious practices and folkways; the best way to do so is by the use of linguistic data.

(b) That an investigation of Ashkenazic religion and culture suggests that most of the elements are either recognizably or demonstrably of non-Jewish origin, specifically, that they were *inherited* primarily from the Slavs, the major contributors to the Ashkenazic ethnogenesis, and not later *borrowings* from the Slavs. Other minor ethnic components, e.g., Romance, Greek, Turkic and Germanic, and perhaps others, were also acquired in the Balkans and the Germano-Slavic lands and possibly even in Asia Minor.

Neither claim has been pursued with any rigor up to now. The first claim is not likely to arouse objection, though some readers (especially historians) may balk at the suggestion that linguistics could provide the best means to reconstruct prehistory and poorly documented early history. The second claim will arouse debate because it represents a radical departure from "received tradition" and because it takes both Jewish and Slavic historical and linguistic research into largely uncharted waters.

The hypothesis of a non-Jewish origin for the two languages of the Ashkenazic Jews—Yiddish and Medieval/Modern Hebrew—has never been raised by linguists. Until my attempt to derive Yiddish from Sorbian in 1991, only a handful of linguists had even spoken of Sorbs, Polabians (two major Slavic groups coterritorial with Germans) and Jews in the same breath, but without questioning the Germanic classification of Yiddish (the earliest mention of *sorbin, -m* 'Sorbs' in a Jewish document is found in *Josippon*, a 10th-century anonymous Hebrew historical narrative from southern Italy; only German sources provide an earlier attestation of this ethnonym). For example, the Yiddishist Max Weinreich noted parallels between Sorbian and Ashkenazic folk culture (1924:170–1—see also chapter 5.2 below) and the Slavicist Roman Jakobson identified occasional Polabianisms in allegedly Czech Hebrew writings of the 10th–13th centuries (1957:2, 7); both of these scholars also displayed a keen interest in one another's disciplines (see Jakobson 1953; M.Weinreich 1956b). A lone ethnographer who took an independent interest in both Sorbs and Jews—but without proposing genetic or historic links between the two groups—was Richard Andree (1874, 1881).

The hypothesis of a non-Jewish origin for the Ashkenazic Jews that I am proposing here has almost never been raised before, either by historians or others. The few attempts to do so in the past have met with resounding criticism—and rightly so, since their authors were never able to furnish convincing evidence (most recently, in 1976, Arthur Koestler sought, unsuccessfully I believe, to establish the Turkic Khazar origins of the Ashkenazic Jews). The present study, in contrast, will offer detailed linguistic and ethnographic motivation for the hypothesis of a predominant *Slavo*-Turkic origin of the Ashkenazic Jews. Moreover, while Koestler placed the transformation of the Turkic Khazars into Ashkenazic Jews in the area between the Caspian and Black Seas, I will argue that the Balkans and the mixed Germano-Slavic lands were the major cradles of the Ashkenazic Jews and that the Turkic component was secondary to the Slavic component.

The book is not free of problems and imprecisions, in part because of its novelty, in part because of the paucity of historical documentation. The present study generates a host of new research questions, which I hope will be addressed jointly by linguists, ethnographers and historians of Jews and Slavs. I am aware that discussions of ethnic reconstruction and the origins of religious and superstitious practices often provoke emotional reactions; this is especially true when traditional views are being challenged. I came to my conclusions on the basis of studying the existing linguistic and non-linguistic data, without preconceived biases, and hope that they will be judged in a dispassionate atmosphere.

The reader who is sceptical about my claim that a Slavo-Turkic population underwent Judaization during the first millennium A.D. bears the burden of explaining how and why the alleged north European Ashkenazic descendants of the Palestinian Jews could have undergone the incontrovertibly intensive Slavicization that they did. Whatever the source of the Slavic component in Ashkenazic culture, religion and language, it deserves far more attention than scholars have given it heretofore.

The plan of this book is as follows:

In chapter 2 I will summarize the *traditional views of the origins of the diaspora Jews in general, and of the Jews in the Slavic lands in particular,* and motivate my dissatisfaction with these views.

In chapter 3 I will explore how the study of *Jewish languages* is an indispensable tool for historians by proposing new interpretations for known facts of early Jewish history and by widening the data base.

I will motivate the hypothesis that the Ashkenazic Jews are predominantly of Slavic, and secondarily of other Indo-European, Turkic and Palestinian, origins—*on the basis of linguistic evidence* in chapters 4 and 5, and *on the basis of Ashkenazic religious and folk practices* in chapter 5. The Slavic origins of many Jewish religious and folkloristic practices, as well as many of the Jewish terms for these practices, will be elaborated for the first time. Because the hypothesis proposed here is both novel and provocative, it is essential to present a wide variety of linguistic and ethnographic evidence. The data are meant to be illustrative rather than exhaustive.

In chapter 6 I will collect and assess in detail the evidence of *individual and group conversions to Judaism in Asia Minor and Europe* from around the time of Christ up to the beginning of the second millennium, with special attention to areas inhabited historically by Slavs. The major venues of conversion to Judaism corroborate the findings of chapters 4 and 5 that were based on linguistic and ethnographic data.

In chapter 7 I will examine *the inherited Palestinian Jewish patrimony of the Ashkenazic Jews* and define the phenomenon of *Judaization,* whereby originally Slavo-Turkic and other religious practices and folklore were reshaped according to Old Palestinian norms, and Yiddish was flooded with a host of Hebrew and Judeo-Aramaic borrowings. I will also explore the chronology of and motivations for Judaization.

In chapter 8 I will summarize my findings and offer *an agenda for future research.*

The present book brings together a dizzying array of peoples who are ordinarily not recognized as partners with the Jews in a common history: the partly Turkic Avars, the Iranian Scythians, the Magyars, Slavic tribes such as the Obodrites, Polabians and Sorbs,[2] and other Indo-European groups such as the Dacians, Illyrians and Phrygians. Along with these ethnic groups, the Eurasian landmass now thrusts up many new placenames in the face of the historian of the European Jews and Slavs, e.g., Aphrodisias and Čelarevo. I will identify historical figures and toponyms mentioned in the text that are apt to be unfamiliar to students of either Jewish or Slavic history.

In citing contemporary Hebrew names and references, I follow current Israeli pronunciation norms, but in citing Hebrew etyma, I may use an etymological notation (e.g., historical *ḥ*, *ṭ*, *q* and *ə* rather than modern *x*, *t*, *k* and *e*, respectively.) In examples transliterated or transcribed from non-Latin alphabets, I employ *j* for the front glide except in the case of Arabic, where *y* is traditionally used in this capacity, and *j* represents the consonant of English *Jew*.

2

THE ORIGINS OF THE DIASPORA JEWS: A REASSESSMENT OF THE TRADITIONAL VIEW

The concepts "Jew" and "Judaism" need little introduction. The average educated person who might falter in identifying ethnic groups such as the Druze, the Dinka or the Dogon would have no difficulty citing some fact about the Jews. He would probably readily respond that the contemporary Jews are in the main the direct descendants of the Palestinian Jews of biblical and talmudic times, that modern Judaism has evolved from Palestinian Judaism (the very religion widely believed to have contributed to the formation of Christianity and Islam), and that Modern Hebrew is a revived version of the Old Hebrew that had died out in Palestine around the 3rd century A.D.

Most of us also believe that the history of the Jews is characterized by a number of unique features. The Jewish people are said to be unique because they maintained their group identity for close to two millennia in the face of global dispersal and no common territorial base, retained their ancestral religion and culture more or less intact during the long period of "exile" that extended over some 1900 years, recreated an independent state in their original homeland (where only a trivial number of Jews had resided between the Islamic conquest and early 1950s), and successfully "revived" Hebrew, their ancestral language, which had lain dormant as a spoken language for close to two millennia. This at a time when other peoples that were never uprooted from their homelands could not achieve national independence (witness the Sorbs or Kurds), or resuscitate a language abandoned by most of its speakers (witness the Irish).

In assessing the impact of non-Jews on the Jews, most scholars make a sharp distinction between language and other domains. Scholars agree that the non-Jewish origins of the approximately two dozen Jewish languages, e.g., Yiddish, Judeo-Spanish, Judeo-Arabic, etc., attested across Europe, Africa and Asia, are so obvious that no demonstration is required. But they do not agree on the non-Jewish origins of the Jewish religion and folk cultures, or of the Jewish people itself. It should not come as a surprise if the latter proved to be of the same origins as the Jewish diaspora languages themselves.

Despite the many differences in genetic makeup that must separate the Old Palestinian Jews (as far as the facts can be reconstructed) and all the contemporary diaspora Jews, the latter continue to be regarded by and large as descendants of the Old Palestinian Jews. Most Jews and non-Jews also assert that the religion and folk culture of the north European Jews, while not visibly Palestinian in all their details, have incorporated only a modest number of largely insignificant non-Jewish features. I argue for an alternative to these asssertions about the origins of the Jews, their religion and folklore. Since there is no simple way to measure discontinuities in genetics, culture and religion, I will turn to the evidence of the Jewish languages. In language it is often easier than in other media to distinguish between two independent and unrelated phenomena, and two chronological or geographical variants of the same phenomenon.

The evidence provided by the Jewish languages strongly suggests that there is little basis for the claims that the contemporary Jews of Europe, Africa and Asia, as well as their religious practices and folklores, are "evolved forms" of the Palestinian Jews and their culture of two millennia ago. On the contrary, the contemporary Jews, like their religions and folk cultures, appear to be overwhelmingly of non-Jewish origin.

While the basis for my new hypothesis is generated by Jewish linguistic history, the latter alone cannot always provide full confirmation. I need to substantiate hypotheses generated by linguistics through independent channels—such as historical demography and settlement history, ethnography, folklore and religious practice, and even genetics. In short, there is an interlocking relationship between linguistics and other disciplines, in which the linguist often plays the role of *primus inter pares* 'first among equals'. This is so because only the linguist is in possession of the rich empirical material necessary to motivate any innovative hypotheses; but the results of the linguist's investigations can and should be checked against data derived from a cross-disciplinary search for new facts and interpretations. The present work will show how the varied linguistic and non-linguistic data, in part supplemented by knowledge of the approximate age of many contemporary Jewish religious practices, together can offer support for my hypothesis and refute the *opinio communalis* that the contemporary Jews are a people possessing an uninterrupted history of three and a half millennia—a chronological depth which would make the Jews possessors of one of the longest recorded histories of any people on earth.

In the present book I have chosen the north European or Ashkenazic Jews as the object of research since they constitute the overwhelming majority of the Jews in the world and research on their histories, cultures and languages is much further advanced than those of other Jewish communities. I have no doubt that linguistic evidence could enlighten us considerably about the early and pre-histories of the non-Ashkenazic Jews as well, and from time to time I will speak about these groups, in particular the Iberian (or Sephardic) Jews (who I believe are largely of Arab and Berber descent).

The present book makes two original contributions, pertaining both to methodology and to the findings themselves. In methodology, the originality lies in harnessing diverse linguistic and non-linguistic data for the first time in support of an innovative hypothesis.

The original findings are two:

(a) The Palestinian Jewish community that took root in Asia Minor, North Africa and southern Europe shortly before and after the destruction of the Second Temple in Jerusalem in 70 A.D. at the hands of the Romans succeeded in surviving as a group thanks to the incorporation of overwhelming numbers of indigenous non-Jews who repeatedly joined the Jewish fold all throughout the first millennium of this era. (I purposely use the ambiguous formulation "joined the Jewish fold" since I do not always have evidence concerning the nature of the association—formal conversion, or informal association with the Jewish community and its religious practices. In the discussions below, I will use the terms "convert" and "proselyte" for both types of association.)

Of all the non-Jewish ethnic strains that participated in the ethnogenesis of the contemporary north European, or Ashkenazic, Jews, the Slavo-Turkic strains stand out as the most significant.

(b) In order to appreciate why the Ashkenazic Jews now see themselves largely as descendants of the Old Palestinian Jews, it is expedient to break the history of the diaspora Ashkenazic Jews into two periods.

The first period extends from the founding of the first Ashkenazic Jewish diasporas (by the 6th century in the Balkan Slavic lands, and by the 9th century at the latest in the German and Germano-Slavic lands) through the first two centuries of the second millennium of our era. This was the time when the European Jews (i.e., both ethnic Palestinian and Eurasian converts) derived their languages, religious and folk patterns for the most part from the coterritorial pagans, Christians and Muslims.

In the second period, from about 1100, the Ashkenazic Jews started to define themselves and other Jewish groups in southern Europe, Africa and Asia (which also consisted of varying mixes of Jewish and non-Jewish stocks), as members of a single dispersed Jewish people which was heir to the Old Palestinian Jewish people. The Jewish descendants of the Slavs and others eventually subjected their beliefs and folkways to a process of Judaization.

In the case of folkways and religion, Judaization meant providing biblical or talmudic pedigrees or links; in the case of language, Judaization meant flooding Yiddish with a host of Hebrew loans, reshaping existing non-Hebrew vocabulary according to Hebrew models and extending Hebrew grammatical processes to non-Hebrew vocabulary. In the case of the community itself, Judaization meant the erection of barriers against Christianity, by discouraging proselytism, by fostering the ideal of the "purity of the race" and a growing infatuation with the belief in a Jewish people that had links to the Jews of biblical and talmudic Palestine.

Among some Ashkenazic Jews in the late 19th century, the process of replacing the Yiddish lexicon by Biblical Hebrew went so far that Yiddish came to be called "Modern Hebrew". While the extreme Judaization (i.e., "Hebraization") of Yiddish had taken place many times before in the past, this was the first time that a growing number of Ashkenazic Jews actually called for the "giving up" of their ancestral Yiddish in favor of spoken "Hebrew"—at least in their colonial Western Asian outpost in Palestine.

Parallel processes of Judaization existed in some south European and Afro-Asian Jewish communities as well, though not always in all domains. For example, intensive linguistic Judaization seems to be limited to the Germano-Slavic Jews. Thus, the illustrious Iberian Arab Jewish grammarian, Jicxak ben Josef ibn Barun, who flourished in Zaragoza around 1100, sought Arabic and Aramaic etymologies for native Hebrew words, just the reverse of the Judaization processes characteristic of Medieval Yiddish society, while his famous contemporary compatriot, Avraham ibn Ezra (c.1089–1164), described Hebrew as unadulterated Arabic and derived numerous Biblical Hebrew words from Arabic (Weil 1968:ii–ii). Medieval Karaites in the Near East transliterated the Hebrew Bible and liturgy in Arabic rather than Hebrew characters, perhaps as a means of expressing their separatism from non-Karaite (or Rabbanite) Jews (Khan 1992:170; see also examples in Hoerning 1889).

If they are Judaized artifacts of pagan, Christian and marginally Muslim origin, then European Jewish religious and folk cultures can hardly be the latest link on a long, unbroken chain of evolution leading back to Palestine. Much of the allegedly "Jewish" content of contemporary Jewish language and culture was not predominantly Jewish in origin. Moreover, between the "Jewish people in Old Palestine" and the "Jewish people of the 20th century" stands a very long period of history which witnessed the creation of many heterogeneous "Jewish peoples" consisting of various mixes of Jewish and non-Jewish ethnic groups.

As I will show in greater detail below, many scholars had already voiced some of these claims in the 19th century. For example, there is a wealth of studies of mass and individual conversions to Judaism in Europe, Africa and Asia in the first millennium, and of the history and evolution of non-Jewish folk culture and religion among the Jews (I am thinking of the research carried out since the 19th century primarily by Jewish scholars such as L.Blau, M.Brück, M.Gaster, T.H.Gaster, M. Grünbaum, M.Grunwald, M.Güdemann, F.S.Krauss [also a major contributor to Slavic ethnographic literature], A.Landau, J.Z.Lauterbach, N.Prilucki, A.Rappoport, I.Scheftelowitz and J.Trachtenberg).

In addition, the process of Judaization of religion and folk culture has been occasionally discussed in the literature, though the term itself never enjoyed wide circulation in this meaning (Weinryb appears to be the first to have used the term in my sense, to be sure, sparingly: 1974: 953). The term is also found in other meanings in the literature, e.g., Nadel used *judaizirung* to mean conversion to Judaism (1960:54), while for Blumenkranz, *judaïsation* denoted the replacement of Roman soldiers by Jews in medieval Christian illuminations of the crucifixion (1966b:102). For other writers, Judaization also denotes the espousal by non-Jews of selected Jewish practices or beliefs. The derivative "Judaizer" has a particularly long history reaching back to the Greco-Roman period. It either denoted a non-Jew who followed Jewish practices, or served as a negative epithet applied to one's adversaries, with no reference to Jewish content, e.g., Nestorius, the founder of the Christian sect of Nestorianism and the patriarch of Istanbul in the early 5th century, was so labeled by his opponents (Baron 1964:8; Kraabel 1982:464). In the 15th century, the label "Judaizers" was given to a heretical Christian group in Russia by their opponents, but was never employed by the group itself (H.Birnbaum 1985:8, fn 17).

The term "de(-)Judai(ci)zation" also enjoys limited popularity. Freund has used the term to denote the process by which the European Karaites institutionalized their split from rabbinic Judaism and declared themselves to be descended from Turkic (Khazar) tribes (1991; see also chapter 6, fn 3 below). I also used it to define the process whereby the Dutch Jewish descendants of the Marranos (Iberian Jews who converted to Catholicism between the late 14th and 15th centuries but clandestinely maintained elements of Judaism) replaced distinctive Jewish linguistic features in Marrano Portuguese and Spanish by standard Portuguese and Spanish elements respectively (Wexler 1987a; on the de-Judaization of Iraqi Jews in the Far East, see my 1983c). While the term "Hebraization" is not used to denote the receptivity of Yiddish to Hebrew, "de-Hebraization" has been used to denote the Soviet policy of eliminating Hebraisms in Soviet Yiddish that was initiated in the early 1930s (see Peltz 1985).

The hypothesis of a Slavo-Turkic component in the Ashkenazic ethnogenesis is both old and new: old in that the Slavic and Turkic Khazar theories have been in the public eye individually for the last century (though without adequate corroboration, see Renan 1883 on Slavic and von Kutschera 1910, Koestler 1976 on Turkic); new in that I am proposing *both* Slavic and Turkic components at the same time and suggesting that proselytes from these two groups probably outnumbered the ethnic Palestinian Jews throughout Eurasia. The Turkic converts to Judaism became largely submerged in the coterritorial Judaized Slavic majority—both in the Ponto-Caspian steppelands as well as in the Balkans and Central Europe.

The present book recasts the thesis expounded by Arthur Koestler in his *The Thirteenth tribe* (London 1976), that the Ashkenazic Jews—who constitute over 80% of the world's Jews today—descended largely from the Turkic Khazars who converted to Judaism *en masse* in the 8th century in the area between the Black and the Caspian Seas. Koestler assembled a host of (mainly unfounded) evidence, repeatedly voiced over the last century (see von Kutschera 1910 and Poljak 1951 and discussion of *pεsaḥ* in chapter 5.12 below). Arab reviewers of Koestler's book, such as Šaki 1981, acclaimed the book on the grounds that it denied the Jews any historical rights to settle in Palestine, and urged the Jews to return to Itil, the capital of the former Khazar kingdom (near modern Astraxan', Russia). Koestler was right about a Turkic component in the Ashkenazic ethnogenesis, but he was wrong on three important counts: (a) he overemphasized the role of the Turkic component—which was far less significant than that of the Slavic; (b) he located the Turko-Slavic ancestors of the Ashkenazic Jews in the Caucasus—whereas the evidence points to the Balkans and the mixed Germano-Slavic lands as the cradle of Ashkenazic Jewry; and (c) he ignored the tradition of conversion to Judaism that had begun in Asia Minor and Greece shortly before the birth of Christ, which was to contribute significantly to new Jewish peoples all over the world.

The significant role that the South and West Slavs (among the latter, specifically the Sorbs and Polabians) have played in the ethnogenesis of Ashkenazic Jewry and their language and culture is both overt and covert. At the same time the European Jews have been largely oblivious of their Slavic (and Turkic) roots for the last several hundred years and have felt no sense of loyalty to the peoples who spawned them. Nor have the latter usually recognized the Jews as kinfolk—no doubt because of religious hostility. Most contemporary Jews genuinely believe that they are descended from Palestinian Jews and that the heterogeneous forms of diaspora Judaism are evolutions of Old Palestinian Judaism. Unfortunately, there is no way of knowing how diaspora Jews defined themselves in the millennium prior to the escalation in the Judaization processes. The Slavic contribution to Jewish religious practice, and even to the linguistic behavior of the Ashkenazic Jews, was probably not immediately apparent to Jews in the second millennium of our era because of the cyclical processes of partial language shift and the intensity of Judaization processes. Yet, both Yiddish and Modern Israeli Hebrew (as opposed to Old Hebrew) are demonstrably both dialects of West Slavic. As the evidence for these two revolutionary claims was provided elsewhere (Wexler 1990f, 1991b), I will offer only a summary here (in chapters 3 and 4 below). The present book will use these linguistic findings to motivate the claim that the Ashkenazic Jews themselves, as well as their religion and folk culture, are largely of Slavic origin.[1]

Of course there once was a people known as Jews—or Hebrews, Israelites—whose historical national territory was on the southeastern shores of the Mediterranean Sea. But such large numbers of Palestinian Jews had been making their way abroad—to North Africa, Arabia, southern Europe and other parts of Western Asia—that by the time of the Roman conquest of Judea in 70 A.D., the overwhelming majority of Jews were residing outside of Palestine. Some of these Jewish diaspora communities were centuries old by the time of the Roman invasion.

Given the conditions of their dispersal, frequently tenuous links with their Palestinian homeland and the widespread ignorance of their original languages, Hebrew and Aramaic, it is not surprising to find that most of the Jews outside of Palestine assimilated to the coterritorial cultures, religions and languages, though Christianity, still retaining a marked Jewish tone in its early stages, ultimately became the dominant religion of the diaspora Jews, while Greek became the language of most

European, Western Asian and North African Jews in the first centuries of the Christian era.

The task of the researcher cannot be limited to explaining why the Old Palestinian Jewish immigrants to Europe nearly all disappeared. The fact is that millions of people today define themselves as Jews, and as such have become heirs to a Palestinian past; among the latter are many who practice forms of the Jewish religion. Hence, I will also need to explore the phenomenon of Judaization in detail. On the latter subject a number of new challenging questions suggest themselves. I will address some of these questions in the following chapters; others will have to be left for future study:

(a) Under what conditions and in what times and places did most Jews who left Palestine cease to identify themselves as Jews?

(b) Under what conditions and in what times and places did large numbers of non-Jews find Judaism an attractive religion? What were the ethnic origins and the relative weight of each group of proselytes? Could the diaspora Jews have survived as a distinct group without proselytizing?

(c) What was the nature of the "Judaism" that the proselytes espoused, and what was the nature of their membership in the Jewish fold?

(d) What mechanisms did the Jews develop to Judaize non-Jewish religions, folk cultures and languages? Were there significant differences among the diasporas? How did Judaization among the north European Jews change through time and space? Was contact with Jewish communities with a higher level of Jewish scholarship or the possession of a relatively larger percentage of ethnic Palestinian Jews prerequisites for the success of Judaization? What were the reasons for implementing Judaization? To what extent did Christian intolerance and persecution of the Jews contribute to this process? The widespread ignorance among the Ashkenazic Jews in all historical periods of the Slavic origins of their religion, folk cultures and languages is eloquent testimony to the success of the process of Judaization.

(e) How, when and where did separated groups of Judaized proselytes, of disparate ethnic and cultural origins, succeed in developing the now almost universally accepted notion of a single Jewish religion and people? Did the chronology of "nation building" differ in diverse areas? What was the role of non-Jews in formulating the notion of a Jewish people?

How did proselytes succeed in largely shedding their native ethnic identities when they joined the Jewish fold? To be sure, numerous "communal" differences remained to stamp a unique profile on each new "Jewish" diaspora community, see, e.g., Sephardic (Iberian) vs. Ashkenazic vs. Arab Jews, etc. Significantly, Jews have never been characterized as "full" vs. "partial" (except perhaps for the actual converts, but not their descendants, who often had an inferior status within the Jewish community).

(f) A very small vestigial north European Jewish diaspora population generated an enormous number of progeny by the beginning of the second millennium—in spite of the persecutions, mass conversions to Christianity and Islam (both voluntary and forced) and settlement upheavals that came in the wake of events such as the Crusades and the Black Death in Germany and neighboring Slavic lands. Could this population explosion have taken place in the absence of largescale proselytism?

(g) Many of the properties that allegedly establish the uniqueness of the Jews emerge as neither unique nor justified. I cited three examples above: the contemporary Jews are the direct descendants of the Old Palestinian Jews, contemporary Judaism—especially in its "orthodox" manifestations—represents an evolutionary stage of Old Palestinian Judaism,[2] and Modern Israeli Hebrew is a "revived" form of Old Palestinian Hebrew. The reasons for the widespread belief in these erroneous claims need to be uncovered.

(h) Are there parallels to Judaization among other cultures? Comparison with groups that lack a single territorial base (such as the European Romá or Gypsies), or with groups that have sought to reestablish links with their earlier, now abandoned traditions (such as the Welsh), or with groups that elected to establish links with someone else's patrimony (such as the Greeks or Cypriots) offer particular promise.

Considerable evidence has been available for some time now that might have prompted scholars to question the claim that the Old Palestinian Jews were the source of the bulk of the contemporary Ashkenazic Jews. Consider just two facts:

(a) Yiddish, like most other Jewish languages, uses non-Jewish terms to designate aspects of the Jewish religion, including the kosher food laws, the synagogue and elements of its internal architecture. Yet, it is counterintuitive to believe that Palestinian Jews who practiced the tenets of normative Judaism would want or need to accept originally non-Jewish terms to designate these and many other allegedly primeval

Palestinian Jewish concepts upon their removal to Europe. The only conceivable explanation for these "non-Jewish" terms is that the bulk of the Ashkenazic Jews do not derive from Palestinian Jewish stock, and/or that the Jewish practices in question are not originally of Palestinian origin. As I shall show below, the Yiddish speaker often utilizes precisely terms which had clear pagan associations in German or the Romance and Slavic languages to denote aspects of the Jewish religion and folk culture.

(b) Palestinian Jewry was sorely depleted at the beginning of the common era by two events. First, the destruction of Judea at the hands of the Romans in the first century A.D. undoubtedly accelerated Jewish emigration abroad and assimilation. Secondly, large numbers of Jews, both at home and abroad, appear to have adopted Christianity—a contemporaneous form of Judaism which divorced itself fairly promptly from the Jewish fold altogether and developed, at different times and places, a hostile stance towards the surviving forms of Judaism. Unlike their Palestinian brethern, the remnants of the Jewish people in Europe did not suffer from the ravages of war, despite the embarrassment of losing their national homeland in 70 A.D. at the hands of the Romans (assuming diaspora Jews regarded Palestine as their "national homeland"). It is these diaspora Jews, who in certain areas and periods drew considerable numbers of non-Jews, mainly pagans, to their ranks. It is hard to believe that many non-Jews would have espoused Judaism had they regarded it as the religion of a captive, exiled and humiliated nation. The convert population, who far outnumbered the ethnic Palestinian Jews and constituted the bulk of most diaspora Jewish communities, might not have seen themselves as members of a Palestinian Judean people.

A lamentable terminological confusion conceals the many discontinuities which divide the Palestinian and diaspora Jews. Since most researchers assume that the latter constitute a "continuation" of the Palestinian Jews—though subject to varying non-Jewish influences at different periods—they choose to speak of a "modern-day evolution of the old Jewish people". I submit that it may be more accurate to speak of the creation of newly Judaized "peoples" (in the plural) in Europe, Arabia, North Africa and the Fertile Crescent, when small bodies of Palestinian Jews merged with larger numbers of indigenous non-Jews. Only a handful of scholars have regarded the diaspora Jews as a collection of peoples:

> "...it is correct to affirm the existence of a Jewish religion, a Jewish community of peoples, a continuity of cultural forms, and other non-biologic entities. It is on a completely different level of analysis to point out that linguistically and biologically the *Jewish peoples* have often changed into forms indistinguishable from the Gentile people around them" (M. Jacobs 1942:54—italics supplied).

It is important to select a clear terminology in defining the relationship between the Palestinian and diaspora Jews; there are two conceivable solutions:

(a) I could distinguish Palestinian from diaspora Jews by variants of a common term, say "Jews I" and "Jews II". The Yiddishist, Max Weinreich, recommended (1973) just such a nomenclature to capture the radical changes that Jewish languages underwent when they were transported out of their native habitats. For example, the exile of the Jews from the Iberian Peninsula between 1492–8 resulted in a weakening of the bonds between Judeo-Spanish and Iberian Spanish, and exposure of the former to the new influences of Balkan languages and Turkish; the gradual, largely voluntary migration of Ashkenazic Jews from the German lands into the monolingual Slavic lands, beginning with the 12th century, resulted in the weakening of ties between Yiddish and High German dialects and the establishment of new contacts with Slavic and the Low German dialects spoken in Eastern Europe. Sephardic and Ashkenazic non-verbal culture also underwent dramatic metamorphoses as a result of these migrations. In recognition of these dramatic events, Weinreich proposed to speak of "Sepharad I and II" and "Ashkenaz I and II"—the Medieval Hebrew names for Spain and Germany, respectively. Weinreich's nomenclature may be appropriate for describing the evolution of an original "Sepharad" or "Ashkenaz" that continued its existence in new colonial contexts, but it is inappropriate if the two stages were originally unrelated for the most part, so that "links" between them are largely due to diffusion, or borrowing, of features rather than to inheritance and evolution.

(b) Many Greek and Roman writers in the first post-Christian centuries used "Hebrew" to denote the ancient Jewish people in Palestine and the term "Jew" in the meaning of the Jewish or Judaized peoples of the diasporas. This fact suggests that they recognized the growing chasm between Palestinian and non-Palestinian Jews. Moreover, Greek *hebraîos* also denoted primarily a Jew who spoke Hebrew or Aramaic in opposition to *hellēnistḗs* 'a person who used the Greek language; a Greek Jew' (both terms appear in Acts 6:1). At the same time, some writers (exclusively of Jewish origin?) used the terms "Hebrew" and

"Jew" interchangeably. For example, Saint Paul, born in Tarsus on the Black Sea (d.67?) of Greek- and Aramaic-speaking Jewish parents, called himself alternatively a "Hebrew", a "Jew", and even an "Israelite" in Philippians 3:5, Galatians 2:15 and 2 Corinthians 11:22, respectively. Undifferentiated nomenclature may have suited Paul's missionary goals, unless the differences between the two groups had not yet crystallized. The earliest Christian literature usually makes a distinction between "Israelite" (a Jew who accepts Christianity) and "Jew" (a Jew who is hostile to Christianity); see the passage in John 1:47 (c.95–105 A.D.).

In Rome, the "synagogue of the Hebrews" was specifically a synagogue whose members claimed descent from a community of Palestinian emigrés or one in which Hebrew or Aramaic was the language of prayer. Alternatively, among non-natives "Hebrew" could also define a religious group, or an inhabitant of Judea, while "Jew" designated either a person who lived according to Jewish customs, but was not necessarily an ethnic Jew (Mayer 1967:746), or a Christian whose faith was wanting (Meeks 1975:183). Recently, Kraemer has noted that "Jew" in Greek and Latin often denoted a pagan adherent to Judaism (1989:35). Medieval Latin usage also permitted free variation between *hebraeus* 'Hebrew', and *iūdaeus* 'Jew'; the latter might or might not carry a distinctly ethnic, as well as religious, meaning (see Blumenkranz 1955:81, fn 5; Solin 1980:307). On the term *ioudaïsmós* 'Judaism' found in Judeo-Greek literature and on inscriptions in Italy and Stobi, Macedonia, see Amir 1982.

Significantly, Medieval Jewish writings, mainly in Hebrew, prefer the term "Jew" as the native ethnic epithet. On differences between the Russian terms *evrej* 'Jew, Hebrew' and *žid* 'kike' (formerly non-pejorative; there is also *iudej* 'Israelite'), see H.Birnbaum 1985; Wexler 1987b: 142, fn 196; the first term comes from Hebrew *ʿivrī* 'Hebrew', the other two from Hebrew *jəhūdī*.

The scholarly literature of the last century or so varies widely in the use of precise terms for "Jew". For example, many historians (both Jews and non-Jews) have insisted on the chronological progression of the entities "Hebrew", "Israelite" and "Jew", e.g., Graetz 1897–1911 and Wellisch 1937:784; but Wellhausen 1894 and Sellin 1896 used the terms "Israelite" and "Jew" interchangeably for the period up to the Bar Koxba revolt in 135 A.D. Leopold Zunz, the eminent 19th-century German Jewish historian and the founder of the scientific study of Judaism, recognizes the distinction between the periods of "Israelite/Hebrew" and "Jew", but his terminology is imprecise, since he declares that it was "Jewish" history that terminated in Palestine in 135 A.D. (1919).

The ambiguous use of the word "Jew" to denote two historically distinct populations is not unusual; consider the Germanic tribal name *Frank* which denotes a Romance-speaking population in France, as well as the German-speaking area known as *Franken* 'Franconia', while the native Hungarian ethnic name *Magyar* denotes a territory populated by several related Finno-Ugric tribes, of which the Magyars were a major component (Boba 1967:75). At different times in history, the term *Rus'* has been associated variously with the historical Kiev-Polesie, Novgorod-Suzdal' and Polock-Rjazan' territories—now inhabited by the present-day Ukrainians, Belorussians and Russians. Currently, the term "Arab" is applied (by natives and non-natives alike) to Moroccans (many of whom are of Berber origin), Egyptians (of Egyptian, Nubian descent, etc.) and Iraqis (descendants of the Babylonians, Sumerians, etc.).

Similarly, it is imprecise to use the single term "Judaism" for the religion of both Palestinian and diaspora Jews, since the two types of Jewish religious expression were not a single phenomenon which evolved through time and place; rather they were for the most part distinct religions which only later became intertwined through the processes of "Judaization" cited above (for details, see chapter 7 below). I have no doubt that the use of the common language name "Hebrew" to denote both the Semitic Old Hebrew of the biblical and talmudic periods and the non-Semitic Hebrew spoken now in Israel contributes to the popular misconception that these are two chronologically distinct forms of the same language; I suspect the choice of the name "Hebrew" by most 19th–20th-century Zionists was not accidental.

In principle, I am in sympathy with any nomenclature that distinguishes explicitly between Old Palestinian and diaspora Jews. Yet, since my definitions of "Jew", "Judaism" and "Hebrew language" can easily be understood according to period and place, i.e., within or outside of ancient Palestine, there is little to be gained by creating a new terminology. For the European diasporas, an epithet like "Judaized pagano-Christianity" might be preferable to the term "Judaism" since it emphasizes the historical discontinuities, but it is too cumbersome. Hence, I will use the terms "Jew", "Judaism" and "Hebrew language" indiscriminately for all periods and origins. The following chart summarizes the relationships between the two periods:

Chart 1. The relationship between the Palestinian and Ashkenazic diaspora Jews in religion, language and ethnic make-up.

Palestinian Jewry up to about the 3rd century A.D.		Ashkenazic Jews (including their colonial offshoots in Israel, the Americas, etc.) from about the 6th century A.D. to the present
religion:	Judaism (variety of sects)	Judaized (Slavic and Germanic) paganism, Christianity and Islam, with a component of borrowed and inherited Palestinian Jewish traditions
languages:	Semitic Hebrew and Judeo-Aramaic	Slavic Yiddish; Slavic Hebrew (a written language in northern Europe, a written and spoken language in Israel)
ethnic make-up:	Jews (Hebrews, Israelites), consisting of major Near Eastern and minor European and African ethnic components	Jews, consisting of minor Palestinian Jewish and major Slavo-Turkic and other ethnic components

The myth that the Jewish people survived the collapse of an independent Jewish state in the first century A.D. intact is widespread:

> "Not the least remarkable thing about the Jews is their antiquity... As a people conscious of their distinct tradition and of their existence as an entity, only the Egyptians are older than they" (Shapiro 1960:9).

> "Tomorrow an announcement will be issued in Beijing on the establishment of diplomatic relations...between China and Israel. Thus, a visible and official link between two independent entities representing the oldest continuous civilizations in Asia and in the world will be forged" (Merxav 1992).

The discontinuous property of the Jews—through time and space—is not at all unique to the Jews. Discontinuity of one sort or another probably characterizes all ethnic groups. But the discontinuity of the Jews differs from that of ethnic groups that exchanged to some extent race, culture and language (e.g., the modern-day Egyptians), race, culture and habitat (e.g., the Albanians, who once were neighbors of the ancestors of the Rumanians, now reside almost exclusively in the western Balkans), or language and culture (e.g., the Irish Celts). The discontinuous non-Jewish peoples absorbed large numbers of newcomers who brought new cultures, religions and gene pools, and occasionally new languages, but they did not usually also experience widespread geographical dispersal. The absence of a single territorial base caused the Old Palestinian Jews as a whole to become more heterogeneous—racially, culturally, linguistically, ethnographically and theologically—than probably any other previously unified people.

Elie Kedourie defines the ability of the Jews to survive as a people in the face of great odds as their most remarkable feature:

> "[The Jews'] continued survival as a group in these dominant, attractive and yet very frequently hostile [Islamic and Christian] societies, where other groups sooner rather than later were lost without trace—as, for instance, the pagans of Greece, Italy and Western Europe, or the Christian populations of Anatolia and North Africa—must be adjudged remarkable" (1979b:8).

It is imprecise to say that the Jews are "remarkable" for surviving as a widely dispersed people without a territorial base; no such thing happened for the first thousand years of European diaspora history—not until the codification of the belief in a common Jewish people, one major outcome of the Judaization process of the late Middle Ages. If the European diaspora Jews are remarkable, it is for two quite different reasons: (a) for having merged with a variety of non-Jewish groups to produce a quasi- or para-Jewish cultural and religious syncretism, and (b) for later unifying "fragmented Judaized peoples" and cultivating a link between the latter and a largely unrelated people and their religion in ancient Palestine, which eventually ended in the occupation of the latter's territory and the attempt to adopt the latter's long unspoken language—Biblical Hebrew.

The hypotheses that the contemporary Ashkenazic Jews are largely of non-Jewish, especially Slavic, origins, and that Yiddish and its "offspring", Israeli Hebrew, are two forms of a single Slavic language (Sorbian) render the Jews and their languages a fascinating laboratory in which to study the evolution of peoplehood, self-identification (including rewriting of history), and partial language shift (or re-lexification). A number of disciplines will now have new challenges to face:

(a) *Slavists* will be surprised to encounter a new member in the Slavic family of languages: Yiddish/Modern Hebrew. Recent research has set the Jewish-Slavic contacts in the 9th century in Bohemia and in the 12th century in Poland. But in my conception of Yiddish genesis the chronology and geography of Jewish-Slavic contacts could be extended back to the German lands in the 9th–10th centuries and to the Balkans in the 6th–7th centuries.

(b) *Linguists* will have to reclassify the members of the Germanic and Slavic language families, but in the process will gain a major new laboratory in which to study the mechanics of cyclical partial language shift.

(b) Yiddish will retain much of its traditional attraction to *Germanists* for the period *after* the language shift when Yiddish and German moved largely in tandem, and would gain new significance as a non-Germanic language which acquired a massive German component.

(c) *Yiddishists* will need to rewrite significant parts of Yiddish linguistic history, e.g., place the genesis of the Eastern and some of the Western Yiddish dialects in the 9th–13th centuries—possibly several centuries later than the traditional periodization of (Germanic) Yiddish genesis in the 9th–10th centuries.

(d) The field of *Jewish studies* will require redefinition and redirection. Hopefully, students of European Jewish history will begin to recognize the usefuless of linguistics in their research and regard familiarity with the histories of the Slavic, Germanic and European Turkic peoples as prerequisites to writing European Jewish history, since these were the peoples who most interacted with the Palestinian Jewish emigrés and their descendants in Asia Minor and Europe.

Students of European Jewish history have been reared on the notion that Italian and French Jews constituted the major components in the Ashkenazic ethnogenesis (note the familiar cliché "Franco-German Jewry" that allegedly gave rise to Ashkenazic Jewry). They must now address the possibility that most Slavo-Turkic (i.e., Ashkenazic) Jews originated in the Balkans and Eastern Europe and, in part, joined the *Drang nach Westen* of Slavs, Avars, Magyars and others, which was gathering momentum in the 6th century A.D. Hence, Ashkenazic Jewry was not constituted in the Franco-German borderlands, as the popular conception holds. If the uniqueness of Yiddish stems from the replacement of most of its Slavic lexicon by German lexicon and not from the gradual physical separation of Yiddish from its "German" homeland and subsequent attachment to Slavic areas (as proposed by M.Weinreich 1:1973:43), then historians will want to revise their notions of Jewish communal instability and mobility in early Medieval Germany.

Curiously, two scholars writing in the 1880s anticipated to some extent my largely Slavic-origin hypothesis of the north European Jews: one proposed that the Jews in Poland and the East Slavic lands had once spoken a Judaized Slavic analogous to Yiddish, while the other proposed that German Jews had a more intimate contact with Slavs than the Germans:

> "...many words and patterns of speech from Old Slavic are preserved in the Yiddish of the Russian and Polish Jews, which stem from the time in which the local Jews used the Slavic languages as their everyday language. These Old Slavic words form an analogue to the Old German words in Yiddish" (Grünbaum 1882:88, fn 1, citing Harkavi 1865:39).

> "Israel's history remains bound with Germany's name more intimately than with any other in the diaspora, no matter how much people have striven and may still strive to loosen the tightly bound ties. German Jews much earlier than the very sons of Germany worked at the Germanization of the Slavs, of the Slavic East that begins with Bohemia; they are still today in many places on earth representatives of German culture, even though they have had to suffer no small amount of injustice for that" (Frankl 1884:5).

It has taken just over a century to come full circle—to recognize anew the kernel role that Jewish-Slavic contacts played in the genesis of the Ashkenazic Jews.

3

THE JEWISH LANGUAGES AS TOOLS FOR RECONSTRUCTING THE ORIGINS AND SETTLEMENT HISTORY OF THE SLAVO-TURKIC JEWS

All historians of the diaspora Jews have voiced their deep frustration over the fragmentary knowledge of European Jewish history in the first millennium of this era. But they do not agree on the prognosis for Jewish historical research.

Some scholars, like Cecil Roth, expected better documentation to improve our knowledge of early European Jewish history; others, like Bernard Weinryb, asserted that no amount of documentation could eliminate the fragmentary quality of historical descriptions.

In describing our state of knowledge of the Jews in Western Europe between 711 (the Muslim invasion of Spain) and 1096 (the First Crusade), Roth wrote:

> "...we are driven to rely unduly in this period on arguments *e silentio.* Some element of uncertainty therefore frequently remains. We have for example no references over much of this period to Jewish settlements in a great part of Western Europe. Is this to be interpreted as evidence that no such settlements existed, or that if they existed they were of negligible importance? Or is it a question only of the restricted nature of our sources? Jews were to be found in the late classical period in France and Germany as well as in Italy: to what extent were the Jews residing in these countries in the Dark Ages descended from them, and to what extent were they descended from recent arrivals? We simply do not know, and are driven to conjecture" (1966a:7).

Turning to the Jewries of Eastern Europe at this time, Roth painted no less hazy a picture:

> "The record of the earliest settlement of the Jews in Eastern Europe is involved in obscurity to an even greater extent. We know that Jews traveled there for purposes of trade, we have vague statements that Jews resided there, we are told legends regarding the antiquity of the Jewish settlement there. It is out of these ludicrously sparse elements that we have to reconstruct the pre-history of what was to become the most

numerous and most vital section of the Jewish people, which had a memorable influence on the history of the Western world" (1966a:8).

"It will be noticed that there is...no allusion to the Jewish settlement in Poland, later to be a principal center of Jewish life and cultural productivity over so many generations. That there were Jews there in the period is not unlikely. But in fact we know nothing whatsoever of them, other than a couple of later and improbable legends, a vague reference to Jewish slave-dealers in the region (in 1085), and an unsubstantiated report of the presence of Jews in Gnesen [Gniezno]. All this illustrates yet further the difficulty of building up a consistent picture of Jewish origins in medieval Europe, even in those areas where their presence was later so significant" (1966b:304).

Roth was wrong to characterize the references to Jewish slave dealers as "vague" and few in number. There are many such references, and they are far from vague, as I will show in chapter 6 below. In the above passages Roth was alluding to three problems:

(a) Except for portions of the New Testament, we lack significant Jewish literary remains from Asia Minor in the Hellenistic and Roman periods, and we have no Jewish written evidence in any language from Europe until the 10th–11th centuries.

(b) There are no regional chroniclers from either German or Slavic Europe in the first millennium A.D. who left detailed accounts of Jewish life (see also Čerikover 1939). The accounts of a single Catalonian Jewish visitor, Ibrāhīm ibn Jaʿqūb, in the 10th century, are fragmentary and embedded in the writings of later Arab authors (see chapter 6.2 below).

(c) The extant source materials on Jewish life in Europe in the first millennium are not always easy to interpret since most of them come from the pen of pagan and Christian writers, whose negative attitude towards the Jews often resulted in skewed reports. Weinryb's prognosis for Jewish historiography is even more pessimistic than that of Roth, since for him it is the inherent unreliability, rather than the paucity of data, that constitutes the obstacle:

"Written history is doomed to be fragmentary because of the incompleteness of records. Events are only partially observed, only a part of what is observed is recorded, and only a part of what is recorded is preserved... Instead of trying to ascertain the facts,..writers projected what they thought they should have been. The result is a record of what might have happened. Like the anonymous authors of...legends and

> myths, they invented artificial constructions responding to needs, real or imagined, of their time. Most of the theories and hypotheses may reflect the climate of opinion of the author and their times, but are of little, if any, value to the understanding of the history of the Jews in eastern Europe" (1962b:500).

Here and in other writings, Weinryb also casts doubt on the reliability of the primary sources: many documents were copied down or recopied several centuries after the events they described, and unfamiliar words and toponyms were often garbled by later scribes ignorant of the original languages (1957, 1962a, 1962b; for further discussion of the problems of historical research, see D.Lowenthal 1985:214ff).

Roth is right that the discovery of new documents and archeological sites could provide important clarifications, and Weinryb is right that the new data are likely to prove no less fragmentary than the old. I suppose, though, that Weinryb would have admitted that a large collection of fragmentary data is better than a small collection.

No one can predict what new data will become available to future historians of the Jews, though in recent years two remarkable archeological discoveries—separated by about 1000 miles and five centuries—were made. These are the Jewish Greek inscription from Aphrodisias (in present-day southwest Turkish Anatolia), dating probably from the 3rd century A.D., and the numerous brick fragments with Jewish artistic motifs and one Hebrew inscription from the Avar necropolis at Čelarevo, Vojvodina (Serbia), thought to date from the 8th century A.D. and consisting of 263 graves. The find at Aphrodisias was discovered in 1976, but its description and assessment were only published in 1987; the Jewish artifacts at Čelarevo were discovered in 1972, and the results were published between 1972 and 1980.

The findings at Aphrodisias and Čelarevo have expanded our understanding of Jewish life in Asia Minor in the early first millennium and the northern Balkans in the late first millennium. The Aphrodisias inscription confirms the existence of a community of "God-Fearers", non-Jews who had accepted some of the doctrines of Judaism and were closely associated with the local Jewish community, though had not formally joined it, and testifies to widespread Jewish proselytizing in Asia Minor in the early Christian period. The Avar burial ground is the first historical evidence of contacts between Jews (possibly of north Monoglian stock, in the view of the archeologists Bunardžić and Živanović) and the Avars—the part-Turkic conglomerate that overrode much of Central Europe and the Balkans between the 6th and 8th centuries and propelled the Slavs to spill out of their primeval habitats in Eastern Europe into Western and Southern Europe in the 6th century (I will return to these finds in chapter 6 below). Archeological evidence is of paramount importance to the historian of the European and Asia Minor Jews because it is often as old as the last Palestinian written sources, and the only direct Jewish evidence available in Europe and Asia Minor from the first millennium.

If we accept Weinryb's scepticism about the historian's ability to make plausible reconstructions of historical events buried deep in the past, much of historical research will be paralyzed. I share Weinryb's frustration, but I believe that there is a way of testing old hypotheses as well as providing fresh interpretations for the extant data—*namely, through the findings of linguistics.*

There are three reasons why the study of languages offers the historian a unique opportunity to advance new hypotheses about the early history and pre-history of a people:

(a) Language, by preserving evidence of its own earlier stages, can reveal historical contacts between speech communities more faithfully than the chance survival of historical documents and archeological sites.

(b) Historical linguistics provides the tools to reconstruct the hypothetical forms of a language that predate the oldest linguistic evidence—even if only in general outline and tentatively.

(c) Only with language data are we able to distinguish native from borrowed elements with a high degree of certainty.

It is primarily archeologists and students of poorly documented remote periods of history who have appreciated the contributions that linguistics can make to historical reconstruction, as the following statements by the Near Eastern archeologists Albright and Lambdin demonstrate:

> "The study of language content needs no special justification, since the written records of antiquity are our most valuable source of information concerning the peoples and civilizations which form the object of historical investigation. But language as a formal structure, like the tools and institutions of a society, represents a kind of transmitted organism and as such falls into the category of data which can be ordered in typologically related sequences. Thus, for the historian, who is interested primarily in tracing interacting continuities, the study of the history and development of a language, apart from its use as a vehicle for oral and written traditions, provides useful and sometimes unique evidence of otherwise undiscernible ethnic and cultural affiliations" (1966:3).

"...cultural interference of even a slight degree may leave their traces on the languages of the affected communities in the form of loanwords or, less commonly, of borrowed grammatical features. The detailed study of loan material serves, therefore, to corroborate the existence of cultural contacts which are indicated by other data and, in those cases where other indications are lacking, to suggest contacts which would otherwise be unknown" (1966:8).

Few historians of the Slavs or the European Jews recognize the usefulness of linguistic data in doing historical research. At best, we encounter occasional fascination with proper and place names (see the historians Šiper 1924, Stasiewski 1934:243 and Weinryb 1974:962–5). Thus, having convincingly identified flaws in all the theories proposed for the arrival of the Jews in the East European lands, Weinryb opted for a relatively late German Jewish presence in the Polish lands in the 12th century. Yet, other than occasional onomastic data, he did not consider evidence from Jewish languages like Yiddish and Judeo-Slavic (by the latter I have in mind a set of barely attested extinct languages that were Judaized possibly as early as the 6th century in the Balkans but first attested in the West Slavic lands in the 10th century), or from non-Jewish languages like German and the Slavic languages. Had he done so, he might have been tempted to posit a Jewish presence (I believe of Balkan origin) in a number of locales throughout the West Slavic lands before the 10th century.

With linguistics, the historian is always in a "no-lose" situation: his hypotheses are strengthened if the linguist can corroborate them by independent means; if the linguist contradicts the historian's hypotheses, then the historian gains the opportunity of examining new hypotheses which he otherwise might not have been led to formulate.

The Jews (also called Hebrews or Israelites) emerged on the stage of recorded history in approximately 1500 B.C., as speakers of Hebrew, a West Semitic language. The thorny question of whether Hebrew was their unique language, or was borrowed from another Semitic people resident in Palestine, e.g., perhaps from the Canaanites, need not detain us here. Beginning with the 6th century B.C., we find significant numbers of Hebrew speakers in Palestine switching to a related Semitic language, Aramaic. There are several reasons for this: the latter was a closely related language that enjoyed international status throughout the Near East, and was the native language of the mounting number of Jews living outside of Palestine and possibly of the returnees to Palestine from Babylonian exile after 536 B.C. Even the original Hebrew alphabet was replaced by the Aramaic alphabet before the Christian era (see details in Diringer 1950); it is the Aramaic alphabet which now serves the Jews everywhere as their "Hebrew" writing system.

By the time of Christ, most Palestinian Jews were speakers of Aramaic or Greek (in Judaized versions of the languages, so we are entitled to speak of a "Judeo-Aramaic" and "Judeo-Greek"); a minority, probably mainly resident in the north of Palestine, in the Galilee, continued to speak Hebrew. Most scholars concur that Hebrew definitively ceased to be a spoken language in Palestine by the 3rd century A.D., though at times thereafter it had liturgical and literary functions. The obsolescence of Hebrew was brought about not just by the popularity of Aramaic; many speakers of Hebrew were exterminated or uprooted from Judea after the unsuccessful Bar Koxba revolt against the Romans in 135 A.D.

Aramaic remained the primary language of Palestine and adjacent lands both to the east and west until the rise of Islam in the 7th century A.D., when it was displaced for the most part by Arabic. It is still the native language of a handful of Christians in Syria and of several hundred thousand Jews and Christians in Kurdistan. In addition, a dialect of Aramaic, Syriac, continues to serve as the liturgical language of Christians in a wide area linking the Middle East to southwest India. This is a shrunken domain in comparison with the territory in which Aramaic, in a wide variety of not always mutually comprehensible dialects, was spoken and written at its peak at the close of the first millennium A.D.: from the eastern Mediterranean, across modern-day northern Pakistian, all the way to the Xijiang Uygur Zizhiqu (the Uighur Autonomous Region) of western China. Aramaic also died out among small pockets of speakers on the European continent and Malta by the 5th–6th centuries. Judeo-Aramaic (early documents of which have been discovered in western Afghanistan and western China) is the only language other than Hebrew that acquired liturgical status among the Jews, since the Talmud, some parts of the Bible and a number of prayers were composed in that language. In fact, the functional equality of Hebrew and Judeo-Aramaic is reflected by the use of a common name for the two languages in Yiddish, e.g., *lošn kojdeš* 'Hebrew, Aramaic', literally 'the holy language'. Some Yiddish words which could be equally from Hebrew or Judeo-Aramaic even share both Hebrew and Aramaic meanings, when these differ, e.g., Hebrew and Judeo-Aramaic *mədīnāh* > Western Yiddish *medine* 'city' (the Aramaic meaning) and 'state' (the Hebrew meaning, and the only meaning in Eastern Yiddish).[1]

It is not difficult to understand why the first Jews who emigrated from Palestine (presumably as speakers of Aramaic in the main, and of Hebrew and Greek secondarily) gave up Hebrew and Aramaic in favor of a local European language. Migration is often accompanied by language shift. All the immigrant languages brought to North America have tended to disappear within a generation or two, with the exception of Spanish, which survives only because of the fresh migration from Spanish-speaking countries that guarantees a living Hispanic culture. But there is nothing automatic about language displacement under the conditions of migration. Many of the five-odd million descendants of the Romá (Gypsies) who left northwest India about a millennium ago still speak their native Indic language, Romani, in Europe and the Middle East; the Hungarians continue to maintain their Finno-Ugric language in an originally Latin- and later Slavic-speaking territory surrounded exclusively by speakers of Indo-European languages; the North and South Americans continue to speak English, Dutch, Spanish or Portuguese, in forms that remain mutually intelligible with the home dialects of these languages.

There is no way to determine either the chronology of the loss of Hebrew and Judeo-Aramaic outside of Palestine, or the extent to which Palestinian Jews arrived in Europe as speakers of Greek, or marginally, Latin. However, I can think of three reasons why the first Jewish settlers in Europe (like other transplanted Near Eastern speakers of Aramaic) would have given up their Semitic linguistic baggage fairly soon, and why subsequent immigrants, especially those coming after the collapse of an independent Judea in 70 A.D., would have failed to impose Hebrew and Judeo-Aramaic on the European Jews:

(a) Greek was already spoken by certain segments of the Jewish population in Palestine.

(b) Hebrew and Judeo-Aramaic could not compete in Europe with international languages of culture and government like Latin and Greek.

(c) Most significantly, the Jewish diaspora communities had rapidly grown thanks to the inclusion of large numbers of non-Jewish proselytes, to the point where probably the majority of the European Jews by the 3rd century were of proselyte origin. It would have been unlikely that such people could acquire non-European spoken languages like Hebrew and Judeo-Aramaic. At best, the later Palestinian and Babylonian Jewish immigrants to Europe and Asia Minor might have succeeded in imposing the use of *liturgical* Hebrew and Judeo-Aramaic on the diaspora communities, but the non-existence of texts in these languages from Europe before the end of the first millennium suggests that even in non-spoken functions, the two Semitic languages enjoyed little or no popularity in Europe. If Cecil Roth is correct that a Judeo-Hispanic iconographic tradition found in 14th–15th-century Hebrew Bibles has roots in Roman and Hellenistic Jewish art (1953), then we can assume European Jews had access to the Hebrew/Judeo-Aramaic Bible during the first millennium, though no examples are known.

The large proportion of proselytes in the European Jewish communities could also explain the blatant absence of Hebrew inscriptions on tombstones in southern Europe until the 8th–9th centuries (the oldest extant Jewish cemeteries in northern Europe, at Mainz and Worms in the monolingual German lands, date from the late 11th century and have only Hebrew inscriptions), the absence of European Hebrew documents prior to the 10th–11th centuries and the relatively low level of Hebrew letters among the German Jews through the 13th century (in opposition to the Iberian Arab Jews, who shared the Arabs' love for philology). There are no Jewish cemeteries in the lands occupied by the Slaves that predate the 1500s.

The large Israeli diasporas that have developed after 1948 provide a modern parallel: Hebrew is used exclusively by the most recent Israeli immigrants abroad, but is almost never acquired by indigenous Jews. It is unclear to what extent the children of Israeli immigrants continue to speak Hebrew.

A remarkable feature of the Jewish experience outside of Palestine is that the loss of spoken Hebrew and Judeo-Aramaic did not regularly result in the adoption of a new non-Jewish language. Rather the Jews idiosyncratically selected material from the coterritorial non-Jewish language, incorporating in it a few elements from Hebrew and Judeo-Aramaic, and other Judaized languages. The result was that in most diaspora communities the Jews came to speak a unique form of the coterritorial non-Jewish language. Semitic Hebrew and Judeo-Aramaic (continuously, intermittently, or only since the early second millennium?) served as the non-spoken languages of Jewish liturgy (the "Hebrew" and "Judeo-Aramaic" of original literature in the diaspora communities were really dialects of the users' native languages: see below) and became modest sources of enrichment for the new spoken languages of the Jews (an exception is Yiddish which has an enormous Hebrew component—see more on this in chapter 4 below).

Scholars call the languages which the Jews adapted from neighboring non-Jewish languages (i.e., languages spoken exclusively by Jews other than possibly ancient Hebrew) "Jewish" or "Judaized". I list alphabetically, without regard to historical periodization, the Jewish languages of Indo-European and non-Indo-European stock (the former family comprises the bulk of the Jewish languages); the languages differ widely in the extent of their written remains, functions and body of speakers. A few uncertain examples are listed with a question mark:

I. Judaized Indo-European languages:

(a) The Germanic family: Yiddish has traditionally been cited as an example of a Jewish language of Germanic stock, though I prefer to classify it as a form of Judeo-Sorbian; therefore I will list it among the Judaized Slavic languages. The motivation for my claim will be given in chapter 4 below. On mildly Judaized Germanic languages, see the discussion below.

(b) Greek: this is the oldest attested European Jewish language, spoken by Jews from the 4th century B.C. up to the present (though perhaps with interruptions), both in Greece and in many non-Hellenic areas of Europe, as well as in Egypt and Palestine.

(c) The Indo-Iranian family: Judeo-Marathi (in west central India), Judeo-Persian (in Iran and Afghanistan, and for an unknown period of time in the Jewish communities in China as well—up to the 16th century?), Judeo-Tadjik (in Tadjikistan and Uzbekistan), Judeo-Tat (in Azerbajdzhan).

(d) Latin and the Romance family: Judeo-Latin, Judeo-Catalan, Judeo-French, Judeo-Italian, Judeo-Provençal, Judeo-Spanish (now natively known as Judézmo, Judyó, Jidyó, Ḥakitía), Judeo-Portuguese (after 1498 spoken only by Jewish converts to Catholicism in the Iberian Peninsula, some of whom subsequently returned openly to Judaism outside of the Peninsula; the speech of the converts, which came to differ from the Judeo-Portuguese of unconverted Jews, might best be labeled "Marrano-Portuguese", after *marrano*, the term of opproprium, perhaps meaning pig, by which the Iberian Christians called them) and the now extinct Judaized dialects of Aragonese, Leonese, etc.[2]

(e) The Slavic family: Judeo-Belorussian, Judeo-Czech(?), Judeo-Sorbian/Yiddish (originally spoken in the eastern German lands), Judeo-Ukrainian.

II. Judaized non-Indo-European languages:

(a) The Afro-Asian family: Judeo-Amharic(?), Judeo-Arabic (in a wide variety of dialects spoken from Morocco and Spain to Yemen and Iraq), Judeo-Aramaic, Judeo-Berber (spoken by Jews primarily in Morocco and Algeria), Judeo-Coptic(?) (derived from Ancient Egyptian, possibly the native language of Saadya Gaon 882–942, the famous Jewish writer and translator of the Bible into Judeo-Arabic, who was a native of al-Fayyūm), Judeo-Kwara(?) (formerly spoken by the Ethiopian Jews). *Note that I do not cite Old Hebrew as a Jewish language, on the assumption that it was not adapted from a non-Jewish language through a process of linguistic Judaization.*

(b) The Caucasian family: Judeo-Georgian.

(c) The Sino-Tibetan family: Judeo-Chinese.

(d) The Turkic family: Judeo-Khazar(?) (on this Turkic people in the region to the north of the Black and Caspian Seas who converted to Judaism in the 8th century, see remarks in chapters 4, 5.11, 5.12, 6, 6.2 and 6.6 below), Judeo-Krimčak (spoken in the Crimean Peninsula). (On Karaite, see below.)

(e) The Dravidian family: Judeo-Malayalam (spoken in Kerala State, India).

In addition, when Jews abandoned their traditional Jewish languages, they often created mildly Judaized languages of the non-Jewish successor languages which often survived for several generations, before being replaced by standard variants of the non-Jewish language. Examples of these transitional, moderately Judaized Jewish languages are Judeo-Dutch, Judeo-English, Judeo-Frisian(?), "Ashkenazic" or Judeo-German (not to be confused with Yiddish which it replaced in the 18th–19th centuries), and North African Judeo-French which replaced the local Judeo-Arabic, Judezmo and Judeo-Berber (preserved for the most part today in metropolitan France—and quite different in component structure from Medieval Judeo-French which became extinct during the 15th century, cited in category Id above). Slavic examples are Judeo-Polish, Judeo-Russian, and new Judeo-Belorussian and Judeo-Ukrainian in the 19th century (see Wexler ms a).

I can expand the list still further if I include the languages developed by the Karaites, adherents of a sectarian form of Judaism which developed in Iraq in the 8th century, which rejects the authority of the Talmud. The contemporary non-European and Turkish Karaites alone define themselves as members of the Jewish people (a characterization the non-Karaite Jews accept). The north European (in the western Ukraine and Belorussia and in eastern Poland) and Crimean Karaites deny any connection with the Jewish people and are not now usually recognized by non-Jewish political authorities as Jews; they often claim, without convincing evidence, to be descended from Khazars (see Zajączkowski 1961: chapter 1). The Karaites speak a number of languages, all of which are presently obsolete or obsolescent: Karaite, a form of Qypčaq Turkic, spoken in the Crimean Peninsula and northern Slavic Europe, (Kareo?-)Arabic (spoken in Egypt and Iraq) and (Kareo?-)Greek (spoken until recently in Istanbul). I have no information on the languages spoken and written by another Jewish sectarian group—the Samaritans, who are today reduced to a few hundred members in Israel (Holon, outside of Tel-Aviv) and Palestine (Nablus, the biblical Sh[e]chem). The Samaritans maintain a unique pronunciation of Hebrew, and a variant of the original Hebrew alphabet (unlike the Jews who write Hebrew and the Jewish languages in alphabets which are derived from the Aramaic, rather than the Hebrew, writing system, as I noted above); the native language of the Palestinian Samaritans is Arabic, but I have no information as to whether the latter differs from the dialects spoken by the coterritorial Arabs.

Since Jews have created Judaized languages in most diasporas, the absence of Judaized forms of English and most other modern European languages are marked exceptions which have yet to be explained. Four factors have been proposed to account for the creation of Jewish languages, i.e., for the failure of the Jews in most territories to assimilate fully to the linguistic norms of the coterritorial non-Jewish population:

(a) Jews lived in relative isolation from the dominant non-Jewish population, so that they could not acquire the linguistic norms of the latter fully; imitating non-Jewish norms was especially difficult when the Jews moved away, either voluntarily or under duress, from the areas where the cognate non-Jewish dialects were spoken, e.g., when Judezmo became spoken only outside the Iberian Peninsula after the expulsions of the Jews in 1492–8, or when Yiddish came to be spoken almost exclusively in the Slavic-speaking lands by the mid–19th century, as most German Jews had by then shifted to standard German.

(b) The maintenance of a unique religion encouraged separation from the non-Jewish surroundings and the use of Hebrew and Judeo-Aramaic; the latter, as natural sources of enrichment for the spoken languages of the Jews, could lead (together with other linguistic factors) to the creation of Judaized languages.

(c) The Jews often enjoyed a relatively unstable settlement history due to persecutions and expulsions, which brought them into contact with a greater variety of coterritorial dialects than most non-Jews; as a result, the Jewish languages assumed a more merged dialectal character than any single non-Jewish dialect.

(d) Because the Jews no longer had their own national spoken languages, Hebrew and Judeo-Aramaic, Judaized languages were intended to enhance their separate ethno-linguistic profile, thus insulating the small, scattered Jewish settlements from the surrounding majority non-Jewish cultures.

I find only factors (c) and (d) convincing. Factor (a), isolation from the non-Jewish population, which was both enforced and voluntary in Medieval Europe, is not at all a convincing factor in the genesis of most Jewish languages since it tends to date several centuries after the creation of the latter. Legislated segregation of the Jews was rare in the Slavic lands (except for the "Pale of Settlement" in the Russian Empire). For example, many observors cite separation from the non-Jewish dialect as the major cause for the creation of Judaized Spanish after 1492, but separation from Spanish is irrelevant since Judezmo existed in Spain before 1492, while Morocco, a haven for many Spanish Jewish exiles, hardly lies at a great distance from Spain. (A similar "isolation theory" was also long advocated to explain why many Blacks in North America spoke a form of English that differed from the speech of White Americans; the argument of racial segregation rightly fell into disfavor when linguists realized that already in Africa Africans [and Europeans] had created creolized forms of English out of English, Portuguese and African languages.) Of course, isolation can have an important effect on a Jewish language after its creation—by impeding the spread of non-Jewish linguistic innovations to Jewish speakers. In addition, after Jews became relatively more isolated from non-Jews in Europe, we begin to detect the beginnings of both linguistic and non-linguistic "Judaization"—i.e., the attempt by Jews to eliminate elements from their language and culture which they believed had markedly pagan, Christian or Muslim associations (see chapters 5.2 and 7 below). For example, contemporary Judezmo uses the Arabism *alxat* (literally 'the first [day]') for Sunday. Synonymous Spanish *domingo,* while known to many present-day speakers of Judezmo, is shunned by them because of its historical association with Christ (the ultimate source is Latin *dominus* 'lord').

It is noteworthy that the Jewish languages are scarcely consistent in their purging of pagan, Christian or Muslim terms. For example, Yiddish preserves a host of Jewish religious terms which are of Slavic Christian and pagan origin, e.g., Yiddish *praven* 'conduct a religious ceremony' is from the Slavic root which originally meant speak, e.g., Polish *prawić* (now 'sermonize; conduct', as in *prawić mszę* 'conduct the mass'), Russian *spravit'* (now 'conduct', as in *spravit' pominki* 'invite guests to the funeral meal in honor of the deceased': see these and further examples in chapter 5.11 below).

One might expect factor (b), religious separatism, to increase the receptivity of a Jewish language to Hebrew vocabulary, but the fact is that aside from the Eastern dialects of Yiddish (see the definition in footnote 1 above), no Jewish language has ever regarded Hebrew as a favored source of enrichment. The lexicon of standard Eastern Yiddish today has approximately 15% Hebraisms, and these elements by no means predominate in the domains of religion or philosophy.

Common typological features and patterns of historical development among many Jewish languages of diverse genetic stock and structure encourage linguists to conceive of the discipline of "comparative Jewish linguistics". The process of developing a Jewish variant of a non-Jewish language was repeated over and over again during the last two and a half millennia on a broad territory stretching across Asia, Africa and Europe, though most languages belonged to the Indo-European family.

Except in a few cases, e.g., "Yiddish" (literally 'Jewish'), we do not know the native names of the Jewish languages. Hence, I will arbitrarily use the prefix "Judeo-", e.g., "Judeo-Latin", "Judeo-Slavic", etc. Jews themselves have historically not used this formula to create glottonyms, but non-Jews frequently do, see, e.g., German *Judendeutsch, Jüdischdeutsch,* etc. (literally, 'the German of the Jews'). The nomenclature "Jewish" is sometimes also found in non-Jewish languages, see, e.g., Russian *evrejskij* 'Yiddish; Jewish'.

Since Jewish language names formed from the adjective "Jewish" are relatively recent (e.g., the Yiddish name *jidiš* 'Jewish' is not found before the 16th century, and the synonymous Balkan Judezmo *džidyó* or *džudezmo* 'Judaism' are not found among Sephardic Jews before the Expulsions of 1492–8), they may have been coined during recent periods of intense Judaization when Jews sought terms that explicitly distinguished their languages from the coterritorial non-Jewish languages (on Judaization, see chapter 7 below). Other older names for

Jewish languages, e.g., Hebrew *lešon ʾaškenaz* 'Yiddish' (literally 'the language of Germany'), known from the 11th century, or Judezmo *ladino* (literally 'Romance; Latin; intelligible language', which denoted the unspoken Judezmo translation of the Hebrew/Judeo-Aramaic Bible, first known from the early 15th century), suggest that the Jews may not have initially recognized their speech to be strikingly different from that of non-Jews; hence, no special glottonym was needed. This could support my proposition that the diaspora Jews were largely of non-Jewish origin. (On the possibility that proselytes may have played a major role in the development of Jewish languages, see discussion below and in chapter 4.)

Moreover, the north European Jews were as a rule aware of the heterogeneous components of their language, and may have preferred names that were non-committal as to its origin. I am tempted to say that the name "Yiddish", by not committing the language to either the Germanic or Slavic family of languages, reflects the uncertainty speakers may have felt regarding the genetic affiliation of their language after the re-lexification of Judeo-Sorbian to High German vocabulary (see details in chapter 4 below).

The above enumeration would be incomplete if I did not state that in most communities, the Jews created a *variety* of Jewish languages, each with well-defined functions. The colloquial Jewish language, by enjoying also limited (usually secular) written functions, entered into a state of complementary distribution with written and liturgical Hebrew and Judeo-Aramaic, which were almost never spoken (except perhaps artificially among Jews from different lands who had no other language in common). But there was always a need to translate some of the original Old Hebrew and Judeo-Aramaic liturgical literature into the vernacular for the many Jews who did not understand these languages. In the Jewish tradition, the Bible was usually not freely translated into the spoken language; rather, it was translated into a newly created, unspoken form of the vernacular which faithfully imitated the word order and derivational patterns of the original Hebrew or Judeo-Aramaic text, and shunned the use of almost all Hebrew and Judeo-Aramaic words, even words commonly used in the colloquial Jewish language itself. The result was a translation language which was essentially incomprehensible to a speaker of a Jewish language who did not understand the underlying Hebrew or Judeo-Aramaic text.

The only part of the Jewish Bible translation language which comes from the Jews' spoken language is the lexicon and phonology, while the grammar is a faithful imitation of the original Hebrew (or Judeo-Aramaic) text. Hence, it is more precise to define Jewish translation languages as bizarre *dialects of Hebrew*—bizarre because they are syntactically and derivationally Hebrew-like but almost totally devoid of Hebrew words (the first to appreciate this fact seems to have been the French abbé, Fleury 1683:268). Thus, each Jewish community has at least two Jewish languages, which are usually genetically distinct. For example, spoken Judezmo, a Judaized form of Castilian, coexists in the same community with non-spoken Ladino, which should be defined as an Iberian recension of "Hebrew" (see also chapter 5, fn 1). Conversely, the original Hebrew texts penned by native speakers of Judezmo, by following the latter's syntactic, derivational and phonological structures, should be classified as unusual forms of Judezmo and not as dialects of "Medieval Hebrew". As far as I know, no one has proposed such a classification of the Jewish translation languages and the "Medieval Hebrew" recensions. The names given by Jews to the traditional language of translation vary, but are usually based on the words "intelligible" or "explanation" (sic!), see, e.g., *ladino*, literally 'Romance; intelligible', Judeo-Arabic *šarḥ*, literally 'explanation'.

By the same token, I would define Medieval Latin, which imitated the syntax and pronunciation of the language of the non-native writers, e.g., Polish, French, Swedish, etc., as bizarre dialects of Polish, French, Swedish, etc. (see Wright 1982); if Medieval Latin is not an extension of native colloquial Latin, there is little justification in using the label "Latin", though this *was* the name given to the written language in the Middle Ages. The use of a common language name, e.g., "Latin" or "Hebrew", for both the native and non-native medieval periods, was no doubt motivated by the belief in a universal Christian or Jewish religious community, i.e., in Christendom and the Jewish people, or by the desire to create such a community (see Horvath and Wexler ms).

Finally, distinctive variants of the spoken Jewish language could come into existence depending on the proportion of Hebrew and Judeo-Aramaic loans utilized. I said above that, except for Eastern Yiddish, Jewish languages display a negligible Hebrew-Aramaic component. However, in German areas where Yiddish was understood to some extent (despite the Slavic syntactic and phonological norms and the relatively large Hebrew and Judeo-Aramaic corpus), it became necessary for the Jews to develop a variant of Yiddish for cryptic purposes, e.g., in the market place. The cryptic variants of a Jewish language characteristically show an abnormally high Hebrew-Aramaic component, that could reach as high as 85%. But the artificial explosion of Hebrew-Aramaic components in a Jewish language does not guarantee incomprehension on the part of the non-Jews. Often, sizeable elements of the crypto-Jewish language have been expropriated by the non-Jews for use in their own cryptic dialects, e.g., (non-Jewish) German and Iranian slang lexicons have extremely high proportions of Hebraisms. This means that the Jews and non-Jews may share a Hebrew slang lexicon, if not their usual vernacular language. Indeed, the non-Jews may even create new "Hebraisms" which could be borrowed back by the Jews, e.g., Yiddish *šaxer-maxer* 'wheeler and dealer' < German *Schacher-Macher* 'ibid.', ultimately < Hebrew *saxar* '(to) trade' + German *Macher* 'dealer; maker', but the change of Hebrew *s* > *š* was committed by Germans, for most of whom *s* at the beginning of a word was ungrammatical (on the spread of this and other Germanized Hebraisms to the Slavic languages, see Wexler 1983a). When Hebrew *saxar* is the basis of a term composed by Yiddish speakers, the result is with *s*, e.g., Yiddish *saxren* 'to trade', since initial *s* is grammatical in Yiddish. Israeli Hebrew has now "Hebraized" German *šaxer-maxer* into *saxar-mɛxɛr,* literally 'trade' + 'sale' (see further discussion in chapter 5.11 below).

The reader may note that I have refrained from listing Old Hebrew as a "Judaized" Semitic language (see category IIa above). If the definition of a Jewish language is an originally non-Jewish language that has become "Judaized", then Old Hebrew is probably not a "Jewish" language. *Modern Hebrew, invested with spoken functions in the 1880s, is, however, a Jewish language—but not of the Semitic family.* The *opinio communalis* views Modern Hebrew as a direct continuation, or "revival" of Biblical and Mishnaic Hebrew. I argue that it is impossible to "revive" a language which has ceased to be the native language of a community, because there are no native speakers to supply a native norm. Thus, Modern Hebrew cannot be a "continuation", or "rebirth", of the unspoken Semitic language, Old Hebrew. Modern Hebrew simply embodies the syntax and sound system of the Eastern Yiddish language spoken by the first Modern Hebrew language planners in Ottoman Palestine, while its lexicon (about 75% German, 15% Hebrew—much of it original to Yiddish—and 10% heterogeneous Slavic, of which only Sorbian is native) was systematically replaced by Biblical and Mishnaic Hebrew vocabulary. The Slavic syntactic and phonological norms of Yiddish, the features which define the membership of a language in a family, and not the lexicon which is easily replaceable, have remained essentially unchanged. Now, since I will define Yiddish as a dialect of

Judeo-Sorbian (see more in chapter 4 below), I will have to define Modern Israeli Hebrew as a dialect of Judeo-Sorbian as well—with its roots extending back to the time when Judeo-Sorbian was spoken (in approximately the 9th–13th centuries). While I am the first to propose a Slavic origin for Modern Palestinian/Israeli Hebrew (1990f), others before me have classified the language as "common Indo-European" (see Bergsträsser 1928; ʿAmara 1967:72–3).

The use of a common name in English and Hebrew (see *ivrit* 'Hebrew') for both Old and Modern Hebrew confuses the issue. (I do not know the age of this term in the Jewish diasporas, or of Hebrew *ləšon qodɛš*, literally 'the holy language'—the traditional epithet for non-spoken Old Hebrew and Judeo-Aramaic.) The early Hebrew language planners were Zionists who maintained that the contemporary Jews were heirs to the Old Palestinian Jews, their historic homeland and national language, Semitic Hebrew. These early language planners purposely sought to encourage the identification of their "revived" spoken Hebrew with Old Semitic Hebrew by using a common language name, *ivrit,* though for a while a few early Hebrew language planners did propose a different term for Modern Hebrew, e.g., *sfat ɛvɛr,* literally 'the language of the Hebrews', but this never took hold. Only a few non-Jewish languages and Yiddish use separate terms for Old and Modern Hebrew, see e.g., Russian *drevneevrejskij* (literally 'Old Hebrew'—in opposition to *evrejskij* 'Yiddish; Jewish') and *ivrit* (< Modern Hebrew), or Yiddish *lošn kojdeš* (which also means 'Judeo-Aramaic') and *ivres,* respectively. But the double nomenclature may reflect the wish of Russian and Yiddish speakers to distinguish historical periods of the two spoken "Hebrew" languages—separated by some 1600 years—and not the recognition that the two forms of Hebrew belonged to two entirely separate language families.

I am convinced that the study of Jewish languages—individually or in a comparative framework—can make an original contribution to general linguistics and the study of the non-Jewish source languages. There are two reasons:

(a) The documentation of Jewish languages often predates that of the coterritorial non-Jewish speech. To cite a few examples, the earliest extant colloquial-like Arabic, Belorussian, Castilian Spanish, Czech, French and Modern Persian were recorded by Jews, usually in Hebrew-derived alphabets. Still, specialists of Arabic, Belorussian, etc. must utilize these data with extreme caution because of the idiosyncracies of

Judaized speech that I alluded to above; hasty extrapolation from one speech community to the other must be avoided (see Wexler ms b).

(b) Jewish languages tend to display features in a more developed or extreme form than non-Jewish languages. For example, the student of bilingual interference could find in Yiddish a particularly interesting laboratory, since Yiddish provides far more dramatic and varied contact phenomena than most languages. Three of the reasons are: (i) Yiddish has borrowed as much as 75% of its vocabulary from German and roughly another 15% from Hebrew and Judeo-Aramaic, plus a smaller percentage from Slavic languages (other than its native Sorbian); (ii) as a group, the speakers of Yiddish have remained in constant, uninterrupted contact for a thousand years with most of the languages which provided the bulk of their vocabulary, and (iii) tend to be fluent in the coterritorial non-Jewish languages. The last two factors especially tend to arouse the curiosity of many Yiddish speakers about the etymology of their words. In sharp contrast, English, which incorporated a huge corpus of Latin and French loans, has been spoken for centuries by a largely monolingual population which is not especially interested in the origins of its lexicon. The list of distinctive properties of Yiddish (and many of the other Jewish languages) could be expanded but this would take us much beyond the present discussion.

As I suggested in chapter 2 above, linguistics can provide invaluable help to the historian and archeologist. This is because the latter can only study extant documentation, while the linguist is in the unique position of being able to reconstruct stages that predate his oldest records. Even in the absence of any historical documents, the linguist can reconstruct quite a bit of the pre-literary stage of the language from examples of contemporary speech. In addition, the linguist can also reconstruct aspects of the external history of a language (e.g., where and by whom it was first used, its status in the community, its contact experiences with other languages, especially the possibility of partial language shift or relexification), and, through the latter, the outlines of the migration and settlement history of earlier speakers. Despite the assistance that historical linguists can render historians, the latter too frequently have ignored language data in writing history, bemoaning all along their inability to reconstruct more than a fragmentary and highly partial picture of past events. The problems of historical reconstruction are especially acute in Jewish history, where the historical (and even linguistic) records tend to be even spottier than in the coterritorial non-Jewish societies.

I am confident that the comparative study of Jewish languages will make major contributions to disciplines beyond Jewish and general linguistics, especially to the fields of Jewish history, ethnography and religion. I am not the first to appreciate this fact. Matthias Mieses, the insightful Polish Yiddishist murdered by the Germans in 1945, remarked in 1924:

> "From the analysis of the phonetic, inflectional and lexical state of affairs of the [Yiddish] language we have arrived at historical results, which future specialists in history may consider, in order to create from the fragments of the Jewish exile fate a synthetic, pragmatic, coherent whole standing on the level of European historical science" (1924:318).

A half century later, the Yiddishist, Marvin I.Herzog, in characterizing differences among Yiddish dialects, emphasized the

> "significance of the [Yiddish] language...boundaries—boundaries that might otherwise remain the only evidence of the very events which we invoke to explain them" (1979:56).

Avraham Poljak, in recognition of the prime importance of language data, appended a chapter on the origins of the Yiddish language to his book in Hebrew on the alleged Khazar origins of the Ashkenazic Jews (1951:315–23). His "disciple", Arthur Koestler, also urged the study of the Yiddish language in his English popularization of Poljak's thesis (1976:246).

The study of Jewish languages offers historians and archeologists precious evidence which will either corroborate their theories of migration and settlement history using independent data and methodologies, or provide fresh hypotheses for their consideration. The linguistic evidence is invaluable, in view of the otherwise scant documentation. If the hypotheses proposed by the linguist differ from those profferred by the historian or archeologist, even to the point of irreconcilabilty, I do not hesitate to give greater credence to the hypotheses of the linguist. The evidence of language, subject to verification and analysis through a system of interlocking oppositions, is usually more reliable than that of the chance documentation available to the historian or archeologist.

As I will show in chapter 4 below, the study of Judeo-Sorbian/Yiddish has thrust on center stage new hypotheses of Jewish settlement history, migration and the genesis of the Yiddish language that differ markedly from all the hypotheses that have been propounded thus far by historians and archeologists. The importance of Judeo-Sorbian/ Yiddish lies in the fact that this Jewish language probably came into existence by the close of the first millennium. *As such, it is one of the oldest surviving artifacts of the Ashkenazic Jews, even though there are no running texts in Judeo-Sorbian and the first Yiddish texts date only from the 15th century* (texts in Judaized, or "Ashkenazic" German are slightly earlier); as I said above, the first north European Hebrew texts also date from the beginning of the second millennium—but European Hebrew is best defined as an unspoken "variant of Judeo-Sorbian" (see above).

The hypothesis arrived at by a linguistic analysis of Yiddish prompts reassessment of the familiar findings gathered by students of Jewish history, religion, folklore (in particular, of superstitions and mythology), demography and population movement. The implications of the new hypothesis are significant, since the Ashkenazic Jews have constituted for several centuries the most numerous "Jewish ethnic group"; even today they make up the overwhelming bulk of world Jewry, despite the nearly total annihilation of European Jewry, most of whom were Ashkenazic, by the Germans and their collaborators during World War II. These were the Jews who historically spoke, and to some extent, still speak (or have passive knowledge of) Yiddish, the Jewish language with by far the largest body of speakers ever recorded—reaching 10 million on the eve of World War II. These Jews were the first to create a colonial dialect of a Slavic language in Western Asia, now known popularly as "Modern Hebrew".

All languages shed light on the early settlement history and prior abodes of the speakers. For example, Yiddish has unique Romance, Greek and Slavic components that are either not found in coterritorial non-Jewish languages which are themselves also receptive to enrichment from these sources, or are found in the coterritorial non-Jewish languages with radically different form and/or meaning. There are also a few unique words of Arabic and Iranian origin which must have become lodged in Judeo-Sorbian (and hence Yiddish) thanks to a Turkic intermediary agent. These components allow us to postulate channels of Jewish migration from the Mediterranean basin to the German lands through the Balkan Peninsula and Hungary, though we cannot say for sure what the first Jewish settlers in Germany spoke: Balkan Romance, South Slavic and/or Greek. In addition, the geographical distribution of these heterogeneous elements in Yiddish leads me to the conclusion that from the eastern reaches of Germany, i.e., from the originally mixed Germano-Slavic lands, the Jews fanned out westward to the monolingual German lands and down into northern France, southward into northern Italy, and back to the east across the monolingual Slavic lands.

The progressive reassignment of the Hebrew ethnonym *ʾaškenaz* (first cited in Jeremiah 51:27) is poignant testimony to the westward path that Jewish migration cut across the north of Europe. The term shifted from a designation of the Iranian Scythians to become that of Slavs and Germans by the 11th century—and finally of "German" (Ashkenazic) Jews in the 13th century; the Hebrew language name *lešon ʾaškenaz* 'the Ashkenazic language' first denoted Slavic and then German (and Yiddish).[3] The fact that the label *ʾaškenaz* could be applied both to Jews and non-Jews is testimony to the possible non-Jewish origins of most north European Jews. Other terms for "German(y)" used by Medieval European Jews (related to French *allemand* or Common Slavic **němьcъ* 'German') early went out of use in the face of the term "Ashkenaz(ic)".

The Jewish languages contain another sort of invaluable information for the historian of the Jews. For example, Yiddish contains a significant corpus of pagan and Christian vocabulary designating Jewish religious and superstitious beliefs which are of Slavic, Turkic, German, Greek, or Romance origin (the latter three often Slavicized).

Most of the components of the Judaized languages of Europe were undeniably adopted from non-Jewish languages. A host of linguistic and non-linguistic evidence leads me to the conclusion that a broad body of religious practices, superstitions and folklore shared by north European Jews with non-Jews in northern Europe and the Balkans is also of non-Jewish origin—diffused to the Jews when large numbers of indigenous non-Jews converted to Judaism. As I will show below, there is considerable evidence that when the common folk displayed no readiness to drop customs and religious practices disapproved of by the rabbis, the latter were often obliged to sanction them, imbuing the practices with new "Jewish" interpretations and elements.

Hence, contemporary Judaism is best defined not as the continuation of the Judaism which served as an antecedent of Christianity and Islam, but as a newly Judaized variant of European (mainly Slavic) paganism and Christianity; similarly, Modern Hebrew must be defined as a dialect of Slavic, and not as a direct descendant of Old Hebrew. Conversely, most of the features of Old Palestinian Judaism and Semitic Hebrew to be found in Ashkenazic "Judaism" and Medieval Ashkenazic/Modern Israeli "Hebrew" were latter borrowings rather than original inheritance.

Paradoxically, 19th-century reform and conservative (liberal) Judaism, by simplifying the religious services, abandoning many talmudic laws and allowing men and women to pray together are in some ways closer in form and content to forms of Old Palestinian and early diaspora Judaism than contemporary orthodox Judaism. A striking example is the equality of women as practitioners of the Jewish religion in both early diaspora and Old Palestinian Jewish communities on the one hand, and in reform and conservative Judaism on the other—in contrast to the restricted role of women in the male-dominated orthodox culture that developed in Medieval Europe (see Brooten 1982 and Yiddish *rebecn,* in category I, Greek 1 in chapter 5.11 below).

The accretion of non-Jews to the Jewish community was a major factor in the survival and eventual growth of the European Jewish communities. As I will show in chapter 6 below, the prime centers of proselyte activity were, in chronological order, Asia Minor, the Balkan Peninsula (including Greece and Hungary at either extreme), and finally, the mixed Germano-Slavic lands (corresponding to the territory of the former German Democratic Republic and neighboring areas of the Federal Republic up until 1990). This order matches the ever northwestward migration of the Jews within Europe. Assuming physical links between successive areas of proselyte activity, I could conclude that the overwhelming majority of the north European Jews descended from a mix of Greeks, Romans, indigenous Balkan peoples (e.g., possibly Illyrians, Dacians, Phrygians), East European and Asian peoples who migrated into central, eastern and southern Europe during the 6th century (e.g., the Avars, Khazars and Slavs), and to a lesser extent, Germanic tribes. In this motley of peoples, the Slavs appear to have played the major role.

Since Ashkenazic ethnographic evidence reveals greater Slavic and Romance than Greek and German components, I would not rule out the possibility that the bulk of the Ashkenazic Jews might trace their roots only as far back as the last two major centers of proselyte activity, e.g., to the Germano-Slavic and Balkan areas, but not to Asia Minor; this question requires further study. In any event, the link between the European Jews and the Old Palestinian Jews (= Hebrews, Israelites) is highly tenuous (more on this topic in chapter 4 below). Theoretically, Judeo-Sorbian (Yiddish) in turn might be a re-lexified form of Judaized South Slavic, but this is probably impossible to determine (see Wexler 1992b).

The present discussion permits us to formulate a new intriguing question for linguistic research: Did proselytes play a role in the genesis and development of Jewish languages in Europe, Africa and Asia? If so, in what sort of Jewish languages: the vernacular languages learned at birth, or the calque translation languages acquired by adults? Or in both?

A positive answer to this question would oblige us to distinguish terminologically between languages created by Jews and those created by non-Jewish proselytes to Judaism—say, "Jewish" vs. "Judaized languages", respectively (up till now, I have used these two terms interchangeably). Before examining the historical and ethnographic evidence in support of the hypothesis of a large proselyte component in the Ashkenazic Jewish ethnogenesis (see chapter 6 below), let me consider the implications of the proselyte hypothesis for our understanding of Jewish language creativity.

I will begin with the Jewish languages of literal Bible translation, the so-called calque languages. The reason given for the rise of this type of non-spoken language is that some Jewish males and almost all females were unfamiliar with Hebrew and Judeo-Aramaic and required a translation in order to understand the Bible and the prayers. But it seems to me that the reduced opportunities for women to play a role in the performance of Jewish rituals in northern Europe since the 12th century could not have provided an internal motive sufficient to warrant the creation of calque translations. Only in the Greco-Roman world and early northern Europe, where women played a more significant role in the religious life of the community and proselytes were extremely numerous (without necessarily knowing Hebrew?), might there have been serious motivation for producing such translations (see also discussion of Yiddish *rebecn* in category I, Greek 1 in chapter 5.11 below).

The first attested Jewish translation of the Bible, the Greek Septuaginta, done in Alexandria, Egypt, some of it as early as the first half of the 3rd century B.C., was characterized by a relatively free rendition of the original Hebrew text; this translation enjoyed popularity for several centuries. All subsequent translations of the Bible for use among the Jews slavishly imitated Hebrew syntax and word-derivation; the tradition of calque translations remained in vogue among the Jews until the end of the 18th century. It is curious that the earliest calque translations were composed by proselytes (a point that Schürer first made in 1909; see also Fuchs 1927 and Cassuto 1929). The first known example is the Greek translation of the Bible made by Aquila, a 2nd-century A.D. Greek proselyte to Judaism from Sinope (on the Black Sea, now Turkey). According to Jewish tradition, he made his translation—which remained in use in synagogues until the middle 6th century—because the Jews had become dissatisfied with the Septuaginta translation, once it had become widely quoted by Christians to justify the new religion. In Aquila's translation we see the first signs of what was to become a hallmark of Jewish translations for many centuries: the search for translation equivalents which were similar in both sound and meaning to the original Hebrew and Judeo-Aramaic words.

A second translator who may also have been a proselyte was Theodotion, a Greek contemporary of Aquila who possibly hailed from Ephesus (south of modern Izmir, Turkey) or Pontus (the province of Cappadocia, on the Black Sea, Turkey); his translation drew from the Septuaginta and was less bound to the Hebrew original than that of Aquila.

A third Greek translation was done in the second half of the 2nd century by Symmachus (or Symmachos), who was believed to have been either a member of the Judeo-Christian sect of Ebionites in Jordan or a Samaritan convert to Judaism.

The Judeo-Aramaic translation attributed to Onkelos (1st century A.D.) may be another proselyte achievement. I have no evidence about the identity of those who made the translations of the Bible into Yiddish or Judeo-Slavic known since the 14th century. That proselytes were among the intended audience for translations is suggested by the remark in the diary of the English writer, John Evelyn, relating his meeting with a Burgundian Jew in 1641 who had translated Jewish devotional literature (into "Judaized" English?) for his Kentish proselyte wife (1: 1901:26); unfortunately, no samples of this text survive.

A distinctive feature of all Jewish calque translations of the Bible is the near-total absence of Hebrew and Judeo-Aramaic words, including those very loans ordinarily used in spoken Jewish languages. For example, if contemporary spoken Yiddish normally expresses the concept of inheritance by the Hebrew loan *jeruše*, the earliest Yiddish Bible translations preserve the German term *arb*—cognate to Modern German *Erbe*. There is really no reason why colloquial Yiddish Hebraisms could not have been retained if the calque translations were made by native speakers of Yiddish. Their absence makes sense only if the translations were composed by and for proselytes, most of whom would have had knowledge of the languages spoken by the Jews but not of Hebrew and

Judeo-Aramaic (in later periods, when the volume of Hebrew in Yiddish rose considerably, German-speaking non-Jews certainly experienced difficulties in comprehending Yiddish). Alternatively, I might assume that the calque translations were composed by ethnic Jews before Hebraisms such as *jeruše* were borrowed by Yiddish, but this argument is problematic, since a number of Hebraisms (including this term?) surface in the earliest stages of a number of Jewish languages.

The tradition of calque translations, possibly initiated by newly converted non-Jews, was carried on by the descendants of Jews and proselytes even after widespread conversion in Slavic Europe had virtually ended by 1200, see e.g., the Yiddish calque translations of the 14th century and the East Slavic translation (the so-called Vilna Codex #262) that was probably done by Jews in the late 15th-early 16th century. The Judeo-Slavic text survives in a Cyrillic-alphabet version, which is unusual, since most Jewish languages, calque and vernacular, at least those attested since the 11th century, are traditionally written in the Hebrew alphabet (a manifestation of mounting Judaization?); the use of the Cyrillic alphabet might indicate widespread ignorance of Hebrew writing and language among the Jews, or a religious document intended for, or commissioned by, (Judaizing) Christians or (prospective) proselytes. (It is worth remembering that almost none of the Judeo-Latin and Judeo-Greek inscriptions and documents before the second millennium were recorded in the Hebrew alphabet. This fact supports a hypothesis of proselyte origin for the translators.) Future research should determine where and when Christians took an interest in the Jewish calque translations of the Bible and where Christians commissioned Jewish translations for their own use (see the example of Arragel's Judeo-Castilian Bible translation in Latin characters from the early 15th century, or the Christian publication of the last Western Yiddish translation of 1679 in the *Biblia pentapla* of 1711, discussed in detail in Wexler 1987c).

There are no extant Jewish translations of the Bible into any language from Europe between the Judeo-Greek Bible translations of the early first millennium and the Yiddish, Judeo-East Slavic and Judeo-Ibero-Romance (Ladino) translations of the 14th–16th centuries. Given our knowledge of when Judeo-Ibero-Romance and Judeo-Sorbian/Yiddish probably developed, there is no reason to push a calque language tradition in these languages back before the 10th–11th centuries. No Judeo-French translations are known. The absence of Bible translations for some 800–900 years suggests that there was no, or little Hebrew language tradition in the European diasporas (see also the absence of

Hebrew inscriptions or documents from Europe during this period). On the origins of European Hebrew literature, see the discussion of Judaization in chapter 7 below.

In his classic study of 1925 which continues to retain its relevance today, David S.Blondheim discussed at length the development of calque translations among the Jews, in particular, those into Judeo-Romance. He advanced the thesis that the Judeo-Latin translations—none of which survive—must have influenced the early Christian Latin Bible translation, known as the *Vetus latina.* He took as his evidence the preference for a literal translation (see, e.g., the Bibles of Tertulian and Saint Cyprian, which preserve a strong Hebrew-Greek syntactic imprint) and the use of many words, including neologisms, in the *Vetus latina* that surface in the much later surviving Judeo-Romance Bible translations. Blondheim imagined that the Jews could have influenced the Christian Bible up until about the 4th century thanks to their superior status in pagan society, their probable numerical superiority over the Christians, and close links between Jews and Christians.

Blondheim's hypothesis that Jewish converts to Christianity initiated the Christian calque translation tradition (1925:cxxiv) is reasonable, given that Christians made use of the Septuaginta and other Judeo-Greek translations, but is difficult to prove since only the Christians preserved a Bible rich in Judeo-Greek influences. I submit, alternatively, that the detailed lexical parallels between the Christian *Vetus latina* and the Judeo-Romance (and even Yiddish) translations of the Bible that survive from the late Middle Ages could just as well reflect the influence of Christian converts to Judaism on the first Judeo-Roman Bible translation(s). My interpretation seems more plausible than that of Blondheim, in view of two facts: (a) the existence of original Christian ecclesiastical terms in the Jewish translations and (b) early Jewish translations into Greek, known to have been made by proselytes. Blondheim assumed, arbitrarily, that original Jewish terms later became Christian ecclesiastical terms, while he seems to have been unaware of the proselyte authorship of the Judeo-Greek Bibles.

I should also stress that a translation language does not exist in the absence of a Jewish vernacular language. Most of the European Jewish languages appear to have been formed by 1000–1200 A.D. at the latest—precisely during the period of intense proselytism. In contrast, colloquial Jewish languages created after this period show a minor Jewish linguistic profile. The last European language to become Judaized—Judezmo (Judeo-Spanish)—was created when Judeo-Arabic and Judeo-

Catalan speakers began gradually switching to Castilian in the 11th century; this process of full language shift lasted until the early 1400s, about a century before the expulsions of the Iberian Jews (1492–8). I have no evidence of Arabic-speaking Jews leaving Spain in the wake of the expulsions. But the Castilian component of Judezmo is extremely close to Catholic Castilian norms; only the non-native components derived from the original Judaized languages of the Iberian Peninsula—Judeo-Arabic, Judeo-Catalan and Judeo-Greek—display some originality vis-à-vis the respective donor languages.

The fact that Judezmo is a weakly Judaized form of Castilian suggests that the Castilian Jews may not have undergone a strong Judaization process. The absence of Judaization among the Sephardic Jews could be interpreted in three ways: (a) A significant proselyte component was lacking among the Iberian Jews so that no artificial means were required to heighten the distance between Jews and non-Jews. (b) The nation-wide pogroms of 1391 (though they totally destroyed organized Catalan Jewry) did not lead to widespread segregation of Jews and non-Jews in the Peninsula, hence there was little difference in the dialects of the two groups. (c) Iberian Jews were in the process of becoming Christianized in language, culture, and perhaps in religion.

The only Jewish language that is radically distinct from the coterritorial non-Jewish dialects is Yiddish. In its (borrowed) Germanic lexicon, which constitutes approximately 75% of the total vocabulary of the contemporary Eastern European Yiddish dialects, there are numerous deviations from German semantic norms—even though Yiddish and German look quite similar on the surface. Consider the pair Yiddish *blien* and German *blühen* 'to bloom'; both verbs can be combined with a common verbal prefix, Yiddish *far-* and German *ver-* ([fer-]), yet the meanings of the resulting compounds are quite different: see Yiddish *farblien* 'bloom forth, on' vs. German *verblühen* 'cease blooming, fade'. The Yiddish verbal prefix has a perfective force—a common feature of verbal prefixes in Slavic (including *za-*, with which *far-* is productively linked; see Wexler 1964, 1972). Even in its minor Slavic lexical component, Yiddish differs from the coterritorial Slavic languages, e.g., Yiddish *trejbern* 'clean the meat of ritually unpure parts' vs. Old Czech *triebiti* 'remove defects, errors; bring to completion; improve, cultivate, purify (usually in relation to the harvest)', Upper Sorbian *trjebić* 'cleanse; clear (forest); castrate (fowl)' (see also discussion in category I, Slavic 6 in chapter 5.11 below).

It is striking that the "gap" between Yiddish and the coterritorial non-Jewish languages is greater than that between any other Jewish language and the coterritorial non-Jewish languages that supplied its major components. No scholar has accounted for this fact. I believe the massive gap between Yiddish and High German can be explained by the partial language shift, or re-lexification, from Judeo-Sorbian to High German lexicon; *the partial language shift, in turn, could have been prompted either by ethnic Jews or proselytes.* It is significant that of all the European Jewish languages, only Yiddish appears to have developed in a community comprising so many proselytes.

4

THE BALKAN ROUTE OF THE JEWS TO THE GERMANO-SORBIAN LANDS AND THE RISE OF JUDEO-SORBIAN/YIDDISH

The student of early Germano-Sorbian Jewish history needs to answer three questions:

(a) Were the Jews who first settled in Europe of immediate Palestinian origin or were they descended from Jews and prosleytes who had sojourned for generations in other areas? To what extent did Jews and non-Jewish proselytes from southern Europe and Asia Minor participate in a "*Drang nach Norden*"?

(b) What routes did the Jews follow in their trek to the Germano-Slavic lands? Via the Balkans and Central Europe, the Black Sea and Asia Minor, France and Italy?

(c) Where did Yiddish arise and what is its genetic classification?

In light of the fragmentary historical evidence, the best way to answer these questions is to examine the evidence provided by the Jewish languages; I will first summarize my answer to each question:

(a) All scholars have assumed that Palestinian Jews—to a modest degree mixed with indigenous European and Asia Minor non-Jews—made the long journey from the Eastern Mediterranean to northern Europe. I will argue, exploiting an array of linguistic and non-linguistic data from the Germano-Slavic lands and the Balkans (e.g., settlement history, religion, folk culture and demography), that the Ashkenazic Jews must have consisted of a mix of Greek, Balkan Romance and Balkan Slavic, Germano-Slavic and Turkic (Khazar, Avar) converts to Judaism and their descendants and only a minority of ethnic Jews—many of whom in all probability came from other parts of Europe rather than from Palestine itself. The north European Jews, separated from Palestine and for the most part from the major centers of "Jewish" scholarship (in Babylonia, Spain and northern France) developed various non-normative forms of Judaism, based on some inherited Palestinian Jewish customs and a Judaization of European and Asia Minor pagan and Christian religious practices.

(b) Traditionally, most linguists and historians have proposed France as the major, and Italy as the minor, immediate conduits for Jewish immigration into the southwest, and marginally southeast, German lands. I will show briefly why this view is untenable and will propose that the Jews chose the Balkans and Central Europe as the routes by which they travelled to the *southeast* German lands—the latter populated at that time by both Germans and West Slavs.

(c) Most scholars readily define Yiddish as a derivative of High German. The evidence of both Yiddish and comparative Jewish linguistics belies such a genetic assignment. On the basis of an analysis of the component structure of Yiddish, I argue that the language began originally as a dialect of Sorbian that became re-lexified to High German by the 13th century at the latest, but probably several centuries earlier in some locales. This claim is the basis for my belief that the Slavs played a major role in the ethnogenesis of the Ashkenazic Jews.

It is to five groups of scholars that we owe the standard explanation of a Franco-Italian Jewish settlement in the German lands and the genesis of Yiddish in the Rhineland on a Judeo-Romance substratum:

(a) Historians have combed the existing documentation relating to the Jews.

(b) Ethnographers have explored the roots of Ashkenazic Jewish folk traditions (though usually only in comparison with German folkways).

(c) Archeologists and historians have studied the extant Jewish material artifacts—cemeteries, synagogues and ritual baths—with an eye to establishing the origins of the architectural styles.

(d) Linguists have studied the three textually attested languages used by the German Jews (Hebrew, German, Yiddish) for clues to the direction of settlement within the German lands as well as to the original indigenous and imported languages of the first Jewish settlers in the German lands. The belief that Yiddish was a form of High German prompted linguists to ignore altogether the Slavic languages spoken in Germany, and to ascribe all Slavic features in Yiddish to much later contact with Czech, Polish, Belorussian, Ukrainian and Russian.

(e) Paleographers have studied the shapes of letters in the earliest Ashkenazic Hebrew documents. Curiously, the field of paleography, which enjoys the largest number of artifacts, is poorly appreciated by historians. Salomon A.Birnbaum, the well-known Austrian-born specialist in Yiddish linguistics and Hebrew paleography, who studied the shapes of the letters in the earliest German Hebrew documents, identified a French and Italian origin in the style of writing of these manuscripts (1954–7:300–1, 1979:66–7) and expressed his confidence that paleography would "shed light on the settlement history of the Jews and especially on the dark area of early Jewish history in Europe" (1931: 276).

While there is some disagreement over details, all specialists have traditionally concurred that the first German Jewish communities were founded by Jewish settlers hailing from France and/or Italy (see the reputed migration of a famous rabbinical family from Lucca, Italy to Mainz); the dates given vary from the 8th to the 10th century. Historians have also repeatedly pointed to a Jewish presence in the Rhineland during the Roman period, which appears to have been interrupted after the withdrawal of the Romans. The evidence consists of a mention of Jews in Cologne in an edict of Constantine the Great in 321–31 (known as the Codex Theodosianus, preserved in a 5th-century text) and 4th-century lamps possibly manufactured in Trier, which have Jewish motifs, e.g., the *mənōrāh*, a seven-branched candelabrum commonly used as a Jewish national symbol in the Greco-Roman period (see Unversagt 1919, table 6, ##181, 183, Reusch 1965:77–80 and Künzl 1988a:424, fn 3; on the *mənōrāh*, see also category I, Germanic 6, in chapter 5.11 below, under *māgen dāvid*).

The first known discussion of the Romance origin of the German Jews and their Yiddish language surfaces in the writings of the Hebrew grammarian Elia Baxur (Levita) (c.1468–1549), who noted that Rhineland Jews, by using French vocabulary unknown to his Bavarian Jewish compatriots, were clearly of French origin. The "*liaison française*" (with or without a minor Italian component) has enjoyed unquestioned popularity ever since the 16th century, in no small measure due to Baxur's enduring prestige. In the late 19th and 20th centuries, the theory of the southwestern German lands was to find additional support in the fact that the oldest extant Jewish cemeteries, synagogues and ritual baths were located in today's States of Hessen, Pfalz and Rhineland. This body of evidence meshed well with the desire of many historians and linguists to find the roots of the German Jews in Western Europe and to ensure the participation of the Jews in the *Drang nach Osten* of the Germans, in force since the 8th–9th centuries.

I will label the popular view of German Jewish and Yiddish genesis the "Romance hypothesis". During the last eighty years or so, linguists have proposed no less than seven variants of this hypothesis; I will add an eighth:

I. The "Romance hypothesis":

VARIANT A: The Jewish settlers who came to the Rhineland, and marginally to Regensburg in Bavaria in the 9th–10th centuries were of French and Italian Jewish stock who spoke Judaized variants of these two languages. This is the view of Max Weinreich (1956a, 1973). Yiddish was created when the French- and Italian-speaking Jews switched to German. Judeo-French could have become extinct in the southwest German lands by the mid 15th century, since the Jews were definitively expelled from the Kingdom of France and Franche-Comté in 1394. I see no evidence that German Jews ever spoke Judeo-Italian, though some probably became exposed to the language when they migrated to northern Italy between the 14th–16th centuries. Italian Jews have developed their own dialects of Italian, but there is disagreement over the age of these dialects; the linguistic behavior of the Jews in France also remains a subject of debate (see Wexler 1989: preface).

Jews allegedly adopted/adapted the German dialects of the Rhineland, adding a small Judeo-Romance substratum and Hebrew-Aramaic elements—both inherited from Judeo-Romance and newly borrowed from texts by Yiddish speakers. As this Judaized German amalgam was brought by settlers to the central and southeast German lands, the German component became almost exclusively High German.

In the 12th century, the Jews are said to have established contact with Slavic languages. While the Slavic contribution to the total spoken Eastern Yiddish lexicon probably never exceeded 10%, Slavic—along with Hebrew—was held responsible for the dramatic reshaping of Yiddish phonology, semantics and syntax that produced such a marked gap between those dialects of Yiddish spoken in the Slavic lands and all of the German dialects from which Yiddish was supposed to have been derived. The physical separation of Yiddish in the Slavic lands from metropolitan German was also said to have contributed heavily to the retention in Yiddish of German archaisms and deviations from German norms (M.Weinreich 1956b, U.Weinreich 1958; this last claim ignores the fact that both High and Low German were spoken alongside Yiddish in many areas of Eastern Europe for some seven centuries).

VARIANT B: This variant is identical to variant (a) except that the Jewish settlers were regarded as exclusively of French stock who spoke (Judeo-)French. Linguists such as Bin-Nun 1973 and S.A.Birnbaum

1979 have promulgated this variant; among historians, Salfeld and Bein speak only of a putative French Jewish immigration to Mainz (1934: 176).

VARIANT C: The Jewish settlers were of Italian stock, spoke Italian and settled in Bavaria. This view was first proposed by Matthias Mieses, though he did not speak of a specifically Judaized Italian (1924:106). After a long period of oblivion, this theory has emerged with heightened popularity in the 1970s and 1980s, see, e.g., the writings of Bin-Nun 1973, Faber and King 1984 and King 1987.

VARIANT D: The Jewish settlers were only of French stock, and spoke Judeo-French, but they did not become speakers of German. Variant (d) differs from variant (b) in regarding the syntax and phonology of Yiddish as essentially Judeo-French and Hebrew *(sic!)* in origin; the German component is limited mainly to the vocabulary. This view was proposed by Š.M.Lazar (1913:55–7). Except for a brief mention by Matthias Mieses (1924:246), no scholar has ever referred to Lazar's theory of "partial language shift" or "re-lexification" (my terms) from Judeo-French or Hebrew to German lexicon. As I will show below, Lazar was right about the mechanism of re-lexification, only his proposal of a French or Hebrew starting-point was erroneous.

VARIANT E: The Jewish settlers were speakers of Italian and/or Rhaeto-Romance. Denman, who proposed this view in 1991, was more categorical than I had been a few years earlier when I tentatively proposed a Rhaeto-Romance origin for a few Yiddish Romanisms (1988:94, 123, 126, fn 227; for my most recent formulation, see variant [h] below).

VARIANT F: The Jews who were noted as residents in the German lands in the 9th–10th centuries were descended from a Jewish community that was established in the Roman period. These Jews spoke Judeo-Latin for centuries after the withdrawal of the Romans, switching to German only around the 11th century. The sole protagonist of this view was Leo Fuks 1987 who never provided a shred of evidence.

VARIANT G: The Jews came from Italy as speakers of a Germanic language—Langobard. The sole protagonist of this view is Šmuel Hajle 1990, who, like Fuks in variant (f), never provided evidence.

VARIANT H: I find all seven variants unacceptable (see my 1987b, 1991b, 1992b). I believe that if the initial Jewish settlers to the southeast Germano-Sorbian lands spoke Romance at all, it was most likely a Balkan Romance variant (or else Balkanized Friulan or Venetian), alongside South Slavic and Greek (ibid.:1992b).

The alleged migration of Romance Jews into the German lands in the west is matched by purported migrations of Jews into southeastern Europe from the Black Sea or what is all too often improperly called "southern Russia", i.e., from southern Rus' (the contemporary Ukraine). These theories offer both a replacement for, and an ancillary conduit to, the alleged Romance channels of migration. The "Ukrainian" Jews are held by many scholars to have merged with the Yiddish-speaking Western European Jews on the territory of Poland and the East Slavic lands. The "Ukrainian" theory introduces Jews into the East Slavic lands in four variants (sources and details are provided by Weinryb 1962b).

II. The "Ukrainian" hypothesis:

VARIANT A: Jews came from Scythia or the Caucasus c.600 B.C.

VARIANT B: Jews came from Babylonia and Iran in the early Christian period.

VARIANT C: Jews came from Byzantium or Palestine in the 7th–10th centuries.

VARIANT D: Jews came from the Khazar Kingdom in the 10th century.

How should we evaluate these proposals? It is doubtful that new historical discoveries will ever tip the scale in favor of one proposal or another. It is also doubtful that an anthropological or genetic study of Ukrainian Jews can assist in evaluation. Only a careful analysis of the linguistic and ethnographic data can lead us out of this labyrinth of hypotheses and counter-hypotheses. First I will explain why I reject the variants of the Romance hypothesis which posit a (Judeo-)French origin and a southwest German homeland for Yiddish:

(a) There are hardly any southwest German dialect features in any dialect of Yiddish.

(b) Western Yiddish is relatively monolithic compared to the extreme heterogeneity of the coterritorial west German dialect landscape, which hints at a late arrival of Yiddish in the area (on the definition of Western and Eastern Yiddish, see chapter 3, footnote 1 above).

(c) Yiddish comprises a very minor French component—primarily in its southwest German, Swiss, Alsatian and Dutch dialects; in other Yiddish dialects, Gallicisms are limited to a handful of names, e.g., *sime* feminine < Hebrew *śimḥāh* (/ḥ/ was pronounced as zero by the French Jews, vs. /x/ by Yiddish speakers; see discussion in chapter 5.12 below). Other non-native components, both minor and major (e.g., unique non-French Romance, Greek, West Slavic and occasional "Oriental" components), surface throughout all the Western and Eastern Yiddish dialects—a fact which points to the (south)east German lands as their conduit (Wexler 1988:chapter 2).

(d) There is no evidence that the Romance speech of the Jews who settled in the German lands was uniquely "Judaized" as Max Weinreich claimed. The nature of the French spoken by the Jews prior to the expulsion of the Jews from the Kingdom of France and Franche-Comté in 1394 is uncertain; in Italy, the Jews developed their own dialects of Italian, but Yiddish offers no clear reflection of the latter.

The dialect of French spoken in Lorraine, an area reputedly settled by the Jews who may have migrated to the adjacent German lands, contains features which are not attested in the unique Romanisms in Yiddish. The problem with the claim that small numbers of Jews from Lucca, in northwestern Italy, settled in Mainz by the end of the first millennium is that Luccan Italian features are not present in the corpus of unique Yiddish Romanisms. Lorraine French continues Latin *ka*, and changes *ū* > *u*, while Yiddish Romanisms point to a newer *ča* and *ü*, respectively; features of Yiddish Romanisms such as these, as well as the *pl*-cluster and the retention of the *-s* plural, are not found (at least not now) in Luccan Italian.

Very few historians have proposed a migration of German Jews south into the northern French lands (a rare exception is Schwarzfuchs 1980). Nevertheless, such a migration is strongly suggested by the fact that numerous Germanisms (not to speak of Slavisms—unless these were later inserted into the text by Slavic speakers) appear in the Hebrew writings of Rashi, the famous Champagne-born commentator of the Bible and Talmud (1028/1040?–1105). As I showed elsewhere (1992b), there is also reason to suppose that Balkan and Italian names used in Yiddish were diffused to the French lands. The strong imprint of French Jewish rabbinical literature on the German Jews is undeniable, but it does not require the migration of French Jews into Germany! Hence, I reject the popular term "Franco-German Jewry"—the allegedly uniform population which formed the nucleus of Ashkenazic Jewry (used by Spiegel 1949:540, Baron 3:1957:174, *inter alia*). As I will argue below, the northern French Jewry, originally bearing few connections to the Provençal Jewry in the south (which could well be of Roman origin), should be regarded primarily as a colonial offshoot of German Jewry.

The diffusion of Jews from the German to the French lands is paralleled by the spread of linguistic features from north to south among the Christians. Consider the diffusion of Judeo-Christian terminology from Germany into France, as, e.g., French *samedi*, Old French *sambedi* with *m* < German *Sam(stag)* < Judeo-Greek *sambata* < Hebrew *šabbāt* 'Saturday'—in opposition to most other Western Romance languages which lack *m*, e.g., Italian *sabato*, Spanish *sábado* < Latin < non-Judaized Greek *sabbata*.

(e) The German spoken by the Jews in the southwest German lands appears to have had a distinctly different origin from Yiddish (see below). Elsewhere (1981a), I labeled this Judaized German by the term "Ashkenazic German", on the basis of the late 18th–19th-century native language name in use among the German Jews. Thus, the southwest German lands were home to French Jews migrating north and Sorbian-speaking Jews coming from the east of Germany.

(f) The variants of the Romance substratum hypothesis which advocate an Italian or Rhaeto-Romance origin and a (south)east German homeland are plausible, but there is no evidence that Jews spoke either Judeo-Latin or Langobard in the 9th–10th centuries. The small unique Romance component of Yiddish which has attained for the most part a pan-Yiddish status, together with a small corpus of unique Grecisms known in most Yiddish dialects, suggests that the most likely path of Jewish migration from the Mediterranean to northern Europe was through the Balkans, Hungary and Bohemia, and not through France (see also below). So far approximately fifty unique Romance elements have been identified in Yiddish, many of which could be of (Balkanized?) Italian origin. "Unique Yiddish Romanisms" are elements not found among the Romance borrowings of coterritorial German and West Slavic—the sources of most of the (non-unique) Romance component in Yiddish. A number of Yiddish Romanisms may be from Friulan or Dalmatian. Moreover, the existence of probable Italianisms in Yiddish does not necessarily require an "Italian" origin for the first German Jews, since a number of prospective Italianisms show evidence of being accepted by "pre-Yiddish" (= South Slavic?) in the Balkans and not in the Italian Peninsula.

Consider only two examples:

(i) For pan-Yiddish *benčn* 'bless' M.Weinreich opted for an Italian source, due to the presence of *-č-*; French *bénir* 'bless' is a late learned borrowing from Latin and thus is an unlikely etymon (1: 1973:34, 2:68, 4:96–9). Yiddish *benčn* has close formal links with south Italian *benedicere* (~ standard *benedire*), but the geographical distance poses a problem. A Balkan venue for the borrowing is motivated by the fact that both *bene* and *dīcere* are found in Balkan languages (e.g., Albanian *bekoj*, Serbo-Croatian *dìčiti [se]* 'to praise'), and all the Balkan languages have translations of the Romance expression, e.g., Bulgarian *blagoslavjam*, Rumanian *binecuvînta*, literally 'well' + 'speak'.

(ii) M.Weinreich derived Yiddish *frimzl* 'noodle' from (Judeo-) French *vermeseil*, itself a borrowing from Italian; the earliest Yiddish example dates from the 12th century. I doubt that this can be the etymon since the earliest French attestation dates only from 1675. I prefer to derive Yiddish *frimzl* directly from Italian *vermicello* (plural *vermicelli*) but the change in the order of syllables from *ver-* > *fri-* can be motivated in either a South (or West) Slavic milieu. Moreover, native Serbo-Croatian *cȓn* 'worm' is the basis of the term *crvìna* 'section of noodle dough', *cŕvić* (diminutive) 'noodle'—parallel to Italian *vermicello* 'little worm; noodle' < *verme* 'worm'. I owe these data to Skok 1:1971:276, who provides no dates. According to Hope 1:1971:227, the oldest example of Italian *vermicelli* is from 1553, but the Yiddish datum suggests that the Italian derivative could have been considerably older. On Slavo-Romance symbiosis among Balkan non-Jews, see Skok 1934: 130.

See also the discussion of Yiddish *nitl* 'Christmas', *lejenen* 'read' below. Further details are given in Wexler 1992b. Future studies should compare the model of Romance substrata in Yiddish with the hypothesis that Bavarian German developed on a Rhaeto-Romance substratum (Markey 1988).

Curiously, the evidence of a Jewish presence in the mixed Germano-Sorbian and Germano-Polabian lands since the mid 10th century, most of which was already known in the late 19th and early 20th centuries, has not been able to shake the hypothesis of a "southwest" cradle of Yiddish and German Jewry, except to elicit the occasional concession that Jews settled in Regensburg and along the Elbe River at about the same time that they did in the Rhineland. I am thinking of the evidence of a Jewish presence in Salzburg, to judge from the Salzburger Formelsammlung (798–821), of peripatetic Jewish merchants in Raffelstetten (in Upper Austria, between Linz and Enns) c.906 (though there may not have been a permanent settlement here), in Magdeburg and Nienburg, Anhalt (the latter known in Slavic as Novgrad) from approximately 965 (recorded in the Arabic writings of the Catalonian Jewish traveler, Ibrāhīm ibn Ja'qūb); there are also sedentary Jewish communities noted in Merseburg, late 10th century, Meissen and Halle, early 11th century, Bamberg 1097–8, Erfurt 1137 and Leipzig, 12th century. The Salzburg source may contain the earliest reference to a "Slavic Jew", if the passage *medicum iudaicum vel sclavianiscum* 'a Jewish (or) Slavic doctor' refers to a single individual (see Aronius 1902:29ff, #80; Löwe 1988:168). The text is ambiguous since *vel* can mean or, even, actually, especially.

In many areas early settled by Jews, Slavic was still spoken as late as the 14th century, e.g., in northeast Bavaria. In many other areas, Slavic died out only in the early 15th century (e.g., in Brandenburg, Meissen, northeast Bavaria, on the island of Rügen)—but was still spoken in the Lüneburg area up to the late 18th century. There are also a number of indications that Jews in the mixed Germano-Sorbian lands were speakers of Slavic. For example, a reference to Jews in Spandau (near Berlin), possibly from the 12th century, states that Jews were obliged to take an oath "in German"; this suggests that the indigenous Jews may have spoken Slavic (Sorbian, Polabian?) as a matter of course. As I noted above, Slavic glosses also appeared in the Hebrew writings of the French scholar, Rashi (1028/1040?–1105), who hailed from Troyes, Champagne.

There are no records of Judeo-Sorbian, but traces of the language can be found in Medieval Hebrew documents (most of which have traditionally been described as "Czech"—see M.Weinreich 1956b, Jakobson 1957 and Jakobson and Halle 1964) and in non-Jewish languages (e.g., German and Slavic). Until approximately the 13th–14th century, Sorbian speakers inhabited the eastern half of the present-day German lands in various strengths; today, the Sorbian population numbers some 70,000 bilinguals in the Nieder- and Oberlausitz (in Brandenburg and Saxony, respectively).

The *historical* evidence from the Germano-Sorbian lands sketched above allows us to question the alleged primacy of a primeval southwestern German Jewish community—since clearly the east was settled at the same time as the west—but does not enable us to reconstruct the paths of Jewish migration within the German and Germano-Sorbian lands. As I said above, barring the discovery of new documents or artifacts, it is unlikely that historians or archeologists will be in a position to formulate new theories. New thinking on the origins of the German Jews and Yiddish can only come from linguistics (on the contributions of ethnography, see chapter 5.2 below).

My analysis of Yiddish has led me to propose a Sorbian origin for this language and a Balkan, probably Slavic, origin for its speakers. Hence, I follow Matthias Mieses (given in Romance variant [c] above) and propose a new variant (h), which sees the lands between the Danube River in Bavaria and the Saale and Elbe Rivers in Saxony as the homeland of Yiddish. In addition, I insist on two further innovations:

(a) Yiddish is not a "form of German", and

(b) the German lands were settled by Jews in the southwest and (south)east *independently,* though possibly simultaneously. The two groups shared some sort of Romance linguistic background *(inter alia),* but developed very diverse linguistic profiles in their new homelands.

The language known as Yiddish (since the 16th century) developed in the bilingual Germano-Slavic lands in the 9th century as a Judaized form of Sorbian, and the local Jews were probably overwhelmingly of Balkan origin (see variant [h] above). The original immigrants could have spoken Balkan Slavic, Romance or even Greek—but Slavic seems to be the best guess. (This might explain the preference of the Jewish immigrants to merge with the Sorbian—rather than with the German-speaking community.) I reach this conclusion on the basis of convergent linguistic and historical data, and because there is no substance to the claims made for a French substratum in Yiddish.

Aside from Yiddish evidence, the importance of the Balkan zone is borne out by facts in many of the European Christian languages. For example, Hebrew *jəhūdī* 'Jew; Judean' is not the immediate basis of the ethnonym Jew in most European languages. Rather, derivatives of Latin *iūdaeus* (mentioned in chapter 1 above), specifically north Italian *giudeo,* are used in most European languages, especially in languages with uninterrupted geographical links to northern Italy (keep in mind that north Italian dialects were early diffused to the northern Balkans), e.g., French *juif,* Hungarian *zsidó,* Polish *żyd,* Serbo-Croatian *Žȉdov.* A north Italian source for "Jew" is plausible since this area was important in the early settlement history of the European Jews. Even Balkan Judezmo *džidjó* and Yiddish *jid* 'Jew' may be derivatives of the north Italian word—in counterdistinction to Spanish *judío* (with *u* in the first syllable) and German *Jude.* Yiddish also shuns the Hebrew word *jəhūdī*, see, e.g., *jid* 'Jew' and Eastern Yiddish *jidišn* ~ Western Yiddish *jid(i)šn*, *jičn* 'circumcise' (literally 'make Jewish'—though 'circumcision' is expressed by the Hebraism *bris* < Hebrew *brīt*, literally 'covenant'). If Yiddish *jid* had been taken from German, I would have expected *Jüde* in German; the latter exists, but only in dialects spoken at a distance from German Yiddish (but see standard German *Jüdin* 'Jewess'). We might then postulate a Slavic origin for Yiddish *jid* (on *dž*> *j*, see Italian *gentile* 'noble' > Yiddish *jente* woman's name). H.Birnbaum recently rejected a link between Slavic *žid* and Yiddish *jid* on chronological grounds (1985:5), but there is no problem if we accept the hypothesis of a Sorbian origin for Yiddish. A few languages, e.g., Greek, Russian and Belorussian, use the term "Hebrew" to denote the Jews (in general).

Judeo-Sorbian underwent "re-lexification" to High German, at various times and in various locales, beginning with the 9th–10th centuries, but at the latest by the early 13th century. The result of such a *partial language shift* was the grafting of High German vocabulary (reaching c.75% in most contemporary East European dialects of Yiddish and even higher in some forms of Western Yiddish) onto a Judeo-Sorbian syntax, phonology, phonotactics, and to some extent, morphotactics. Thus, despite its "German look", Yiddish remains a West Slavic language; its genetic classification hardly changes because of its lexical reorientation, no matter how major. By the mid–13th century, Yiddish was transported for the first time to Poland, and in the late 14th century, to Belorussia.

At the close of the 19th century, a small number of Eastern Yiddish speakers carried out another partial language shift, or re-lexification, this time from Yiddish (German) vocabulary to Biblical and Mishnaic Hebrew vocabulary; they called the resulting language "Modern Hebrew". Within merely a century of the rise of Modern Hebrew, we witness the incredible fact that Hebrew has become the native or second language of several million Jewish, Arab, Druze and Circassian residents of Israel and the second language of a large population of Arabs living in the occupied Palestinian and Syrian lands and in Egypt (the Sinai). Recently, Hebrew has also become a "colonial" language, since it is the primary language of perhaps as many as one million Israelis who have created a modern diaspora abroad since 1948.

The notion that Modern Hebrew represents the "revival" of Biblical and Mishnaic Hebrew is trumpeted from every side in our days, but common sense must stand firm against this erroneous view. I reject the *opinio communalis* that Modern Hebrew was "revived" as a modern, defrosted version of Biblical or Mishnaic Hebrew—the last stage of colloquial Hebrew in the 3rd century A.D.—since no language can be "revived" in the absence of a body of native speakers. The so-called process of "revival" only involved the transplanting of vocabulary from one language to another; this is a commonplace development, though not usually to the massive extent that Modern Hebrew *borrowed* from Biblical and Mishnaic Hebrew. The syntax and phonological system of Modern Hebrew remain Yiddish (i.e., Slavic). Just as Yiddish was a dialect of Judeo-Sorbian which had been re-lexified to High German, Modern Hebrew must be defined as a dialect of Yiddish which recently became re-lexified to Biblical and Mishnaic Hebrew. In both acts of partial language shift, the new resulting speech form did not—in fact, could not—belong to another language family: thus, both Yiddish and Modern Hebrew are dialects—to be sure, bizarre because of their lexicon—of Sorbian (see Wexler 1990f, Horvath and Wexler ms).

My proposed genesis of Yiddish can be supported by a variety of evidence, which I present here in an abbreviated form; further details are available in my 1987b, 1991b, 1992b:

(a) There is a small, possibly West Slavic component in Western Yiddish dialects which cannot be convincingly attributed to Eastern Yiddish migrants to Western Europe beginning with the mid–17th century, as has been widely proposed (e.g., by Beranek 1961:275, fn 25 and Bin-Nun 1973:46–7). These words can be smoothly derived from Sorbian. A few examples are Alsatian Yiddish *bā*, Eastern Yiddish *babe, bobe* 'grandmother' (~ Upper Sorbian *baba*); Eastern Yiddish *blince* 'pancake' (see also Silesian German *plins[en]* ~ Upper Sorbian *blinc*); Old Western Yiddish, Eastern Yiddish *bok* 'non-Jewish God' (this component surfaces in German *Bockshorn*, now understood as 'goat's horn', but originally a euphemistic replacement for tabu *Gotteszorn* 'the anger of God' ~ Upper Sorbian *bóh* 'God'; this may be the basis of the association of 'devil' and 'goat' in German *Bock*). Other examples are Western Yiddish (Regensburg 15th c), Eastern Yiddish *dunaj* 'Danube' (~ Upper Sorbian *Dunaj* vs. German *Donau*), Eastern Yiddish *jojx* 'broth' (vs. German *Jauche* 'sewer water' ~ Upper Sorbian *juška*), Western Yiddish *kawleč*, Eastern Yiddish *kojleč* 'festive bread' (see Thüringen German *kalatsche* 'baked goods' ~ Upper Sorbian *kołač*, and Yiddish *kojleč* in category I, Slavic 3 in chapter 5.11 below).

On the possibility that some of these Yiddish Slavisms might have been acquired by the Jews in the South Slavic lands, see below.

(b) Yiddish dialects (especially in the east) possess an inordinately large Hebrew component that finds no parallel in any other Jewish language. In addition, Hebrew exercises "component dominance" over other components—including the majority German lexicon—which takes the form of formal and/or orthographic Hebraization of non-Hebrew components, as well as their outright replacement by Hebrew loans. For example, Yiddish *nitl* 'Christmas', of Romance stock (see standard Italian *Natale*, dialectal Italian *nedal*, Old Dalmatian *nadal*, etc.), is widely regarded as the result of reshaping to Hebrew *nitlāh* 'hung', a derogatory reference to the crucifixion of Christ. The first example of the reshaping is the French Hebrew spelling *njtl* (instead of the expected phonetic spelling *njṭl*) in a 14th-century document from Vesoul, Franche-Comté (Loeb 1884:193). Yiddish has no examples with a vowel other than /i/ in this word.

The sweeping use of Hebraisms might have been motivated by the desire of the Sorbian Jews to come to terms with the rising tide of Germanization which threatened complete language shift to German (the fate of most of the German Slavs), a development presumably unattractive to the Jews since Germanization was tantamount to Christianization. See also the discussion of Yiddish *gojlem* in category II, Slavic 1 in chapter 5.11, and *homen(-taš)* and *nedan* in chapters 5.13 and 5.14, respectively.

(c) Yiddish tends to use Hebraisms (and occasionally unique Romanisms) where Sorbian uses Germanisms. An example is Yiddish *lej(en)en* 'read' < Italian *leggere* (~ north Italian *lejere*) or Balkan Romance vs. Upper Sorbian (archaic) *lazować* < German dialectal /lazen/ (~ standard German *lesen*; on *lejenen*, see also category II, Romance 4 in chapter 5.11 below). The widespread overlap in the distribution of borrowed lexicon—not found between Yiddish and any other Slavic language—suggests that Jews and Sorbs must have once been coterritorial, and that each group responded to the common inroads of Germanization in its own way. Jews may have succeeded better than most Sorbs in resisting the pressures of Germanization because of their close ties with the Slavic-speaking Jewish communities in the Czech lands. (But then, why were most Sorbs not so affected? Had German settlement by then interrupted the territorial continuity of the Sorbs, Czechs and Poles? Also, German missionary efforts may have been directed primarily or exclusively at the conversion of pagans, not Jews, to Christianity.)

(d) A number of Slavisms in Polish Yiddish which are clearly not of Polish origin have usually been derived from Belorussian and Ukrainian, possibly via the local Yiddish. Diffusion from Eastern Yiddish dialects is an unattractive hypothesis, since the Slavicisms are widely known in Yiddish in areas far from the two East Slavic languages. But there are no linguistic obstacles to regarding the bulk of the "East Slavisms" in Polish Yiddish as Sorbianisms. For example, Yiddish *mučen* 'torment' on phonetic grounds could in theory be derived from Ukrainian *mučyty* or Belorussian *mučyc'*, but the presence of Yiddish *mučen* in western Poland makes Upper Sorbian *mučić* a more attractive etymon; Polish *męczyć* must be excluded as an etymon on formal grounds.

(e) The contemporary Belorussian-Baltic Yiddish dialects (except for Kurland Yiddish which has strong affinities to Western Yiddish) have a higher "Judeo-Sorbian profile" than the Polish Yiddish dialects. The former were introduced into their present location by the first wave of German Jewish immigrants in the 13th–14th centuries; present-day Polish Yiddish continues the relatively more Germanized Yiddish introduced into Poland in the 1600s, which supplanted the original Yiddish brought there in the 13th century. Significantly, the Judeo-Sorbian imprint is stonger in those Yiddish dialects which were coterritorial with German for the shortest period of time. The Yiddish that continued to be spoken in Germany underwent extreme Germanization, resulting in the incorporation of many German syntactic and phonological features, thus facilitating the complete shift to High German that took place between the late 18th and early 19th centuries.

(f) There is evidence that the Jews themselves were uncertain of the relationship of their language to coterritorial German and Slavic:

(i) A non-committal language name *jidiš*, literally 'Jewish', has been in use since the 16th century.

(ii) The language has been broadly receptive in the last hundred years to Hebrew elements, but relatively closed to Modern German and new Slavic influences. Nevertheless, the latter two components are utilized ambivalently. For example, Old Yiddish words with a Slavic verbal infix are replaced by a synonymous German morpheme, e.g., the verbal infix *-eve-* > *-ir-* (thus creating a distribution for *-ir-* that differs from that of German *-ier-*), but *-eve-* still plays a role today in generating Yiddish neologisms (see Wexler 1982c).

(g) The attested Jewish settlements in southern Europe in the early Christian period and those in northern Europe that emerge in the 9th–10th centuries can best be linked by a presumed migration through the Balkans and northeastern Italy.

During the first millennium, Jewish settlements are attested at various locations in Macedonia, Thrace, Bulgaria, Serbia, Croatia and Hungary (south and west of the Danube River). Switzerland (Roman Rhaetia) is conspicuously free of Jewish settlements, even though this was an important link between Roman Italy and Bavaria. It is significant that Jewish settlements in northern Italy are extremely rare until the 12th century; examples are Aquileia (3rd–4th centuries), Milan, Tortona (4th century), Grado (late 4th-early 5th centuries), the Padua region, Turin, Genua, Ravenna (5th–6th centuries), Imola (7th century), etc. Though a significant break appears in Jewish settlement history in several locales, e.g., in Aquileia and throughout Hungary (Roman Pannonia). The reason for the latter may be the dislocating affects of the Germanic, Avar and Slavic invasions between the 5th and 7th centuries. This would also account for the gap of several centuries between the dates of Jewish settlement in the Balkans and the Germano-Slavic lands. There appears to be no evidence of a Balkan Jewish migration to the north before these invasions. Apart from the mention of Salzburg and Raffelstetten, Jews are not noted in Austria until the early 11th century in Kärnten, Steiermark and Lower Austria.

The French-speaking lands are an unlikely source for the German Jews since settlements in the north of France date only from the early 11th century—with the exception of Metz and Paris in the mid 4th and late 6th century, respectively. Finally, the extent of documented Jewish presence in the northwest Balkan Peninsula and Hungary during the first millennium is more impressive than that of the Italian Peninsula.

The discontinuity in European Jewish settlement history raises doubts about a significant northward Jewish migration into the mixed Germano-Slavic lands by the 9th–10th centuries. Hence, I suppose that the German Jews were descended from a small Balkan and Mediterranean Jewish population which was augmented by a large body of converts of varied origins—first and foremost among them being the pagan Western, and possibly also Southern, Slavs. This means that converts to Judaism in Asia Minor and southern Europe may have only played a minor role in the ethnogenesis of the Ashkenazic Jews. It is unlikely that Jews would have had a unique pattern of migration, barring, of course, instances where they alone were expelled from a territory. Indeed, the Jews may not have been the only Balkan immigrants to Germany: in the course of the 7th–8th centuries, South Slavs apparently also migrated north into the German lands, to judge from the existence of common Slavic placenames in the German lands and the Balkans (Kunstmann 1987:187ff); note also the similarity of the Slavic ethnic names *sorb* (in the German lands) and *serb* (in the Balkans). The northern migration of South Slavs offers further support for the hypothesis that the first Jews in the Germano-Slavic lands were Slavic-speaking; conversely, the Jewish data add support to Kunstmann's thesis.

Baron's charge (4:1957:86, 90) that "masses of Jews" settled in northern Europe during the 12th century is devoid of corroboration (as I.A.Agus 1962:3, fn 2 rightly complained). Nor is there a speck of evidence in the rabbinical literature of the 12th and 13th centuries of any sort of cultural clash or confrontation between indigenous German Jews and "foreign" Jews emanating from the Middle East or elsewhere. Hence, any increase in the German Jewish population during that period should be ascribed primarily to local factors. (The suggestion that heightened Judaization was made possible by Near Eastern Jewish immigrants to Europe [see chapter 7 below] need not require a sizeable immigration.)

There are other demographic problems which should have alerted scholars to the implausibility of the traditional Romance-origin theory of the German Jews.

Since the late Middle Ages the Slavic lands have harbored most of the world's Jews (e.g., 80% in the Polish Commonwealth at the time of its first partition in 1772). It is difficult to see how the latter could be descended from the tiny Jewish communities in the monolingual west German lands. There is also no evidence of large-scale Jewish migrations into the Slavic lands from other regions, the four "Ukrainian" hypotheses notwithstanding. This conundrum prompted Koestler in 1976 to posit the Khazars who allegedly settled in large numbers in both the Western and Eastern Slavic lands as the major component in the ethnogenesis of the Ashkenazic Jews. Unconvinced by the Khazar hypothesis, Faber and King 1984 had to suggest that the original Jewish population in the east German lands prior to the eastward migrations must have been substantially larger than hitherto supposed. I share their scepticism over a significant Khazar connection and welcome their suggestion.

The linguistic evidence discussed above is compatible with the hypothesis that the relatively small German Jewish population might have been larger than expected. The larger numbers of Jews hypothesized by

Faber and King would have included West Slavic converts to Judaism. (On the reasons why Sorbs might have converted to Judaism, see chapter 6 below.)

While a major Khazar connection cannot be established on linguistic grounds, there is a tiny "Oriental" component in Yiddish which would find no easy explanation within any of the frameworks proposed by historians of the German Jews. See, e.g., Eastern Yiddish *šabaš* 'tip paid to musicians by guests who dance at a wedding'—with surface cognates (in other meanings) in German, Dutch, Hungarian, and most of the West and East Slavic languages (discussed in category 1, Turkic 2 in chapter 5.11 below). Moreover, the small unique Greek component in Yiddish has few parallels with that of the Judeo-Romance languages; hence, I assume independent channels of Hellenic diffusion for Yiddish and Judeo-Romance. If the latter inherited its Grecisms indirectly from Judeo-Latin, Yiddish may have acquired its Grecisms directly from Balkan Greek.

(h) The widely held view that the German Jews migrated in tandem with the Germans into the monolingual Slavic lands is unconvincing due to the different chronologies of the two eastward migrations: the German Jews migrated into the Polish lands primarily in two waves, in the 13th and 16th centuries, while the Germans settled the Sorbian lands from the 9th century, expanding into monolingual Slavic, Baltic and Hungarian territories between the mid 12th and 14th centuries (see Elbogen 1930:974, Tykocinski 1934:258, Higounet 1989 and Wexler 1991b for details).

There are several reasons why a "Sorbian" origin of many German Jews and of Yiddish has never been entertained—despite the mass of evidence that Jews dwelt in the Germano-Slavic lands at least as early as those in the monolingual southwest German lands:

(a) Unlike the southwest monolingual German lands, there are no early Jewish material remains, artifacts or records from the eastern, originally mixed Germano-Slavic, regions of present-day Germany.

(b) Many historians of the German Jews (both Jewish and non-Jewish) were outspoken in their hostility to Slavic cultures, which impeded serious consideration of an eastern origin. A particularly obnoxious example of anti-Slavic racism comes in the statement by Eppenstein:

> "By steadfastly maintaining the German language and capacity of intellect brought over from Germany, Polish-Lithuanian Jewry has formed a

lasting protective wall against Slavic barbarism up to the present time" (1919:186).

Such views echo the condescending attitude towards Slavs that was common in contemporaneous German circles as well. An example is the proposal of Mielke, a National Socialist sympathizer, to attribute the positive features of "Slavic" rulers to a putative German origin or influence:

"...many Slavic rulers and nobles were renegades or derived from descendants of the Germanic [tribes] who remained behind...indeed even the Polish rulers, the most illustrious of whom, Bolesław Chrobry, had many Germanic characteristics...appear to have been of Germanic origin" (1927:238).

(c) A Slavic theory would have required positing a migration of Jews within the German lands from east to west, which contradicted the prevailing view that the Jews had participated in the *Drang nach Osten* and that the oldest Jewish settlements were in the southwest German lands.

(d) The overwhelming majority of Yiddish vocabulary is of German stock. The Slavic element in Yiddish, primarily restricted to the phonotactics, semantics and syntax after re-lexification of the language to German, is less visible to the speaker, and, in any case, was never suspected to be from Sorbian, a language whose existence was unknown to most Yiddishists and historians of the German Jews. Yet, it is precisely this sort of distribution—of a Slavic element in all components of the language *except the lexicon*—that favors a Slavic origin for Yiddish.

At most, the presence of a large German component in the Yiddish lexicon which deviated from German norms prompted some observors to classify Yiddish as an extreme distortion of German, but never as a "non-Germanic" language! This may be because observors tended to blame Hebraisms as the cause of Yiddish deviance from German norms. Consider the comment of the Christian Hebraist Johann Christoph Wagenseil (1633–1705), who stopped short of reclassifying Yiddish as something other than German:

"With no language are the Jews so abusive, people are prone to say, as with our German language, since they have given it a totally foreign tone and sound; the good German words they have botched up, speak badly, perverted; they have invented new words unknown to us, as well as mixed into German innumerable Hebrew words and figures of speech, so that in such a form, whoever hears them speaking German can think only that they are speaking pure, undefiled Hebrew, since almost no single word comes out intelligible" (1699:7).

(e) The Yiddish literary language up until the early 19th century was based on Western Yiddish norms which were much closer to standard German than the Eastern Yiddish dialects were. The very fact that the literary norms of a minority of Yiddish speakers in the West could be attractive to masses of Eastern Yiddish speakers attests to the immense popularity of things "Western" among the Eastern European Jews. In Germany itself, many speakers of Sorbian/Yiddish preferred to write in German (standard or Judaized) or Hebrew, much as Sorbian and Polabian speakers wrote in German and Latin.

(f) Despite some major research in the late 19th century, the serious study of Judeo-Slavic linguistics and Slavic settlement history in the German lands did not come into being until the 1950s. The paucity of extant Judeo-Slavic materials also impeded a proper evaluation of the Judeo-Slavic component in Yiddish.

(g) Germanists paid more attention to the development of German dialects in the East European lands than to the origin and chronology of the Slavic component in those dialects.

(h) Until recently, the phenomenon of partial language shift has been poorly understood by linguists and has barely surfaced in the Yiddish linguistic literature (see Thomason and Kaufman 1988 for a general discussion of the phenomenon).

(i) With the exception of M.Weinreich (1956a, 1956b, 1973) and S.A.Birnbaum (1979), there was little interest among Yiddishists in the comparative aspects of Jewish language creativity, which might have aroused doubts about a Germanic affiliation of Yiddish.

(j) Dialect geography is a major tool for recognizing the historical act of language shift from Judeo-Sorbian to German, as well as reconstructing the original territory of Judeo-French/Ashkenazic German, yet only in the last few decades have major linguistic atlases become available for Belorussian, Polish, Sorbian, Ukrainian and Yiddish.

The "Slavic"-origin hypothesis of the German Jews and Yiddish flies in the face of all previous proposals. There is little historical documentation that might corroborate the Slavic hypothesis, though much linguistic, ethnographic and religious data do strongly support the hypothesis. I do not regard the lack of historical support as a weakness. In principle, I find hypotheses based on linguistic considerations more attractive than those based on historical considerations. As I cited in chapter 2 above, while historians are always bound by the nature of the extant documentation, historical linguists alone are in a position to reconstruct earlier, unattested stages of a language. This is because a language retains clues of earlier strata and sociolinguistic conditioning factors. Thus, the absence of important centers of Jewish learning in the historical Sorbian lands prior to the 13th century need not eliminate those areas as the cradle of German Jewish settlement.

The first seven variants of the "Romance hypothesis" outlined above as variants (a–g) envisage Yiddish as the sole Jewish language to take root in the southwest German lands. In many of the variants of the Romance hypothesis, Yiddish was carried eastward from the Rhineland into the monolingual Slavic lands. I believe that the Jews in the southwest German lands were originally not involved in the development of Judeo-Sorbian/Yiddish, though the fates of the two speech territories were later intertwined. Originally, southwest Germany was settled by French Jews between the 10th century up until their expulsion from most parts of France in 1394. By the mid–15th century these Jews had either become speakers of (a) Yiddish when the latter spread into the Rhineland, Alsace and western Switzerland, or of (b) a mildly Judaized (i.e., Gallicized) "Ashkenazic" German, based on the immediately coterritorial German dialects; Ashkenazic German was eventually supplanted by Yiddish. Prior to the final expulsion of the Jews from France and the Franche-Comté, I would entertain the possibility that knowledge of German spread to the French Jews as a result of Jewish migration from the German lands (see, e.g., the presence of German/Yiddish glosses in the Hebrew writings of the French scholar Rashi 1028/1040?–1105).

Ashkenazic German, with written records dating from the 14th–15th century (in the form of native texts as well as French and Hebrew words embedded in early German slang), shows neither signs of extreme component fusion nor a native Slavic component; its small unique French component, still marginally found in some Western Yiddish dialects, is, except for a few personal names, entirely unknown in the Yiddish of other areas. In the contacts that developed between Ashkenazic German and the rapidly Germanizing Judeo-Sorbian, it was the latter which played the role of purveyor of linguistic enrichment, e.g., Sorbianisms surface in Yiddish/Ashkenazic German spoken quite far to the west of Sorbian (and Polabian) territory—as in Alsace, western Switzerland, southwest Germany and Holland (see the examples given above). This means that the Jews in the southwest German lands played a distinctly *passive* role in their linguistic relations with the Jews of the Germano-Slavic lands—in contrast to a more *active* role in religious and philosophical matters.

The hypothesis that Yiddish began as a Judaized dialect of Sorbian necessitates a break with the traditional conception of Yiddish language genesis. At present, the only part of the traditional view of Yiddish history that strikes me as correct is that there were some "Western Yiddish" dialects (my "Ashkenazic German") created in the absence of a Slavic substratum when French- (and possibly some Italian-)speaking Jews shifted *completely* to German.

The ethnography and religion of the Jews cannot corroborate the theory of a Franco-Italian origin of the German Jews. They do provide evidence in support of the proselyte hypothesis:

(a) There are Slavic words in Yiddish which are connected with basic aspects of the Jewish religion, though it is not always clear when these terms acquired their religious meanings in Slavic or Yiddish. If the designated ritual precepts were of Palestinian origin, European Jews would presumably not have needed new Slavic words to denote them; Slavic proselytes to Judaism, on the other hand, might have introduced these terms (along with the concepts) into Judeo-Sorbian/Yiddish.

(b) The existence of so many pagan and Christian Slavic customs among the Ashkenazic Jews also suggests that numerous Slavs were incorporated into the Jewish community.

There are two important goals confronting ethnographers of the Jews:

(a) Ethnographers need to ascertain the geography and relative chronology of each custom. This would allow them to identify with greater accuracy the Slavic and German origins of the customs. Unfortunately, few studies (i) appreciate the need to distinguish between Jewish customs practiced in originally monolingual German and bilingual Germano-Slavic territories, or acknowledge that numerous Jewish customs (ii) have Christian and pagan origins, and (iii) that many German customs are of Slavic origin (a blatant example of these failures is Pollack 1971; see chapter 5.2 below).

(b) Ethnographers need to distinguish between possible Slavic ethnographic substrata and adstrata among the Jews. I would expect that in the Germano-Slavic milieu, Jews might have been inclined to maintain primarily Palestinian customs and folklore which could be supported by similar or identical customs and folklore in the coterritorial non-Jewish cultures, while discarding religious practices and customs which had no support in the new environments. For example, breaking a glass at the wedding ceremony is cited on two occasions in the Talmud (though not as a "custom"!). The practice of breaking a glass was, until recently, known almost exclusively among Ashkenazic Jews; other Jews may have acquired the practice later from Ashkenazic Jews. I suspect the glass custom was first introduced to the Ashkenazic Jews by their Germanic and Slavic neighbors or converts who had this practice; the talmudic "pedigree" would have been a later development (see chapter 5.2 below).

Historians should also explore the possibility that the Jews were the carriers of Slavic and east German linguistic features and cultural traditions to the west German lands. It would also be interesting to know if the profound "Slavicization" of the Ashkenazic Jews has a parallel in the non-Jewish component in the religion and folkways of the Jews in the Arab, Berber, Chinese, Ethiopian, Indian, Iranian, Romance or Turkic lands.

I was motivated to replace the traditional French and Italian hypothesis of German Jewish and Yiddish origin because of my inability to resolve a number of stubborn contradictions between demographic and linguistic data, or to accept unsubstantiated claims inherent in the first seven variants of the Romance-origin hypothesis. Substratal relics in Yiddish and Ashkenazic German enabled me to propose an eighth variant (h)—a Balkan Romance/Slavic origin for the first Jewish settlements in the German lands—and to postulate the existence of Judeo-Sorbian.

Uriel Weinreich argued that the Yiddish language and Ashkenazic folk culture became highly "receptive" to Slavic influences in Eastern Europe, while the language and culture of the millions of coterritorial Germans in Eastern Europe remained relatively closed to Slavic influences (1958). Yet, if the German Jews were largely Sorbs "by birth", then at least a part of their Slavic baggage would have been an "inheritance" from Sorbian, and Uriel Weinreich's claim that the Jews "borrowed" more heavily from the Slavs than the colonial Germans would have to be reconsidered; it might still be true with regard to the relative receptivity of Jews and Germans to Polish and East Slavic influences.

All scholars have assumed that it was the Jews who developed Yiddish. Above I assumed that one motive why Jews might have created Judaized languages was the desire to strengthen their separate ethnoreligious profile, having given up their ancestral languages, Hebrew and

Judeo-Aramaic. Still, the hypothesis of a Jewish origin for Judeo-Sorbian or Yiddish is not entirely convincing for a number of reasons (see below), though this does not mean that the hypothesis that proselytes to Judaism created the Jewish languages is problem-free. At this stage I am unable to resolve definitively the question of who developed the Jewish languages.

Six problems confront the hypothesis that the Jews were the creators of the Jewish languages:

(a) How could ethnic Jews have created a unique Judeo-Sorbian and Yiddish if the majority of north European Jews at this time were already of Slavic and other proselyte origins? As the majority, one would have expected proselytes to impose their speech norms on the ethnic Jewish minority, rather than adopt the unique speech of a Jewish minority.

(b) If Jews had relatively unimpeded contacts with non-Jews in most of Europe during the first millennium A.D. (and this must have been the case in order for the Jews to acquire the non-Jewish languages in the first place), how could they have resisted the pressures to speak like the non-Jews with whom they were so closely identified?

(c) In theory, the growing gap between Yiddish and German might be explained by a Jewish population prone to widescale migrations. But forced migrations did not become the fate of German Jews until after the First Crusade in 1096, which resulted in the massacre of numerous Jewish communities, especially in the Rhineland.

The argument of extreme mobility or disparate origin makes more sense with a proselyte population. For example, the extreme geographical and ethnic variety of the proselytes could have easily led to the creation of a form of Slavic or German that was more variegated in component structure than any dialect spoken by the more sedentary Germans or Sorbs who continued to profess paganism or Christianity. (On the varied origins of the alleged proselytes, see chapter 6 below.)

(d) The theory that the segregation of the Jews was a major force in the creation of a Jewish language could account for the lack of diffusion of new speech habits from Christians to Jews. But the problem here too is that the social segregation of the Jews in ghettos began mainly after the Black Plague in 1348–9.

(e) The German component of Yiddish attained its unique profile vis-à-vis German dialects as a result of Judaization—a process presumably carried out by the Jewish descendants of proselytes after segregation from the non-Jewish populations had become institutionalized and proselytizing had become too dangerous in view of intense Christian opposition (on Judaization, see chapter 7 below).

(f) In the mixed Germano-Slavic lands, the pagan Slavs were under pressure to accept the German language along with the German religion, Christianity. Slavs in the mixed Germano-Slavic lands who became Christians could have acquired native German norms when they became monolingual speakers of German, and eventually became submerged in the general German population—though often not before imparting some influences to the coterritorial German dialect, or some folkloric elements to the majority superstratal culture. Sorbs could have considerably improved their chances of surviving as Slavs if they joined the Jewish community, since most or all of the Jews were presumably Sorbian-speaking, and since as Jews the Sorbs would not have constituted the main object of Christian missionary activity.

There are three reasons why Slavic language loyalty would have been especially high among the German Jews: (i) the Jews were Slavs; (ii) there was an important community of Jewish coreligionists in the neighboring Slavic territories, e.g., in the Czech and South Slavic lands (the latter included Hungary), who could reinforce Slavic language loyalty among the German Jews (especially if immigration to Germany from these areas was still in force); (iii) the existence of two unique written (and liturgical) languages, Hebrew and Judeo-Aramaic (especially after the 11th century), would have reduced the dependence of the Jews on the written languages of the German missionaries—Latin and German.

Since Sorbs would have been more threatened by Germanization than Jews, they may have engineered the partial language shift prior to, or during conversion to Judaism—as a means of decelerating the Germanization of Sorbian and impeding the complete shift from Sorbian to German. If so, the influx of Sorbian-speaking proselytes to Judaism might have served as a *sine qua non* to preventing the local "older" Jews (of Balkan extraction) from undergoing a total language shift to German. On the other hand, if the Balkan Jewish immigrants were the last group in the mixed Germano-Sorbian lands to retain a Slavic language after the bulk of the Slavs had accepted German language and religion, they might have been the ones to engineer the partial language shift to High German lexicon. Theoretically, the partial language shift might have been inspired by sizeable numbers of German-speaking Slavic prosleytes to Judaism (see chapter 6 below).

There were presumably three factors which facilitated the partial, rather than the full, language shift, regardless of whether ethnic Jews or proselytes were the prime movers:

(a) Ignorance of native German norms (there may have been few or no native speakers of German to emulate in the former Slavic areas of Germany for a certain period).

(b) A plethora of dialects spoken by the German settlers in the Sorbian lands favored linguistic fragmentation in the former Sorbian lands.

(c) Unwillingness on the part of the Jews to merge totally with the German-speaking population.

I have argued that a colloquial Jewish language is a prerequisite to the creation of a Jewish language of translation, and some early Jewish translation languages can be attributed to non-Jewish proselytes. It is thus conceivable that proselytes could have also been the major force behind the creation of some *colloquial* Jewish languages. I could also readily envision the possibility that in some Jewish communities only the language of translation might have been created by proselytes, whereas in other communities, both the colloquial and translation languages could have been created by them.

Hence, it is premature to say whether the practice of using the terms "Jewish" or "Judaized" as synonyms is ill-advised. Future research should determine the usefuless of defining languages created by ethnic or "old" Jews as "Jewish", while reserving a different term, say "Judaized" or "para-Jewish" (or "proselytic"?), for languages created by recent proselytes to Judaism. This is of course predicated on the assumption that a linguist could distinguish Jewish languages created by existing Jews and new proselytes on the basis of distinctive features, e.g., the presence or absence of Jewish religious terminology of established non-Jewish origin, and that "newer" and "older" Jews may have even formed initially distinct communities—parallel to the separate communities of Spanish *cristianos viejos*/ Portuguese *cristãos velhos* 'old Christians' and Spanish *cristianos nuevos*/ Portuguese *cristãos novos* 'new Christians' (of Jewish origin, many of whom retained Jewish practices clandestinely in 15th–16th-century Spain and Portugal).

The creation of such a diagnostic test is the goal for the future. Consider, for example, the different treatment of Hebraisms in Judaized and non-Judaized languages used by Jews. For example, when speakers of Jewish languages borrow Hebrew participles, they normally prefer the masculine singular form; to this now indeclinable word, Jewish languages add a non-Hebrew auxiliary, e.g., 'to be' which is conjugated for person, number and tense, as in Yiddish *bojdek zajn* 'inspect' (< Hebrew *bōdeq* 'inspecting'). In a Hebrew document (known as F.12. 135, in the library of Trinity College, Cambridge) containing Germanic-language glosses written in Hebrew characters which appears to be from the 13th–14th century, a Hebrew participle appears unexpectedly in the masculine plural form. This document has few features which are found in unmistakably Old Yiddish texts. I would define the Hebrew-character glosses as (non-Judaized) German, though Bar-El, who recently studied the document (1992), regards them as Yiddish. Hence, the integration of Hebrew participles might serve as a diagnostic test for distinguishing Jewish (or Judaized) languages from non-Jewish languages spoken by Jews which happen to be recorded in Hebrew characters. For a parallel example from a Castilian document in Hebrew characters from Valladolid 1432, see Wexler 1988:117, fn 186. In German slang (Rotwelsch), Hebraisms are never integrated in the periphrastic conjugation with 'be' described above (see Wexler 1971, 1988: chapters 2–3).

For the time being, the following three questions must remain open: were ethnic and "old" Jews or new converts the prime movers behind (a) the creation of colloquial Judeo-Sorbian, (b) the partial language shift from Judeo-Sorbian which gave rise to Yiddish and (c) the Yiddish (and Judeo-Sorbian?) calque translations of the Bible? Future research in Jewish linguistics, in addition to uncovering more details of the historical evolution of the Jewish languages, could profit too from comparisons of synthetic cultures. For example, a possible parallel to the Jewish/proselyte symbiosis may be the interaction that developed in Florida in the 18th century when refugee African slaves joined the Seminole Indian communities; as a result the Creole English of the Africans was transmitted to the Indians, at the same time that the Africans adopted the Indian culture. Each race remained distinct despite living together for over a century and intermarriage (see Dillard 1972: 150–5).

5

THE EUROPEAN ROOTS OF THE JEWISH RELIGION AND FOLK CULTURE IN THE BALKANS AND GERMANO-SLAVIC LANDS

5.1 Evidence from language

In his pioneering discussion of Yiddish and Colonial German in Eastern Europe, Uriel Weinreich wrote as follows about the Slavic terms that denoted religious concepts in Yiddish:

> "...the occurrence of Slavicisms with Jewish ritual connotations (e.g., *trejbern* 'to remove the veins of [meat]'...) shows that the Slavic origin of words—recognizable to many bilingual Jews—did not disqualify them from application even to sacred objects" (1958:387).

Weinreich assumed that the religious concepts and objects existed before the Slavic terms were acquired by the Eastern European Jews. In my opinion, the Slavic ritual terms in Yiddish very likely suggest a Slavic origin for many of the practices denoted, and are not relatively recent borrowings. The weakness of Weinreich's assumption is the absence of any plausible motivation for Jews to borrow Slavic pagan and Christian terminology for allegedly Old Palestinian Jewish religious practices which should have had Hebrew, Judeo-Aramaic or possibly Greek names.

5.11 Yiddish terms of European and Turkic origin

Yiddish words of non-native origin are invaluable evidence of contact, direct or indirect, between Jews and speakers of the source languages. Ascertaining the origin of a term is often tantamount to ascertaining the origin of the concept or practice itself. Terms designating concepts associated with the Jewish religion which are *not* derived from Hebrew or Judeo-Aramaic also carry a clue to the relative chronology of the borrowing. For example, in Karaite, the Turkic language spoken by a small number of Karaites at Halyč (Ukraine), Trakai (Lithuania), and in the Crimean Peninsula, the name for a Karaite synagogue is from

Arabic while the non-Jewish house of prayer is borrowed from the language spoken by the religious group in question, see, e.g., Trakai, Halyč Karaite *ken(e)sa*, Crimean Karaite *kėnėsa* 'Karaite synagogue' < Arabic *knīsa* 'church' vs. Crimean Karaite *k(i)lisė* 'church' < Greek; however, in the Trakai dialect of Karaite, 'Catholic church' is expressed by native *jėgjuv*, literally 'good house'. Might the use of this original native expression for Catholic church indicate close Catholic-Karaite ties, or a Christian origin for some Karaites? Were there Christian speakers of a Turkic language who might have provided the Karaites with the model? Trakai Karaite also uses native *jėxkjun*, literally 'good day', to designate Sunday, which also has a Christian ring to it. In any case, the Karaite naming of the synagogue by an Arabism points to the Iraqi Arabic origin of the sect (in the 8th century), or to contact with Arabic speakers at an early historical period. Note that Karaite *ken(e)sa*, etc., differs in meaning from non-Judaized Arabic *knīsa* 'church' (vs. *knīs* 'synagogue'). May we assume that *ken(e)sa* underwent a change in meaning from church to synagogue?

The interpretation of linguistic data is not always straightforward:

(a) Non-Jewish terms with cult meanings could have been taken into a Jewish language where they are given altogether different, non-cult meanings or borrowed in ignorance of non-Jewish cult meanings in the donor languages; in the latter case it would be inappropriate to speak of direct non-Jewish religious or cultural influences. For example, Jews seem to have accepted the mystical functions of the numeral 13 from the Christians without appreciating the connection of the numeral with Judas Iscariot's betrayal of Christ (Staerk 1922:202). In practice, it is not always easy to distinguish between cases where the Jews consciously reshaped and/or redefined Christian or pagan terms to suit their own needs, and cases where they unwittingly accepted non-Jewish innovations.

(b) Non-Jewish terms may enter Yiddish through a second language, thus complicating the search for the ultimate origins. The centuries-long mixing of peoples and languages in the Balkan Peninsula has created an arena for diffusion (including back borrowing by the original donor language) which often makes the precise identification of origin well-nigh impossible. For example, Balkan Greek loans could have entered the Balkan language(s) spoken by the Jews either through a Romance or Slavic intermediary. Romanisms acquired in the Balkans could have passed through either a Greek or Slavic filter. In chapter 4 above I suggested that archaic Yiddish *frimzl* 'noodle' could come ultimately from Italian *vermicello*, a diminutive formation of *verme* 'worm'. But the form of Yiddish *frimzl*, with the cluster *fri-* vs. Italian *ver-*, suggested a Slavic (possibly Balkan) impact, since only the Slavic languages subjected original clusters of {consonant + vowel + *r*} to reordering. The hypothesis of a Balkan venue of Yiddish *frimzl* is further strengthened by the fact that only Serbo-Croatian denotes noodles by the diminutive form of the native word worm, possibly under the influence of Italian.

Another problematic locale is the mixed Germano-Slavic lands. As the indigenous Slavs became incorporated into the larger German mass, their languages and cultures became Germanized, but the Slavs influenced the culture and language of the Germans prior to their total assimilation (compare the Balkanization of the Iberian Jews cited in chapter 1 above). Hence, the Slavs may have been purveyors to the Jews not only of original Slavic terms and practices, but of Slavicized German terms and practices as well (see the discussion of Western Yiddish *barxes* ~ *berxes* in category I, Germanic 1 below), while the Germans may have actually passed on originally Slavic customs to the Jews. Finally, the existence of not a few practices shared by Balkan and German populations further complicates the recovery of origin. On Jewish knowledge of Slavic practices in the 11th–13th centuries, see Jicxak ben Ašer (Speyer, c.1050–c.1130), Josef Kara (northern France, early 12th century) and Moše de Coucy (northern France, c.1200–1260: see Kupfer and Lewicki 1956:96–100, 101–23 and 263–7, respectively).

(c) We need to try to determine whether the Jewish or non-Jewish group used the term first, and whether the practices or institutions were also borrowed by the Jews along with the terms; if so, what was the relative chronology of the borrowing of the terms and concepts?

(d) Using linguistic data to establish historical contact between Jews and non-Jews, even to the extent of reconstructing reciprocal influences, is not the same as corroborating the hypothesis of largescale conversion to Judaism. Ultimately, any interpretation of linguistic material requires a comparison of Jewish and non-Jewish terms as well as concepts.

It is striking that Hebrew terms are not used for many basic aspects of the Jewish religion, especially since in Medieval Christianity and Islam, religious terms were mainly preferred from, or modeled on each group's liturgical language—Latin and Arabic respectively—or, occasionally, vernacular language. Jewish examples are Slavic terms connected with the ritual food laws of the Jews, not all of which are mentioned, incidentally, in Old Palestinian Jewish writings. A Slavic word in the domain of kosher food rules suggests that the practice in question may actually have originated among Slavic Jews and is not of pre-diaspora Palestinian Jewish origin—talmudic and biblical precedents notwithstanding. We need additional non-linguistic evidence to determine if the innovation originated among non-Jews or Jews. A complication is that terms used by both Jews and non-Jews often denote one another's religious practices, as when Modern English *temple* denotes either a church (e.g., a Mormon temple) or a reform synagogue.

Even when Hebrew and Judeo-Aramaic terms are used in Yiddish to designate aspects of the Jewish religion, it should not be assumed that the use of such terms automatically establishes the Palestinian Jewish origin of the practice or concept denoted. First we need to determine the relative chronology of the Hebraisms and Judeo-Aramaisms in Yiddish, especially when non-Jewish synonyms are also available (see the example of 'Yom Kippur' discussed below). Many Hebrew and Judeo-Aramaic terms were introduced into Jewish parlance at a relatively late date in an attempt to Judaize an originally non-Jewish concept. A Hebraism (or Hebraized term from another language) that competes with a variety of Hebraisms and non-Hebraisms alike (see, e.g., *xale* in category 1, Germanic 1 below), is probably evidence that the term was acquired at a relatively late date. *Hence, the decision to replace non-Jewish elements by Hebrew and Judeo-Aramaic terms in a Jewish language can shed light on how the Jews perceived the origins of their religious practices.* Of particular interest are cases of component replacement in one Jewish speech community that are not matched in another, but a detailed comparative study is necessarily beyond the aims of the present study. (On the origin of the Hebrew and Judeo-Aramaic literary tradition that is a prerequisite to the process of Judaization, see discussion in chapter 7 below.)

The interpretation of shared material becomes particularly acute when the Jews are in the process of a partial language shift—as in the east German lands in the early second millennium; there Jews may have been prompted to accept non-Jewish terminology from the new donor language, German, as a convenient means of filling lexical gaps.

Some scholars have suggested that the relative frequency of use of a term is a revealing mark of origin. For example, Blondheim took the greater use of a term among Jews or the existence of a meaning generally associated with Jews as proof of a Jewish origin:

> "While the word [*schola*] is more or less known everywhere in the non-Jewish population, it seems to have been used primarily by the Jews. The only exception that I have noted is that of Germany, where Luther uses the term to translate *synagōga;* even there the word could be a borrowing from the speech of the Jews" (1925:110).

Blondheim ignored the fact that the first use of the term *schola* with a cult meaning comes from the New Testament, where it refers to a "Judeo-Christian" hall of study (see also Kraabel 1981:119).

I suspect that knowledge of the relative chronology of the terms and the practices, or of changes in meaning or use of the terms in both the Jewish and non-Jewish communities is more revealing of origin than relative frequency. For example, in Christian Latin translations of the Bible, *ara* denotes specifically 'pagan altar' vs. *altare* 'Christian altar' (see the translation of Saint Cyprian, a Christian bishop martyred in Carthage in 258). Yet, *ara* continues to appear in much later Judeo-Romance translations of the Bible (in the passages Exodus 34:13, Ezechiel 43:15), see, e.g., the Ladino (Judeo-Castilian) Bible of 1553, prepared in Ferrara by Portuguese Marrano exiles in Italy in Latin characters (in this translation, Ladino *altar* means high place).[1] What does this example teach us about putative Christian or pagan influences on the Jews? The persistent use of *ara* by Jews might indicate that they were more receptive to pagan influences than the Christians (even though the Christians had absorbed far larger numbers of pagan proselytes into their communities than the Jews). Or that the Christians were more sensitive than the Jews about establishing a clear divide between their terminology and that of the pagans. *In other words, the Christianization of paganism may have preceded by several centuries the Judaization of paganism.* Our ability to interpret the significance of each example clearly gains if we can expand the corpus of examples and languages. Future research will need to compare different Jewish communities in this regard.

Quite a number of terms in the domains of superstition and religion that were used in early stages of a Jewish language are absent in later texts, though the concepts denoted were not necessarily discarded. It is imperative to determine as precisely as possible when and how the old words were replaced; usually the replacements are loans from Hebrew or Judeo-Aramaic. Such cases of "lexical discontinuity" (or "Hebrew component dominance") in the Jewish languages are an important clue to the chronology of "Judaization" (see chapter 7 below).

For instance, Old Bavarian Yiddish *der lange tag* 'Day of Atonement, Yom Kippur' (Margaritha 1530), literally 'the long day', appears to continue old Judeo-Aramaic and Judeo-Greek patterns of discourse, see, e.g., *jōmā᾽ rabbā᾽* and *hē megalē hēmera* 'the great day', respectively; today the Yiddish expression is unknown to Jews, except marginally perhaps in Alsace. While its universal replacement in Yiddish by the Old Hebraism *jom kiper* could be interpreted as a manifestation of "Hebrew component dominance" or Judaization, there was apparently no concomitant change in the celebration or significance of the holiday itself. See also Judeo-(Marrano) Portuguese *dia grande*, literally 'great day', in the same meaning. The expression 'long day', by remaining in use among Christians, now became "Christian by default"; Vollbeding 1804:49 explicitly defined German *der lange Tag*, current nowadays in Bavaria, as "Christian" (on recategorization "by default", see also chapter 7 below). The expression 'long day' for Yom Kippur is also the basis for the standard term in two other nearly neighboring Christian languages, Czech *dlouhý den* and Hungarian *hosszúnap*. The obsolescence of the expression in Yiddish suggests Jews interpreted it as non-Jewish (perhaps because the Christians used the term as well; it would be interesting to know if the source of the Judeo-Aramaic or Judeo-Greek expression was originally Jewish).

Changes in the Jewish term for Friday, after sundown on which the Sabbath begins, may reflect changes in religious practice. The linguistic data inspire the hypothesis, but only non-linguistic data can provide confirmation. For example, Judeo-Latin expressed 'Friday' by *coena pura*, literally 'undefiled meal'; in the Latin of pagan speakers, the term denoted a ritual meal marked by abstinence from certain dishes (Blondheim 1925:lix–lx). The expression survives now only in Sardinian *kenáβura*, etc., with the Jewish meaning Friday. It appears then that when the originally pagan term was adopted by the Jews, it acquired a specifically Jewish meaning, which was subsequently borrowed back by Sardinian (and other?) Christians. The concept "undefiled meal" is not attested as a religious concept in any other European Jewish languages. Would the term indicate that the observance of the Sabbath was once characterized by the eating of a distinctive meal, but not necessarily by universal abstention from work, as orthodox Jews are now wont to interpret the observance of the Sabbath (see also discussion in the paragraph below)? Judeo-Greek *paraskevē* 'Friday', literally 'preparation (usually for war)', has also disappeared from most contemporary European Jewish languages, but remains in (Christian) Greek and Karaite (where the Turkic speakers can obviously not be aware of the original meaning). In some Slavic languages, *paraskevē* serves as a female name (e.g., Ukrainian *Paraskeva*).

The nonexistence (or loss?) of the Greek and Latin concepts "undefiled meal" and "preparation" to designate Friday in Judeo-Romance languages and in Yiddish suggests changes or disruption in religious practice. I wonder if the disruption could be explained by the growing numbers of proselytes who were joining the Jewish communities or the subsequent Judaization processes. I could also assume that proselytes introduced *coena pura* to the Jews in the first place, as well as perhaps the present Ashkenazic Jewish practice of preferring certain foods for the Sabbath meal (see, e.g., Yiddish *gefilte fiš* 'stuffed fish', traditionally eaten by Jews in Slavic Europe on Friday night)—for which there is a Christian parallel in the traditional prohibition against eating meat on Friday. The putative proselyte term *coena pura* may have always been restricted to the Italian-Sardinian area, or, if it was once more wide–spread, its replacement might have been prompted by its pagan associations. But it is curious that "Friday" is not expressed by a Hebraism in any Jewish language, see, e.g., Yiddish *frajtik* (from German *Freitag*), Judezmo *vjernes* (= Spanish *viernes*), Trakai Karaite *baraski* (from Judeo-Greek *paraskevē*)—vs. 'Saturday, Sabbath', which is expressed by a Hebrew term, e.g., Yiddish *šabes*, Trakai Karaite *šabbatkjun'* (literally 'Sabbath day'), Judezmo *saba, šabað* < Hebrew *šabbāt*. Can we deduce from this that the Ashkenazic and other Jews and Karaites never felt a need to Judaize "Friday" (i.e., replace it with a Hebrew term), perhaps because the practice of beginning the Sabbath on Friday at sunset was originally unknown to them (see also the preceding paragraph)?

A major desideratum of Jewish studies is the systematic collection of original terms in different Jewish languages which were subsequently replaced, usually by Hebraisms. If these terms were replaced because Jews perceived them as "Christian", "Muslim", etc., we could reconstruct how and when Jews perceived the "distance" between themselves and their non-Jewish surroundings. For example, Judezmo now uses the Iberian Arabism *alxat* 'Sunday' in place of an earlier (?) *domingo* (pre-1492) which originally was derived from the Latin root for Lord (Jesus Christ) and is the standard term in Spanish. Possibly the Jews used the Arabism without any awareness of Christian connotations in *domingo*. Furthermore, not all non-Jewish terms with religious connotations in a Jewish language are subject to replacement. For example, *trejbern* 'clean the meat of ritually impure elements to render it kosher' is an acceptable Slavism in many Yiddish dialects, though some dialects have alternative terms, including *menakern, menaker zajn* < Hebrew *n-q-r* 'bore'. The latter is probably recent, since other Jewish languages use a different Hebrew term for this concept, see, e.g., Judeo-Arabic Hebrew *n-q-h* 'clean' (~ native Judeo-Arabic *n-q-y;* on the use of different Hebraisms in Jewish languages to denote common practices or cult objects, see chapter 8 below). Earlier speakers of Yiddish dialects that now lack *trejbern* may have regarded it as non-Jewish and thus replaced it. It is interesting that non-Slavic Christians who borrow a Slavic term for sacrifice take the term popularized in Slavic Christian texts, see, e.g., Rumanian *jertfă* < Old Church Slavic *žьrtva*, and never the originally pagan term *trěba*—the basis for Yiddish *trejbern* (see further discussion in category I, Slavic 6 below).

An original non-Jewish impact on the Jewish community and culture can be seen in lexical bifurcation, the use of synonyms to distinguish religious or ethnic agents. In Jewish languages, some terms associated with Jews are expressed by Hebraisms or Judeo-Aramaisms while the non-Jewish counterparts are denoted by non-Hebraisms. By blocking the use of a term regarded as non-Jewish for designating Jewish activities, lexical bifurcation achieves distance between Jewish and non-Jewish practices; as such, it can be defined as a manifestation of Judaization. We will need to check in future if individual instances of lexical bifurcation can be correlated with some non-linguistic event, e.g. a rise in proselytism, a fear of being swamped by the impact of many converts to Judaism (whose religious fervor and sincerity may have been suspect), or a growing segregation of Jews from non-Jewish society (motivated by Jews and/or Christians).

There are also cases of lexical bifurcation where only the non-Jewish agent is designated by a Hebraism. In Yiddish 'pray (by Jews)' is *dav(e)nen* (either from Arabic or Iranian, see category I, Turkic 4 below) vs. *tfile tun, moljen zix* 'pray (by Christians)' from Hebrew and Eastern Slavic, respectively. The absence of a Hebraism to denote Jewish prayer is suggestive of an early proselyte input—prior to the Judaization process. In contemporary discussions, the etymology of the term *dav(e)nen* is widely disputed; Jews may very early have lost the knowledge that *dav(e)nen* was of non-Jewish origin and hence felt no pressing need to replace it when the Judaization process intensified. The term is currently restricted to Eastern Yiddish and some Western Yiddish locales; most Western Yiddish speakers use the Romanism *ōrn* (see category I, Romance 5 below).

Lexical bifurcation seems more widespread in Jewish than in non-Jewish languages; among the latter, Yiddish is especially rich in examples. If English distinguishes lexically between the clergy and houses of worship of different religions, see, e.g., *rabbi; synagogue* (Jewish) vs. *priest; church, cathedral* (Catholic) vs. *pastor; church, temple* (Protestant), Jewish languages tend to have multiple terms for these and many other concepts for which there is no lexical bifurcation in English, e.g., 'cemetery', 'die', 'pray', etc. Moreover, while a non-Jewish language does not necessarily employ loans of a particular source to create bifurcation, Jewish languages usually utilize Hebrew words for this very purpose—often to mark the terms as specifically Jewish.

Even genuine Hebrew words may be targeted for replacement if they lack literary Hebrew attestation. This fact highlights the importance of the old Palestinian Jewish literature on which all Judaization processes were based. An interesting example is the concept of cemetery in Jewish languages. Eastern Yiddish now distinguishes Jewish and Christian cemeteries by different words, e.g., *besalmen, besojlem; bejsakvures* (< Judeo-Aramaic and Hebrew for 'the house of the world' or Hebrew 'house of graves') and *gut(e) ort* (< German 'good place') all denote a Jewish cemetery vs. *cvinter* 'Christian cemetery' from Latin (via Slavic) or *mahil'nik, mohil'nik*, etc. from Belorussian. But as early as the 14th century, in an area bounded in the west by German cities such as Magdeburg, Prenzlau, Spandau and Bernberg (Anhalt), and in the east by Sandomierz, Poland, and possibly even the Eastern Slavic lands, Jews denoted their cemetery by a simple Hebrew term *qɛvɛr* 'grave'—to judge from Christian documentation, e.g., Polish *Kawyory* (near Kraków, late 14th century), Polish Latin *Kawyary* (near Sandomierz 1387, with the Polish plural suffix *-y*), German *Judenkiewer* (with plural meaning, attested since the 14th century; see details in Güdemann 1866:6, 38; Wexler 1987b:211–4).

The area covered by *qɛvɛr* was originally Slavic-speaking; hence the term may have been a Hebrew innovation of the Slavic-speaking Jews. When Slavic languages died out among the Jews, and in the period of accelerating Judaization, the term for 'Jewish cemetery' may have been replaced by *literary* Hebrew and Judeo-Aramaic expressions. Note also that in German, the expression requires the root *Juden-* 'of the Jews', as if to imply that **kiewer* might have once designated non-Jewish cemeteries as well. In other words, the Slavic Jews may originally have had a single term for all denominations of cemetery (on mixed burial grounds, see chapter 6.1 below). Curiously, a singular noun in Old Polish, *okop(ow)isko* 'cemetery' (1424: Urbańczyk 1965–9), from the root 'bury', appears to have special reference to Jews and pagans (which reflects Polish classificatory principles, not necessarily that Jews were derived from pagans; see also discussion of Polish *kierkot*, etc., below). Hence, a Slavic model may be the basis for Hebrew *qɛvɛr*.

In view of the appearance of Hebrew *qɛvɛr* (though not in its original meaning) in Eastern Slavic territories, I would be prepared to entertain, alternatively, a Khazar origin for *Kavyary, -kiewer,* etc. Russian slang has numerous words which appear to be related to *Kavyary: xibara* (Orël, Rjazan', Tambov) 'shanty, hovel, earthen hut', *xavera, xavira* 'den of thieves', *xovyra* 'hiding place', *xavyrka* 'female sexual organ', *kabur* 'theft through a tunnel', etc. The earliest Russian example dates from the 17th century (Wexler 1987b:212–4). If the source of all these Russian terms is not Hebrew *qɛvɛr*, then I would propose Judeo-Aramaic *qabrāʾ* 'grave', which is the basis of Middle Persian *gabr, gaur* 'hole, depression' and Modern Persian *gūr* 'grave'. Note also Czech Romani (Gypsy) *govr* and the derivative Czech slang *govrák* 'grave'.

Lexical bifurcation may also have a non-Jewish origin. For example, Polish *ki(e)rchów, kierkut* originally meant a Protestant cemetery, but now generally designates a Jewish cemetery. The origin is German *Kirchhof* 'churchyard, church cemetery'. The Jewish meaning first surfaces in a Polish Latin manuscript dated 1553 (relating to Jews in Kazimierz, near Kraków). Some Polish speakers distinguished Protestant and Jewish cemeteries lexically, by creating two forms of the original German loan, e.g., *ki(e)rchów* 'Protestant cemetery' vs. *kierkot, -kut* 'Jewish cemetery' (Karłowicz 1894–1905). The semantic shift from Protestants to Jews probably has nothing to do with Jewish linguistic practice. Altbauer could well be right that the change in meaning from Protestant to Jewish cemetery was a result of the waning of Protestantism in Poland in the mid-17th century, thus leaving the Jews as the only substantial minority (1954). However, the semantic bifurcation in the Polish Germanism may have had its roots in German itself, since contemporary Rhineland German has the pair *kerfəɛ* (neutral) 'churchyard; Jewish cemetery' vs. *kerəçhof* 'Christian cemetery' (Wexler 1987b: 139).

The fact that *kierkot*, etc., came to denote a Jewish cemetery suggests that the older *Kawyary*, etc., was either obsolete, or else there was a need to distinguish cemeteries of different Jewish groups: perhaps *kierkot* may have denoted the cemetery of Yiddish-speaking Jews from Germany in the 1600s, while *Kawyary* denoted the cemetery of the indigenous Slavic-speaking Jews, some of whom could have been the descendants of Khazar-Slavic or Sorbian proselytes (on the possibility of two origins for Polish Jewry on anthropological grounds, see Czekanowski 1960).

In mixed ethnic areas, it is interesting to note which non-Jewish communities exert the major impact on the coterritorial Jews. For example, Jews in Spain and China often borrow Islamic terminology to denote Jewish religious concepts; this is a clue to the ultimate Arabic origin of the Chinese and most Spanish (especially Castilian-speaking) Jews (on the latter, see Wexler 1985a, ms c, respectively). Consider the example of Old Judezmo *fadas* ~ *(h)adas*, contemporary Judezmo *fada(s)* 'custom of naming a boy or girl seven days after birth', *fadamjento* 'naming ceremony for a girl' (some of the terms are attested prior to 1492). The fact that only Iberian Jews and Muslims used the term suggests a North African Muslim origin for the Jewish custom. An original southern Iberian zone of radiation is assured from Portuguese Jewish examples and by the absence of the term in Judeo-Catalan in the far northeast of the Peninsula. In view of Muslim usage, the etymon is most likely Arabic *ḥadaθ* 'novelty, event', *ḥadīθ* 'new'; Spanish typically replaces Arabic *ḥ* with *f*—which, at least in Castilian, later became zero (orthographically *h*). Attempts to derive the term from the cognate Hebrew *ḥādāš* 'new' (see Baer 1/2:1936:445) or from Spanish *hada* 'fairy' (< Latin *fata*: see Romano 1933, Veny Clar 1960:181) are less convincing (did fairies have a name-giving function in Medieval Iberian folk culture?).

Alternatively, as Jews became less conversant in Arabic, they could have become attracted to the Hebrew etymon *ḥādāš* out of ignorance, or consciously Judaized the practice by giving it a "Hebrew" name (presumably outside of the Iberian Peninsula). The custom and name survive among the pre-World-War-II Jewish descendants of the Portuguese Marranos in Germany, see *fadas*, but only in reference to the naming of a boy on the evening before his circumcision (references in Wexler 1988:40, fn 191). Could the narrowing of the term to refer only to boys reflect changes in custom among the German ex-Marrano Jews? Relevant is the discussion in category I, Germanic 3 below of Western Yiddish *holekrāš* 'naming ceremony for a child', of pagan Germanic origin. Both the *fadas* and *holekrāš* ceremonies involve the bestowing of a secular name on the Jewish child, as the religious Hebrew name was given the boy on the occasion of his circumcision seven days after birth.

Non-Jewish languages at times retain data that permit us to reveal possible historical changes in the practice of the Jewish religion or superstitions which are not immediately suggested by the Jewish source languages. Naturally, we must be on guard against distorted non-Jewish interpretations of Jewish practice. For example, Hebrew *kāšer* 'kosher, food that is ritually fit for consumption' surfaces in Ossete, an Iranian language spoken by Muslims in the Daghestan Autonomous Republic in Russia (bordering northern Azerbajdzhan), as *kōsart, kūsart* 'ritually slaughtered animal used as an offering for God or guests, or on holidays' (Wexler 1987b:227). Did the Alan ancestors of the Ossetes borrow their current unusual meanings of Hebrew *kāšer* from a coterritorial group of Jews, say Khazars, together with the term itself, or are the unusual meanings of a slaughtered offering or a holiday food Ossete innovations? Disturbed by the semantic discrepancies between Hebrew and Ossete, the noted Iranianist, Emile Benveniste, concluded that a Hebrew etymology for this Ossete term should be dismissed (1956:36–7).

When speakers of coterritorial Jewish and non-Jewish languages share lexical bifurcation, we have the problem of ascertaining the source of the innovation. An example is Moroccan Muslim Arabic *meġāra* 'Jewish cemetery' (< Moroccan Judeo-Arabic) vs. *mqebṛa, ṛūḍa* '(unspecified) cemetery' (native, literally 'graves, garden', respectively). It is difficult to say whether this bifurcation originated among non-Jews or Jews; see Moroccan Judezmo *meʿara* 'Jewish cemetery' (< Hebrew *məʿārāh* 'cave') vs. native Spanish *simenterio* 'Christian cemetery' vs. *emqabar* 'Muslim cemetery' (< Arabic: Wagner 1931:230). Another example is Yiddish *šikse* 'Christian girl' (this "Hebrew" word was invented in Yiddish, on the basis of the existing Hebrew masculine noun *šɛqɛc* 'abomination'; see Petrikovits 1922 and Wexler 1988:150). Curiously, "Judaization" subsequently affected this word in Christian speech, see Viennese German slang *šikse* 'Jewish girl' (vs. native terms for 'girl' in general).

The use of Hebraisms in German (and Yiddish) slang raises intriguing questions. The Hebrew origin of these terms suggests the Christians might have derived the practices from the Jews, even though some of the practices are known to be of Christian origin! I assume that the practices could have died out among the Christians and were later revived through contact with the Jews who still preserved them. Alternatively, the practices may have developed in mixed Jewish-Christian circles; in either case, we have a telling mark of the intensity of the relations between Jews and Christians in the early Middle Ages, especially in the domain of folk culture. (See also the peregrination of Hebrew *saxar* to German *šaxer,* as in *Schacher-macher,* and back to Yiddish, cited in chapter 3 above.)

For example, German slang (Rotwelsch) *passulant* 'bearer of an amulet' (known only from a 16th-century Christian source: Avé-Lallemant 3:1862:154, fn 1), to judge from its form, is of probable Hebrew origin. The closest Hebrew etyma are *pɛsɛl* 'sculpture', *passāl* 'sculptor', *pāsal* 'disqualify, declare unfit'; the latter term is the basis for Yiddish *pasl(en)en* 'declare unfit, invalidate'. Significantly, Yiddish also uses this verb in two phrases with magical connotations, e.g., *pasl(en)en a kac* 'cut off the tail of a cat', *pasl(en)en a kind* 'rub the face of a child with urine', acts which were intended to remove the effects of an evil eye. Despite the Hebrew name, the practices themselves are probably of non-Jewish provenience. For instance, Grünbaum (1877:348) noted that the custom of smearing a child with dirt as protection against the evil eye was practiced in ancient Egypt and modern Greece; the Jews could have gotten this custom either in the Near East or from a Hellenized European society. This raises the possibility that some Mediterranean customs could have been transmitted via the Jews to north European non-Jews. German *passulant* might be derived from the Yiddish verb or from an unattested underlying Yiddish agentive noun **paslen* 'bearer of an amulet'. The ending *-(e)n* of Yiddish nouns that usually denotes the agent performing the action bears strong formal and semantic similarity to the French participial suffix *-ant* (e.g., *parlant* 'speaking'), also borrowed by German; hence, a hypothetical Yiddish noun **paslen* may have been remodeled by Christians into *passulant,* on the model of terms like Berlin German slang *mogelant* 'swindler' < *mogeln* 'swindle' (1925, also of Hebrew origin: Wexler 1988:94, fn 53, 95).

Another Hebraism used to denote a non-Jewish practice among the Christians is German slang (Basle) *klabot* (1411–63), *claffot* (1510) 'garment'; contemporary German slang has *kluft* (first attested in 1687: see Wolf 1956:#2736 for other variants and a slightly different etymology), which occasionally surfaces in Yiddish slang. I recently proposed Hebrew *qlāf* 'parchment; playing card' as the source of *kluft* (see 1988: 151), but related Hebrew *qlīppōt* 'peel; evil spirit', plural of *qlīppāh* (in Yiddish *klipe,* pl *klipes* 'evil spirit; shrew, nuisance') or even *qillūf* 'peeling' may also be the etyma of German slang *klabot, claffot, kluft.* The ending *-ot* in the German forms is unlikely to be the Hebrew plural suffix, since *-t* should have been pronounced as *s* in a Yiddish reading of

Hebrew. Moreover, the plural of Hebrew *qlāf* is normally formed with another Hebrew suffix, *-īm*. A solution would be to derive *-ot* from the Old French diminutive *-ot* (as in *moinot* 'little monk' < *moine* 'monk'). A Judeo-French impact on German slang is plausible since the earliest extant German slang lists were compiled in the area between Basle and Strasbourg, a territory which could have been settled by the French Jews who were definitively exiled from the Kingdom of France and the Franche-Comté in 1394.

I cannot determine when Hebrew *qlīppāh* 'peel' acquired the meaning evil spirit. However, I can envision a link between Yiddish 'evil spirit' and German/Yiddish slang 'clothing' through the current Jewish/obsolete Christian religious practice, known in Hebrew as *tašlīx* (literally 'you will throw'). Among the Jews, *tašlīx* involves going to a body of water prior to the Jewish High Holidays (New Year and Yom Kippur) in order to shake off sins, an act performed by symbolically emptying one's clothing of crumbs intended for the evil spirits. If the practice of *tašlīx* itself is of Near Eastern origin, it may have become obsolete among the Germano-Slavic Jews, to judge from its historical absence among Iberian (Sephardic) Jews. In northern Europe, the custom could have been revived (or reinforced) among the Jews by a similar pagan practice (see further discussion in chapter 5.2 below).

I can conceive of two paths of diffusion for *klabot* from Jews to Christians: (a) French Jews > German Christians > German Jews (who now have only *kluft*), or (b) French Jews > German Jews > German Christians. The Christians who accepted the term 'garment' from the Jews may have also been aware of the supersititious implications current among the Jews, since the Italian poet Francesco Petrarca (1304–74) found the Catholics practicing *tašlīx* as well on a visit to Cologne; unfortunately, he does not give the German Christian term for the practice.

In the German speech of the Jews and coterritorial Christians in southwest Germany, the term *hilūxə* denotes clothes. Matras derived the term tentatively from Hebrew *halīxāh* 'going, gait' (1991:289). The semantic extension from procession to clothing would make sense in the context of the *tašlīx* ceremony. On the other hand, dress and movement are concepts that can be expressed by a single morpheme in some Slavic languages, see e.g., Upper Sorbian *stroj* 'machine, instrument' and *strojić* 'dress, put on'; in German also *gehen* 'go' combines with nouns denoting clothing to mean wear, e.g., *in Nationaltracht gehen* 'go about in national costume' (note the parallel English *go about in*). The cryptic meaning of German slang *haliche* 'secret way of thieves; slippery, illegal way' (1840: recorded by Wolf 1956:#2027) may also be a reference to Jewish *tašlīx*, by this time no longer practiced by the Christians.

The Jews might also have been prompted to ascribe an innovative religious meaning to a loan which was phonetically similar to native Jewish words which did have religious meanings. A possible example is Eastern Yiddish *lajbserdak* 'ritual undergarment for males', consisting of German *lajb* 'body' and *serdak*, which is probably Ukrainian *sardak, serdak* 'sleeveless shirt worn by Carpathian mountaineers' (first attested in Ukrainian in the 16th century). *Lajbserdak* appears to have been invented on the model of phonetically similar wholly German *lajbcudekl*, etc., literally 'body' + 'little covering', which denotes the same ritual object. The original Ukrainian term never had any religious connotations. Subsequently, Yiddish *lajbserdak* spread (back) to Polish and East Slavic languages, where it acquired pejorative non-cult meanings, see, e.g., Belorussian *lapsurduk* 'urchin; Jew (pejorative); torn clothing, rags' (1870). The second part of Yiddish *lajbcudekl* occurs in the Czech speech of Jews as *cidákl* 'amulet, talisman' (Pech 1948), a vivid testimony to the superstitious functions often attributed to the garment (see also the discussion of Hebrew *məzūzāh* in chapter 5.2 below).

The type of component chosen for a concept sometimes allows us to put a relative date on the development of the Jewish practice. For example, the Yiddish term *sandek* for the Jewish godfather who holds the newborn boy at the circumcision ceremony is of Greek origin, even though Greek *sýndikos* 'defender of a community; public advocate' originally lacked any cult meaning. I assume that the role of the godfather during the circumcision may have originated among the Jews during the time when large numbers of Jews were Greek-speaking. It is curious that the Greek term first appears in 10th-century Hebrew texts (as *sandāq*, along with other, now extinct, variants from 13th–14th-century Hebrew texts from both former Slavic and non-Slavic areas of Germany, which were closer to the Greek original: see details in Wexler 1987b:30–1), very soon after the practice of the godfather lifting the neophyte from the baptismal water was introduced into the church ceremony at the Mainz Council in 813 (T.H. Gaster 1980:60, 62, fn *). Note also the use of Yiddish *jidišen* 'induct a male into the Jewish community by circumcision' < *jid* 'Jew'—imitating Slavic Christian terms for 'baptism', which are often derived from the root 'Christian', see, e.g., Upper Sorbian *křćić* 'baptize' ~ *křesćan* 'Christian' (as well as English *christen, Christian*). The 10th century was a period when large numbers of European proselytes were joining the Jewish fold. Hence, a non-Jewish (though not necessarily Greek) origin for the Jewish practice of the godfather holding the infant at the circumcision is in place. It is significant that none of the Slavic languages has a cognate of Yiddish *sandek*; the Slavic term for godfather comes from Latin (see Skok 1930). This fact suggests that the Jews may have acquired the Grecism prior to making contact with Balkan Slavs in the 7th century; if so, the Christian practice may have been performed in the Balkans before 813. Finally, the Jewish Grecism also raises the possibility that the Slavs once used the Grecism.

Yiddish has other terms of Balkan Romance and Balkan or West Slavic origin, and occasionally even Arabic terms (presumably received through a Turkic carrier)—again from areas with either a documented or probable record of widespread Jewish proselytism. Sometimes, a Yiddish Grecism and the original Greek term both lack religious connotations, but a second borrower language has religious connotations; these facts compel us to entertain religious meanings in earlier Yiddish or in other Jewish languages. An example is Greek *ẻpitropos* 'steward, trustee, administrator' which appears in the Talmud as *ʾapīṭrōpōs, ʾapō-* in the meanings tutor, guardian; Yiddish *apetropes, apitropos* have the Hebrew meanings. Parts of the Talmud could have been composed as late as the 8th century, in the view of some scholars. Serbo-Croatian *(je)pitrop* (14th–15th cc) and *potrop* 'person in charge of church money; church guard, director' have ecclesiastic connotations.

Below I will cite non-Hebrew words in Jewish languages under three categories:

CATEGORY I. Jewish loans (or loan translations) with religious and/or superstitious meanings which have parallels in the donor language. I presume the Jews borrowed the practices together with the terms from non-Jews and/or prosleytes.

Examples from Yiddish (cognates from other Jewish languages are cited in the text below) that are discussed below come from Greek (*-ecn (rebecn), šul, tolme/uftolmen, trop, vorokoli/vorkolakas),* Romance (*ant-špojzn, benčn, briv/šmire-briv/kimpet-briv, jičn/jid(i)šn, ōrn, poršn, šar-men/šormen, tečn*), Turkic (*pejsex, šabaš/šibeš, almemer/balemer, dav[e]nen?*), Slavic (*grager/grejger, kowleč/kojleč, praven, sanvi, sansavi, samangelaf, trejbern)* and German (*barxes/ berxes, xale, baxer/ boxer/ buxer, holekrāš/xolekrāš, jorcajt, kobolt, mogen dovid).*

CATEGORY II. Jewish loans (or loan translations) with religious and/or superstitious meanings which lack parallels in the donor language. In this case, either the Jews independently developed the new meanings after acquiring the terms from non-Jews and/or proselytes (with other meanings), or the donor languages lost the original meanings.

Examples from Yiddish come from Greek *(hinūmāh, miniç/mineš, sandek)*, Romance *(čolnt/šālet/šōlet, [ha]čamers, fačejle, lejenen/ lajen, mape, memern, memōrbūx, repetier[en]/ertorn/dertornen, sargenes)*, Turkic *(homen[-taš], jarmlke)*, Slavic *(gojlem, nadn/nedan, par[e]ve, kitke, lajbserdak, oprixtn, opšprexn, šprox)*.

CATEGORY III. Jewish loans with no religious and/or superstitious meanings for which the donor languages do have religious and/or superstitious meanings. I presume that the Jews either originally borrowed both the religious/superstitious practices and the terms from non-Jews, giving up the practices at a later date, or borrowed the terms with neutral meanings before the non-Jews independently developed their own religious or superstitious connotations.

Examples from Yiddish come from Greek *(katoves)* and Slavic *(dejže)*.

I will give Yiddish examples for each category according to the presumed chronological order of the first contact: Greek; Romance; Turkic (only as an intermediary carrier of Iranian, Arabic and even occasionally Hebrew); Slavic; German. Needless to say, some Latinisms could have reached the Jews before some Grecisms, some Germanisms before Slavicisms, etc. In most cases it is extremely difficult to pinpoint the geographical origin of Grecisms and Slavisms in the absence of unambiguous dialectal clues or historical sources. Yiddish has no unique native Turkic words, but does have a few Turkisms also found in neighboring Slavic languages and German, which were presumably the carriers of the Turkisms to Yiddish.

The various loans could have been acquired in the following locales:

(a) Greek terms could have been borrowed in Palestine, Asia Minor and/or the Balkans (in the latter case, possibly through a Slavic intermediary).

(b) Romance terms are primarily of north Italian, Friulan or Balkan Romance extraction; the first two languages were also spoken in the northern Balkans. Occasionally, Yiddish Romanisms show possible traces of a Slavic intermediary carrier.

(c) Iranian and Arabic terms and one Hebrew word were received presumably from Turkic languages spoken in the Balkans or Hungary or transmitted via Eastern Slavic Jews in the Khazar kingdom.

(d) Slavic terms were received from South and/or West Slavic either directly or (in the case of West Slavic) via German.

(e) German terms were received directly from German speakers or indirectly from bilingual or Germanized Slavs.

My purpose here is to illustrate the types of linguistic data that can be mustered in support of the hypothesis that proselytes played a major role in the ethnogenesis of the north European Jewry; hence, I make no attempt to achieve completeness in the listing of examples.

I assume that a large part of the non-Jewish impact on Ashkenazic cultural and religious terminology was eliminated by the imported Hebraisms that flooded Yiddish in the wake of increased Judaization after 1200 (examples of such Hebraisms are given in Wexler 1991b: chapter 3.222). It is interesting that for many of the concepts now expressed in Yiddish by Hebraisms, Sorbian (and to some extent Polabian) use borrowed Germanisms. The parallel penetration of Hebraisms into Yiddish and Germanisms into Sorbian (and Polabian) suggests very strongly that Yiddish (as Judeo-Sorbian) must have been coterritorial with Sorbian when both languages were exposed to Germanization. Many of the missing nativisms in both Yiddish and Sorbian fall into the domain of religious expression and superstition.

CATEGORY I. Jewish loans (and one loan translation) with religious and/or superstitious meanings attested in the donor languages

Greek (via Slavic?) 1. Yiddish *-ecn* female agent, in *rebecn* 'rabbi's wife; erudite woman'; (earlier) 'woman rabbi'(?)

Yiddish *rebe* 'rabbi' is derived from Judeo-Aramaic *rībbī* (literally 'my teacher'), but the formation with the feminine gender suffix *-ecn,* which occurs only with this word in Yiddish, is, I believe, possibly of combined Judeo-Greek and Slavic origin.

Max Weinreich derived Yiddish *-cn* from two synonymous suffixes marking feminine gender: from Italian *-essa/-issa* (see 19th-century Judeo-Italian *rabissa* 'rabbi's wife' as well as modern variants *rubìssa, rabinèssa)* + Yiddish *-(i)n* (as in *kinig* 'king': *kinigin* 'queen'). I might add that Italian *-essa* is a borrowing from Greek *-íssa* that denotes feminine nouns with titles and honors, e.g., Italian *duchessa* 'duchess'. The suffix was particularly productive in Church Latin, including the Latin Bible translations.

I still have the problem of explaining how a Greco-Latin *-s-* became Yiddish *-c-;* there is no such precedent either in Yiddish or in Italian. The *-c-* might have arisen under the influence of South Slavic *-ica,* also a marker of feminine gender, see, e.g., Serbo-Croatian *kral'* 'king': *kral'ica* 'queen'. For many Yiddish speakers, especially in the Western dialect areas, the unfamiliar double suffix prompted the creation of quite a number of replacements, e.g., *rabucindrin, rebeče, rebecin(t)e, rebectn, rebenen, rebesn,* etc. (the data were given in Beranek 1965: map #87); some of these forms involve the Slavic suffixes *-inja, -ač* + possibly Hebrew *-āh* (for possible Sorbian source suffixes, see Kovalyk 1967:87–90). In Eastern Yiddish, the Slavic suffix *-ica* is occasionally encountered, see, e.g. *nudnice* 'bore, pest' (feminine, with a Slavic root), *mefunice* 'fastidious woman' (with a Hebrew root). Slavic *-ica* is occasionally found in Greek with Slavic loans, see, e.g., Serbo-Croatian *vȅverica* 'squirrel' > Greek *ververítsa.*

I do not know the age of any of the variants that now denote the rabbi's wife, but Judeo-Aramaic *rībbī* was used in Greek and Latin-speaking areas, see, e.g., *rebbi,* an honorific title, in a Judeo-Latin inscription from Mérida (Extremadura, Spain), thought to date from between the 6th–8th centuries A.D. The change of *ī* in the first syllable to *e* could have taken place in either Vulgar Latin or Greek. The Judeo-Catalan *reebi* (Girona 1385) is a continuation of the Judeo-Greek form (the Catalan and Valencian coasts had Greek speakers until possibly as late as the 8th century A.D.).

The forebear of Yiddish *rebecn* may have originated in pagan societies, in imitation of pagan religious institutions. In a number of Judeo-Greek inscriptions from Greece, Italy and Malta spanning the period from the 2nd century B.C. to the 6th century A.D., we find repeated use of feminine nouns connected with important community roles performed by women, including forms like Greek *arxḗgissa* '(synagogue) founder', *presbetérēssa, arxisynagṓgissa* 'synagogue elder'; Latin *pateressa* 'synagogue functionary, board member' (from *pater* 'father'!: see Brooten 1982, Trebilco 1991: chapter 5). These forms attest to the equality women enjoyed with men in the performance of functions associated with the synagogue and the Jewish community. Therefore, I speculate that the original meaning of Yiddish *rebecn* and of its Greco-Latin forebears may have been 'female rabbi' (see M.Samuel 1971:58–9). Note that in Yiddish *rebecn* can also denote an erudite woman.

The important role of women in Jewish religious life in the Greco-Roman period is witnessed by the large number of female donors to synagogues. The status of women in this early period stands in sharp contrast to their diminished role in European Jewish societies beginning with the early 13th–14th century. Though in some parts of Europe, the practice of giving both men and women religious instruction may have persisted into the early 15th century. For example, illuminations in the so-called "Darmstadt Haggada" of Upper Rhine origin c. 1430 (Ms. Or.8, fol. 37v and fol. 48v in the Hessische Landes- und Hochschulbibliothek, Darmstadt, an illustration of which is given by Nachama, Schoeps and van Voolen 1992:99) portrays teachers instructing a group of mainly female students.

In the contemporary orthodox synagogue, women are separated from men, usually in their own separate gallery, and cannot participate actively in the service. The women's gallery does not appear in German or Slavic synagogues until after the systematic segregation of Jews from Christian society, in the wake of the First Crusade (1096). Beginning with the 13th century we find women's galleries added to existing synagogue buildings. Thus, the synagogue at Worms from the 11th century acquired a women's section (on the same level as the men's section) in 1212/3, the now destroyed Speyer and Cologne synagogues erected c.1090 acquired women's sections in the late 14th century, and the Pinkas synagogue in Prague dating from the 13th century acquired its women's section as late as 1600. The Regensburg synagogue built in the 14th century (and destroyed in 1519) shows no signs of ever having had a separate section for women (for details, see Krautheimer 1927 and Künzl 1988a:62–3, 65–6, 85, 1988b:89–90). In Poland, the synagogue built around 1400 at Kazimierz (near Kraków) did not originally have a women's section. Only Polish synagogues built in the 16th century (e.g., at Szczebrzeszyn and Zamość) had a female section from the very start. A gallery is found in Iberian synagogues of the 14th century (Toledo's Tránsito synagogue, that of Córdoba), but two illuminated manuscripts from 14th-century Aragón show men and women together in the synagogue (Metzger and Metzger 1982:61—citing the Sarajevo and Kaufmann Haggadas). In the Germano-Slavic lands, the custom of adding a women's section may have spread from west to east, but the paucity of remains makes any such claim tentative.

Greek (via German and/or Slavic?) 2. Yiddish *šul* 'synagogue, school'

The use of the word school to designate the synagogue is characteristic of Yiddish and most of the Judeo-Romance languages; exceptions are

Judezmo, Judeo- and Marrano Portuguese which use an Arabized form of Latin *sinagōga*, a testimony to the Judeo-Arab origins of most Iberian Jews, see, e.g., Dutch Marrano Portuguese *šnoġa*. The term *škola* 'school' means synagogue in most Slavic languages too, which permits us to reconstruct the meaning in Judeo-Slavic. It is also widespread in the Christian Romance languages, including Latin, and in German (see the quotation from Blondheim given above). Some commentators have sought internal Jewish motivation for the use of 'school' for 'synagogue', e.g., on the grounds that the synagogue originally functioned as a house of study (Wischnitzer 1947:25). But such an argument is unnecessary, since Latin *schola* could also denote a meeting place, as well as a school.

The first use of school in the meaning of synagogue dates from the New Testament: "[Paul] took his disciples apart to hold daily discussions in the *school* of Tyrannus" (Acts 19:9). This was apparently because the Jews would not listen to Saint Paul in their own synagogue. The event described took place in Ephesus, Anatolia. The fact that this is not the normal term for synagogue in the New Testament (and is unknown, to the best of my knowledge, in Judeo-Greek inscriptions) has engendered discussion of whether *sxolē* meant in fact a synagogue. The usual terms for synagogue in the New Testament are (a) *synagōgē* (literally, 'place of gathering'), which in Jewish inscriptions denotes almost exclusively the Jewish community rather than the actual building (this usage is the basis for the nomenclature in the European Christian languages and in two Jewish languages: Judezmo and Judeo-Portuguese), (b) *proseuxē* (originally 'prayer'), which is the standard Judeo-Greek term for the synagogue and the manner of discourse in most Afro-Asian Jewish languages—see Moroccan Judeo-Arabic *ṣḷā* (taken from the root 'pray'), Judeo-Chinese *lǐ-baì sì*, (literally 'prayer temple'), and (c) *oĩkos proseuxēs* (literally 'house of prayer'), also attested on Judeo-Greek inscriptions (see Wexler 1981c). The varied terminology may reflect different types of houses of worship (S.E.Johnson 1975:98–9, like English *temple* 'reform synagogue', *synagogue* 'conservative synagogue' and *shul* 'orthodox synagogue'). There are also some geographical differences, e.g., *proseuxē* was used in Greek inscriptions in Egypt, the Aegean region, the Balkans, Spain and the Crimean Peninsula, while *synagōgē* and sometimes *oĩkos proseuxēs* appeared in Central Anatolia. The first example of Latin *schola* 'synagogue' is in the early North African Latin *schola Judaeorum*, literally 'synagogue of the Jews', from the sermons of Saint Augustine (137:6; the latter was born in North Africa, at Tagaste [Souk Ahras, Algeria] 354 and died at Hippo Regius [Bône, Algeria] in 430). Greek *proseuxē* is occasionally used in the meaning of a pagan place of worship, which suggests a pagan borrowing from the Jews (see Trebilco 1991:242, fn 42).

In view of the fact that Greek *sxolē* first appears in the New Testament prompts me to regard the new meaning synagogue as a non-Jewish, i.e., proselyte, innovation. To the best of my knowledge, the only other observor to have made such a claim (though without motivation) was Güdemann (1888:94, fn; see Abrahams 1896:34). The use of *schola* in a number of European Jewish languages (e.g., Yiddish, Medieval Judeo-Catalan, Judeo-French, Judeo-Provençal, Judeo-Italian) supports the hypothesis of an important proselyte component in European Jewish communities. Judeo-Greek *proseuxē* was borrowed by (Judeo-)Latin as *proseucha*, see, e.g., Juvenal (c.60–c.140), but does not survive in Judeo-Romance or Yiddish, either as a loan or model for a loan translation.

I think it significant that Yiddish lacks a common term for synagogue which is modeled on the root 'prayer'—such as we find in the overwhelming majority of Jewish languages—from Moroccan Judeo-Arabic in the west all the way to Judeo-Chinese in the east (see details in Wexler 1981c). I cannot determine the age of the expression *davenšul* 'synagogue' (literally 'synagogue for prayer') which Uriel Weinreich listed in his Yiddish-English dictionary (1968), but in any case it is not the typical term for synagogue in Yiddish.

Written Old and Modern Israeli Hebrew *bēt knɛsɛt* 'synagogue', literally 'the house of the gathering', is thoroughly un-Jewish: *knɛsɛt* is a loan from Aramaic, possibly used in the meaning of Judeo-Greek *synagōgē* 'Jewish community' (unless Greek was patterned on Aramaic).

Greek 3. Old Western Yiddish *tolme* 'bridal chair, canopy', Dutch Yiddish *uftolmen* 'place on a bier'

The etymon is Greek *θalamos* 'bridal chamber'. The only other Jewish language that I know of that has this Grecism is Judezmo *talamo* 'bridal canopy' (expressed in contemporary Yiddish by the Hebraism *xupe*). The Grecism exists in some Ibero-Romance languages, see, e.g., Old Catalan *tàlam*, Catalan *tàlem* 'receptacle for carrying holy relics in a procession', as well as in standard Italian *tàlamo* 'nuptial bed' (13th c) and Abruzzi Italian *tàlëmë* 'stretcher for carrying sacred images'. I suspect that the Yiddish Grecism was borrowed by Ashkenazic Jews in the Balkans, while the Judezmo counterpart comes from neighboring Christian Catalan.

Literature: Wexler 1988:32ff.

Greek 4. Yiddish *trop* 'stress, emphasis; musical accents used in cantillating the Torah'

The etymon is Greek *tropos* 'mode of music'. Since the Grecism is not found in the Hellenistic Hebrew literature from Palestine and there are no grounds for positing a Judeo-Latin intermediary (it is unknown in Judeo-Italian or Judeo-Ibero-Romance; on Judeo-French, see below), I have to assume that the word first entered the lexicon of Balkan Jews who brought it to the German lands. The Balkan Jews preserve the word without the Greek ending *-os,* which is typical of Arumanian *trop* 'manner' (Arumanian is a Romance language closely related to Rumanian spoken today by 350,000 in scattered locales in Albania, Bulgaria, northwest Greece and Macedonia) and Serbo-Croatian *trop* 'poetic genre'—but not of Rumanian *tropos* 'manner' (a language with which I presume Jews did not have contact in the first millennium). From Yiddish, the term passed into Judeo-French (see Wexler 1987b:41–2). In terms of meaning, Yiddish *trop* is very close to Old Serbo-Croatian *tròpârь* (14th c) 'church song' (< Greek *troparion*).

Greek (via Slavic?) 5. Ashkenazic Hebrew *bwrwqwlj* /vorokoli/ (in *Sefer xasidim* of Jehuda Hexasid, died 1217), *bwrqwlʾqʾš* /vorkolakas/ (in *Nišmat xaim* of Eliezer of Worms, died c.1238) 'werewolf'

A common term for werewolf appears to be shared by Slavic and a number of non-Slavic Balkan languages, see, e.g., Serbo-Croatian *vukodlak*; the term is also found in non-Slavic Balkan languages, e.g., Greek *vroukólakas* (in Macedonia, among other locales), *vourkólakas* (Cakonia: see Budziszewska 1991:14), Rumanian *vălcolác* ('demon of the atmosphere'), Albanian *vurvollák* (see also Hanush 1859:195; Güdemann 1880:203 and fn 7, 217, fn 5, 1884:336; Filipović 1960: 261). Vasmer (1953–8) postulated two Slavic words 'wolf' and 'skin' as the etyma. Trachtenberg also regarded the Hebrew word as a borrowing from Slavic and expressed surprise that a "Slavic" word should surface in Jewish writings in west Germany in the early 13th century (1939:279, fn 40). I have no idea whether the term was ever used in colloquial Yiddish. Most recently, Nichols has proposed an Iranian source, consisting of the morphemes 'wolf' and 'person', which was subsequently reetymologized in Slavic (1987). For attempts to derive the Greek term from native Greek roots, see Vlachos 1971:227–8 (who provides additional Greek variants).

The belief in werewolves seems to be most typical of the northern and eastern regions of Germany (once settled by Slavs!) and German-speaking areas of Bohemia (Wuttke 1900:276–7; von Hovorka and Kronfeld 1:1908:425, 429), though the Germans do not use this particular word. On the popularity of the concept among Orthodox South Slavs, see Vlachos 1971:226, fn 48. The second Hebrew example most resembles the Greek form of the Slavism, while the first variant has a syllable structure which better resembles Slavic. It is conceivable the Jews acquired the term from Greek speakers in the Balkans (or received it through Hebrew literature penned by Greek Jews), though I wonder if its retention among the German Jews as late as the 13th century was not due to the existence of cognates in the coterritorial Slavic languages.

Romance 1. Western Yiddish *antšpojzn* 'become engaged' (14th c), 'marry' (16th c)

The ultimate source is Latin *in-* + *sposāre*, but the path of diffusion of the term into Yiddish is unclear. A north Italian source is problematic since these dialects (now) use a different root (e.g., *maritarsi, pigliarsi,* etc.). A Balkan Romance source is also not problem-free, since the root neither appears there nor in any Balkan non-Romance language. Hence, the best explanation is a north Italian source, before replacement of the root there by the current terms. I should also note that both Yiddish and north Italian use a solitary term for 'marry' (see Yiddish *xasene hobn*), in contrast to many other Italian dialects and many Slavic languages which distinguish lexically between 'marry (girl)' and 'marry (boy)', see, e.g., Russian *vyjti zamuž* and *ženit'sja*, respectively.

Literature: Wexler 1992b.

Romance 2. Yiddish *benčn* 'bless'

The source is ultimately Latin *benedicere*, today retained only in south Italian (vs. north and standard Italian *benedire*). A Balkan connection is not to be ruled out, since the components, literally 'well' + 'say', form the basis of Rumanian *binecuvînta* and Bulgarian *blagoslavjam.* Also Latin *dīcere* 'speak' is the basis of Serbo-Croatian *dìčiti (se)* (16th century) and possibly also Hungarian *dicser* 'praise'. A curious parallel with Middle High German is that Yiddish *benčn* denotes, *inter alia*, the saying of grace *after* meals, while Middle High German *benedîz* means the *last* blessing in the mass (the latter appears in the early 13th century: Moser 1964:29). See also discussion in chapter 4 above.

Romance 3. Yiddish *briv* 'letter'; *šmire-briv, kimpet-briv* 'amulet placed in the room of a pregnant woman' (literally 'letter for guarding, confinement', respectively); *brivele* 'little letter; amulet'

Deriving Yiddish *briv* from German *Brief* 'letter' (ultimately from Italian *breve*) is problematic in view of the final *v*, though Middle High German seems to have had variants with both *v* and *f*. Alternatively, I could explain Yiddish *v* as a direct borrowing from Italian with *-v-*. In view of the paucity of German terms in Yiddish with pagan or Christian religious meanings, an immediate Italian origin seems more secure. The meaning of amulet, expressed often by the Yiddish diminutive form, finds a reflection in Old Italian, Old French, Istrian Romance and Austrian German. Andree wrote that among the Jews the amulet was attached to the window and chimney, where the devil might enter (1881:150), but in the Romance tradition, the amulet was hung around the child's neck to afford protection against evil spirits.

Literature: Aly 1927 (for a discussion of German amulets); Kostrzewski 1964a (Slavic amulets); Wexler 1992b.

Romance (via Slavic?) 4. Western Yiddish *jičn*, Eastern Yiddish *jid(i)šn*

On the possibility of a Slavic model, see above.

Romance 5. Western Yiddish *ōrn* 'pray'

This is a Romance church word that became archaic in most Romance languages by the 13th–14th centuries and was replaced by derivatives of Latin *precari* (e.g., Fr *prier*). The term survives rarely in the original meaning of pray, see, e.g., Rhaeto-Romance *urà* 'pray'; Albanian *uroj* has the related meanings of bless, wish.

The geographic details of Yiddish *ōrn*—and synonymous *davenen* (see Turkic 4 below)—are given in Lowenstein 1969: map #7.

Literature: Wexler 1992b.

Romance (via Slavic?) 6. Western Yiddish *poršn*

See Slavic 6 below.

Romance 7. Western German Yiddish (also one instance south of Eisenach, Thüringen < Judaized German?) *šarmen, šormen* 'bewitch'

The source is French *charmer,* with the same meaning. In the Saarland between the two World Wars, Yiddish *šormen* was known to non-Jews as the process by which elderly Jews could cure sick people and horses (Fox 1927:124, 296).

Romance 8. Yiddish *tečn* 'blow the shofar in the synagogue'

The source is Medieval Latin *toccare* 'play a musical instrument'. Religious connotations appear occasionally in Romance, see, e.g., Rumanian *tocă, bate toáca* 'announce a religious service by beating on a wooden or metal board' and Gascon *toucá* 'announce the angelus prayer'.

Literature: Wexler 1992b.

Turkic (Hebraism) 1. Eastern German Yiddish and Eastern Yiddish *pejsex* male name; 'Passover'

See discussion in chapter 5.2 below.

Turkic (Iranianism) 2. Eastern Yiddish *šabaš* 'tip paid to musicians by the guests who dance at a wedding'; *šibeš* 'trifle; small coin'

The etymon of both Yiddish words is Iranian *šabaš* with the identical meaning as Yiddish *šabaš.* The Iranianism is widespread in Muslim languages, e.g., Turkish, Urdu, where it tends to mean bravo, approve, appreciate. The Iranianism is used (often in a truncated form) in most of the East and West Slavic languages, Hungarian, Greek, German and Dutch, usually in their slang registers, and in a variety of meanings always associated with money (sometimes illegally earned), payment or time off—but never with precisely the original Iranian meaning. I am unaware of South Slavic examples. Examples are Bavarian German *schab ab* 'finished; over!' (shouted by masons and construction workers when work was done: 1548), Viennese German *schabn* 'divide booty'; Dutch *voosch* 'good penny' (1547); Hungarian *sáp* 'pimp's share; money for silencing; brothel owner's profit; metal or wood cuttings' (1846); Russian, Belorussian *šabaški* 'wood cuttings taken hóme by carpenters from work'; Russian, Ukrainian *šabaš* 'enough!; rest time; ship oars' (1771; see discussion in Wexler 1990g).

Curiously, there is no evidence of this Iranianism in Polish, though Polish appears to have the oldest corpus of Iranianisms of all the Slavic languages (see Trubačev 1967:81; Nichols 1987:174). This fact suggests that the Slavic Jews and the Slavs may have received Iranianisms from different sources and at different periods.

The fact that Yiddish alone among the European target languages preserves the original meaning suggests that the Jews received the term directly from an Iranian (or Turkic?) source language, spoken presumably in the Balkans or Hungary, in other words, prior to the partial language shift from Judeo-Sorbian to Yiddish. The European non-Jewish languages could have received the Iranianism either from the Jews or a Turkic/Iranian language (Kranzmayer raises the possibility that the Avars brought Iranianisms to Hungary, Austria and Slovenia: 1:1956:59, 65, 200). Yiddish speakers now believe that *šibeš* comes from Hebrew; three etyma can be suggested:

(a) One hypothesis is that the etymon is *šibbuš* 'error, complication', hence the spelling *šjbwš* in the Hebrew manner; the Hebrew etymon is convincing to speakers since genuine Hebrew *šjbwš* would also be pronounced *šibeš* in Yiddish. It occurs to me that the use of the Hebraism *šibeš* in Yiddish might even have been motivated by the existence of the earlier homophonous Iranianism; as far as I know, no other Jewish language borrows this Hebraism.

(b) Many contemporary Yiddish speakers believe Yiddish *šabaš* is derived from *šabes* 'Sabbath' (Liberman 1960).

(c) Among some speakers, the semantic distance between "Sabbath" and "tip" appararently has given rise to the hypothesis that the etymon is an acronym for Hebrew *s(xar)* 'payment' + *b(adxan)* 'jester' + *t(en)* 'give' (Weissenberg 1905:64). This is clearly a more problematic etymology than the first two, but with some adjustments could be made palatable. The initial *s* presents no problem for the etymologizers since /s/ and /š/ are spelled by the identical grapheme in Hebrew and Old Yiddish. The consonants of a Hebrew acronym are linked by vowels, thus yielding /šabat/; the rule that postvocalic *t* in Hebrew words undergoes lenition in the Yiddish pronunciation of Hebrew would then produce an imaginary Hebraism **šabas*, which would be pronounced /šabes/ in Yiddish and is homophonous with the Yiddish pronunciation of Hebrew *šabbāt* 'Sabbath'.

While Slavic languages do not use this word in the meaning tip to a musician at a wedding, the practice of tipping musicians at such an event is attested at Slavic weddings, e.g., in the Ukraine (Piprek 1914: 29), in Macedonia (at Peštani: Leibman 1972:128) and in the (former) Polabian areas, e.g., at Rebenstorf, near Lüneburg (according to a description from 1894, cited by Tetzner 1902:370; see also Fischer 1932: 24). In Rebenstorf, coins for the musicians were thrown into a plate after the third dance (the number three very often has magical functions), with the express intention of smashing the plate (see the glass-breaking ceremony at Ashkenazic and Slavic weddings discussed in chapter 5.2 below). Might the Polabian custom be a unique combination of the glass and tipping ceremonies? The Polabians were a Slavic people in Germany that finally gave up its native Slavic tongue in the Lüneburg area, a mere 30 miles southwest of Hamburg, in the late 18th or early 19th century; originally, the Polabians had settled widely in western and northern Germany, but in most areas they very early became Germanized. Jews could have made contact with Polabian speakers in the Magdeburg area as early as the 9th–10th centuries. On the practice among Germans in south Moravia (1895), see Rottleuthner 1985:40; among west Hungarian Christians, the money is given by the dancing guests to the church primate.

Future research should seek to determine with greater precision in which areas the custom alone survives and where both the custom and the Iranianism are used.

Turkic (Arabism) 3. Western Yiddish *almemer*, Eastern Yiddish *balemer* 'synagogue reading desk'

The source is ultimately Arabic *ʾalminbar* 'the pulpit'. The presence of a cognate in Judeo-French might make an Iberian language (say, Judeo-Arabic or Judeo-Romance) the likely source, but Arabisms are not expected in Judeo-French. An alternative explanation is to derive the Arabism from the early Turkic Muslim population resident in Hungary, Transylvania, Bulgaria and Croatia, which preserved an Islamic identity at least through the 12th century (on Muslims in Bulgaria, see chapter 6 below); Serbo-Croatian Muslims have *mìnber, mìmber, minbèra*, etc., but this may be a more recent borrowing from the Ottoman Turkish Arabism *minber*, etc., after the 16th century (see also the next entry, Eastern Yiddish *dav[e]nen* 'pray').

Speakers of languages who are ignorant of Arabic offer borrow Arabisms with *ʾal-* 'the' attached. For example, compare the many

Arabisms in Spanish with *al-*, matched often by Ladino (the Castilian unspoken calque translation language of the Hebrew Bible developed in Spain during the 15th century) and Judezmo forms without *al-*, an indication that the Iberian Jews who borrowed the terms were conversant in Arabic, see, e.g., Portuguese Ladino *bateha* (Ferrara Bible 1553) vs. Spanish *albudeca* 'watermelon' (but see also Old Spanish *badea* 1423). The presence of *al-* in the Yiddish term weighs against a Judeo-Iberian source—especially since Judezmo (at least now) lacks this Arabism altogether.

The Eastern Yiddish form may least resemble the Arabic etymon due to a merger with synonymous *bime*, a Talmudic Hebrew word of Greek origin. It is curious that the reading desk is given little prominence in Italian Jewish illuminated manuscripts of the 15th century (Metzger and Metzger 1982:74). On folk etymologies proposed for *balemer* in Eastern Yiddish, see Liberman 1967.

Turkic (Arabism or Iranianism) 4. Eastern, rare Western Yiddish *dav(e)nen* 'pray'

The etymology of the term for pray in Eastern Yiddish (with occasional attestation in the Western Yiddish dialect area) has been repeatedly discussed in the literature. Recently, I hypothesized that the source of *dav(e)nen* was Arabic *duwa* 'prayer' (1987b:61–4). A plausible source of this, and other, putative Arabisms would be the Turkic speech of Muslims with whom Jews could have been in contact; see discussion of *almemer* just above and of *dav(e)nen* at the beginning of this chapter.

I am prepared now to propose a second hypothesis. Yiddish may have acquired the verb 'pray' from a Balkan language if *dav(e)nen* could be shown to be cognate with Rumanian *doină* 'sad folk song', which Trubačev derives from an Iranian language (1967:20, fn 96; see Avestan *daēnā-* 'religion', Old Indian *dhénā-* 'voice, speech, prayer'). In this case, an Arabic source would be excluded.

Slavic (via German?) 1. Yiddish *grager, grejger* 'rattle, used to make noise at the Purim holiday upon mention of the name Haman (the anti-Semitic villain in the Purim narrative) during the reading of the Scroll of Esther'

The Yiddish term is of Slavic origin, but it is difficult to say which Slavic language was the donor. Semantically, the closest parallel is with

Polish *grzegotko, grzechotka* 'noise maker used during the week of Easter; a device used in cloisters in place of a bell'. The purpose of the noise was to chase away Judas Iscariot. In Yiddish, the noise maker was recalibrated to mock Haman during Purim, a holiday which occurs in the Hebrew month of Adar (approximately March), and hence does not coincide with Easter (the lack of overlap may derive from the use of different calendars by Jews and Christians). Hence, it may be that the cult meanings associated with the word in Polish and Yiddish are independent. The term is found in other West Slavic languages as well, but with different meanings, e.g., Czech *hrochat,* (Moravian) *gruchat'* 'beat (with a whip)', *rohnouti* 'hit hard with the fist or block of wood'. On the custom of using wooden clappers on Maundy Thursday and Good Friday in the rural Czech lands, see Salzmann and Scheufler 1974: 110. On the parallels between Purim and Easter noise-making customs, see Sartori 1935–6.

The Slavism is also found in Tyrolean German *gragela* 'talk noisily, angrily' (Prilucki 1924:89), Carinthian German *gragg(ez)n* 'raise a din (especially of chicken)' (Lexer 1862), which could support the hypothesis that Yiddish first acquired the term in the Germano-Slavic lands. The practice of noise-making at Purim was also known in the German lands (Güdemann 1880:156, fn 6).

Literature: Landau 1924:329.

Slavic 2. Eastern Yiddish *kitke*

See discussion under Germanic 1 just below.

Slavic 3. Western Yiddish *kowleč,* Eastern Yiddish *kojleč* 'braided festive bread'

This Slavic term is found in all Slavic languages, as well as in dialectal German, Hungarian and some Romance languages, see, e.g., Hungarian *kálacs* 'braided festive bread' and Rumanian *colac* 'kind of fancy bread'. While Yiddish could have acquired the term from Sorbian, I cannot rule out an alternative Balkan Slavic source. In Western and Eastern Slavic, but not in contemporary South Slavic, the term denotes a special sort of bread, but as far as I know, not the specifically Jewish bread; in some Polish Yiddish dialects, *kojleč* does denote the Sabbath bread, which elsewhere is known as *xale* (from Hebrew) or *kitke* (from Slavic: see Germanic 1 and 3 below). Of course, the Jews may still have acquired the term in the Balkans, before the loss of the meaning 'special holiday bread' there (see further discussion under *barxes* below). A holiday connection with this bread is found in the Balkans, since the bride carries the *kolač* as she circles the bridal table in the Serbo-Croatian wedding ceremony (see also the discussion of Yiddish *dejže* in category III below).

Western Ukrainian denotes the Jewish braided bread by *balabux* (standard Ukrainian *balabuxa* 'loaf of bread; small cake, bun' is not marked as specifically Jewish). It is interesting to note that the first component of *balabux(a)* may be of Turkic origin (Sadnik and Aitzetmüller 1963–4 describe *bala-* as a designation for anything large, fat or bloated).

A number of other Turkic words are used in both the Slavic languages and Yiddish in connection with Jewish dress, e.g., Yiddish *jarmlke* 'scull cap', *kaftn* 'long male overgarment' (see category II, Turkic 2 below). On Turkic as a purveyor of other elements to the Jews, see *pejsex* 'Passover', used as a male name, discussed in chapter 5.2 below, and *šabaš* 'tip', *almemer* ~ *balemer* 'synagogue reading desk' and *dav(e)nen* 'pray (Jews)', all discussed above. This evidence supports the Jewish-Turkic links postulated in chapter 6 below—either in Hungary and the Balkans in the west, and/or in the Ponto-Caspian steppelands in the east.

Slavic 4. Eastern Yiddish *praven* 'conduct (a religious ceremony)'

The etymon is pan-Slavic and in many Slavic languages has religous associations, see, e.g., Polish *prawić mszę* 'conduct the mass', Russian *spravit' pominki* 'invite guests to a funeral meal in honor of the deceased'. A Yiddish synonym of German origin is *oprixtn* (vs. German *abrichten* 'train, adjust'), which appears to be a translation of a Slavic expression, see, e.g., Ukrainian *vidpravyty Službu Božu* 'perform the Mass' (Ukrainian *pravyty* = German *richten* 'direct', among other meanings; Ukrainian *vid-* = German *ab-* 'from') or Polish *odmówić* 'say prayers' (from 'from' + 'speak').

Slavic 5. German Hebrew *snvi, snsnvi, smnglf* ~ *snm-* /sanvi, sansanvi, semangelaf ~ senam-/ angel names

These angels are first mentioned in the *Sefer raziel* (12th century). Trachtenberg quotes Schwab's view (1897:201) that the first and second terms were onomatopoeic, in imitation of the twittering of birds, since the names were often written on amulets accompanied by bird-like figures (1939:101). M.Gaster, on the other hand, suggested these were the Hebraized names of three Slavic saints who were effective in driving away the child-snatching witch (see Frau Holle in Jewish and German mythology discussed in Germanic 3 below under Western Yiddish *holekrāš*); in Greek sources they appear as *Anos* ~ *Synodoros, Sisynodoros; Saint Sisynie; Satanael* (1880:558). The ultimate source of these angel names is a Manichaean tale that came into Europe with the Bogomil heresy in southeastern Europe.[2] The names also appear in Bulgarian, Rumanian, Russian, and Old Slovenian folktales (ibid.:558, 560–1, 1971b). These angel names were regarded as protection against the *mora* spirit (Fröhlich 1990:135; see also Germanic 6 *māgen dāvid* below). If Gaster is right, then the association with birds may be a secondary attempt to de-Christianize the terms.

The Hebrew variants *sanoi, sansanoi* and *samangelaf* appear on an early 20th-century Turkish bed cover of a pregnant woman (Nachama and Sievernich 1991:291, #13/19).

Literature: Fröhlich 1990:134; Pócs 1990:111, 113–5, 120–1.

Slavic 6. Eastern and Northeast German Yiddish *trejbern*, Western Yiddish *poršn* (~ Judezmo *purgar*) 'render meat kosher by removing forbidden fat and veins'

The source of Yiddish *trejbern* is either West or South Slavic, see, e.g., Old Czech *triebiti*, Modern Czech *tříbit* 'remove defects, errors; bring to completion; improve'; Upper Sorbian *trjebić* 'clear (forest); castrate (fowl)'; Old Church Slavic *trěba* 'pagan sacrifice, (sacrificial) table', *trěbiti* 'cleanse, purge', *trěbište* 'altar'; Ukrainian *terebyty* 'peel; eat greedily'. Old Church Slavic is an attractive source for Yiddish since the noun in that language has a ritual meaning, but the Upper Sorbian meaning of castrate a fowl is also close to the Yiddish meaning.

An interesting point is that Old Church Slavic *trěba* denotes a pagan sacrifice; the Christian counterpart, Old Church Slavic *žьrtva* '(Christian) sacrifice', which is the basis of Rumanian *jertfă*, is unknown in Yiddish. I cannot decide whether the Jews acquired the word in the meaning offering from pagan Slavs, or in the general meaning of purge after the pagan connotations had become erased. Old Church Slavic *trěba* has cognates in the spoken Slavic languages, but in different meanings, see, e.g., Polish *trzeba* 'need, it is necessary'. The earliest attestation of the Slavic term (*trebo*) is in a Latin text dated 785 (the so-called Paderborn Capitulary: Brückner 1912:170).

Synonymous Western Yiddish *poršn* provides a Romance parallel, see, e.g., Old French *purgier* 'cleanse; sift; purge of impurities; justify; purify (in the moral sense); atone'; the only association with food is 'remove impurities from the wheat' (1190); Italian *purgare* 'purge (animals, holy sites)'; Old Provençal *purgar* 'clean the flour of bran' (14th century); Aragonese and Catalan *purgar* 'sift; fecundate (blossom of the vine, olive tree, wheat)'. Italian alone provides a meaning connected with ritual. The ultimate Latin source is *pūrgāre* 'purge, cleanse', which gives rise to French verbs with *ü*. But Yiddish has no example of **püršn* (or a derived **piršn*); hence, a French source (as is often argued) is unconvincing. A Balkan Romance source is also a possible candidate since Italian *purgare* is the basis for Serbo-Croatian (Dubrovnik) *(is)pùrgati* 'clean' (16th century). This is the only example I know of where two Yiddish synonyms may both be of Balkan origin (Balkan Romance; Old Church Slavic = Old Macedonian).

Germanic (via Slavic?) 1. Eastern German Yiddish *barxes, berxes,* Eastern Yiddish *xale, kitke* 'Sabbath bread'

Two etymologies have been proposed for German Yiddish *barxes, berxes,* first attested in a manuscript of 1504: (a) a derivation of Hebrew *birkat* 'blessing of' (Eckstein 1938–41:950; Maler 1979); (b) a derivation from *Berchta* ~ *Perchta,* the name of a Germanic goddess of vegetation and fertility (Schauss 1938:31). The second theory also asserts that the traditional braided shape of the Sabbath bread is connected to the cult of the Germanic goddess, since in the pagan Germanic rites, women offered the goddess their hair symbolically braided; the form of the bread represents the intertwined braids. For the geography of the term among Jews, see Lowenstein 1969:19 and Herzog 1979:48, figure 2; on the forms and names of this type of bread among Germans, see Höfler 1906:130.

I reject the Hebrew connection on phonological grounds; Hebrew *birkat* would have yielded **birkes* in Yiddish. This interpretation was probably proposed *ex post facto,* in an attempt to make sense out of an unfamiliar root and/or to Judaize the term, so basic to the Sabbath meal. The second analysis is more convincing, especially in light of the German expression *Berchisbrod* ~ *Perchisbrod* 'Berchta's bread' (Trachtenberg 1939:40–1). Kohlbach notes that the custom of the Jews to cover the Sabbath bread prior to uttering the blessing over it on Friday nights might be a vestige of the offering up of the shorn locks to the goddess (1914:268–9).

Even if the Germanic etymology is correct, that would not necessarily mean that the Jews ever practiced the Germanic hair cult; they could simply have assimilated the custom of baking twisted holiday bread. The twisted shape of the bread is popular among Jews in Hungary, Rumania and the Slavic lands as well, though in the local Yiddish the bread is called *kojleč* (from Slavic—see Slavic 3 above) or *xale* (< Hebrew *ḥallāh*) (see Prilucki 1923, fn pages viii–ix, xvi), but the precise geography and chronology of these terms are unknown. In addition, Yiddish (dialectally?) also uses the Slavism *kitke* for plaited bread—see, e.g., Ukrainian *kyt'ký* 'braided strands of hair over the ear' (Želexovs'kyj and Nedil's'kyj 1882-6). The term is common in the English of South African Jews, who are largely of Lithuanian-Belorussian origin, but otherwise I cannot give precise geographical details (the term is also recorded among Baltic Germans as a Yiddishism: see Kiparsky 1936:198). As far as I know, the Slavism never denotes baked goods in any Slavic language. The widespread use of several non-Hebrew names for bread or hair to denote items of Jewish ritual is significant.

I could argue that *xale* is older than *barxes*, since it surfaces in the Talmud and among non-Ashkenazic Jews, e.g., the Persian Jews. I do not know the age of Hebrew *ḥallāh* among the Persian Jews, but among north European Jews, *xale* may be a newer Hebraism intended to replace the pagan *barxes* (several Jewish languages could borrow the same Hebraism independently, at different periods). Kohlbach conjectures that the custom of baking braided bread began with the Greek and Roman Jews, but that the original name *ḥallāh* was replaced by *barxes* in the German lands. The holy day of the goddess, called *Perchtennacht*, falls on the first night of the year. In many parts of Germany, special foods were put out on All Saints eve for the goddess. Old Palestinian rabbis objected to putting out food for gods on the grounds that it was a pagan custom, yet in 17th-century Germany, the Jews practiced this custom as a means of propitiating the demons in the house of a new born boy before the circumcision ceremony (Scheftelowitz 1925:39; see also chapter 5, fn 7 below).

Moreover, there is no guarantee that the Jews acquired the Germanic custom or bread form directly from the Germans, since High German *Perchta* was also known to the Czechs and Slovenians, see, e.g., Czech *perchta* (1418), *peruchta, perychta*—which could be either male or female; (Central Moravian) *šperechta*, (Moravian) *perechta*; Slovenian *prhtra baba, perta* (Karłowicz 1900:184; Eckstein 1938–41:949–

50; Knobloch 1986:22). Conceivably, the custom might have been practiced among the Sorbs in eastern Germany as well (see below). Since the custom of baking braided bread has Greco-Roman antecedants and is also found, on festive occasions, in Dalmatia (e.g., Zara, Croatia: Höfler 1906), I propose that the Jews might have learned the practice in the Greek cultural area, acquiring the German terms for the familiar artifact much later. (On a Balkan origin for the Yiddish *jorcajt* custom, presently named with a German term, see the discussion below.) It is even conceivable that the Germans acquired the custom of baking braided bread from the Jews, since the use of such a festive bread is apparently not attested in the German lands until the Middle High German period (ibid.:147).

Höfler thinks that the sprinkling of poppy-seeds on the bread is now most characteristic of Jewish baked goods, but

> "since poppy-seeds are missing in the Egyptian-Semitic culture area, the sprinkling of poppy-seeds on the "Jewish braided bread" cannot be an original Jewish addition" (ibid.: 139–40).

Note that Balkan Slavs put poppy-seeds around the house as protection against the *mora* spirit (Pócs 1990:126; on the *mora*, see Germanic 6 below).

In view of the tendency in German folklore to equate the two goddesses/witches Frau Holle and Berchta by attributing similar functions to them (e.g., both supervise spinning), I wonder whether the Jews in the German lands might not also have imitated the German practice of calling braided bread after the goddess Frau Holle (one of whose tasks was to inspect the braids of girls during the Christmas season: Wuttke 1900:25), see, e.g., in the Vogtland, northern Franconia, Wetterau, Thüringen and neighboring Lower Saxony (Grimm 1:1900:292), Lausitz (in the Sorbian-speaking territory the German term is *Höllenzopf*) and Swabia (*Höllküchen*: Höfler 1906: 134). If so, then Hebrew *ḥallāh*, which originally denoted the portion of the dough offered to the priest in the biblical temple in Jerusalem or a cake made from semolina, was introduced as a "Jewish" replacement for *Holle*, where it acquired the unique meaning of Sabbath bread (note also Yiddish *nemen xale* 'remove a piece of dough for burning, in a ceremony prescribed for women'; on this practice among Spanish Jews in c. 1483, see Loeb 1889: 235). On *Holle*, see also discussion of *holekrāš* in Germanic 3 below.

Literature (on Jewish and non-Jewish sources): Zingerle 1855a, 1855b; Feifalik 1859; Grohmann 1864:vi–vii, 1–2; Grünbaum 1877: 348;

Höfler 1906; Wuttke 1900:25, 27, 69, 298, 369; Scheftelowitz 1911:378, 1925:38; Schauss 1938:31; Trachtenberg 1939:40–1, 280; Maler 1979; Wolf 1979.

Germanic (Hebraism) 2. Western Yiddish *baxer*, Eastern Yiddish *boxer/buxer* 'Jewish seminary student', etc.

Hebrew (and Judeo-Aramaic) *bāḥūr* 'young man' is a widespread loan in European languages, both Jewish and non-Jewish. Consider, e.g., Old Ukrainian *baxura* (genitive singular, Brėst 1577). In the West and East Slavic languages and Hungarian the meaning is usually 'Jewish seminary student' (on the merger of the Hebraism with a similar-sounding Slavic root, see Laskowski 1966:53, fn 12). A distinctive feature of the Slavic languages is that in East Slavic languages and Polish the word surfaces with /a/ in the first syllable, while in the West Slavic languages, including again Polish, the word has the vowel /u/. The Hebrew vowel diacritic in this word, the *qāmec*, is normally pronounced /a/ in Western Yiddish and /o ~ u / in Eastern Yiddish. The dual pronunciation of the Hebraism in Polish has a fixed distribution: as a simple noun, Polish uses an Eastern Yiddish form, *bucher*, but when a native diminutive suffix is added, Polish switches to the Western Yiddish-like form, *bachurek*. Since it is unlikely that a Western Yiddish pronunciation could have reached the Eastern Slavic languages, the latter might be a borrowing from Ukrainian or Belorussian, following an Oriental, say Khazar, reading norm of Hebrew. In German slang as well, the Hebraism surfaces in two forms: *bacher* '(peripatetic) teacher (of Jewish children); student; official who understands the art and language of thieves' vs. *bochur* 'student' (both 1822). In the case of German, the variant with /a/ could conceivably be either of Judeo-French or Judeo-Slavic origin.

Among the Germans, beginning with the early 15th century, wandering students were called *bachant* from Latin *bacchari* 'to rage, rave; be enthused about'. According to Hampe, the German term, now extinct, survived longer in Austria than in Germany proper (1902:51). Güdemann has suggested that the Jews chose Hebrew *bāḥūr* to create a word meaning wandering Jewish student on the basis of similarity in form and meaning to the German Latinism (1888:58ff). The formal replacement of *bachant* by *bāḥūr* was matched by the semantic replacement of the feature "+Christian" by the feature "+Jewish".

Germanic 3. West-central and South German Yiddish *holekrāš* 'the home ceremony of giving a secular name to a newborn infant on the fourth Sabbath after its birth'; apparently once known in Eastern Yiddish

In 20th-century Germany, the custom applied either to Jewish boys or girls, or to both sexes, depending on the locale (Lowenstein gives the geography of the term without specifying the meaning in 1969:27–8, 30). In the 17th century, the custom applied to both boys and girls in southern Germany but to girls only (and rarely at that) in Austria, Bohemia, Moravia and Poland (Trachtenberg 1939:42–3, 172, 281; M. Weinreich 1967:245). M.Weinreich believes the Jews acquired the term and the concept from the Germans in the area of Hessen, when the pagan custom was still alive (ibid.:246ff).

The ceremony entered Jewish life as early as the 13th century (to judge from the Maḥzor Vitry, a Hebrew prayerbook from northern France). The only Jewish element in the custom appears to be the recitation of biblical verses, which is probably a later addition to the ceremony to give it a Jewish flavor. The Jewish boy receives his Hebrew name on the occasion of his circumcision. The German Hebrew spellings give both *hwljqrjjš* ~ *xwljqrjjš* /holekrāš ~ xolekrāš/ (Lauterbach 1932:359, fn 73). The meaning of the term was already unknown in the early 14th century (Güdemann 1888:104–5; M. Simon 1992:168). Zunz proposed two components in his pioneering etymology (1832:439, fn f): Hebrew *ḥōl* 'profane' (i.e., a secular name) and German *kreischen* 'to shout' (shouting was an effective remedy against the demons in Christian practice: Trachtenberg 1939:280–1; Zimmels 1958:164). Most subsequent scholars have regarded Zunz's explanation as a "folk etymology"—in my terms, an instance of Judaization. I think it makes more sense to derive *hole* ~ *xole* from the German name *Holle*, the witch or goddess with long, matted hair and protruding teeth, who, in medieval Germany, was held responsible, *inter alia*, for gobbling up children and entangling hair at night (see also discussion of *barxes* above). Another possibility is to derive the component *-krāš* from German *Kreis* 'circle', which played a major role in medieval mythology, since a circle drawn around the bed of a woman giving birth or a baby could provide potent protection against the devil; the change of *s* > *š* is typical of some German dialects, e.g., Swabian, and Western Yiddish *ā* = German *aj*, see, e.g., Yiddish *flāš* = German *Fleisch* 'meat'.

Today there seem to be no German Christian parallels to the Jewish naming-custom, though traces, including the association with Frau

Holle, appear in folksongs from western Germany, Lower Austria and Jihlava (Iglau), Moravia (see Landau 1899b:73–4 and von Schulenburg 1934:226–7, fn 1). For references to Frau Holle as a snow goddess in Eastern Yiddish proverbs (where the custom of *holekrāš* is presently unknown), see Sadan 1952:15–6.

The practice of granting two names to Jewish boys—one secular (of any origin) and one (of almost exclusively Hebrew origin) for use in religious contexts—has a parallel among the Slavs, see, e.g., the use of pagan Slavic names for secular use vs. baptismal and canonization names from specifically Old Church Slavic (ultimately of Greek and Hebrew origin; see Rudnyc'kyj 1969; Unbegaun 1970).

On *Holle*, see also *barxes, berxes* in Germanic 1 above.

Literature: Landau 1899a, 1899b; Grunwald 1900; Lauterbach 1932; Trachtenberg 1939:172–3 and fn 42 (with bibliography); M. Weinreich 1967:245–53; T.H.Gaster 1980:36–7.

Germanic (via Slavic?) 4. Yiddish *jorcajt* 'commemoration of the anniversary of a relative's death'

The commemoration of a death in the Talmud involved fasting (a voluntary act) and the recitation of the prayer known as the *qādīš*. In Germany, the tradition of fasting became obsolete (perhaps because it was not practiced by the Christians—though it was still cited in the *Sefer xasidim* in the 13th century); instead, the Catholic custom of lighting a candle (see Yiddish *jorcajtlixt* '*jorcajt* candle') was adopted (in Germany?). On the German use of the candle on the occasion of a death in the Middle Ages, see Franz 1:1909:457. Ja'akov ben Moše Halevi Mölln (known as the Maharil, c.1360–1427) opposed the custom as non-Jewish; opposition continued as late as the 17th century, to judge from the writings of the west German talmudist Jair Xaim Bachrach (1638–1701):

> "One should not ridicule any custom, even though there is no point to it, such as the *jorcajt* light" (cited by Güdemann 1888:128, fn 4).

According to the *Or zarua* (written by the Bohemian Jicxak ben Moše c.1180–c.1260), the custom of lighting a *jorcajt* candle was practiced in Bohemia and the Rhineland, but not in France (see W.Lewy 1927:128). The Sephardic Josef Karo (Toledo 1488–1575) might not have known it, since he does not discuss the custom in his famous codification of laws known as the *Šulxan arux* (1564–5). Despite the opposition of many rabbis through the ages, a number of contemporary scholars ignore the non-native, i.e., German origin of the term and practice. For example, Freehof described the custom as an example of the "ceremonial imaginativeness" of the Ashkenazic Jews (1967:222), while Fishman cited the term as an original Yiddish creation (1991:314). Today, the commemoration among the Ashkenazic Jews involves only the lighting of the candle and the recitation of the *qādīš* prayer for the dead. The earliest reference to the candle is in a Hebrew document from Nürnberg from the 13th century (Stern 1894–6:100, fn 5, 162, fn 3—where the term is Hebrew *ner haššānāh*, literally 'candle of the year'), but the Yiddish word *jorcajt* itself is not attested until the 16th century.

The practice and the Yiddish name have spread to the Sephardic, Italian, Moroccan, Yemenite and Iranian Jews, but I cannot determine the chronology of the diffusion to the non-Ashkenazic diasporas (for data, see Güdemann 1880:111, fn 1; Wagner 1950:101; Bar-Ašer 1978; Rachabi 1982:103, fn 6). In addition, Sephardic Jews call the anniversary in Judezmo by the Grecism *meldado, meldadura* (see category II, Romance 4 below), the Hispanism *anjos* and the Hebraism *naxala*, literally 'the (prayer) read; years; heritage', respectively.

While the name and practice are attested among the Germans (see, e.g., *Jahrzeit* in the Kanton Zug in Switzerland: Ithen 1897:119; *Jahrzeit Buch*, literally 'book containing the anniversaries of deaths' 1678, St. Gallen, Switzerland: Kessler 1916:198; *Jahrestag*, literally 'day of the year': Jungbauer 1931–2b), the practice is also known among the Slavs as well. For descriptions of the Slavic practice of celebrating the anniversary of a death on fixed days of the year, see Dmitriev 1869:213–4, Bogusławski 2/2:1900:820, Dovnar-Zapol'skij 1909:305, Bogatyrev 1929:72 and Lewicki 1952–3:438. On the popularity of the ancestor cult among the pagan Slavs, see Gasparini 1965:148 and Kowalczyk 1968: 133. Krauss, in his description of the Serbian candle, known as *krsna svijeća* 'kin candle', uses the standard German term *Jahreszeitlicht (Jahreszeit* refers now to a season of the year: 1885:594, fn); Wuttke 1900:472 uses the term *Seelenlichtlein*, literally, 'little soul light' in reference to the practice of placing a candle on the hearth on the anniversary of a death in the Alpnach Valley, in Unterwalden, Switzerland; this is precisely the term used in Hebrew, e.g., *ner nešāmāh* (for which I only find contemporary attestation) and Yiddish *nešome-lixt*. I do not know if Slavs other than the Serbs presently have a special term for the candle, but the commemoration service itself (carried out either in church or at home) has a different name in each language, see, e.g., Russian *pominki*,

Belorussian *dzjadý*, Serbo-Croatian *zàdušnice* < *duša* 'soul' (the pan-Slavic practice of using the plural form may account for Judezmo *anjos*, also plural, cited above). The Bosnian Muslims also light a candle on the anniversary of a relative's death (Hangi 1907:255).

It is possible that the custom of candle-lighting was added to the original Palestinian Jewish mourning practice in the Balkans; in the German lands, to judge from the German Hebrew writings, the practice of fasting was discarded, and the standard term in Yiddish for the commemoration was acquired.

Literature: Güdemann 1888:132; Abrahams 1896:140, 156, fn 2; Eisenstein 1904; W.Lewy 1927; Flattau 1931; Avida 1951; Zimmels 1958: 186–7; Steiman 1963:65 and fn 34; Freehof 1967:212, 214–5.

Germanic (via Slavic?) 5. German Hebrew *qwpwlṭ* /kobolt/ 'demonic homunculus which mimics a man's voice to bewilder him; ventriloquist' (13th century)

The Jewish meaning of the Germanism appears to be unique, see German *Kobold* 'imp, hobgoblin; house spirit' and Polish *kobold* 'mythical mountain spirit in the form of a dwarf who guards treasures kept in rich metallic veins; spirit in the form of a bird' (Karłowicz 1894–1905) or 'a dwarf who guards treasures hidden in mountains' (Doroszewski 1958–69). Given the wide variety of meanings in the non-Jewish languages, I am not surprised to encounter a unique meaning among the Jews.

Literature: Trachtenberg 1939:39.

Germanic (Hebraism via Slavic?) 6. Yiddish *mogen dovid*; Hebrew *māgen dāvid* 'star of David' (literally 'shield of David')

The use of the hexagonal star among the central European Jews as a national Jewish symbol appears relatively late. The first known instance is on the flag of the Prague "Altneu" (in Yiddish "Altnaj") synagogue which might date from 1354—but at that time the star probably had a magical or decorative, rather than a national function (Grotte 1922:2–3; Scholem 1949:249). A Prague Hebrew book from 1512 bears the star. In the early 16th century, the star appeared on Prague gravestones of men named David and Menaxem (the latter, literally 'comforter', was a code-name for the messiah), and by the 18th century with graves of men with other names as well (Sadek 1991). In synagogue architecture, the star appears first in Prague, Moravia and Austria in the 19th century (Scholem 1949:244, 249); it never gained popularity in non-Ashkenazic synagogue architecture until recently. The first Jewish mention of the Hebrew term *māgen dāvid* appears in a 12th-century Hebrew work by the Macedonian Karaite, Jehuda Hadasi(s), in the meaning of protective amulet.

The original magical function of the star can be seen from the fact that it adorned the wedding stone embedded on the outer north wall of the synagogue against which the glass was smashed during the wedding ceremony (see chapter 5.2 below). While the symbol is found in many parts of the world among Jews and non-Jews both, see, e.g., Morocco and Spain (in the interior decor of the 13th-century synagogue known as Santa Maria la Blanca in Toledo), it became a national Jewish symbol only in northern Europe, I suspect, under Germano-Slavic influence (see below). If the name 'shield of David' among the Ashkenazic Jews is independent of the term found in Hadasi's book, which seems likely, then the choice of the name David might also be motivated by German practice. (Hadasi was a Macedonian Karaite, and his choice of the name David may have been inspired by the name of the founder of his sect, Anan ben David, who flourished in Iraq in the 2nd half of the 8th century.)[3]

As many scholars have noted, the hexagonal star was used by the Germans at the foot of a bedframe or the floor of an animal pen to frighten away the *Drude, Trude, Drute,* an old witch. Hence, the symbol was called in German *Drudenkreuz* 'the cross of Drude', *Drudenfuss* 'the foot of Drude' or *Alpkreuz* 'the elf's cross'. Another name for the symbol is German *Mahrenfuss,* from Czech *můra,* (Moravian dialect) *mora* 'moth' (embodying a dead person's spirit); see also Sorbian *Mórawa* 'female moth demon' (Machek 1971; for further discussion on the *mora,* etc., see Pócs 1990:125–7). Andree points out that the symbol is particularly common among Jews in the West Slavic lands, and is widespread among Christians in Lower Lausitz (still a Sorbian-speaking area), Hessen, southern and eastern Germany, Rügen, Sweden and Russia (1903). M.Mieses notes that the six-pointed star appeared on the coat of arms of Polish Christian aristocrats (in particular in Volhynia), as well as on that of a converted Jew in 1499 (1991:28).

While the name *māgen dāvid* is very old (see above), I propose that the Ashkenazic use of the regal name David, in Yiddish *dovid ~ duvid,* might have been inspired by phonetic similarity with German *Drude, Drute, Trude* while the choice of *mogen* could have been chosen to match Czech *můra*, etc.; the use of the Hebrew word for shield is a reminder of the original function of offering protection (see also the discussion of the "wedding stone" in chapter 5.2 below). Grohmann notes that in Moravia, the *Drude* was construed as either male or female (similarly for the *mora* in Central Europe: see Pócs 1990: 126); this suggests that the Yiddish male name *dovid* may have been chosen in the Czech lands, then spreading into both the west and east German lands (1864:25). However, a male witch with a masculine form of the name, e.g., *Truder*, is also known from Bavaria (partly Slavic-speaking as late as the 14th century) and Westfalen (Ranke 1936–7:1173).

The Jewish ethnic symbol popular in the Greco-Roman period was the seven-branched candelabrum, known in Hebrew as *mənōrāh*. This symbol enjoyed marginal use in European diasporas as a decoration but only reacquired a quasi-ethnic function in early 19th-century synagogue decor (e.g., in England, Germany, Hungary, Russia and Slovakia), though there is an early example inside the synagogue at Beckhofen, northeast Bavaria, 1733 (see the illustrations in Krinsky 1985). The State of Israel utilizes both the *mənōrāh* and the *māgen dāvid* as national symbols—with preference for the latter (see the national flag).

On the Christian (and Jewish?) practice of writing the phrase *māgen dāvid* on a piece of paper that is baked inside bread and then thrown into the fire as a device for extinguishing fires, see Anhorn 1674:796; Eckstein 1927:1621–2.

Literature: Wuttke 1900:181; Grunwald 1901, 1927, 1936:195–8; Andree 1903–5; Blau 1904; von Schulenburg 1905, 1934:226, fn 1; von Hovorka and Kronfeld 1:1908:422–4, 2:1909:705–7, 890–1; Güdemann 1916; Grotte 1922; Ranke 1936–7; Nusenblat 1939; Scholem 1949; T.H.Gaster 1980:217–21.

CATEGORY II. Jewish loans (and two loan translations) with new religious and/or superstitious meanings not attested in the donor languages

Greek 1. Hebrew *hinūmāh* 'bridal veil'.

The etymon is Greek *hymenaios* 'wedding song, sung as the bride is led to the bridegroom's house'. The Greek meaning, to be sure, is religious, but different from that of Hebrew—hence, I include the example in category two. See also discussion of Yiddish *fačejle* under Romance 3 below.

Greek (via German?) 2. Western Yiddish (and scattered points in the East, e.g., Jutrosin and Kaliningrad) *miniç*, *mineš* 'food that can be eaten with meat or milk products' (see also synonymous Eastern Yiddish *par[e]ve* discussed in Slavic 3 below)

The etymon appears to be Greek *monaxos* 'monk' but the chain of semantic shifts and the period and place of borrowing by the Jews remain unclear. In German (and other European languages) the term 'monk' developed a variety of secondary meanings, partly by way of mocking the monk, e.g., in Middle High German *münich* denoted a castrated horse, an allusion to the monk's abstention from sex. This meaning is also attested in contemporary Swiss Yiddish, but in Old Swiss Yiddish (or Ashkenazic German?), *mūnx* /müneç/ meant theater (1290: Timm 1977:26, 30). One could assume that "neutral food" is an extension of the sexually inactive monk. Even if this hypothesis were correct, it would not eliminate the Balkans as the place of the borrowing. From German, the Grecism has passed to the Slavic languages.

Greek 3. Yiddish *sandek* 'godfather'.

See the discussion in the text above.

Romance 1. Eastern (and at points in Western) Yiddish *čolnt*, Western Yiddish *šālet, šōlet* 'food cooked on Friday to be consumed on the Sabbath, due to the prohibition against cooking on the Sabbath'

In the opinion of Max Weinreich (2:1973:56–7, 59; 4:79–81), the Latin participle *calentem* 'warming' is the etymon. In Judeo-Aramaic and Hebrew, the food was called *ḥammīn*, from the native root 'hot'; either the Latin term could have been modeled on the Semitic naming practice or vice versa (though *ḥammīn*, unlike Latin, is morphologically plural). If the Latinism reached the German Jews via Old French, then the word would have had to enter Yiddish before the 13th century, when Old French *č* > *š*. The Western Yiddish variants *šālet, šōlet* are either later Judeo-French loans, or French restructuring of Yiddish *čolnt*, to judge from the presence of *š* and their restricted Western Yiddish geography.

Contrary to M.Weinreich, I suspect that the French-speaking Jews are not the source of any of these terms: *čolnt* is unlikely to be from French, since French terms are not expected in Eastern Yiddish; as to

Western Yiddish *šălet* ~ *šŏlet*, French Christians (e.g., at Metz) have the form *šalăt* 'broad thin cake cooked in the oven'. Nor is a Judeo-Latin source convincing since the term is unknown in any Judeo-Romance language other than Judeo-French, where it could be a borrowing from Yiddish. To the best of my knowledge, only one other Jewish language, Moroccan Judeo-Arabic, uses the native term "hot" in the meaning of Sabbath food, see, e.g., *sxīna*.

All other Jewish languages designate the Sabbath food by a word that expresses the notion "conceal", see, e.g., Old Judezmo *adefina, adafina* < Judeo-Arabic *ʾaddfīna* (in non-Judaized Arabic, 'the burial, concealment'). The Judeo-Arabic form appears to translate the Hebrew verb *ṭāman* 'conceal' in the phrase *ṭāman ʾɛt haḥammīn* 'conceal the Sabbath food (in a pot)'. Since all Judeo-Arabic dialects favor some word associated with the notion of "conceal" (see also Iraqi Judeo-Arabic *tbīt* < *bāta* 'take shelter during the night'), the exceptional Moroccan Judeo-Arabic *sxīna* may be a translation of an earlier, now extinct, Ibero-Romance term based on the root 'warm' (which would strengthen the hypothesis of a Judeo-Latin etymon). Even before the expulsions of 1492–8, the Iberian Jews had been using Judeo-Aramaic/Hebrew *ḥammīn* in their colloquial Romance speech. Note that the latter is not used in Yiddish. The Iraqi Judeo-Arabic word exemplifies the problems confronting reconstruction. While Old Hebrew *ṭāman* offers a model for the Judeo-Arabic terms, South Iraqi Muslim Arabic has cognates of *tbīt* and Iberian Judeo-Arabic **ʾaddfīna* that could also be the sources of the Judeo-Arabic terms: *báyat* 'food left over from the previous night' and *madfūn* 'food buried in the ground to ripen'. A single Yiddish example of "conceal", *ṭāmūn*, in the food meaning, comes from the Hebrew writings of Iserlin, a rabbi born in either Prague or Meissen, who lived in the southeast German and Austrian lands in the 14th century, and was probably a native speaker of Slavic. *Ṭāmūn* unites the Eastern Yiddish speech territory with Jewish Afro-Asian practice.

The fact that Yiddish *čolnt* is now almost exclusively restricted to Eastern Europe makes a French origin especially unattractive. I am inclined to seek its source in a Romance language other than French. Rhaeto-Romance and a number of north Italian dialects, like most French dialects (including the standard language), underwent the change of Latin *ka* to *ča*. The Rhaeto-Romance, Italian and French developments are in all likelihood independent phenomena. If an Italian or Rhaeto-Romance source seems secure, the place of borrowing is not; either putative etymon could have been borrowed in the Balkans—to judge from the presence of the Romanism in a stretch of non-Jewish Romance and Slavic languages spoken in northern Italy and the Balkans (note the occasional shift in meaning from "hot" to "food [pot]"), see, e.g., Istroromance (Parenzo) *calda* 'polenta', Serbo-Croatian (Istria) *skàldīn* (from Italian *scaldino*) 'hot-pot'; Istroromance *caldera* 'cauldron', *čaldina* 'receptacle for hot foods'.

Literature: Wexler 1978, 1992b.

Romance 2. Old German Hebrew *cmrš, cwmrš* /čamers ~ čomers/, (Worms) *hcʔmrš* /ha čamers/ 'the religious schools' (1387)

The source is Old French *chambre* 'room' (Stern 1894–6:200, fn 5). The *ʔ* and *w* suggest that the source is not German *Zimmer* 'room'. Similarly, the Hebraism *xejder* (< Hebrew *ḥɛdɛr* 'room') is used in the meaning religious school in Yiddish (the age of this meaning is indeterminable). The Hebraism may have been proposed as a means of Judaizing the French term.

Romance 3. Yiddish *fačejle* 'veil' (archaic); 'kerchief, shawl'

The Romanism is also found in German dialects, see, e.g., Old Bavarian German *fatzalet, fatzel, fa(c)zol* 'handkerchief' (15th century). The oldest Yiddish example known to me is Franconian Yiddish *wṭšwln* /fačolin/ 'veil' (in the *Bovo-bux*, 16th century). Differences in form, meaning and register (in Yiddish the term is standard but in German dialectal) mitigate against the assumption that Yiddish received the Romanism via German. The source of Yiddish *fačejle* and possibly German *fatzel, fa(c)zol* (unless the latter are contractions of German *fatzalet*) could be north Italian *faz(z)uòlo* or Balkan Latin **faciola;* the source of the first Bavarian German Romanism is rather standard Italian *fazzoletto*. Moreover, the Old Yiddish meaning veil (unknown in German?) suggests a direct link with tabus of the north Italian or Balkan Slavic speech communities; e.g., Serbo-Croatian *fačel* (15th century), etc., denotes the veil worn by a bride on her wedding day as protection against demons. The meaning of wedding veil is also attested with the Hungarian Romanism *fátyol* and the cognate Friulan term. In the 19th century, the meaning of wedding veil was replaced in some Italian dialects (e.g., in Venetian) by the meaning bathing-gown or cloth covering most of a woman's body. In the Talmud the Grecism *hinūmāh* has the meaning of (bridal) veil, a hint that the custom itself was imported (see category II, Greek 1 above).

There is no linguistic evidence that *fačejle* ever had magical or religious connotations in Yiddish, but we know that among Slavic Jews, the veil (often red in color) was regarded as protection against the evil eye (Scheftelowitz 1925:81; on red, see chapter 5.2 below).

Romance 4. Eastern Yiddish *lejenen,* Western Yiddish *lajen* 'read'

M.Weinreich opted for a French origin for this pan-Yiddish verb (see French *lire*: 1:1973:112, 2:61–2, 4:87–8). In contrast, I regard the source as dialectal Italian, see, e.g., Judeo-Italian *leje,* Friulan *lèi,* etc. (vs. standard Italian *leggere* with /-ždž-/).

The infix *-en-* in Yiddish may provide a clue to the origin. This infix is used productively in Central and Eastern Yiddish dialects to construct verbs from Hebrew verb roots, e.g., Hebrew *bādaq* 'he inspected' becomes Yiddish *batkenen* (the second *-en* is the infinitive suffix). Most Yiddishists derive *-en-* from Hebrew *-ān,* the agent noun suffix (e.g., Hebrew *gazlān* 'brigand' formed from the root *g-z-l* 'rob'). I suspect that Yiddish *-en* is either the Upper Sorbian verbal noun suffix *-nje* or Hebrew *-ān* used according to the Sorbian grammatical requirement of adding a verbal infix to foreign verb stems (1991b). Given the fact that Western Yiddish dialects use *-en-* far less productively than Eastern Yiddish dialects, it is tempting to hypothesize that Western Yiddish *lajen* was a borrowing from Judeo-French, while Eastern Yiddish *lejenen* came from Italian or Balkan Romance, which is reasonable on formal grounds. Note also that the Romanism is used in Balkan Slavic, e.g., Serbo-Croatian (Dubrovnik) *lègati* 'read'. The presence of *-en-* in southwest German dialectal *dǫrmənə* 'sleep' (Matras 1991:289) may also mark this Romanism as a Judeo-Italianism—vs. *dormen,* attested in German since the late 15th century and in Franconian Yiddish, which is presumably of French origin (see details in Wexler 1988:89, fn 27).

The addition of *-en-* to the stem *lej-* suggests that Yiddish speakers may have regarded the word as a Hebraism, though there is no trace of an underlying Yiddish **lejen* 'reader'. Thus, the word may originally have denoted the reading of Hebrew religious books. This is plausible since for centuries there were no non-Hebrew books in use among the Jews. In fact, forms of this verb in some dialects of German Yiddish have the meaning read (aloud) from the Torah (Wexler 1992b: chapter 3.3, fn 178).

The same semantic change of 'read Hebrew books' > 'read' took place in Judezmo and Marrano Portuguese with the Grecism *meldar,* which today often means read (in general), though in some contemporary dialects, and in earlier parlance, it designated specifically the reading of Hebrew, see, e.g., Saloniki Judezmo 'read' vs. Dubrovnik and Moroccan Judezmo 'read Jewish religious texts', Bayonne Marrano Portuguese 'read the Torah'. Note also that the commemoration of a relative's death in Judezmo and North European Marrano Portuguese is called *meldado, meldadura,* respectively (a reference to the reading of Hebrew texts)—corresponding to Yiddish *jorcajt* (see above). The Greek source of *meldado*, etc., is *meletáo* 'be occupied with, exert oneself, study'. Catalan and south Italian dialects also have the Grecism, e.g., Catalan *maldar* 'make a special effort to attain', south Italian *melet(á)ó* 'read' (Reggio, Otranto). A Judeo-Latin origin can be postulated for the Judeo-Romance data, since Judeo-French and Judeo-Provençal also have surface cognates. Curiously, Judezmo *meldar* has, like Yiddish *lejenen,* undergone Judaization, since many native speakers think the source is actually Hebrew *lāmad* 'study'. The Grecism is unknown in Yiddish.

Romance (via German?) 5. Yiddish *mape,* Hebrew *mappāh* 'Torah wrapping'

The ultimate source of the Hebrew Romanism is clearly Latin *mappa* 'linen towel'. Yiddish could have received the term directly from Mishnaic Hebrew, Greek or German *Mappe.* Conceivably, the use of the Hebrew Latinism could have been stimulated by the use of the term in non-Jewish languages; it is apparently unattested in other Jewish languages. The Bavarian Jewish convert to Christianity, Anthoni Margaritha (1530), cited southwestern German Yiddish *mappa* (his spelling) 'Torah wrapping' as a typical Rhineland term, unknown in his own area, which used *menttelin* (see Modern Yiddish *mentele* in this meaning, a diminutive of *mantel* 'cloak; case'). Margaritha regarded the word as one of the many French terms in use among the Rhineland Jews. If the word is indeed of French origin, then the Jews have preserved the original *m*-, which tended to be dissimilated to *n*- in Old French, e.g., *nappe.* Among Christians, the term usually denoted a tablecloth (e.g., Old Liège French *map[p]e* 1440) or napkin (1330). I can cite a Christian ritual connotation in Old French *nappe d'autel* 'linen cover on the altar' (1508), contemporary Liège French *mape di comugnon* 'linen spread before the communicants'. The first depiction of the *mappāh* appears in a late 14th-century German Jewish manuscript (Metzger and Metzger 1982:67, #94).

Romance (via Slavic?) 6. Western Yiddish *memern* 'commemorate the death of Jewish martyrs', *memōrbūx* 'book commemorating the death of Jewish martyrs'

The first example of Yiddish *memōrbūx* dates from 1445. Max Weinreich offered Latin *memoria* 'remembrance, memory' or *memor* 'remember' as the etymon but could not chose between a French or Italian carrier of the term to Yiddish. Today, the term is restricted to the Yiddish of western Germany and a handful of points in the east, at Berlin, Kobersdorf (south of Vienna) and Zabrze (Poland). French *memorie* (12th century) and Italian *memoria* 'memory' (13th century) are not likely sources since they are learnèd Latinisms, an unlikely source of enrichment for Yiddish. A possible source might be Old Italian *membrare* 'remember', though the latter may be disqualified if it turns out to be a Provençal borrowing in Italian. However, the Latin term is widespread, both in Friulan and Italian forms, in coastal Balkan Slavic, e.g., Serbo-Croatian (Istria) *mrmor* 'reason, intelligence', Slovenian *mramoriti* 'care for.' Hence, I regard the Yiddish Romanism as a possible borrowing made by Jews on Balkan territory.

Romance 7. Western Yiddish *poršn* 'porge meant of impurities according to ritual prescriptions' and synonymous cognate Judezmo *purgar*

See discussion of Yiddish *trejbern* in category I, Slavic 6 above.

Romance 8. Old Rhineland Yiddish *repetier(en)* 'repeat as a teaching device in the Jewish (religious) school', with cognates in Judeo-Romance

The earliest Yiddish source of this word is Margaritha 1530. The word is probably of Judeo-French (and ultimately Judeo-Latin) origin, to judge from the existence of cognates in other Judeo-Romance languages, e.g., Bosnian Judezmo *ariftar* 'correct a pupil's reading of a religious text by having him re-read it correctly', Judeo-Italian *rjpjṭjṭw"r* /ripitetor/ 'teacher who has a student repeat' (16th century: Marx 1924: 621). The term is semantically distant from Bavarian German (Munich) *repetieren* 'return to something in a mocking or angry tone' (attested only from the 19th century: Schmeller 1872–7). In the Romance languages, the term means repeat, with no religious connotations, e.g., French *répéter*, Old Catalan *repetir* 'go over the lesson'. Margaritha also cites a Yiddish synonym *ertorn* from French *tourner* 'turn' (see Modern Yiddish *dertornen*). For discussion, see Wexler 1988:122.

Romance 9. Western Yiddish *sargenes* 'shroud'

The source is Italian *sargano* 'serge'; the use of the plural in Yiddish parallels synonymous Hebrew *taxrīxīm*, but I cannot say where the plural usage began.

Turkic 1. Eastern Yiddish *homen-taš* 'Purim pastry'

See discussion of the Ukrainian Turkism *hamán* 'purse' in chapter 5.13 below.

Turkic 2. Eastern Yiddish *jarmlke* '(Jewish) scullcap; cap'

The Yiddish term has cognates in Polish and the East Slavic languages, e.g., Polish *ja(r)mułka* 'cap' (attested since the 15th century), Russian *ermolka* (especially applied to Central Asian realia). Only Ukrainian *jarmulka* ~ *jarmurka* reveals a Jewish connotation, e.g., 'cap (especially worn by Jews)'. The etymon may be Turkish *yağmurluk* 'raincoat; roof over a doorway'.

There are two reasons why it is unlikely that Yiddish, or another Jewish language spoken to the east of Yiddish, would have gotten the term directly from a Turkic language (say in Hungary or in the Balkans): (a) the custom of covering one's head was adopted late (see the discussion in chapter 5.2 below); (b) the term also appears in many Slavic languages with the same meaning (though this fact need not automatically eliminate a Jewish source for the Slavic Turkisms). Hence, I assume that Slavic is the immediate source of this Yiddish term—presumably after Jews began habitually covering their heads in prayer. But I am unable to determine if Yiddish dialects borrowed the Turkism independently from each coterritorial Slavic language (i.e., Belorussian Yiddish from Belorussian, Ukrainian Yiddish from Ukrainian, etc.), or borrowed the Turkism once, say from Ukrainian, and then Ukrainian Yiddish spread the term to other dialects of Yiddish. The western extent of the Turkism in Yiddish seems to be in Eastern Galicia, since large sections of northern Polish and Lvov Yiddish use German *kepl* in this meaning rather than *jarmlke*. Curiously, in the Lvov dialect of Yiddish, *jarmlke* has acquired the narrowed meaning of cap worn by Hassidic Jews; this fact might explain why a newer *kepl* was required in these areas. Prilucki reports that in Polish, *ja(r)mułka* also means a priest's cap (1923:111).

Another Turkic word for clothing in Yiddish (and Slavic) is Yiddish *kaftn*, Polish *kaftan*, Belorussian and Ukrainian *kaptan* 'long outer robe'. It is only in Czech and Slovak that *kaftan* now denotes a type of long overcoat especially worn by observant male Jews. On Turkic styles of dress among the Poles in the 16th century which the Jews retained after they had become obsolete among Christians, see Heler 1939:616 and Zamoyski 1988:58, 107, 125, 197. This appears to be a rare case where Judaization was tantamount to "Turkicization".

Compare the example of Yiddish *šabaš* (category I, Turkic 2 above) where the Jews may have been the purveyors of an Iranianism to the Slavs.

Slavic (Hebraism?) 1. Yiddish *gojlem*, Yiddish Hebrew *golɛm* 'supernatural servant made out of clay; idiot'; in Hebrew also 'amorphous mass; cocoon'

One could assume that Hebrew *golɛm* was formed from the native root *g-l-m* 'mass' which underwent a semantic change from 'mass' to 'supernatural creature (which acts as a servant)' > 'idiot', without any outside interference.

Nevertheless, I suspect that this term was either derived from one of several Slavic roots (and later Hebraized) or was a native Hebrew word which developed the meaning of supernatural creature under the impact of a Slavic term with similar sound and meaning. Possible models are Old Czech *holemek* 'servant; judge's or executioner's helper' and Old Polish *holomek* 'house servant' (attested c.1460), or Czech *holemý* 'strong', Common Slavic **golěmъ* 'large', attested in all Slavic languages beginning with South Slavic (see 10th-century Old Church Slavic: details appear in Skok 1934:76; Zaręba 1965; Rusek 1983). The earliest Jewish account of the story of a *golɛm*-servant seems to be in the 13th-century Hebrew writings of German pietists and mystics. The father of the writer Jehuda Hexasid of Regensburg (d.1217) is the first person to be associated with the creation of a *golɛm* (note also Hexasid's use of the Slavo-Greek term for 'werewolf', discussed under category I, Greek 5 above). Common Slavic **g* changed into *h* in Czech by the 11th century, and in Upper Sorbian by the 12th century, and Slavic-speaking Jews of the period could have been aware of the original *g* pronunciation in the above-mentioned Slavic roots, which would have made possible the association with native Hebrew *golɛm* 'mass'; alternatively, the Jews might have borrowed the Slavism from West Slavic when Czech and Upper Sorbian still had Common Slavic *g, that is, well before the time of Jehuda Hexasid, or from a South Slavic language where Common Slavic *g never underwent lenition to *h*. For example, in Serbo-Croatian, *gòlem* has acquired the modified meaning of gigantic.

Max Weinreich has pointed out that the legend of the *golɛm* may originate in Byzantine Greek sources (1:1973:87, 373; see also Starr 1939:73, 117). Substantiation for this claim is that a *golɛm* story is known among the Italian Jews in the 10th century (Scholem 1971:755). The existence of a similar legend among a number of European peoples, both Jews and non-Jews, highlights the need to study the diffusion of Byzantine folklore to northern Europe within a comparative framework. *Golɛm* stories are associated with rabbis in other areas and periods, e.g., with Jehuda Lejb (Löw) of Prague (c. 1525–1609) and Eliahu Ba ͗al Šem, Chełm (Poland, mid-16th century).

Literature: Jacoby 1931–2 (for Byzantine Greek and later European Christian examples); Trachtenberg 1939:85 (for Jewish sources).

Slavic (Hebraism?) 2. Yiddish *nadn, nedan*, etc. 'dowry'

See discussion in chapter 5.14 below.

Slavic (Germanism) 3. Eastern Yiddish (but also attested in Prague and Regensburg) *par(e)ve* 'food that can be eaten with milk or meat meals'

A number of etymologies have been proposed for this term: Czech *páravý* 'paired' (this would parallel the synonymous Hungarian *páros*), Latin *parvus* 'small (meal)', Middle High German *par* 'naked; empty of content'. The Czech and German etyma are reasonable from the point of view of meaning, but I eliminate a German source since the term is almost unknown in German Yiddish territory. In view of the rarity of Czech components in Yiddish (other than in the dialects spoken in the Czech lands), I prefer to posit Upper Sorbian *parować* 'do without' as the etymon, itself a borrowing from Middle High German *enperen* (= Modern German *entbehren*). The removal of the verbal prefix *en(t)-* is a phenomenon found with other Sorbian Germanisms. A Sorbian origin would explain the nearly exclusive presence of the term in Eastern Yiddish dialects.

Ashkenazic Judaism seems to be unique in having a term for ritually neutral foods. Ashkenazic Jewish food ritual requires that neutral foods, e.g., vegetables, that are cooked in milk or meat pots be consumed with milk or meat dishes, respectively. Iberian Jewish ritual permits vegetables to be cooked in any pot and consumed with either milk or meat dishes. The origin of the Ashkenazic practice requires study.

Slavic 4. Yiddish *kitke* 'Sabbath bread'.

See discussion in category I, Germanic 1 above.

Slavic 5. Yiddish *lajbserdak* 'ritual garment for orthodox men'.

See discussion of this term in the text preceding the examples above.

There is a considerable number of Germanisms in Yiddish used in imitation of Slavic patterns of discourse which express religious connotations in Slavic (but not in German). For the sake of brevity, I will cite only two such examples:

Slavic (via German?) 6. German loan translation in Yiddish: *oprixtn* 'conduct (a religious ceremony)'

See Ukrainian *vidpravyty (Božu Službu)* 'perform (Mass)', which has the same component structure as Yiddish *opšprexn*, and discussion in category I, Slavic 4 above.

Slavic (via German?) 7. German loan translation in Yiddish: *šprox* 'incantation'

The term is a congener of German *sprechen* 'speak' and *Sprache* 'language' which were lacking in Yiddish until Jews borrowed the latter in the 19th century (see Yiddish *šprax* 'language'). In Slavic languages, words for 'language, speech' often acquire quasi-religious connotations, e.g., Czech *namluviti* 'betrothe', *namluviti si* 'court', or a meaning like noisy language; noise, e.g., Old Church Slavic *mlъviti* 'get excited, be upset', *mlъva* 'noise, hubbub, row'; colloquial Czech *řičeti* 'yell, shout', *pořknút* 'blame', Slovak *jazyčit', jazykovat'* 'slander, smear; talk nonsense' (on the tabu of terms for talking, see Liewehr 1954:107). This semantic development may be the source of Yiddish *lošn hore* 'vilification' (literally 'the language of evil').

I know of one German parallel with native *sprechen* 'speak': Bavarian dialectal *Ansprechen* 'false benediction', *Ansprecher* 'person who utters an incantation' (Schmeller 1872–7), but I have no information about its age. Northeast Bavaria had a Slavic-speaking population until about the

14th century. Standard German *absprechen* 'give sentence against; give up; refuse' differs from the meaning of the parallel Yiddish *opšprexn (a bejz ojg)* 'charm away (an evil eye)'; there is no Yiddish simplex **šprexn* 'speak'. Hence, I suggest that Yiddish *šprox*, though a German borrowing, may have developed its meaning on Slavic patterns of discourse, directly or indirectly via Bavarian German.

Other Germanisms used in Yiddish according to Slavic patterns of discourse which I cited above include *šul* (see category I, Greek 2), dialectal *rānigen* (~ *trejbern* in category I, Slavic 6) and possibly *pasl(en)en a kac, a kind* discussed in the text above preceding the examples. Hebraisms which may have developed meanings based on Slavic patterns of discourse that I discussed above before the presentation of the examples include southwest German slang *hilūxə* 'clothes' and Yiddish *apetropes, apitropos* 'tutor, guardian'.

CATEGORY III. Jewish loans with no religious and/or superstitious meanings for which the donor language does preserve religious and/or superstitious meanings

Greek (via Slavic?) 1. Yiddish *katoves* 'jest' < Greek *katavasia* 'church hymn'

The Yiddish Grecism cannot be derived from Russian *katavasija* 'confusion, jumble', since 16th-century Bavarian Yiddish has the term. An earlier Balkan Slavic intermediary is conceivable since the Grecism is widespread in those languages.

Slavic 1. Eastern Yiddish *dejže* 'kneading trough'

In 1991b I derived this Yiddish Slavism from Upper Sorbian, but since the object plays a role in Balkan and other Slavic wedding ceremonies, I would now propose Balkan Slavic as an alternative source. In the Serbo-Croatian wedding ceremony, *díža, dîžva* (currently in the meaning of watering trough or wine container) is enclosed in the "magic circle" drawn around the bridegroom by the wedding guests (Schneeweis 1935:158–8; on the circle, see also discussion of Yiddish *holekrāš* in category I, Germanic 3 above). The kneading trough plays a role in other Slavic wedding ceremonies, e.g., among Poles, Ukrainians, Russians (see Krauss 1885:95, Piprek 1914:40, 58, 185–6, Vovk 1928, Schneeweis 1931:37ff and Wienecke 1940:132). Wuttke records this custom in Thüringen (1900:386), an area inhabited by Slavs until the 12th–

13th centuries. There is no trace of this custom now among Ashkenazic Jews.

The term and the wedding custom may have been acquired by the Jews in the Balkans and then brought to the Germano-Sorbian lands, where the practice became obsolete due to lack of reenforcement by the coterritorial Sorbs, who (at least now) lack the wedding custom (though they preserve the Slavic term in the Yiddish meaning). The association of the kneading trough with birth is also widespread, and finds reflection in Biblical Hebrew, to judge from the fact that both meanings are expressed by the word *ʿarīsāh* (Patai 1944).

5.12 Christianized Hebrew names, Hebraized non-Jewish names and Turkic naming practices in Yiddish

Parallel to the Christian practice of using Biblical Hebrew names, Ashkenazic Jews in the Middle Ages borrowed back Christianized forms of Hebrew names for use as secular names; the original Hebrew names continued in use, e.g., in the synagogue when men were called to read from the Torah. An example of a secular Christianized Hebrew name is Yiddish *zalmen*, a Germanized form of Hebrew *šlomoh* (see German *Salman[n]* 14th century), the cognate of English *Solomon;* Yiddish also has the Hebrew name in the form *šlojme*. Yiddish speakers believe that *zalmen* is a Hebrew name, hence they spell it without vowels, the manner in which Hebrew words are spelled both in Hebrew and in Yiddish; a native Yiddish word would be spelled with vowels. The Hebraization of this name was probably facilitated by the fact that most words in Yiddish with the form CVCC*en* (C = consonant and V = vowel) are Hebraisms, e.g., Yiddish *lamden* 'learned man, scholar' < Hebrew *lamdān*.

Another Hebraized non-Jewish name is Yiddish *kalmen*. For the same reason as *zalmen*, *kalmen* also came to be spelled without vowels in the Hebrew manner. The source is Greek *kalonymos*, literally 'good name', a name borne apparently only by Greek Jews and preserved in two forms by the north European Jews: *kalonimos* in the west German lands, and the Germanized, truncated *kalmen* (consisting of *kal-* + an unstressed form of German *man[n]* 'man', a productive suffix in German and Yiddish names) in the west and east German lands and in Slavic Europe. The full form *kalonimos* acquired a "Hebrew" status among Ashkenazic Jews and was one of two non-Hebrew names (the other was *alɛksandɛr*) by which men could be called to read from the Torah in the synagogue. A Greek diminutive of *alɛksandɛr, sender*, was also popular in Yiddish, but lacked any ecclesiastical status. It is interesting to note that Greek and Arabic names could be used in the synagogues of those respective communities, but German and Slavic names were unacceptable in the Ashkenazic synagogues (see M.Simon 1992: 167). This fact reflects differences in the relative intensity of the Judaization processes in diverse Jewish communities. It is interesting that newly coined European Hebrew names (attested roughly only from the close of the first millennium A.D., e.g., *xaim* and *šem ṭōv*, literally 'life' and 'good name', respectively), are also acceptable in the synagogue ritual, though they were originally translations of Christian and Muslim names of the same meaning.

While Jews occasionally Judaized (Hebraized) Christian names, Jewish converts to Christianity often practiced de-Judaization of their original Hebrew names; this topic deserves a separate study. An example is the family name of the early 16th-century Bavarian apostate Anthoni Margaritha; *Margaritha*, like the female name *Margaret*, is derived from the Greek word for pearl; his grandfather, a well-known rabbi from Nürnberg, called himself by the Hebraized form of the same Greek word which is a common Ashkenazic name even today—*margoles*. As a proper noun, the Grecism is unknown both in Yiddish and German. The change from *margoles* > *margaritha* shows that the meaning of the names was still understood in the early 16th century.

In most Jewish communities women use a higher percentage of non-Hebrew names than men (for examples from Caucasian Jews at the turn of the century, see Čaxčir 1905:138–8). The explanation is not that men required a Hebrew name for use in the synagogue and within the Jewish community. Alongside this name, Jewish men might have another name of any origin for use in the non-Jewish society (which surfaces in most Christian documents; see also discussion in category I, Germanic 3 in chapter 5.11 above); looking only at the "external" male names, we would probably still find a larger percentage of Hebraisms. (The relatively reduced use of Hebrew names by women also characterizes contemporary secular Israeli society. Lawson has noted that in Israel about 70% of the 104 most common male names come from the Bible, while only about 40% of women's names are of biblical origin. Most of the non-biblical names are of foreign origin or are newly created Hebrew names: 1991:108, 119, 123.)

I suspect that the higher frequency of non-Jewish names among Jewish women reflects the fact that women were more often proselytes than men; circumcision, demanded of male proselyte candidates, tended to dissuade many non-Jewish males from formally joining the Jewish community. Moreover, women proselytes had no need for a Hebrew name, since they were not allowed to read from the Torah in the synagogue. This analysis implies that at certain periods the Jewish community would have contained more women than men. There is no way to prove this. But the non-Jewish spouses of converted females would not have had a negative impact on the Jewish population in the long run, since the offspring of married women who converted to Judaism could still be considered Jews by Jewish religious law even if their husbands remained non-Jews, since Jewishness is transmitted through the mother. A surfeit of unmarried women might explain the practice of polygamy among the north European Jews through the first millennium. I wonder whether the decision of the Mainz scholar Geršom ben Jehuda (born in Metz c.965–1028) to ban polygamy was motivated by the disfavor of the Christian community, or by the fact that the number of women and men in the Jewish community had by then become about equal. Polygamy was also practised by the pagan Slavs, but I do not know whether the practice terminated immediately with the advent of Christianity.

The practice of naming a child after the holiday on which it was born is attested in a great many societies, see, e.g., French *Noël* male, *Noëlle* female, Italian *Natale* male, from the native terms for Christmas, though this naming pattern is not particularly productive in the Christian languages; Old Hebrew *šabtaj*, Yiddish *šeftl* male come from Hebrew *šabbāt* 'Saturday', *ḥagaj* male from *ḥāg* 'holiday'. The 3rd-century Judeo-Greek inscription from Aphrodisias also shows an enthusiasm among Jews, Christians and God-Fearers alike for names derived from the names of the Hebrew festivals and the Sabbath. Here there are names based on Greek *heorté* 'Feast (of Tabernacles)', e.g., *Hortásios*; see also *E̓usabbáθios*, literally 'good Sabbath' (and the similar Yiddish *jomtof* male name from Hebrew *jōm ṭōv* 'good day; holiday'—pronounced in Yiddish *jontef* in the meaning holiday: compare Trakai Karaite *jėxkjun* 'Sunday' < 'good day' —with Yiddish interference?— cited in chapter 5.11 above). In other inscriptions, the related name *Heortasios* was used by Greek-speaking Christians and pagans without any apparent Judaizing sympathies. Čaxčir cites the Caucasian Jewish girl's name *purim* from the Hebrew name of the holiday (1905:139); in these Tat communities the holiday of Purim came to be called *hmwnw* /hamonu/ (?—not vocalized in the source available to me), following the name of the anti-Jewish figure in the Purim story, or *nisonu* (= the Hebrew month *nīsān*?—which follows the month in which the holiday falls; see also Čorni 1884:8–8, 261). The practice of naming children after the holidays on which they were born seems to be particularly widespread in Turkic societies, see e.g., Belorussian Tatar *Bajramsuba, Ramazan* family names from Turkish *bayram* 'festival', *ramazan* 'month of Ramadan'.

The Ashkenazic practice of naming a child after the holiday on which it was born could go back equally to Jewish Palestine, Europe or Asia, and in the latter two instances, to non-Jewish practices. However, one male name, Yiddish *pejsex*, from Hebrew *pɛsaḥ* 'Passover' looks suspiciously like a Turkic naming convention, despite the Hebrew origin of the name (unless *pejsex* was originally a shortened form of the Hebrew name *ptaḥjāh*, pronounced *psaxje* in Yiddish, as Golomb 1910: 306 proposed).

There are four reasons why the Yiddish male name *pejsex* is likely to be derived from a Khazar Jewish naming practice:

(a) The oldest example of this word as a male name comes from a Khazar Hebrew document from Kiev, thought to date from approximately 930; the document contains several signatories with the name (see Golb and Pritsak 1982). After the Khazar datum of 930, there are no further examples of the name until the 12th-century.

(b) The distribution of the name within the German lands suggests that it must have reached Yiddish either directly through contact with the Khazars (possibly from those who allegedly emigrated to the present-day Hungarian and Slovak lands, together with the ancestors of the Magyars), or through the intermediary of Judeo-Slavic, in which case the latter could have borrowed the term in the Khazar homeland or in the monolingual East Slavic lands. In Europe, the Yiddish male name *pejsex* is productively used in the Slavic lands; it is rare in medieval Germany, except in the eastern, originally Slavic-speaking, regions; in the monolingual west German lands it is only found sparingly among Jews known to have come from eastern Germany. I am familiar with examples from Budapest 1278, east Germany and Austria in the 15th century (in the writings of rabbi Iserlin); examples from non-Slavic areas of Germany include Fulda early 13th century, Bavaria 13th century, and the Rhineland, as early as the 12th century.

(c) In the Slavic lands, Hebrew *pɛsaḥ* often shows adjustment to Slavic phonological norms, e.g., *ḥ*, which the Ashkenazic Jews pronounced as /x/, was replaced by *k;* this is reminiscent of an Old South Polish rule whereby final and preconsonantal *x* became *k* (first attested in Polish manuscripts of the 15th century, but undeniably earlier still). A Jewish example is the name *Kusko Pyeszakowicz* ~ *Pesachowicz* (literally 'son of Pejsex') from a Polish-language document from Pinsk (Belorussia) 1553–5. The Jewish name with final *k* also appears in German documents, though this is not a requirement of the German sound system, since words with final *x* are grammatical (e.g., *nach* 'after'), see, e.g., *Petsak* in a German document from Wiener-Neustadt (Austria) 1455. These facts suggest the name could have diffused from east to west, sometimes in a Polonized form, perhaps from the Khazar Jews to Slavic-speaking Jews in east Germany, in keeping with the Jewish migration patterns that I sketched in chapter 4 above.

(d) The use of Hebrew *pɛsaḥ* as a male name is unknown among Jews in the Romance countries or North Africa. Its occasional presence today among Balkan Sephardic Jews may be due to contact with local Ashkenazim. The name is common among the Turkic- and Arabic-speaking Karaites in the Ukraine, Belorussia and Egypt (the local Jews in the first two areas were largely Ashkenazic), but is presently unknown among Karaites in Turkey (who were, until recently, Greek-speaking) or in the Crimea (Karaite-speaking).

The use of the Hebrew holiday name *ḥannūkāh* as a personal male name is also found in the same Ukrainian Khazar document of 930 along with *pɛsaḥ*; as a family name, see contemporary Slavicized Tat *Xanukaev* (Ixilov 1950:192; for examples from other Jewish communities, including a single 16th-century Czech source, see Wexler 1987b: 75).

Often, the geography of Hebrew names used in Yiddish can reveal the geographical origin of the naming practice. For example, Hebrew *śimḥāh*, literally 'joy' is a male name in Eastern European Yiddish (*simxe*) but a female name among Jews resident in Western Yiddish and Romance territories (borrowed by Eastern Yiddish in the form *sime*—reflecting the Judeo-French pronunciation of Hebrew *ḥ* as zero). This distribution reflects the fact that the Slavic languages productively form male names from the masculine root 'joy' (from which feminine names may then be derived), while the French Jews who settled in southwest Germany follow the French practice of deriving feminine names from the feminine root 'joy'.

The dividing line in the gender assignment of Yiddish *simxe* in Medieval Germany seems to have passed through Bavaria, to judge from the names derived from 'joy' in the late 13th-century Nürnberg Hebrew texts published by Stern (1894–6:108). Here we find German *wrwjdʾ*

/frejde/ female (but the noun is Yiddish *frejd* ~ German *Freude* 'joy'); Hebrew *cymhh* /cimxe/ male and female (the change of *s-* > *c-* is due to German influence since most dialects of German disallow words with initial *s-*); French *jwjʾh* /džoje/ female (see French *joie* 'joy'). A Slavic translation of Yiddish *simxe* is found in the writings of the Slavic-speaking(?) rabbi Iserlin (1390–1460): *wwʿslj"n* /veselin/ male. This was also the name of a Slovenian Christian cleric who converted to Judaism around 1005 (Golb 1964), and has a parallel in the contemporary Sorbian male and family name *Wesełу* (see Schlimpert 1978:153 for attestation from 1318; Wenzel 1987:76). The final *-n* was originally a patronymic or possessive marker (Eichler 1985:349). There is no trace in Yiddish of Slavic *rad-* 'joy', which is the basis of many names (e.g., Slovenian *Rado* male).

A related topic that calls for immediate study is the Hebraization of non-Jewish names taken from ethnic and geographical names that are borne by Jews (either uniquely or along with non-Jews), since such names could provide valuable clues to the ethnic origins of the Ashkenazic Jews. One example is *zaks* < 'Saxon(y)' (common among Germans as well, and not just in Saxony); this name is often reinterpreted as a Hebrew acronym, *z(εraʿ) q(odεš) š(mō)*, literally 'his name is holy seed', a reference to a martyred Jew. This interpretation is unlikely since the resulting acronym should have yielded **zakš*. Another example is the complex of Jewish names *valax/blox/blok*, derived from the Slavic form of a German ethnonym (itself of Celtic origin!), see, e.g., Serbo-Croatian *vlah*, Czech *vlach*, Polish *włoch*—all of which designate a Romance group (on a Hebrew acronymic interpretation for this name, see Unbegaun 1972:353). In Slovenian, the term is *lah*, which may be the basis of the Jewish family name *laxman*, with *-man* 'man' added (for Slavic details, see Skok 1934:89, Vasmer 1953-8 and Machek 1971; for the suggestion that *laxman* is derived from the Hebrew male name *naxman*, see Briling 1953).

Finally, Yiddish uses many nouns for constructing male and female names, of native and non-native origin, which are not found among the Germans; translation equivalents are, however, frequently attested as names in the Slavic, Romance, Greek and Turkic communities. Examples are Yiddish *blume* female, literally 'flower' (which is in Yiddish now *blum*) or *golde* female, literally 'gold(en)' (also popular in Israel today in Hebrew translations, *zehava, zehavit*; for other examples, see Wexler 1987b:chapters 3.16–3.163; for examples of parallel 14th-century Sorbian family names, see Schlimpert 1978:74, 161).

See also discussion of Yiddish names such as *levi, kojen* and *kaplan* (< Hebrew *levī, kohen* and Slavic *kaplan*) in chapter 6.3 below.

5.13 Non-Jewish terms for Jewish holidays, practices and artifacts which deviate from Palestinian Jewish usage

The non-Jewish names for Jewish holidays and practices which deviate from normative Jewish practice are extremely important because they offer clues to non-normative Judaism and Jewish culture, many elements of which could have been developed by Jews of proselyte origin. The chronology of Hebrew translation equivalents in Yiddish should be checked, but I suspect that most Hebraisms will prove to be relatively recent loans in Yiddish. Hebrew holiday names often appear in Old Palestinian writings, but these could have been lost in Europe, only to be freshly resurrected in a later period of Judaization.

In principle, the non-Jewish terms may be classified into three types:

(a) Original Jewish terms which became obsolete among the Jews but survive among the non-Jews as designations of Jewish holidays.

(b) Original Christian terms which denote both Jewish and Christian practices.

(c) Original Christian terms which denote Jewish customs or artifacts uniquely.

Non-Jewish terms that are not in use among Jews, are presumed, by Jew and non-Jew alike, to be "Christian" terms. Terms which prove to be of Jewish origin can help us to put a relative date of obsolescence on the concepts denoted. An example is the expression "long day" for Yom Kippur in the German, Hungarian and Czech speech of non-Jews which I mentioned in chapter 5.11 above. These three contiguous languages show that Jews must have called Yom Kippur by the expression "long day" after settling in the German, Hungarian and Czech lands, i.e., after the 9th–10th centuries. To be sure, this is only a rough chronology, but no other information is available for fixing the date. The term may well have been brought by Balkan Jewish settlers to northern Europe, since there is a Judeo-Greek precedent for the expression, e.g., *hē megalē hēmera*, literally 'the great day'. The fact that neither the expression "long day" nor "great day" is known in most other areas of Germany (the former surfaces only in Alsace) might mean that when Jews moved westward across the German lands from Bavaria, they were no longer regularly using these expressions for Yom Kippur. The standard Yiddish holiday name *jom kiper* comes from written Hebrew; it may have always prevailed in Ashkenazic written Hebrew but may not have been used in colloquial Yiddish until the period of Judaization. Perhaps "long" or "great day" were Judeo-Slavic expressions which were suppressed in the monolingual southwest German lands by the originally French-speaking Jews there who developed an influential center of Hebraic studies which could have served as a focal point for subsequent Judaization activities.

Another interesting example is the Eastern Yiddish expression *homen-taš* for the distinctive pastry eaten on the holiday of Purim, which means literally 'Haman's pocket(book), pouch'—an illusion to the wealthy Iranian villain in the Purim narrative who tried to destroy the Jews in the 5th century B.C. *Homen* 'Haman' could be the expected Eastern Yiddish pronunciation of Biblical Hebrew *hāmān*, yet coterritorial Christians pronounce the name as *haman. Homentaš* is the only term known now in Eastern Yiddish, though the standard Western Yiddish term is 'Haman's ear', see, e.g., Dutch Yiddish *hamansor*. The use of the term 'ear' is probably an allusion to the chopping off of a criminal's ears, related in the Mishnah. This pattern of discourse is also found in other Jewish languages, e.g., Judeo-Italian *orrechio di Aman*, and is the basis for synonymous Modern Israeli Hebrew *ozen haman*. In addition to Western Yiddish, Ukrainians and Poles also call the Jewish pastry 'Haman's ear'—*hamanove vuxo* and *hamanowe ucho*, respectively; this shows that (Ashkenazic) Jews in these areas must also have once called the pastry by this name.

Given the ubiquity of the expression 'Haman's ear' among European Jews, I would imagine that Eastern Yiddish *homen-taš* was a local innovation possibly motivated by the form of the pastry, which usually has a filling in the center *taš* 'pocket'. While *homen* indeed could be smoothly derived from Hebrew *hāmān*, the etymon may actually have been homophonous Ukrainian *hamán* '(leather) purse, money bag', which some etymologists regard as a Turkic loan (see Rudnyc'kyj 6:1967:553). *Haman* 'purse' could have attracted the Yiddish term *taš* 'pocket' at a time when Jews still understood the meaning of *haman*. There are a number of compound nouns in Yiddish, consisting of synonyms of different component origin, e.g., Yiddish *fis-nohe* 'jellied calves' feet' < German + Belorussian 'feet'. Yiddish speakers during a later period of Judaization, perhaps no longer familiar either with a Turkic language or Ukrainian, could have reinterpreted Ukrainian *haman* as the Hebrew form of the name, thus yielding *homen* in Yiddish.

Alternatively, I could assume the original basis for the expression was indeed Hebrew *hāmān*, which Ukrainians learned from non-

Ashkenazic Jews who pronounced it as *haman*; such Jews might have been Turkic- or Iranian-speaking Jews, of possible Khazar proselyte origin. There are other examples of *haman* in Christian terms for the Purim holiday, see, e.g., 19th-century German *Hamansfest*, literally 'Haman's holiday' or Belorussian *Purim-Aman* 'Purim-Haman' (R. 1850 and Nikiforovskij 1897:22, fn 345, separate pagination, respectively). (See also discussion of Tat *hamonu* and *nisonu* 'Purim' among Caucasian Jews cited in chapter 5.12 above.)

If the origin of Yiddish *homen-taš* was ultimately Ukrainian *haman* 'purse', then I could assume that the pastry itself was originally a Slavic (or Turkic) food and that Eastern Yiddish *homen-taš* and Western Yiddish *hamansor*/Eastern Yiddish **homensojer* were originally distinct types of pastries with independent names.

On Slavic *haman* in the meaning giant, see also discussion in chapter 6.2 below.

Belorussian (or West Russian) *(židovskie) stojany/styjany* (literally '[Jewish] standing') were recorded in the Vicebsk district at the close of the 19th century in the meaning day of Jewish prayer recited by the water preceding the Jewish New Year (ibid.:9, fn 141, separate pagination), i.e., the *tašlīx* service that is discussed in chapters 5 above and 5.2 below. In a slightly different form, the term designates a Christian holiday, see, e.g., Russian *stojan'e* 'nocturnal vigil in the church on the Thursday or Saturday of the fifth week of Lent; recitation of the Gospels; praying while standing; prayer' (Sreznevskij 1893–1903). Nikiforovskij also notes that *tašlīx* is better known among the Belorussians by the picturesque, though cumbersome, expression *tres' (trjasti) blox u vodu* 'shake the fleas into the water' (1897:9, fn 141).

A Christian name for a Jewish holiday which does not also designate a Christian holiday is Old Ukrainian *(holosnie) trubky* 'Jewish New Year', literally '(noisy) trumpets' (late 17th century: Kopczyńska-Jaworska 1986:88; Wexler 1987b:135–6). This term contrasts sharply with normative Yiddish *rošešone*, literally 'head of the year', from Hebrew *rōš haššānāh*. The Ukrainian name is also matched by parallel expressions in the Belorussian and Russian recensions of Old Church Slavic, see, e.g., *prazdnikъ trubъ*, literally 'the holiday of the trumpets' as well as in Polish, see, e.g., *Święto trąbek* or simply *trąbki*, literally 'trumpets'. The expression is an illusion to the Jewish practice of blowing the ram's horn, the *šōfār*, in the synagogue on the New Year, but as far as I know no Jewish group presently coins such a name for the holiday. The Slavic practice may not be original, since a precedent exists in Latin and

Greek of the late 1st century A.D. and Middle Ages, and in Medieval Spanish, see, e.g., Spanish *pascua del cuerno*, literally 'festival of the horn' (late 15th-early 16th century). An intriguing question is whether such an expression could have been coined by proselytes (or, in the case of Spanish, by Marranos or crypto-Jews). The widespread use of the expression in so many separated areas suggests it is very old. I hypothesize that 'holiday of the trumpets' was an original Jewish term (of proselyte origin?), later superseded in Jewish languages by a written Hebraism *rōš haššānāh* during a period of intensive Judaization.

Particularly interesting are Christian terms for the synagogue. The common term in most European languages is derived from Greek *synagōgē*, which among Jews themselves denoted the Jewish community. *Synagōgē* means literally 'gathering together', which is the meaning of written Hebrew *bēt knɛsɛt*, where *knɛsɛt* is of Aramaic origin; I cannot say whether the Greek or Hebrew expression is original (see chapter 5.11 above). *Synagōgē* enjoys no circulation in Jewish languages, except for Judezmo and Judeo-Portuguese, which use the Greek term in an Arabized form. The Southern Slavs also use translations of 'gathering' to denote the synagogue, e.g., Old Church Slavic *so(n)myšče*, Serbo-Croatian *sàjmište jèvrejsko* (with the adjective 'Jewish'; the first word also means market square, bazaar), *skùpština* (literally 'assembly'), *zbórnica* (literally 'meeting room'); I presume these were all modeled on Greek *synagōgē*.

The Slavic Christian languages are also particularly rich in terms for synagogue that are derived from the native roots for 'God' and/or 'prayer'; a proselyte origin could be entertained for these expressions (in most Jewish languages, the term for synagogue is based on the word for prayer, as in Judeo-Arabic *ṣlā*, Judeo-Chinese *lǐ-baì sì)*. Examples include Czech *modla, modlitebnicě, modlitevnicě* < 'pray', Ukrainian *bohomil'nycja* < 'God' + 'pray' (which also denotes 'devout woman; oratory, place of prayer'), Belorussian *bahamol'nja, inter alia.* None of these terms is used by the coterritorial Jews (but see "Judeo-Belorussian" *bogomolie* below in a different meaning). The Western and Eastern Slavic languages also use the term *škola* (from Greek *sxolē*), used by the Slavic-speaking Jews themselves, for both 'school' and 'synagogue' (see also the Ashkenazic family-name *škol'nik* < Slavic and the translation equivalent *šul'man* < German, literally 'caretaker of a synagogue'). Alternatively, the Christian use of *škola* for 'synagogue' might have been lifted out of the Slavic New Testament, where it was a proselyte innovation (see category I, Greek 2 in chapter 5.11 above).

I should also note that two roots 'God' + 'pray' (not a single root as in the case of *škola*) also serve in some Slavic languages to denote (a) the Jewish prayer shawl (Hebrew *tallīt*, Yiddish *tales*), which has to be worn by Jewish males during certain prayers (either inside or outside the synagogue), see, e.g., Ukrainian *bohomilje* (19th century), Belorussian *bahamolle*, as well as (b) the phylacteries, also required by Jewish males in the recitation of certain prayers (usually outside of the synagogue), see, e.g., Ukrainian *bohomillja* (this is the plural of the term for 'prayer shawl' given above and matches the Yiddish name *tfiln* < Hebrew *tfillīn* which is morphologically plural; the phylacteries actually comprise two leather straps, to be worn on the left arm and forehead). I can cite a Slavic song sung almost uniquely by Jews in the Barysaw area of Belorussia (transcribed in 1928 in Yiddish characters), containing the word (Judeo-Belorussian) *bogomolie* 'phylacteries' (in the singular and with *g*, which is not native to Belorussian!: see Goldberg 1928:596–7). I suppose that the use of the expression 'God' + 'pray' developed the meaning of synagogue by extension as the place where Jews wear the prayer shawl and phylacteries. I do not know the age of the practice of wearing prayer shawls in the Germano-Slavic synagogues.

For further examples from Slavic languages, see Wexler 1987b:118–50.

5.14 Unique Hebrew features of European Jewish languages

I have already noted that expressions that denote aspects of the Jewish religion in the European Jewish languages as a whole occasionally differ from the patterns of discourse in Jewish languages in Africa and Asia (see chapter 5.11 above). These expressions are very important for showing the uniqueness of the European Jewish diasporas. An example was Yiddish *šul* 'synagogue'—a loan translation of Judeo-Greek *sxolē*, literally 'school' (through the intermediary of Slavic *škola*?). Translation equivalents of Greek *sxolē* existed in medieval Judeo-French, Judeo-Provençal and Judeo-Catalan. In contrast, the Jewish languages spoken in Africa and Asia usually denote the synagogue by the native or Hebrew term for prayer (see details in Wexler 1981d).

Another example of the uniqueness of the European Jews as a whole is the terms for food prepared on Friday for consumption on the Sabbath, due to the prohibition of working on the Sabbath. Jewish languages fall into two groups: those which use the adjective 'hot' and those which use the term 'conceal' or a semantically related term (e.g., 'take shelter at night; hem of clothing', etc.). European Jewish languages tend to fall in the first group, Afro-Asian languages in the second. As with the term 'synagogue', Judezmo and Judeo-Portuguese form a minority subset within Europe, since they employ an Arabic term derived from the root 'conceal'—evidence of a North African Arabic origin for most Iberian Jews. Conversely, in opposition to all the other Judeo-Arabic dialects, Moroccan Judeo-Arabic alone prefers the adjective 'hot'. The fact that Judeo-Arabic in Morocco follows a European naming pattern suggests that the southern Judeo-Ibero-Romance languages, Spanish and Portuguese, may have once gone together with northern Judeo-Ibero-Romance, i.e., Catalan (see also discussion of Yiddish *čolnt, šālet ~ šōlet* in category II, Romance 1 in section 5.11 above).

I will not speak at length here of the many innovative Hebraisms used by speakers of Yiddish, since most of these were (a) very likely relatively late neologisms intended to replace non-Jewish patterns of discourse and terms which had become objectionable to the Jews (see the discussion of Judaization in chapter 7 below), or (b) translations of Christian terminology, e.g., Hebrew *qādōš* 'holy' came to denote a 'martyr to the Jewish religion (usually a person killed in a pogrom for refusing to convert to Christianity)'. The Medieval European Christian origin of the second meaning is suggested by the fact that in Mishnaic Hebrew the term for martyr was *nɛhɛrag, harūgē malxūt,* literally 'killed (for the kingdom)' (Blau 1924:234), which (in Latin or Greek translation) is unknown in the earliest Christian writings.

The geography of quite a few Hebrew words in Yiddish reveals early boundaries between the original monolingual French-speaking (later to become Judaized German-speaking) Jewish communities in the extreme southwest of Germany and the Sorbian-speaking (later to become Yiddish-speaking) Jews in the eastern mixed Germano-Slavic lands. An example is the Yiddish expressions for 'dowry': reflexes of Judeo-Aramaic *nədūnjāʾ* predominate in the Western Yiddish dialects (as well as in Judeo-Romance and Judeo-Arabic), while reflexes of a possibly Hebrew *nādān, nədān* surface in the Yiddish of the east of Germany and the Slavic lands. *As far as I know, Eastern Yiddish is the only Jewish language to use this "Hebraism" for dowry.* I theorize that Palestinian Jews may have brought the colloquial Judeo-Aramaic term *nədūnjāʾ* to the Romance lands, where it survived intact since the proselyte component in the local Jewish communities was relatively low. In the Slavic lands, the Jewish proselytes may have originally expressed the concept dowry by a native word. Eastern Slavic languages have a term for dowry that is phonetically similar to contemporary Hebrew *nādān, nədān,* see e.g. Ukrainian *prydane* from *-dane* 'given' and *pry-* a prefix meaning drawing near, a little more. Note also Ukrainian *nadanyj* 'given as a free gift; bestowed', *nadannja* 'granting', *nadaty za molodoju*, West Ukrainian *nadaty za dočkoju* 'give a dowry' (literally 'bestow on a bride/daughter') (< *nadaty* 'give plenty of, bestow'). Hebrew *nādān*, *nədān* also mean sheath, which may have been the original meaning; the latter may have been given the additional meaning dowry in order to Judaize the similar-sounding Slavism (there is no evidence that the dowry and the sheath were in any way connected in ancient Slavic wedding ceremonies). This is tantamount to claiming that *nādān*, *nədān*, in the meaning dowry, are Hebraized Slavicisms and not genuine Hebraisms. (For other examples of the linking of similar-sounding Hebrew and Slavic words, see the discussion of Hebrew *-ān*/Yiddish *-(e)n* ~ Upper Sorbian *-nje* and Hebrew *golɛm* ~ Serbo-Croatian *gòlem*, etc. above.)

Another fissure dividing Western and Eastern Yiddish dialects is the meaning of the Hebrew/Judeo-Aramaic loan *mədīnāh*. In most Western Yiddish dialects, the term means 'city', following Judeo-Aramaic and Arabic practice (with parallels in the Afro-Asian Jewish languages, including Ukrainian Khazar Hebrew) vs. Eastern Yiddish which prefers the meaning 'state' (which is the modern normative written Hebrew meaning as well). In the eastern German lands, both meanings of *mədīnāh* often coexist, as for example in the 15th-century Hebrew writings of rabbi Iserlin. Other Hebraisms which might have been unique to the Slavic-speaking Jews are the term *qɛvɛr* for a Jewish cemetery and Yiddish *pejsex* male name, cited in chapters 5.11 and 5.12 above, respectively.

To conclude, Western Yiddish appears to follow Judeo-Romance and Afro-Asian Jewish languages in the inventory and meanings of Hebrew and Judeo-Aramaic terms and models for translation more closely than Eastern Yiddish, which displays some idiosyncratic terms. Taken as a group though, the European Jewish languages stand apart from the non-European Jewish languages in their corpus of Hebraisms. These two facts suggest the long-standing independence of the north European Jewish diasporas and are fully compatible with my Slavo-Turkic proselyte hypothesis for the Ashkenazic Jews. Indeed, the preference for (literary) Hebraisms over (colloquial) Judeo-Aramaisms in Eastern Yiddish might be a sign that the Hebraisms were later borrowings, introduced under the impact of a Judaization process which delighted in Hebrew component dominance (see the example of *medine* above and chapter 7 below).

5.2 Evidence from religion and folk culture

As I noted in chapter 3 above, the ability to distinguish between native and non-native elements in a language by comparing sets of related languages has no counterpart in the domains of religion and folk culture. Identifying the origin of religious practices, superstitions and folk customs shared by two groups is fraught with difficulties since there is no sure way to distinguish drift between cultures from native inheritance. If, in confronting the similarities between individual Catholic and Jewish prayers, we choose to speak of the diffusion of Jewish practices to early Christianity, that is mainly because the historical relationship of the two religions is known to us, and not so much because the internal "structures" of the two religions provide clues to the origins of common features.

Kraabel, a historian of religion, was well aware of these problems, though he did not propose that linguistics might play a significant role in reconstructing the early history of a religious movement:

> "It is notoriously difficult to comprehend what happens when one religious tradition comes in contact with another. The problem arises first of all from the fact that we approach such a confluence either from one tradition or from the other" (1981:113).

In non-linguistic domains, it is not so clear what sort of elements are more amenable to borrowing by another culture—though scholars write freely as if this were the case. For example, the Jewish musicologist, Idelsohn, suggested that while the folk music of the Jews in any area tends to be heavily influenced by non-Jewish norms, music of the synagogue and prayer resists foreign influences longer (1922:5, 1923:28, 1967:175, 385). Idelsohn does not explain why this should be so. The Jewish folklorist, Rappoport, seems to follow Idelsohn by claiming (again without evidence) that the diffusion of non-Jewish practices predominated in the domain of "Jewish folklore", in opposition to the relatively less permeable, and hence purer, "official/true Judaism" (1937:ix–xi). On the other hand, Baron has written that Jews in Islamic lands entered into all sorts of compromises with the beliefs of the Muslims that resulted in the formation of syncretized beliefs and sectarian deviations in Judaism (5:1957:179). In principle then, Jewish religious music could also be of Muslim provenience.[4] The very fact that

Iberian and Germano-Slavic Jews differ to such an extent in ritual matters suggests that many ritual practices were not originally Palestinian Jewish practices, unless the differences are to be explained as later independent interpretations of common inherited traditions (see Zimmels 1958 and Goldstein 1985:8).

Eidelberg noted that when the rabbis, as the keepers of normative Judaism, failed to extirpate what they regarded as non-Jewish practices, they gave them arbitrary "Jewish interpretations" (1962:99, fn 4). The very act of Judaization exemplifies the ease of cultural diffusion. Identifying the Jewish origins of Jewish customs is a problem in view of subsequent Judaization, i.e., the search for Jewish antecedents for non-Jewish customs in the Palestinian Hebrew and Judeo-Aramaic literature—the Talmud and the Bible. Hence, I cannot agree with Perles that if medieval Jewish practices enjoy a talmudic precedent, they must be, *ipso facto*, of talmudic origin (1880:429). Freehof recognizes that the non-Jewish cultures of Europe might determine which Palestinian Jewish practices would be retained or altered, but by ignoring the non-Jewish origin of most of the Ashkenazic religious and folkloristic practices and by failing to recognize the need to distinguish between genuine inheritance of Palestinian Jewish practices and later borrowings through Judaization, he repeats Perles' error:

> "Of course, as is the case of many medieval [European] ceremonies, there is a foundation or a hint in the Talmud" (1967:216).

Jacob Katz assumed that Judaization was a device for protecting an existing native Jewish religious tradition from the influence of Christianity (1961:46), but the evidence suggests exactly the reverse progression of events, namely, that Judaization was a reaction to the Jewish adherence to non-Jewish beliefs and practices.

Medieval German Jews seem to display a greater awareness of the non-Jewish origins of many of their religious and folkloristic practices than contemporary scholars, and often articulate an interest in eliminating or "Judaizing" them. The process of Judaization in the medieval Ashkenazic communities involved three strategies, which could be activated individually or in pairs:

(a) Reinterpreting elements of the non-Jewish practices in concert with precepts and customs expressed in ancient Palestinian Jewish literature, e.g., the Bible and the Talmud, or by linking passages from the

Bible and Talmud with contemporary practices as a kind of "statement of origin".

(b) Expropriating non-Jewish practices as "genuinely Jewish" whenever they had become obsolete among non-Jews.

(c) Combining elements of non-Jewish and Jewish practices to yield original forms of religious and cultural syncretism.

If we rely exclusively on the Talmud as a repository of Jewish folklore and religious practice, we are apt to get a distorted picture of Jewish culture in the early centuries of our era. Some elements of Palestinian Jewish culture and religious expression that did not find a place in normative Judaism have been incorporated in Christian art and religion (on Christian art forms as a clue to the nature of early Jewish religious art, see Blau 1924, 1926:158, 169, Goodenough 1953–68, Roth 1953 and Hadas 1966:75–6). In some cases, Christian sources provide the only information available to us about non-normative forms of Judaism. On the basis of the rabbinic writings, one would have predicted that the art work found in the synagogue of Dura-Europos in northeast Syria (mid-3rd century A.D.)—with its hundreds of human figures, not a few with pagan associations—would have been impossible due to the orthodox Jewish prohibition of graven images. The frescoes at Dura-Europos are an intermediary stage between pagan and early Christian art. It is worth noting that the famous Hellenistic Alexandrian Jewish philosopher Philo (c. 20 B.C.–c.40 A.D.) is not mentioned once in the rabbinic literature, though he is a Jew whose beliefs might constitute a transition to Christianity; his writings are preserved only in Christian sources. (On the survival of non-normative Jewish practices among non-Jewish populations in Palestine in the early 1st millennium, see discussion below.)

Few researchers have paid attention to the geography and relative chronology of shared phenomena in the coterritorial Jewish and non-Jewish communities. This makes the exploration of the origins of Germano-Slavic Jewish folk customs and religious practices difficult. There is little sensitivity to the question of how to distinguish originally Slavic and Germanic practices and reciprocal influences resulting from several centuries of contacts between Slavs and Germans in the east German lands. Ultimately, we will need to compare Jewish, German and Slavic ethnographic practices as composite systems rather than atomistically feature by feature.

Pollack's work on Jewish folkways is a good example of the methodological imprecision that characterizes much current research in Ashkenazic ethnography. In his investigation of German Jewish folkways, Pollack explicitly states that he will ignore geography, diffusion and local innovations unless the facts are readily known (1971:xiv). He defines as "German" Slavic areas that were at times under German political control or subject to German cultural influence. Thus, he places Bohemia and Moravia on a par with monolingual German areas, and views Jewish culture in Eastern Europe as an extension of German Jewish culture:

> "Bohemia and Moravia were of course influenced [*sic!*] by Slavic culture, but we shall not deal with the Slavic elements in these countries. Bohemia and Moravia will be viewed in terms of their relation to German cultural life, for in the 17th and 18th centuries they were part of Germany [*sic!*]. This geographical area can be regarded as a cultural unit, with Yiddish as the vernacular" (1971:xv).

The failure to appreciate that the "German lands" were (a) populated by both Germans and West Slavs, (b) that the new German ethnic groupings that developed in the east German lands were created through the merger of Germans and Slavs (see Dralle 1991:91), and (c) that Slavs have, throughout recorded history, constituted the majority of the population in Bohemia and Moravia characterizes much of the Jewish scholarship of the last century. For this reason, scholars have tended to equate Ashkenazic Jewry with *German* territories. Consider the remarks by Friedrich S.Krauss, an ethnographer, Max Grunwald, a famous rabbi and folklorist, who founded the Society of Jewish Folklore and the Hamburg Jewish Museum, and Marvin Lowenthal, an American historian of the German Jews, all of whom ignore a "Slavic connection":

> "The majority of Jewry belongs ethnographically to the German people, a minority to the Spanish, Portuguese, Italian, Arab, Persian, Indian, Chinese, Ethiopian, Middle and North African people" (Krauss 1897: 284).

> "Just like the language of the German Jews, their tales and stories, their customs and practices, so too are their superstitions German to the core" (Grunwald 1900:7).

> "Orthodox Jewry as the western world knows it today is to a great extent the heir, when it is not the creation, of German Jewry" (M. Lowenthal 1936:ix).

The claim that Eastern European Jewry is an extension of German Jewry is only true in terms of population movements; in terms of ethnic makeup, the German Jews were probably of Slavic origin, and Ashkenazic customs acquired in the German lands were largely of Slavic origin.

Pollack's investigations are very nearly worthless due to his vague geographical characterizations. In discussing the secular name-giving ceremony for children, which he calls "*holekreisch*" (a Germanized pronunciation of the correct Western Yiddish form [holekrāš]), Pollack writes that it was practiced in "southern Germany, which, roughly speaking, was between the Rhine, the Main, and the Danube" (1971:27). At the time of writing in 1971, the approximate geographical boundaries of this custom in the pre-War period were known. Moreover, Pollack could have considerably improved the quality of his discussion had he recognized the original Slavic origins of much of the population and folklore of the eastern German lands, rather than nonchalantly incorporate Bohemia and Moravia into a "German" zone in the spirit of the early medieval German *Drang nach Osten* or the National Socialist policy of *Lebensraum.*

Pollack's myopia is not unique. Jisrael Ta-Šma's recent study of early Ashkenazic ritual and custom makes only a few passing references to Slavic and German "influences" on the north European Jews (1992:23, 102, 257–8). Ta-Šma rather prefers to ascribe Ashkenazic practices not recorded in the Babylonian Talmud to an Old Palestinian Jewish tradition (on the alleged uniqueness of Ashkenazic religious culture, see ibid.:13, 16, 18).

I am not sure if we can always expect success in identifying pagan Slavic customs among the Jews since many Slavs in the German lands became heavily Germanized and Christianized at an early date; many German folk practices, especially in the east German lands, are in reality of Slavic origin (see Brunner 1925). A clue to the origin of a shared Germano-Slavic custom may come from the linguistic evidence. For example, the male marriage broker characterizes both German and West Slavic societies, but Germans in Bohemia and Silesia productively use Slavic terms for this profession (see paragraph 8 below and Schwarz 1932–3:329–330 and in more detail Bellmann 1971:170, 242–7 under *družba*, etc.). Still there is nothing automatic in the interpretation of linguistic data. For example, Germanic terms such as Yiddish *xale* and *holekrāš* need not rule out an ultimately Balkan Slavic origin of the practices and artifacts (see discussion in category I, Germanic 1 and 3 in chapter 5.11 above).

I submit that the Jews may be a good repository of Old Sorbian folk culture—not because they allegedly "absorbed" Sorbian customs and beliefs, but because they *were* largely Sorbs who preserved their folk culture in a relatively less Germanized and Christianized form. A rare mention of Sorbian-Jewish parallels appears in an early article by Max Weinreich (1924:170–1, citing von Hovorka and Kronfeld 1:1908:75), regarding the shared habit of licking a child's forehead and spitting three times as a protection against the evil eye (see also below on a similar custom among Palestinian Bedouins), but Weinreich stopped short of proposing a link between the shared customs of the two communities. The late Hungarian rabbi and folklorist, Alexander Scheiber, also cited a probable Slavic origin in the practice of parishioners remaining seated for a short while prior to leaving the synagogue (1972). The first citation of this practice comes from the writings of the Frankfurt rabbi Juzfa Hahn (d.1637); the custom was known in Hungary and in the Slavic lands as well, and Scheiber adds a Russian non-Jewish example. Scheiber, however, like most scholars of north European Jewish history and folklore, habitually regarded any custom shared by German and Slavic Jews as a German Jewish custom. However, this time, the existence of the Russian practice encouraged him to prefer a Slavic *non-Jewish* origin for the Jewish practice: "one may presume that the Jews acquired this custom from Slavic circles, even though we first encounter attestation in a German-Jewish writer" (ibid.:205).

The linguistic evidence for the Slavic origin of Yiddish and for the initial migration of Jews within the German lands from east to west should convince scholars of the usefulness of treating old Jewish customs that are practiced in both the German and Slavic lands as probable Slavic customs. Thus, Jewish linguistics and ethnography promise rich rewards to the study of comparative north European religion and folklore.

A particularly neglected aspect of Jewish folklore studies is the relative chronology of the non-Jewish and Jewish elements that go to make up a composite Jewish ritual or superstitious belief (as, e.g., the merger of Palestinian Jewish, Slavic and German pagan/Christian elements that we encounter in the *jorcajt* ceremony of commemorating the anniversary of a relative's death, which I discussed in category I, Germanic 4 in chapter 5.11 above). While a few folklorists, mainly trained in German-speaking universities in the late 19th-early 20th century, have displayed sensitivity to geographical and chronological details (e.g., Max Grunwald, Moritz Güdemann, Alfred Landau and Isidor Scheftelowitz), the current neglect for the precise chronology and origins of Jewish customs is widespread.

The following statements by three contemporary scholars—Pollack, Weinryb (who was aware of the camouflaging goals of Judaization) and Fishman—reflect the general disinterest in chronological precision:

> "There is no apparent conflict between the Jewish cultural and religious heritage and the influences that the German environment had on the preparation of foods. The integration of the tradition of the past with the culture of the present to become part of everyday life is no unique development in Jewish history" (Pollack 1971:112).

> "Contradictions between actual practice and the religious prescriptions which were grounded in the Talmud developed early in Europe. The adopted deviant usage was, however, made acceptable by a fictitious means which helped maintain the unbroken continuity of tradition—making Jewish life appear to be a continuation of that of earlier times. In this way tradition remained unaffected" (Weinryb 1974:968).

> "...each [Jewish language]...has adapted the raw material derived from its linguistic determinant in accord with the needs of its own Jewish cultural framework. Thus, while the Yiddish word [*jorcajt*] is derived from the Germanic determinant of Yiddish, the Yiddish meaning of this word is not native to German and the meaning of the German lexical parallel *(Jahreszeit)* has an entirely different meaning [*sic!*] (= "season of the year") than that of the Yiddish word (= "ritually observed anniversary date of the demise of a relative or a famous Jewish personage"). Obviously [*sic*!], Germanic culture could not provide the word [*jorcajt*] with its Jewish cultural meaning. The number of such words with new (Jewish) cultural meanings is legion, in Yiddish and in all other Jewish diaspora languages" (Fishman 1991:313–4).[5]

Some scholars have assumed that many alleged German customs were adopted by the Ashkenazic Jews in waves, e.g., first after the Crusades in the 12th century and again after the recovery from the ravages of the Black Death in 1348/9. Others have seen the Crusades and Black Death as the cause for the widespread decline in spiritual values and scholarship among the German Jews in the late 14th century (Zimmels 1958:45; Eidelberg 1962:97). Scholem has suggested that German Jewish pietism, or Hassidism, developed in southwest Germany as a reaction to the pogroms and expulsions that came in the wake of the Crusades (1966:41–2).

Often we can recover the chronology of the customs in the Jewish and non-Jewish communities by studying the attitudes of each group to one another's practices. For example, Christians in the late 15th century regarded much of Jewish superstition and magic as somehow special (Hsia 1988:6); almost three centuries later, Schudt (1714) was mocking Jewish customs as "oddities". From such characterizations we can surmise that original German (or Slavic) practices among the Jews had by then become obsolete in the Christian community, and so could be interpreted as "uniquely Jewish". In addition, some German Jewish superstitions of Sorbian origin might never have been known to Germans living in the western, monolingual German lands. *Hence, the practice of Slavic customs by German Jews could enable us to plot the gradual migration of German Jews from east to west within the German lands.* A future goal would be to try to plot the spread of Slavic customs to French Jews. It is reasonable to assume that Slavic customs did indeed reach the French Jews since many Slavic terms are found in French Hebrew writings (see, e.g., Rashi, 1028/1040?–1105); a possible example is given in paragraph 9 below.

An intriguing question is whether the Christian churches were more or less successful in condemning parasacramental eucharistic devotion than the rabbis were in Judaizing pagan customs. Wiehl has shown that much pagan Slavic terminology does not continue in use in the Slavic Christian literature (1974). The fact that the Ashkenazic Jews never conducted witch trials as the Christians did periodically suggests that they may have been more accepting of superstitious practices (Pollack 1971: 116, 288, fn 25). Even after the termination of widespread proselytism, there is evidence that Jews continued to consult Christian priests for cures and incantations (Zimmels 1952:33, 35 gives examples from Poland and Italy in the 17th–19th centuries).

It is important to distinguish between the obsolescence of pagan practices and pagan terms. Often pagan practices persisted with new Christian labels (some of which referred uniquely to these practices), which shows that the church was unsuccessful in extirpating the practices. At the same time, some pagan terms were retained with new Christian meanings, which suggests that the original pagan practices had become obsolete. Hence, the use of a pagan term by Jews would not necessarily be proof of a pre-Christian borrowing by the Jews. In the German lands, a large number of pagan terms continued in use among Christians up to the 12th–13th century (Moser 1964:12, 14, 20-8; Masser 1966:41).

Jewish sources can also shed light on the relative chronology of folklore diffusion from the Christians to the Jews. If the rabbis labeled

Christian practices as "heathen", this is a sign either of dissatisfaction with the fact that the Jews practiced the custom or unfamiliarity with the customs in question. For example, the Jews prohibited bathing in "unclean water", i.e., water upon which a Christian priest had invoked the name of Christ before using it for the water-ordeal (Trachtenberg 1939:227).

Jehuda Hexasid (Speyer 1140-Regensburg 1217), the author of the famous *Sefer xasidim*, observed that the behavior of the German Jews was everywhere like that of the Christians (see Edelmann 1966:63). Such a statement suggests that Judaization had not yet become a productive process. However, the Hebrew language of *Sefer xasidim* is noticeably original in style and syntax, and not all the peculiarities can be explained by interference from the author's presumably native Rhineland German dialect (ibid.:60–1). Hence, I could assume that this book might have been an early Hebrew translation of a text composed originally in a language other than German (e.g., Slavic?), which has since been lost. This might account for the presence in the text of a Greco-Slavic term for werewolf which is unattested in coterritorial Christian literature (though the concept was certainly known to the Germans; see category I, Greek 5 in chapter 5.11 above). All of the western German Hebrew literature of the period should be reexamined for its possible retention of a differential Slavic impact unknown among Christians. Hexasid's claim may well have been imprecise.

An important question is the synthesis of pagan-Christian and Jewish customs in Medieval northern Europe. In general, the likelihood that Palestinian Jewish customs (in varying forms of purity) could survive in their new northern European locale largely depended on the degree of overlap with the coterritorial non-Jewish practices. Maximal overlap could guarantee the retention of a Palestinian Jewish custom in the German lands; Palestinian customs that enjoyed no backing in the new environment would be likely to fall into disuse, despite their talmudic pedigree. This would account for the anti-talmudic stance of the *Sefer xasidim* on a number of practices, e.g., Hexasid mocked the talmudic belief that if the hearth fire were high, or if sparks flew out of the oven, this was a sign of an imminent visit (Scheftelowitz 1925:134–5). Another example is Iserlin's preference for a white rooster in the expiatory *kappārōt* ceremony even though the Talmud hinted against it (Avoda zara 13b; see Eidelberg 1962:49 and further discussion below). Jicxak of Tyrnau (late 14th century, of Austrian or Slovak descent) even stated that folk customs might take precedence over the laws of the

Torah (see the introduction to his *Sefer minhagim,* reprinted Warsaw 1909, cited by Eidelberg 1962:97; see also Heler 1939:604). Note the Yiddish saying, *a mineg brext a din* 'a custom overrides the law', for which a Hebrew translation equivalent is attested in the 11th century (see Ta-Šma 1992:30). Thus, numerous Old Palestinian customs recorded in the Talmud are now missing among the Ashkenazic Jews (see examples above). Future research needs to determine the extent to which Jewish practices could maintain inherited or innovative elements not supported by parallel Christian customs.

Quite a few Old Palestinian customs (regardless of their ultimate origin) that were discarded by diaspora Jews still survive among some Palestinians, Bedouin Arabs and Samaritans (the latter now number only about 500 members). For example, members of the Jawārīš tribe of Bedouins in Israel believe that they are descended from Jews (Kressel 1992:83). The custom of putting the saliva of a holy man into a child's mouth and breathing on him as a means of protection against evil spirits and of imparting properties of the holy man to the child was practiced by Jews in Palestine in the talmudic period and was still attested among Bedouin in the late 19th century (Blau 1898:34–5, 208, fn 8; see also Finkelstein 1938 and the comment by M.Weinreich above). On the Old Palestinian Jewish custom of painting the cattle red as protection against the evil eye, see Morgenstern 1973:8, 162, 195, fn 16, 261, fn 231 (on the color red, see paragraph 1 below). A number of scholars have noted that the Samaritans retain some popular beliefs and traditions that were once current among the Jews during the Second Temple period (M.Gaster 1971a:727; on genetic studies of the Samaritans, see Bonné-[Tamir] 1966, 1980), while Kahle regarded the Samaritan pronunciation of Hebrew as a means of reconstructing the earlier pronunciation of Hebrew among Jews (where?) in the early Middle Ages (1956:181). The Samaritans have also been held up as the racial standard of the ancient Jews (though usually in impressionistic discourse devoid of factual underpinning):

> "...it may be reasonably hypothesized that they [the Samaritans] more closely resemble the Hebraic people of the Old Testament than do the much more heterogeneous and widely disparate Jews of North Africa, Iraq, India, and especially of Europe" (Jamieson 1982:147).

Another important goal of Jewish folklore research is to determine which customs shared by Jews and Christians are the result of diffusion (or even rediffusion) from the Jewish to the Christian community (see

Güdemann 1880:211, 218). We can identify instances of (re)diffusion only if we can be sure of the ultimate Jewish origin of the practices. For example, the Christian superstition against starting a new job on Saturday, since that was the end of the week, could conceivably be of Jewish origin; there is a Babylonian Jewish precedent for this belief as well, but since Babylonian customs cannot spread directly to north European Christians, a Jewish intermediary could be postulated (see Scheftelowitz 1925:136). Russian slang and Bavarian German have terms used in the meanings of holiday, Friday or Saturday—the two days which overlap with the Jewish Sabbath when work is proscribed, e.g., Orel Russian (slang of saddlemakers) *piterik* 'holiday' seems to be from *pjat'* '*five*', the basis for *pjatnica* 'Friday' (literally, 'the fifth day'); Bavarian German *Feierabend* 'Saturday' ~ standard German 'eve of a holiday, evening of rest, time for leaving off work'. For a detailed discussion of possible Jewish influence in Balkan Slavic names for 'Sunday', see Flier 1985.

An important goal of comparative Jewish ethnographic research is to determine the relative receptivity of each Jewish diaspora to coterritorial non-Jewish superstitions. Blau thought that the Greek Jews in the Hellenistic period were more receptive to non-Jewish superstitions than their Palestinian coreligionists (1898:96), while Lieberman believed the Old Palestinian Jews practiced fewer superstitions than the Babylonian Jews (1942:110). Scheftelowitz singled out Babylonia and Germany as areas where the resident Jews had undergone considerable change under the influence of the neighboring religion (1925:vii–viii), and Ta-Šma reckoned that non-Jewish occult practices had more impact on the German Jews than on Babylonian or Old Palestinian Jews (1992:103). Babylonia, Greece and the Germano-Slavic lands were all areas of active Jewish proselytizing (see chapter 6 below).

Positing the age and origin of north European Jewish customs can be facilitated by studying Jewish folklore in a comparative framework. For example, the growing of sidelocks by orthodox Jewish males, known as Yiddish *pejes*, Hebrew *pē'ōt*, is found, *inter alia*, both in northern Europe and in parts of Libya (Andree 1881:205). Could the similarity between the two Jewish groups be coincidental, rather than inherited? Among Libyan Jews, we might reckon with an Arab custom, while the European Jews may have been following a now discarded Christian custom. Alternatively, the talmudic precepts may have been continued without interruption in one Jewish community, but lost and later reinstated under non-Jewish influence or through subsequent Judaization in another Jewish community (see also discussion of *pejes* and the breaking of the glass in North Africa below). In many instances, we can posit a relatively late diffusion of Judaized Ashkenazic customs to the Sephardic Jews, see, e.g., the practice of (Yiddish) *tašlex, kapores, jorcajt* (the last term was also diffused), and the breaking of a glass at a wedding (see Zimmels 1958:8 and discussion under paragraph 2 below).

The eleven examples of Jewish folklore, superstition and religious practices that I will discuss below presumably had a European non-Jewish origin. Wherever possible, I will cite attempts by Ashkenazic rabbis to give a genuine Jewish "pedigree" to the non-Jewish customs. Customs which involve interesting linguistic data were already discussed in chapter 5.11 above. The examples are intended to be a preliminary sample of the relevant data; I expect that the corpus will expand as additional customs are studied.[6]

1. The color red

The color red had magical properties in Palestinian Jewish culture. For example, the Talmud approved tying red knotted strings around a child's neck to protect against illness, but condemned the tying of a red string on the finger as a pagan custom and did not recommend the color red for men's garments (Scheftelowitz 1912:47). A fox tail, because it was red, had similar powers of protection against spirits (ibid., 1925:63, fn 1). Liljental reports that in talmudic times trees from which fruit fell down were painted red as a sign of the evil eye (1924:251–2). There are parallels among the European Jews: a red bridal veil was favored by Slavic Jews for protection against the evil eye (ibid.:81; see also discussion of Yiddish *fačejle* in category 2, Romance 3 in chapter 5.11 above); the color red also has negative connotations in two Yiddish proverbs (Bernstein 1908:62, 256).

In Europe the Jewish superstitions connected with the color underwent change, under the influences of coterritorial pagan and Christian traditions. Despite the talmudic prohibition against tying a red string around the finger, European Jews did tie a red string around the waist as protection against the evil eye—in a wide area encompassing Austria, Bohemia, Germany, Poland (including Silesia) and Rumania. In Serbia and Hungary, non-Jewish women during pregnancy tie a red ribbon on their middle finger. Sosnovik reports that among Polish Jews a red thread around the neck or head checked a nosebleed (1924:168, #38; for a similar practice in Germany, see Taylor 1:1949:447). Among Christians the negative quality of the color red found expression in the tradition that Judas Iscariot had red hair (Mellinkopf 1982:46). See also paragraph 2 below.

In the Leipzig *Maḥzor*, an illuminated Jewish prayer book produced in southwest Germany between 1310–30, a Jewish male is portrayed wearing a *tallīt*, or prayer shawl, with red stripes (see the illustration in Krüger 1968:37; Metzger and Metzger 1982:142, #197). Usually the stripes on the *tallīt* are blue or black, and this color preference continues in force today. Metzger and Metzger made the following comment: "The red stripes that appear in the Leipzig *Maḥzor* can only be due to an unexplained fantasy of the painter" (ibid.:150). Curiously, the two Metzgers make no comment on the red stripes on the prayer shawl depicted in a manuscript from Florence 1492 (New York, Jewish Theological Seminary of America, MS, Acc.No.03225, folio 125 verso) which they reproduce on p.142 (#197). In view of the properties of the color red in both the Palestinian Jewish and pagan European traditions, it should not be surprising to find red stripes on the *tallīt*. The extreme rarity of a prayer shawl with red stripes in Jewish illustrations suggests that the non-Jewish preference for red as a protective color may have been successfully extirpated by the rabbis. On the impossibility of red *tfillīn*, or phylacteries, see Abrahams 1896:274 (they are customarily made of black leather).

On the function of red in Jewish and other cultures, see Elworthy 1895:135, 137; Preuss 1910; Scheftelowitz 1912:45–7, 1925:63; Mengis 1935–6; Marmorstein 1936:421–2; Trachtenberg 1939:135, 137; Rowe 1972:357-8; Scholem 1972:28; Morgenstern 1973:284–5; Hadas-Lebel 1979:466; Mellinkopf 1982.

2. The smashing of a glass against the wedding stone on the outer north wall of the synagogue or on the floor at the close of the wedding ceremony

This custom illustrates vividly the difficulty of identifying the origins of a custom due to the multiplicity of potential sources:

> "It is difficult to say if also this breaking of the glass, like the mourning garb of the bridal pair, dampens the overflow of joy, and should remind one of death and seriousness, as it was once said in the Talmud, or was intended to represent the grieving over Zion and Jerusalem, or finally was a symbol of the legality of the performance of the wedding ceremony, as in the old German law the breaking of a staff marked the legality of the expressed judgement" (Holzer 1934:178–8).

It was the practice at an Ashkenazic Jewish wedding to fling a glass against a fixed point on the outer north wall of the synagogue, known as the "star stone" (see also the discussion of the *māgen dāvid* in category 1, Germanic 6 in chapter 5.11 above). In this practice, the Jews were following the widespread non-Jewish tradition of regarding the north as the direction from which the devil was likely to appear; the noise of the glass breaking was intended to ward off evil spirits. Nevertheless, some Jews attempted to give a different interpretation to the north. Ja'akov ben Moše Halevi Mölln (the "Maharil", c.1360–1427) saw the significance of the north in the passage of Job 37:22, stating that out of the north came golden splendor; one should face the north to acknowledge the source of one's sins (see Steiman 1963:90–1). The earliest reference to the (inner!) north wall ceremony comes from a description from Mainz provided by a student of Mölln's (see Güdemann 1880:125, 127). An Italian prayerbook produced in Pesaro, Italy in 1481 mentions the ceremony in the text but the accompanying illustration of the conferring of the marriage contract does not allude to the custom (Metzger and Metzger 1982:293, fn 124). Kretzenbacher descibes the Christian belief that the devil came from the north, noting that between the 10th and 13th centuries there were occasional attempts to neutralize the north in church liturgy and architecture (1987:307, 321). An open question is whether the disappearance of this belief among Christians paralleled the diminishing use of the northern synagogue wall for the glass-smashing ceremony among Jews.

Feuchtwanger assumes that the glass-breaking ceremony originated in Palestine, from where it was carried to the diaspora communities (1986:31). In that case, the innovation of non-Jewish German origin would have been the addition of the north wall as the target for the glass. However, Babylonian Jews put ashes on the bridegroom's head to deceive the demons into thinking that the wedding couple were in mourning and not about to celebrate a joyous event (see Lieberman 1942:105). This fact suggests that the glass-smashing ceremony against demons may have been a European Jewish innovation that replaced the ash ceremony (if the latter was ever transported from Palestine to the European Jews).

At an unknown date, the glass came to be broken against the floor in certain areas. The floor was used in Frankfurt at least by 1714, since Schudt mentions it in his book of Jewish customs (see also Andree 1881:145, and illustration #21 of the synagogue in Edelfingen, northern Württemberg, Germany, in P. and H.Goodman 1965). The floor is also favored (since when?) in Eastern Europe, but Jews in Franconia, a locale intermediate between Eastern Europe and Frankfurt, used the wall (ibid.). In linguistics, the significance of such a geographical pattern would be that the exceptional feature in the center was an innovation, while the common practice found at the two extremities of the territory was original. Teimanas claims that the wedding ceremony among the East European Jews was originally conducted outdoors in the synagogue courtyard (1933:148).

In his description of the 13th-century synagogue in Worms, Böcher writes that the east wall of the synagogue originally held the wedding stone in the form of a lion (1959:35). This is the only reference in the literature to an eastern wall. Could Böcher have been in error, or was he recording an attempt to Judaize the custom by substituting the east—with its reference to Jerusalem—for the pagan north?

To judge from the early rabbinical literature, the rabbis were initially antagonistic to the glass-breaking ceremony which they defined as non-Jewish; unable to extirpate the custom from among the folk, the rabbis sought to imbue the custom with a Jewish interpretation. Namely, that the purpose of the glass-breaking was to remind the wedding couple of the sorrow over the destruction of the Temple in Jerusalem and had nothing to do with neutralizing the intentions of the devil. The rabbinical literature frequently cites talmudic references to two weddings in which glasses were broken in protest against the lavishness of the affairs. These references were meant to give a Jewish underpinning to the pagan wedding custom. The artificiality of the rabbinic interpretation is clear from the fact that while the Talmud has two mentions of glass-smashing, it does not recommend institutionalizing the glass-breaking as a religious act (on the search for talmudic passages, see Freehof 1967:216–7, 221, Holzer 1934 and Feuchtwanger 1986:31). The original anti-demon function still remains clear; after all, if the destruction of the Temple were the original issue, then why would the wedding stone at Memmelsdorf, Unterfranken 1729 bear a Hebrew text that read "voice of bliss and joy, voice of groom and bride", which hardly fits with the destruction of the temple? Also, after the glass had been smashed, the guests traditionally shouted *māzāl ṭōv*, Hebrew for 'good luck' (Raphael 1974:194).

Quite a number of explanations for the custom continue to circulate in the literature, alongside the "official" rabbinical interpretation. Andree suggested that the pieces of glass symbolized the removal of hatred and jealousy (1881:145). Consider also an English Christian's description of the signing of the Jewish betrothal agreement in the early 18th century, an act marked by a similar crockery-breaking ceremony (which has immediate Christian parallels in the German lands):

> "A priest [i.e., rabbi] takes a glass of wine in his hand, and pronounces some prayer and then takes a new pipkin [small earthenware pot], and flings it down on the floor, before the feet of the bridegroom, with a force that breaks it into many pieces. Bachelors generally strive to carry off a bit of the broken pipkin believing it likely to promote their being married soon after" (Mears 1738:20, first set of pagination).

In his comment on the wedding ceremony itself, Mears comments on the significance of the glass ceremony: "by way of putting himself [the bridegroom] in mind, that we are only like brittle ware made of earth, glossy without, and ruff within" (1738:19). This is a novel interpretation. but Mears hastens to add that the glass-breaking wards off bad luck (compare the symbolism of "fragility of matrimonial bliss" attributed to the breaking of a soup terrine among south Moravian Germans in 1895 described by Rottleuthner 1985:34). A few years earlier, in Germany, Kirchner had written that the breaking of a pot on the floor at the Jewish engagement ceremony was a symbolic act; just as a broken pot could not be put back together, so too could a promise not be taken back. Also the couple took shards of the pot for friends and parents; if one of the latter died in marriage, pieces were to be placed on the eyes of the deceased (1726:172, 218, fn c).

The breaking of crockery at the signing of the marriage contract has characterized German practice at least since the Middle Ages (Drechsler 1:1903:244) and is also a part of Slavic wedding practice. The analogous German custom is known as *Polterabend*, and is also practiced by the Sorbian population in east Germany (Schneeweis 1953:24, 39, 107; on *Polterabend*, see Güdemann 1888:130, Wuttke 1900:185 and Trachtenberg 1939:160). Among Germans, especially in the north and central regions, according to Wuttke (1900:369), the ceremony of *Polterabend* is performed before the house of the bride and the groom on the night before the wedding (or on *Fastnacht* 'Shrove Tuesday': ibid.:84). The belief is that the more pots broken, the more the money accumulated for the wedding couple (Gander 1890:456). In East Prussia, Poles also break a glass the day before the wedding (Szyfer 1976:421). On the breaking of a goblet (by throwing it over a horse or one's shoulder) in the Ukrainian wedding ceremony, see Stscherbakiwskyj 1952–3:335, 337–8 (note the feature of "throwing behind one's back" in the cemetery ceremony, discussed under paragraph 9 below). Curiously, European Romá (Gypsies) regard the broken glass as bad luck (T.H. Gaster 1980:119–21). Note the Yiddish expression *brexn teler* 'enter into a betrothal' (literally 'to break dishes').

The parallels of the Jewish glass-breaking custom with wedding customs practised by both Slavs and Germans are striking. Consider Krauss' description of the South Slavic practice of smashing the glass at a wedding over a century ago:

> "The husband's brother invites the bridal couple to eat and entertains them. After eating, the bride, following a command of the master of ceremonies, undresses the groom; the latter takes off the garland from the bride's head, braids up her hair and unties her belt. The master of ceremony places them in the bed, covers them and locks the doors upon withdrawing. As soon as he steps back into the room with the guests, he takes up a full glass of wine, offers a toast before the godfathers to the wellbeing of the bridal couple, empties the glass in one gulp, and flings it with full force against the doors, so that it smashes to pieces" (1885:458–8).

Wuttke has the following description of the glass-breaking ceremony performed after the wedding ceremony in the church in various parts of Germany—all of which, except for Pfalz, once had Slavic settlements:

> "Both [bride and groom] must drink a glass with one another, so that harmony remains between them (East Prussia); they are presented with two glases of wine; the one who takes the glass and drinks it down first gains control (Thüringen, Upper Pfalz); then the glass is passed from hand to hand; the last person throws it away, so that the marriage will be happy (Upper Pfalz), or the bride throws it backwards over her head; if it smashes, then the marriage will be happy; for that reason people also smash it with force (Upper Pfalz, Vogtland)" (1900:373).

The ceremony of breaking some vessel at the wedding was recorded among Christians in Milan in 1565 (H.Lewy 1927:194, 1930:247). Güdemann (1888:122) related a similar custom practiced by the Jews in Tripoli, Libya in the late 19th century, which called for the smashing of a pot with water on the street in memory of the temple and the throwing of an egg by the bride on the outer and inner wall of the bedroom. This appears to have been a custom also practiced by Muslims as protection against the evil eye. It is unclear how old this practice is and whether it is historically related to the Ashkenazic practice at the contractual ceremony. I am reminded of the fact that in parts of Serbia, the *koljivo*, a dish holding food for the dead, is also broken on the ground—perhaps a contemporary parallel of the broken vessels found in open graves in the zone of the so-called prehistoric Lausitz culture (Schneeweis 1953:68).[7]

The relative preference for breaking glasses and crockery among Jews and Christians should be checked in each area; it would be interesting to ascertain whether Jews consciously sought to distance themselves from the specific practices of their immediate Christian neighbors. Sometimes Jews and Christians share conceptual elements but differ in the details of the actual practices. For example, among Germans in Bielsko-Biała (German Bielitz, southern Poland) the bridal couple on their way to the ceremony had to "buy" permission to circumvent a rope blocking the road; the rope was intended to keep witches and demons from following the couple to the church (the rope corresponds to the breaking of the glass in the Jewish ceremony); often the rope was decorated with red bands (Kauder 1923:37—on the properties of the color red, see paragraph 1 above).

Contemporary illustrations of the German Jewish ceremony of breaking the glass and crockery or the star stone exist since the early 1700s. For example, Kirchner shows a picture of an outdoor procession and synagogue stone (1726:179), the view under the wedding canopy (ibid.:180), the throwing of the glass against the star stone of the synagogue (ibid.:185), the star stone called *sigillum Salomonis* with the caption that the stone has power against the devil (thus, it is also called the *Scutum Davidis* or *Schild Davids* 'shield of David, *māgen dāvid*' : ibid.: 184–5—on the *māgen dāvid*, see also category I, Germanic 6 in chapter 5.11 above); see also Liebe 1903, 77, #62 (c.1700), 102, #82 (Fürth 1705—the old synagogue, constructed in 1616, but remodeled in 1697—hence the age of the star stone is unclear), 110, #90 (Nürnberg 1726); P. and H.Goodman 1965, illustrations #20 (Bingen), #21 (Edelfingen—where the stone was embedded in the floor of the synagogue); K.Katz et al. 1968:211, #180 (Kirchner's etching); 212, #181 (Bingen, c. 1700); Eschwege 1980, 68, #28 (Fürth 1705); 74, #40 (Memmelsdorf, Unterfranken 1729); 84, #58 (Nürnberg 1713–66—etching by Paul Nusbigel). See also Landau 1898. It is significant that all the etchings were done by Christians. I would theorize that the absence of Jewish illustrations may be because the ceremony was associated primarily with the lower classes, or was still regarded fairly widely as part of the pagan heritage that had not yet been thoroughly Judaized. Curiously, an Italian Jewish document from Pesaro 1481 (Budapest, Hungarian Academy of Sciences, MS.A 380/II, folio 27 recto) omits depiction of the glass-breaking ceremony, but does depict the sacrifice of the cock during the New Year (*kappārōt:* see paragraph 6 below).

In the Ashkenazic Jewish ceremony the benediction over the bridal couple is pronounced while the latter are standing under a bridal canopy, called in Yiddish *xupe* (< Hebrew *ḥuppāh*). However, in Sephardic circles, the couple are seated under the canopy, called in Judezmo *talamo,* (North African) *talamon* (< Greek *θalamos* 'bridal chamber': see category I, Greek 3 in chapter 5.11 above). In non-Jewish Catalan, the Grecism denotes a receptacle for carrying the (seated) holy relics in a procession, e.g., Catalan *tàlem.* I wonder whether the early Ashkenazic Jews also had the custom of sitting rather than standing under the canopy. In Yiddish, the Grecism is found in the western dialects, but in the meaning of a bier, see, e.g., Dutch Yiddish *uftolmen* 'place on a bier'—which matches Sicilian Italian *tàlamu* 'bier'. The differences between the Sephardic and Ashkenazic use of the wedding canopy (and their possible origins) have yet to be studied. Illuminated manuscripts from the late 13th century show the Ashkenazic couple standing (P. and H.Goodman 1965, illustration #24), but Ašer ben Jexiel (c. 1250–1327) mentions that the couple sat before the ceremony (Freehof 1963).

3. The house amulet

Jews are enjoined to attach an amulet containing biblical pasages on each doorpost in their home. The amulet is called in Hebrew *məzūzāh,* Yiddish *mezuze.* In parts of Europe, the *məzūzāh* was believed to have protective power (e.g., in late 12th-century Metz, France). The Iberian Jews, however, objected to the tradition of ascribing protective functions to the *məzūzāh* (see the writings of Moše ben Majmon, better known as Maimonides, the famous Iberian philosopher, Córdoba 1135-Tiberias 1204). The belief in protective functions may have spread from Palestine and Babylonia to Europe (Aptowitzer 1910; Trachtenberg 1939:153). The condemnation of associating protective functions with the amulet in northern Europe (e.g., by a number of French and German rabbis, such as the French Ja'akov ben Meir Tam, c.1100–71, and Meir of Rothenburg, c.1220–83: see Baron 5:1957:58, 317, fn 72 and 318) may explain why the *məzūzāh* was rarely shown in Jewish illuminated manuscripts (an early exception is an Italian manuscript, possibly from Ferrara c.1470: K.Katz 1968:201, #170). In northern Europe the belief that the *məzūzāh* had magical properties disappeared by the 15th century (Baron 5:1957:149).

In Babylonia, the rabbis had to accept the interpretation of protection against demons in order to get the lax Babylonian Jews to use the *məzūzāh* (Bank 1894:94, fn 1). The rabbis sought to neutralize the belief in protection against demons by connecting the amulet with biblical passages, such as Deuteronomy 6:4–19 and 11:13–20 (Trachtenberg 1939:146). The phylacteries, Hebrew *tfillīn*, apparently were also ascribed magical functions by the Jews, since the Church Council of Laodicea (near Denizli, Turkey) in the 4th century outlawed them as magical amulets (Feldman 1989:296).

A Slavic equivalent of the *məzūzāh* is the Sorbian horseshoe (Schneeweis 1953:153); also pagan Slavs placed a female cult figure in a corner of the dwelling (see Wustrow, cited by Łosiński 1975:643). On the rural Czech practices of placing small coins in the foundation of a new house, or a horseshoe on the frame of the window, door, or doorstep, or placing pussy willows behind a picture- or doorframe, see Salzmann and Scheufler 1974:110, 114.

4. Sidelocks and beards grown by orthodox males

There is considerable disagreement over the chronology of the orthodox Jewish practice of growing sidelocks (Hebrew *pēʾōt*, Yiddish *pejes*) and beards. This is because rabbinical exhortations in the medieval literature were not necessarily followed by the masses of Jews and because the positive identification of sidelocks on medieval representations of Jews is often difficult. For example, Raddatz claims that sidelocks and beards were advocated since the 11th century in the spirit of talmudic injunctions (1990:788), but Metzger and Metzger date the practice of growing sidelocks to the late 16th century (1982:147). While Blumenkranz did not identify sidelocks in medieval Christian illustrations of Jews after the 15th century (1965, 30, #27; 37, #38; 51–2, #61—the last is a late medieval fresco from Landau/Pfalz), he did claim subsequently to be able to identify sidelocks in Christian depictions of Jews as early as the 12th century (1966b).

The requirement to grow sidelocks is not mentioned in the Old Testament, nor is it found in Old Egyptian depictions of Jews. Presumably, it is a post-biblical practice. The passage in Leviticus 19:27 is not a clear precedent, since it merely forbids cutting the head hair in a circle (Gressmann 1920). Bearded Jews are common in Christian manuscripts since the 13th century, but this might have been stereotyped practice and thus need not prove that Jews generally wore beards.

Jews are also portrayed frequently in medieval illuminations without beards (e.g., in Margaritha 1530). Rabbi Iserlin regarded long hair as a non-Jewish custom (Eidelberg 1962:121), and thus recommended that Jews should cut their hair short (ibid. and fn 33). But in 13th-century woodcuts, Jews often appear bearded (ibid.:122). In the illustrations of a Polish Jewish prayer book from the late 15th century, Jewish males are not shown with long hair (Fishof 1986-8:79, #13), though figures are bearded (ibid.:81, ##15, 19).

The Slavs traditionally did not cut a child's hair before the age of seven, for fear that the child would lose its intelligence (Glapa 1970: 250). Slavic priests were distinguished by their long hair and beard while the laiety wore short hair (Potkański 1895:330–422; Urbańczyk 1964; Swoboda 1970b:489). On the style of wearing hair long in 15th-century Poland, see Zamoyski 1988:58. See also paragraph (c) of chapter 6.3 below. The practice of orthodox Jewesses shaving their heads upon marrying and of wearing a wig perpetually has a partial parallel in the practice of some Slavic societies whereby a bride cuts her hair upon marrying (but not permanently: see Stscherbakiwskyj 1952–3:345).

I wonder if the fact that bearded Jews are usually portrayed in Jewish illuminations while performing a ceremonial act (see illustrations in Metzger and Metzger 1982) is a sign that beards (and long hair) were originally most characteristic of the clerical class—as in pre-Christian Slavic societies.

Literature: Pollack 1971:256–7.

5. The water ceremony of washing away one's sins during the High Holidays

This custom, known in Hebrew as *tašlīx*, Yiddish *tašlex*, was first mentioned in Mölln's *Minhage maharil* (c.1360–1427). The Iberian scholar Josef Karo (Toledo 1488–Palestine 1575) has no mention of it, which suggests either that he disapproved of it or was ignorant of the practice altogether. Unable to eliminate this non-Jewish custom, Ashkenazic rabbis made up the story that the fish, to which one threw crumbs of food from one's garments during the ceremony, were like man caught in the net (Scheftelowitz 1914b:373). Lauterbach shows that the *tašlīx* ceremony in its present form dates from about the 14th century (1936:302–3), while the prayer itself does not appear to be earlier than the Middle Ages (ibid.:314). The *tašlīx* custom was practiced by

Christians in 13th-century Cologne, to judge from an eye-witness account by the Italian writer, Petrarca. In some Slavic communities, there was also a belief in a water-goddess, see, e.g. Old Russian **beregyn'i* (R.Eckert 1977).

The non-universality of this practice among non-Ashkenazic communities suggests that *tašlīx* may be relatively recent among the Ashkenazic Jews. Future studies in Jewish ethnography should collect and map the geographical distribution of other propitiatory customs (see Baumgartner's description of the "Adonis gardens" among Italian Jews, which had a precedent in Old French Jewish writings of the 11th century: 1946:136–7; see also Lévi 1911).

Herzog notes that in some areas of northern Poland, Yiddish speakers pronounce the custom *tešlex*, presumably under the influence of the homophonous Yiddish *tešlex* 'little pockets' (1965:51–2 and figure 3.2). Herzog explains the confusion with 'little pockets' by the fact that the custom involved cleansing oneself of sins by symbolically emptying one's pockets into the water. He further assumes that the more widespread Yiddish name of the custom, *tašlex*, is the original term, derived from Hebrew *tašlīx* (literally 'you will throw'), the first word of the prayer pronounced on the occasion. A problem with this analysis is that it is unusual to denote a religious custom by the first word of a Hebrew prayer; at best, only a major prayer might be so called (e.g., *kol nidre*, the opening words of a major prayer pronounced on the eve of the Yom Kippur ceremony). Hence, I submit that the term 'little pockets' might have been original, and Yiddish *tašlex*, Hebrew *tašlīx* constitute a later attempt at Judaization (see Lauterbach above on relative chronology). As Herzog notes, the name *tešlex* survives in precisely those areas where Yiddish speakers do not use *tešlex* as the diminutive plural of 'pocket'; here, the term for 'pocket' is *kešene* (which Herzog derives from Polish *kieszeń*, but the Belorussian *kišėnja* might be more appropriate). Unfamiliarity with the meaning of *tešlex* might have preserved the term, at least as the name of the custom. Unfortunately, ignorance of when *tešlex* 'small pockets' became obsolete impedes establishing a relative chronology for the Judaization process in northern Polish locales. The striking number of idiomatic expressions involving the term "pocket" in Polish and the Eastern Slavic languages calls for a study of the role of the pocket in pre-Christian Slavic folklore.

The custom of burning a straw doll and then throwing it into the water or burning it as a symbol of throwing out the old year is found among Slovaks in the area between Nitra and Košice and among Hungarians. In Slovak, the doll is known as *kyseľ*, in Hungarian as *kisze* or *kiszi* (Manga 1956:448). By containing the elements of water and turning over of the new year, the Slovak-Hungarian custom resembles both Jewish expiation customs of *tašlīx* and *kappārōt*.

See also the discussion of German slang *klabot*, etc. and *hilūxə* in chapter 5.11 above.

Literature: Brück 1837:23ff; Trachtenberg 1939:165–6; Sadan 1960.

6. The ceremony of sacrificing a fowl during the High Holidays as a scapegoat for man's sins

Medieval rabbis differed in their attitude towards this practice, known in Hebrew as *kappārōt*, in Yiddish as *kapores*. It was opposed by Josef Karo, following condemnation by the Catalan scholars Nahmanides (1194–c.1270) and Šlomo ben Adret (1235–1320—who noted that the custom was formerly practiced in Barcelona: see also Scheftelowitz 1925:32, 47ff and Zimmels 1958:81, 248).

On the other hand, the Babylonian Jewish scholar Haj Gaon (c.1000) and German rabbis like Mordexaj of Nürnberg (13th century), Ašer ben Jexiel (c.1250–1327) and Ja'akov ben Moše Halevi Mölln (the Maharil, c.1360–1427) favored the practice. In his 16th-century commentary to Josef Karo's *Šulxan arux*, Moše Iserles (c.1525–72) removed Karo's objection (Scheftelowitz 1925:50). There is an illustration of the practice in an illuminated Jewish prayerbook from Pesaro, Italy 1481 (Metzger and Metzger 1982:247).

Mears, a Christian observor of the English Jews in 1738, described how a Jew would swing a live cock three times over his head and say: "This is my sex; in exchange for me, fowl dies and I go to a life of goodness and peace" (38). The woman did the same with a hen. The butchered fowl was given to indigent Jews, which was also the custom of the German Jews (Scheftelowitz 1925:51).

While the custom has Near Eastern roots, its apparently uninterrupted survival in northern Europe (as opposed to the Iberian Peninsula) may be due to a Slavic and/or Germanic impact. Hens and roosters play a major role in pre-Christian and Christian Slavic and German culture. Up to the end of the 19th century Slavs were daubing a rooster's blood on four corners of a dwelling, in an attempt to soften the anger of the house god (Seweryn 1964:516); the cock was also a typical offering among the Balkan Slavs, when building a home, well or bridge (Grohmann 1864:75; Güntert 1931–2:453). In some Slavic communities, the cock was regarded as a bird of augury (see discussion of Belorussian *kabán* in the basin of the Cna river, a left tributary of the Prypjac' river, in Ossowski 1968). The Eastern Slavic practice of sacrificing a cock to cure sick animals involved walking the animal around in a circle three times (Haase 1939:78; the number three was also noted in Mears' description above).

German Slavs in the pre-Christian period regarded the cock as the personal animal of their god Svantevit (Grohmann 1864:74; Wuttke 1900:34, 291; Güntert 1930–1:1331; see also the discussion of Altenkirchen in paragraph 10 below). The association of the cock with Svantevit may hold a clue as to where the Old Palestinian Jewish custom might have been initially reinforced and restructured in the Germano-Slavic lands, since Svantevit was worshipped primarily on the island of Rügen (north Germany: Wienecke 1940:257). Of course, the worship of this god could have been brought south by Slavs sold into slavery and acquired by Jewish households. Wuttke noted that the Slavs slaughtered a cock at weddings (1900:291), and Kostrzewski (1964b:559) noted that a blackrooster or hen was a pagan Slav offering for spirits on the occasion of a birth, marriage or funeral, but neither author gives geographical details (see also Lewicki 1963:58–9). Note also the Polabian expression *sjǫtə t'übə* 'holy spirit' (17th century) where the second term (< **koba* 'bird of augury') apparently denoted an apparition in the pre-Christian period (Heydzianka-Pilatowa 1971:60).

Germans in the 12th century thought it unhealthy to sleep on a cock's feathers, since the animal was used as a sacrificial offering; hence, the preference for duck or goose feathers (Biegeleisen 1930:140; Wienecke 1940:94). Both Germans and Slavs practiced the custom of slaughtering a hen at different times of the year; thus, at the harvest time, the Sorbs call the cock by a German loan, e.g., Upper Sorbian *honač*, Lower Sorbian *honak* < German *Hahn* (Wuttke 1900:84; von Schulenburg 1934:221–2; Schneeweis 1953:160–1). The earliest mention of the term *kappārāh* 'expiation' (singular of *kappārōt*) in a German Christian source dates from 1494 (Timm 1991a:507). On the killing of a hen during the carnival time in western Hungary, see Lukács 1985.

Literature: Brück 1837:25, 27, 29; Scheftelowitz 1914a, 1914b; Lauterbach 1935; Trachtenberg 1939:163–4; Seweryn 1964:516.

7. The practice of a Jewish male covering his head during prayer, or perpetually

There was no law in the Talmud or Bible which required the covering of the head upon entering a sanctuary or during a religious ceremony (Lauterbach 1928:589). The custom first arose in Babylonia, probably as a carryover from non-Jews (ibid.:590). In Europe, non-Jews regarded the custom as "Jewish". This is a good example of the accidental Judaization of an originally non-Jewish custom as a result of migration, from Babylonia to Europe. The first attestation of the practice in Europe appears to be from Muslim Spain, e.g., the Córdoba-born Maimonides was in favor of the practice, though a late 13th-century Castilian Jewish illumination shows Jews in a building (synagogue?) with uncovered heads (Zirlin 1986-8:66, figure #21). Differences between the Jewish practices of Muslim and Christian Spain might account for the two views.

Most Ashkenazic Jews disagreed with Iberian Jewish practice. The Czech Jicxak ben Moše (c.1180–c.1260) wrote that a bare head was acceptable when praying and some German rabbis agreed, see e.g., Meir of Rothenburg (1215–83: Lauterbach 1928:599), though his German contemporary, David ben Jehuda Hexasid, related that the Ashkenazim, in opposition to the Sephardim, prayed with covered heads (Zimmels 1958:102). Jisrael ben Ptaxja Iserlin of Regensburg (1390–1460) wrote that in saying the benedictions after meals, one should put regular headgear over the scullcaps (see Eidelberg 1962:100). As late as the 16th century in Germany and Poland, Jews often went bareheaded, which was the preference of Šlomo Lurja (a Jerusalem-born Ashkenazic Jew 1534–1572; see Abrahams 1896:280). Covering the head becomes especially common in northern Europe only in the 16th century (Raddatz 1990:788).

A clue to the reason for the change in head-covering norms comes from rabbinic writings. According to David ben Šmuel Halevi (c.1586–1667, active in Lvov, Ostrih and Poznań, and the author of *Ture zahav*), one should always cover one's head in order to draw a clear distinction between Jewish and non-Jewish modes of behavior (Lauterbach 1928: 600; Levy 1963:133; for other examples, see Ta-Šma 1992:140). This practice illustrates clearly how Christianity could influence the formulation of European Jewish religious practice.

Literature: Marmorstein 1928; Jungbauer 1931–2a:532 (for Christian practices).

8. The custom of engaging a marriage broker (usually male), known in Hebrew as *šadxān*, Yiddish *šatxn;* the category of co-parent-in-law

The legal status of this profession dates from the Talmud, but in Europe only from the 12th century (Kahan 1938:77; Zimmels 1958:175;

Steiman 1963:45). The custom still persists among the Jews in Germany and Slavic Europe (Andree 1881:144). It also appears among the Sephardic Jews in Turkey beginning with the 16th century, but the Sephardic custom need not be due to contact with the Germano-Slavic Jews. It is interesting that the practice of engaging a primarily male marriage broker is also characteristic of Slavic societies, e.g., the Sorbs and Ukrainians (see Stscherbakiwskyj 1952–3); on the institution in the pagan Slavic period, see chapter 5.12 above and Russocki 1967:159. On the use of borrowed terms for this profession in Yiddish (from Hebrew) and Sorbian, Polabian and Czech (from German), see Wexler 1991b: 56.

In addition to language-specific terms like Upper Sorbian *družba* 'marriage broker' (see above), there is also a Common Slavic term for the profession which surfaces in Russian and Ukrainian as *svat* masculine, Russian *svat'ja*, Ukrainian *svaxa* feminine. Unlike *družba*, these words also denote a co-parent-in-law, i.e., the term by which the parents of a married couple call themselves. This kinship relationship by marriage seems to be uncharacteristic of Hungarian or German. Curiously, while Yiddish *šatxn* has only the one meaning of marriage broker, Yiddish does share with Slavic the concept of "co-parent", see, e.g., (Eastern) *mexutn* masculine, *mexuteneste* feminine (< Hebrew *məḥūtān, məḥūtɛnɛt* + Judeo-Aramaic *-tāʾ* feminine agentive, respectively). The absence of the concept in Dutch suggests that Dutch Yiddish *mexoten, mexotones(te)* were diffused from German Yiddish, i.e., Judeo-Sorbian; it is unlikely that such kinship terms would have been brought to Dutch Yiddish by Eastern Yiddish-speaking immigrants in the 17th century. To the best of my knowledge, other Jewish languages lack this concept; for example, Turkish has this concept, *dünür*, but it appears to be more common among Muslims than among Turkish-speaking Jews. Note also Romani *xanamík* for 'co-parent' (Hancock 1976:93).

Literature: Güdemann 1888:115; Abrahams 1896.

9. Funeral practices: (a) pouring out the water from the home of a deceased person; (b) ripping up grass and throwing it behind one's back upon leaving the cemetery

The first practice, which is found in a wide variety of cultures in the world, was not mentioned in Jewish sources before the 13th century (Güdemann 1888:210 and fn 6). The Jewish practice has been given a number of interpretations. According to Schudt 1714 (cited by Andree 1881:165, fn 1), the angel of death cleans his poisoned sword in the water found in the home of the deceased, thus rendering the water dangerous. This view appears in the writings of Iserles (though it opposes the Tosefta, a supplement to the Mishnah: Scheftelowitz 1925: 73). A second interpretation claimed that if the water in the house were thrown out after the corpse had been removed the corpse demons would be confused and would not endanger the survivors. A third reason given was that the practice prevented the return of the deceased. Similar ideas predominated in Greece, among the Arabs, and, what is relevant for us, in Germany, to judge from attestation from 11th-century Worms. The custom was known also in France, and earlier than the first Jewish attestation (Trachtenberg 1939:176).

The second custom, involving the ripping up of grass at the cemetery, was observed by Jicxak ben Dorbelo (Dorbolo) in the 12th century when he visited Olomouc (Moravia). He says this custom also presented a problem in Paris where Christians had accused the Jews of practicing magic (Bretholz 1934:66). Had Dorbelo not convinced his Christian interlocutors that the custom was related to the Jews' belief in the resurrection of the dead and had no magical purposes, the custom might have had to be abandoned under Christian pressure. That would have meant that Christian attitudes towards Jewish "sorcery" could have dictated the practice of Jewish burial customs (see also paragraph 7 above and Mann 1927). Wuttke writes that German Christians practiced the custom in the 12th century as a way of driving away pursuing demons (1900:93ff; see also T.H.Gaster 1980:175, fns 101–2). According to Güdemann (1880:211 and fn 2), the Jewish custom is of German origin and had the same purpose. Attempts to Judaize the custom by invoking passages in Psalms 72:16 and 103:14 were probably inspired afterthoughts (T.H.Gaster 1980:175).

The reference to Olomouc suggests that the practice may have been of Slavic origin. In fact the practice of not looking back at a grave upon leaving a cemetery is recorded among South Slavs (Krauss 1892:187), Poles (Biegeleisen 1930:96), Moravians (Schneeweis 1953:67-8; see also Niederle 1953:226), as well as Germans (Wuttke 1900:466—who, unfortunately, ignores the specific geographical facts within Germany). Of particular importance for establishing an immediate Slavic origin of this Jewish practice is a German Christian source of the 13th century which lamented that this "pagan" (i.e., "un-German") custom was being practiced by Sorbs who outwardly observed Christianity (related by Grosser 2:1714:10).

10. The prohibition against consuming pigmeat

The pig was prohibited food in a number of cultures other than Jewish Palestine, since it played a role in religious purification, see, e.g., the ancient Egyptians and Greeks, Phrygians and Celts (Cobern 1917: 418; Ní Chatháin 1979-80:201; Hamp 1987). The Greek biographer Plutarch (c.46–c.120) raised the question of whether the Jews abstained from eating pork out of reverence or aversion for the pig (Grant 1980: 302). The prohibition against consuming pigmeat among the Palestinian Jews could have found reinforcement in Europe, where a similar prohibition existed. Thietmar, the bishop-chronicler of Merseburg (975–1018), mentions that a wild boar was an object of veneration among the Slavs (Kostrzewski 1964b). A 12th-century church at Altenkirchen on the island of Rügen (northern Germany), on the site of a pagan Slavic temple which was destroyed by the Danes in the late 12th century, has a relief of a pig (and two black cocks—the symbol of the god Svantevit) on one of its upper walls—which local lore regards as a pagan Slavic representation.

Despite the prohibition against eating pigmeat, Jews were often allowed to utilize magic remedies which required parts of a pig (see Pollack 1971:127, 295–6, fn 85, 304, fn 128). Pig refuse was also permitted for purposes of making an apothecary (Güdemann 1880:216). However, the *Sefer xasidim* (13th century) opposed the use of non-kosher food or animal blood for such purposes (Trachtenberg 1939:129; Schatzmiller 1982:589). The use of non-kosher food in magic is a clue that the practices were of non-Jewish origin, and suggests that the prohibition against consuming pigmeat may not always have been maintained in the European Jewish communities.

Blumenkranz cites a 13th–14th-century capitol from the cathedral in Uppsala, Sweden showing a Jew sucking the teats of a pig, which he interprets as an attempt to mock the Jews' abstinence from eating pig meat (1966b:67; see other references, ibid.:143, fn 47). However, as Blumenkranz himself notes, no such example is known before this date; moreover, Christian legislation did not force Jewish converts to Christianity to consume pigmeat. Rather than mockery, I wonder if the Uppsala sculpture was not simply recording the fact that the Jews were among the last peoples in Europe to continue the practice of revering the pig as a holy animal. On representations of a Jew and a pig in Christian art, see Peuckert 1931–2:827.

Whatever the origin of Jewish ritual food laws (in addition to the prohibition of the pig), the latter do have the effect of heightening the separation of Jews and non-Jews (see Fleury 1683:100; Andree 1:1878:

118; Eckstein 1936–7:203). As a device for enforcing religious separation, the chronology of food law observance would smoothly fit into the period of intensive Judaization.

11. The belief in house spirits who dwell in the oven hearth

This belief is widespread among Germans, Sorbs, Ukrainians and Russians, in addition to Jews (Scheftelowitz 1925:5); it also finds expression in the Talmud. In the early 20th century, Hessian and Galician Jews hesitated to demolish an oven.

On Slavic stove demons, see Zelenin 1927; Biegeleisen 1930; Wróblewski 1961:336. On the home god among the Slavs in the 12th century, see Seweryn 1967 and Urbańczyk 1970:59.

See also the discussion of the overlap in pagan Slavic and Jewish practices in chapter 6.3 below.

5.3 *The significance of the linguistic and ethnographic evidence presented in chapters 5–5.2*

I would like to explore briefly the significance of the linguistic and ethnographic examples cited in chapters 5–5.2 above.

(a) Examples in category III are far rarer than examples in category II (see chapter 5.11 above), though I remind the reader that the corpus makes no claim to completeness. Hence, I cannot say whether the statistics accurately reveal the non-Jewish contacts that the Jews experienced. I also cannot say whether the Jews were quick to lose the religious-superstitious connotations of their loanwords from Greek, Romance, Slavic, Turkic and German (see the examples of all sources in category I) since I have no way of knowing whether any loans originally in category I were shifted to category III. I do not know how to interpret the examples in category II—where Jewish languages have religious or superstitious connotations for loanwords while the original sources do not: either these reflect the fact that the Jews ascribed new religious-superstitious connotations to the loanwords independent of non-Jewish linguistic or cultural practice, or the Jews conservatively retained the original religious-superstitious meanings, after they were abandoned by the non-Jewish donor languages. This is not a trivial point: I suspect, on independent grounds, that the Jews were more tolerant of pagan loans/concepts than the Christians (see the discussion of Latin *ara* above). Original Jewish linguistic developments are occasionally visible (e.g., see the distinctive Yiddish meaning of German *Kobold* in category I, Germanic 5 above).

To the best of my knowledge, this is the first time that anyone has proposed using Jewish data to reconstruct European pagan and early Christian practices and terminology. The Jewish data are particularly important in view of the rarity of recorded Slavic pagan prayers (for an example, see Pauliny 1964:32, citing the 11th-century Persian writer Gardīzī).

(b) The Jews did not acquire customs, superstitions, or religious practices from all non-Jewish environments equally. I think the data—in descending order of importance from Slavic to Romance, Greek and German—reveal a correlation between the sources of linguistic enrichment and the major zones of alleged conversion activity in Europe during the first millennium A.D. Greek-speaking Asia Minor emerges as a relatively minor contributor to Ashkenazic culture. (On Babylonia/Iraq, an area with historically documented widespread conversion to Judaism, as a source of many customs practiced by the coterritorial Jews, see chapter 6 below).

(c) For Yiddish, the quantitatively most important foreign suppliers of terms with religious-superstitious meanings are Slavic, Latin and the Romance languages. The importance of Slavic increases if I add Romanisms, Grecisms and Germanisms which appear to have reached the Jews through a Slavic intermediary or possibly Balkan Slavic customs which the Jews now name by Germanic terms. Then follow a small set of words of Turkic, Arabic, Hebrew and Iranian origins (I take them together since Turkic is presumably the carrier to Yiddish of Arabisms and Iranianisms, as well as one or two Hebrew names). Finally, it is significant that there are only a handful of Grecisms and Germanisms which show no signs of a Slavic intermediary.

(d) The paucity of Turkic (i.e., Arabic-Iranian) terms suggests that the Muslim population of the Balkans and Hungary had minor contacts with Jews, though the acceptance of a basic term such as *dav(e)nen* 'pray (Jews)' might point to early contacts in the domain of religious practice. The Judaized Khazars seem to have been the source of one or two Hebrew names in Yiddish and Judeo-Slavic (see chapter 5.12 above). Curiously, a number of native Turkic words which surface in Yiddish may have reached the Jews via a Slavic non-Jewish intermediary (see, e.g., Yiddish *jarmlke, homen-[taš]*).

(e) Finally, the source languages can provide a rough idea of the time and place of the borrowing. Jewish borrowings from Greek could have been made in Palestine during the talmudic period, in which case, we usually find the Grecisms in Palestinian Hebrew texts as well (e.g., Yiddish *sandek*, Hebrew *sandāq*), in Asia Minor, Greece and/or the Balkans from Byzantine Greek, up to the 9th–10th centuries. Balkan Greek loans can be tentatively identified from their presence in other Balkan languages.

Jewish borrowings from Latin could also date from the talmudic period in Palestine, or subsequently from Rome. I have no idea whether Balkan Jews spoke Latin (in either a standard or a Judaized form).

The next source language in chronological order of its contacts with the Jews was Slavic—first in the Balkan area with South Slavic after the 6th century, when the Slavs encountered local Jews during their southward migrations into the Balkan Peninsula. Contacts between Slavs and Jews would have continued in the mixed Germano-Slavic lands and Hungary when the Balkan Jews arrived there by the 9th century at the latest. It is almost impossible to distinguish Balkan from West Slavic loans in Yiddish since most of the Yiddish Slavic corpus is pan-Slavic.

German influences could have reached Yiddish directly or indirectly through the Germanized Slavs after the 9th century. This late date of contact between Jews and Germans might explain the paucity of German terms free of a possible Slavic intermediary connection (but note German Jewish names probably translated from Slavic, Greek, Romance or Turkic names that are unknown among German Christians cited in chapter 5.12 above). By the 9th–10th centuries, Christianity had become established in the German lands, and the Germans themselves were engaged in missionary colonization of the Slavic lands to the east, so that German society was unlikely to provide significant numbers of proselytes to Judaism. I know of no German words in Yiddish which have religious or superstitious meanings in Yiddish but not in the source language. The weakness of the German imprint may also have been a function of the fact that the number of Jews resident at the beginning of the first millennium A.D. in the monolingual west German lands was much smaller than in the Germano-Slavic east. Of course, my classification of terms as "Slavic" and "German" has to be taken with a grain of salt, since German-origin customs and terms may have reached the Jews from the Germanized Slavs, while Slavic customs could have reached the Jews directly from Slavicized Germans.

(f) The fact that Yiddish retains so many terms that could have been acquired by the Jews in the Balkans gives grounds for suggesting that Ashkenazic Jewry began in the Balkans several centuries before the formation of the Germano-Slavic Jewish diaspora. If this is so, then we can speak of a relatively conservative nature of Ashkenazic Jewish culture after it was brought north to the Germano-Slavic lands. Note that historians universally date the rise of "Ashkenazic" Jewry to the 10th century in the contiguous Franco-German lands, even though the term "Ashkenazic" referred to Slavs, and before that to Iranians (see Wexler 1991b: chapter 2).

6

CONVERSION TO JUDAISM IN ASIA MINOR AND EUROPE IN THE FIRST AND EARLY SECOND MILLENNIUM A.D.

The purpose of the present chapter is to collect and assess the historical evidence for conversion to Judaism in Asia Minor and Europe on both an individual and group basis. Because the historical evidence is often sparse and prone to ambiguous interpretation, it is the weakest link in the chain of evidence for conversion to Judaism. If I incline to the side of those historians who regard the historical documentation as a reliable reflection of widespread conversion to Judaism in Asia Minor and Europe during the first and early second millennia, it is because of the compelling linguistic and ethnographic evidence that I mustered in chapters 4–5 above.

I must also state at the outset that I am using the term "conversion" loosely. There is no description of the act in either Jewish or non-Jewish sources. In some locales and periods, conversion may have involved an informal association of a non-Jew with Jewish institutions, e.g., the synagogue. In other locales and periods, conversion may have been carried out according to prevailing Jewish custom (Rajak 1992:19ff). The fact that non-Jews are sometimes required to perform Jewish rituals for the sake of Jews (see Ta-Šma 1992:138) provides an opportunity for non-Jews to become acquainted with Judaism. We need not assume that all Judaizers joined existing Jewish groups; some could have formed entirely new Jewish groups.

My major finding is that there is a correlation between most of the known areas of major conversion to Judaism and the reputed origins of Ashkenazic folk culture as suggested primarily by the linguistic and ethnographic evidence of Yiddish. These areas are Hellenic-speaking Asia Minor, Greece and the Balkans (the latter also Romance-speaking), and the Slavic-speaking Balkan and German lands.

The non-native contribution to the ethnogenesis, religion and culture of the Hebrews in Palestine is generally admitted today without dispute. Who has not heard, for example, of the impact of the Babylonians, Canaanites, Egyptians, Hittites and Philistines on Hebrew culture, religion and population make-up? But scholars disagree sharply over the significance of conversion to the diaspora Jewish communities; and few scholars suggest that proselytism might account for the many blatant differences in religion, culture and language that separate Old Palestinian and diaspora Jews, or groups of diaspora Jews from one another.

There are two fundamentally distinct approaches to conceptualizing the relationship between Palestinian and diaspora Jews:

(a) One approach assumes that only a minor non-Jewish component was added to the ethnic makeup and culture of the Palestinian Jews in the diasporas. The overwhelming majority of scholars espouse this view. There are even major studies of Jewish history which ignore the topic of proselytes altogether, e.g., there is no such entry in the index of Margolis and Marx 1927, except for a brief mention of ancient Rome.

Here are two examples of the claim that proselytes did not play a significant role in the formation of diaspora Jewish communities:

> "Individuals by the thousand joined the Jewish fold in every generation throughout the Second Commonwealth [from c.500 B.C. to the Christian era], but two normal elements of proselytizing were absent. The Jews did not set in motion a concerted effort to convert the Gentiles, and there were very few mass conversions to Judaism, save those carried out by force. Some Arab tribes embraced Judaism, southern Arabia had a Jewish king [Dhū Nuwās] who died in the year Mohammed was born, the ruling dynasty of Palmyra [Syria] and the governing elite of Khazaria were converted; some Berber tribes, some East African Negroes, some Dravidian tribes in southern India—these constitute the only known cases of group-conversion to Judaism" (J.B.Agus 1:1963:34–5).

> "We strongly doubt that there ever was a large and broadly based group of gentiles known as God-Fearers [in the Hellenistic and Roman periods]" (MacLennan and Kraabel 1986:48).[1]

(b) The second approach recognizes that the impact of the non-Jewish component was of such magnitude that it is more appropriate to assume that in the diasporas (all, most?) Jewish immigrant communities in Europe were preserved from disappearance, and new non-Palestinian "Jewries" were established, through the merger of a minor Palestinian Jewish entity with non-Palestinian peoples. Many of these new Jewish entities of European, West Asian and North African extraction sought links with Palestinian Jewish culture and religion, at different times in history and with different intensities.

The immediate goal of research should be to reconstruct the venues of major conversion to Judaism and to plot the subsequent geography and chronology of the Judaization of non-Jewish languages, religious practices and folkways. The second approach to the conceptualization of proselytism in the history of the Jewish diasporas has only been recommended by a handful of scholars, and it is the one I myself espouse:

Here is a sample of views, spanning almost three centuries:

> "The Jews were mixed with several nations... Moreover, there were always Gentiles from time to time who converted [to Judaism] and became proselytes. Thus, the Jews were no longer, strictly speaking, a single people, using the same language and the same customs; rather, several peoples began to resemble one another under the same religion" (Fleury 1683:526).

> "There were no doubt Jewish emigrés in Gaul who crossed the Rhone and Saône rivers, and served as a sort of leaven; but there was also a mass of people who became attached to Judaism through conversion who did not have a single ancestor in Palestine... This conversion of the Khazar kingdom has considerable importance for the question of the origin of the Jews who inhabit the Danubian lands and the south of Russia. These regions contain large masses of Jewish population who, ethnographically, probably have nothing, or next to nothing, Jewish about them" (Renan 1883:22–3).

> "Is it possible to believe that [the estimated 1,000,000 Egyptian Jews at the time of Christ] might be descended, in the final analysis, from Palestinian Jews?" (Loeb 1885).

> "In the initial period of Jewish propagandizing, [conversion] was probably quite substantial, since the enormous spread of Judaism can hardly be explained by an increase of the people alone" (Schürer 3:1909:176 7).

> "Among the Jews in fastnesses, the predominant element in the life and in the blood of the community seems to be the contribution of the indigenous proselytes" (Toynbee 2:1935:406).

> "There was hardly a synagogue anywhere in the Diaspora [during the Roman period] but provided space for [pagans who observed Jewish rites]... Very frequently, the children of such half-Jews were brought up by their parents to be Jews in every respect. This helps to explain the large number of Jews in the Diaspora" (Grayzel 1947:142–3).

> "In the Diaspora there was an increasing number, perhaps millions by the first century, of *sebomonoi (metuentes, [j]ereim*—God fearers), gentiles who had not gone the whole route towards conversion" (Hertzberg 1971:55).

> "There must have been numerous conversions of the hitherto pagan Arabs to the Jewish faith, but we cannot, solely from historical records, tell how extensive these were. Blood-group data, however,..suggest that the conversions were extremely numerous" (Mourant, Kopeć and Domaniewska-Sobczak 1978:30).

Which view is correct? A comprehensive collection of all conversion phenomena, both individual and group, awaits a conscientious scholar (see Feldman 1989:298, fn 103). But plenty of evidence is already in from both Jewish and non-Jewish sources to support the claim that the majority of the contemporary north European Jews were very likely of European and Asian proselyte origins.

It is puzzling why so few scholars have been willing to draw the proper conclusions from an ever growing body of data. Of course, references to non-Jewish conversion to Judaism are not the same as hard statistics, and hard statistics we will never have. Hence, the student of Jewish history should treat independent linguistic evidence as the arbitrator in interpreting the conversion data.

I believe that proselytism had three important impacts on the composition of diaspora Jewry:

(a) Converts radically changed the ethnic compositon of the Jewish communities. The input of a non-Jewish gene pool was particularly significant wherever the Jewish population was extremely small (Shapiro 1960:28). Hence, statements such as that of the eminent American anthropologist, Carlton Coon, that "among the Ashkenazim one can pick out Palestinian types that could readily be drawn from the courts of Solomon and David" (1942:32) borders on science fiction, given both our ignorance of the racial make-up of the ancient Palestinian Jews and the documented prevalence of diaspora conversions.[2]

(b) Conversion prevented the total disappearance of the Jewish people. For example, Wacholder assumes that between the 7th and 11th centuries the number of Middle Eastern and North African Jews doubled due to the conversion of slaves (1956:106).

(c) Proselytism led to radical changes in the Palestinian Jewish culture and religion imported to Europe, Africa and other parts of Asia.

Before I examine the evidence for conversion, let me mention two other non-Jewish sources for the Jewish population, whose quantitative impact also cannot be measured with any accuracy: the offspring of rape victims and non-Jewish concubines kept by Jews. Both factors have been cited a number of times in the literature (see Fishberg 1911:191, Ankori 1979:43 and Patai and Patai-Wing 1989:50 on the first topic; Zimmels 1958:257–8 and Baron 11:1967:81, 86–7 on the second).

6.1 The nature of proselyte Judaism in the diasporas

Discussions of conversion to Judaism in the early diasporas rarely specify the sort of Jews with whom non-Jews might have had contact. There could have been two types of Jews:

(a) *Ethnic Jews*, often but not exclusively of Palestinian origin, who had only recently emigrated abroad. I expect these Jews would have intermarried with indigenous populations within a few generations.

(b) Non-Palestinian *non-ethnic Jews* of proselyte origin and their descendants.

This dichotomous classification differs somewhat from the three-way classification Joseph Jacobs proposed over a century ago (1885:24–5), which has often been cited in the literature. Jacobs divided the Jews into Jews (a) by religion and birth (his examples were the Ashkenazim, Sephardim and possibly the Samaritans), (b) by religion only (Ethiopians, Karaites, Beni-Israel of Bombay, Black Jews of Cochin) and (c) by birth only (Marranos).[3] Jacobs' classification is not useful, since, in my view, there have been no examples of "Jews by birth"—his first and third categories—for more than a millennium (except possibly for the Samaritans in category one, who do not as a rule identify themselves as "Jews"); hence, only the second category exists. Furthermore, since Yemenite and Iranian Jews, themselves descended largely from non-Jewish converts, in turn converted small groups of Indians and Chinese to Judaism respectively (Yemenite features surface in the Hebrew reading norms of the Chinese Jews: see Wexler 1985a), Jacobs might have added a fourth category to his classification: proselytes converted by former proselytes.

The differences between Palestinian and many Jewish diaspora communities were often enormous—in ethnic makeup, language and religious practice. It is imperative to remember that most Jews in the diaspora, regardless of their ethnic origins, were geographically far removed from Palestine, often out of touch with developments there, and practiced forms of Judaism which deviated widely from the normative rabbinic (or pharisaic) Judaism that was developing at that time in Palestine. For example, most of the Jews in Rome in the early Christian era knew no Hebrew or Judeo-Aramaic (the few who did were members of the Hebrew- or Aramaic-speaking "Synagogues of the Hebrews" in the city) and had little familiarity with rabbinic lore. Judaic and pagan religious traditions were often mixed in the diasporas; an example is the cult of Sabazios in Phrygia, which spread to Rome as well (see Cumont 1906, Oesterley 1935 and Rankin 1935:189–90; note also the mention of Vincentius below).

Baron anticipated that the greater the distance from the Palestinian homeland, the greater the impact of non-Jews on the racial content and religion of the Jews:

> "The farther away from Palestine a country was situated, the less pure racially and ethnically its Jewish settlers were... A large section of Syrian Jewry, and probably a still larger section of the Jewries of Asia Minor, the East Mediterranean islands, and the Balkans, must have consisted of former proselytes and their descendants. The same is true of the Jews in Italy, Carthage, and Armenia..." (1:1952:283–4).

Baron's formulation is puzzling; after all, the East Mediterranean islands are quite close to Palestine and Syria is a neighboring territory. I suspect that the age of separation from Palestine and the population make-up of the Jewish diaspora settlements were the major factors that determined the racial makeup of a diaspora Jewish community. Geographical proximity is not always a convincing factor; note that the enormous Jewish population in neighboring Hellenistic Alexandria, Egypt, estimated as high as one million at the time of Christ, disappeared as a group in the early centuries of the first millennium.

Anatolian Jews especially had weak ties with Jerusalem, though they were connected to the Palestine landmass. For example, the Jews of Aphrodisias lacked local rabbis and learnèd leaders, even though their Judaism may, on occasion, have been close to talmudic Judaism. The Talmud relates that when a certain rabbi Meir came to Aphrodisias from Palestine in the mid 2nd century A.D., he found that the local Jews had no Scroll of Esther to read at the holiday of Purim (which celebrates the deliverance of the Jews of Persia from a plot to kill them in approximately the 5th century B.C.; the holiday was first referred to only in the 1st century B.C.). The Jewish community in Babylonia must have been particularly close to normative Palestinian Judaism, considering that it was here by the middle of the first millennium A.D. that the Babylonian Talmud was compiled (its scope surpasses by far that of the Palestinian Talmud). The "independence" from Palestine of many Jewish diaspora communities was long-standing. To cite just one example, the Jewish community of Sardis (near modern Denizli, Turkey) had a history of almost 1000 years when the town was destroyed by the Persians in the 7th century A.D.

Even when substantial numbers of Palestinian Jews were emigrating from Palestine after the Romans destroyed the Second Temple in 70 A.D., most new diaspora communities were still being founded by non-Palestinian, rather than by freshly expatriated Palestinian Jews. The Illyrian (north Balkan) Jews came from Italy, Greece and the Roman town of Apamea (just east of Jabla, Syria), while the Jews of Intercisa (now Dunaújvaros, Hungary) hailed from Emesa (now Homs, Syria); numerous Roman Jews in the 2nd century A.D. hailed from Lebanon, Phrygian Laodicea (Anatolia) and North Africa. The Jewish historian, Josephus (37–100?), relates that the Jews of Sardis came originally from Babylonia. Hence, I assume, with Melville Jacobs (1942:44, 50), that by 1000 A.D. few if any Jewish families in the Balkans or Italy could have boasted a "pure" Palestinian origin.

If I accept the population estimates of Baron (1:1952:170–1), that in the 1st century A.D. almost two-thirds of the estimated 8 million Jews in the world resided abroad, so that 1 out of 10 in the Roman Empire and 1 out of 15 in the Hellenistic East was a Jew (other scholars, e.g., Shapiro 1960, posit a smaller total of 5 million Jews), then the number of non-Jews acquiring Judaism from diaspora rather than Palestinian Jews becomes very high. The bulk of the Jews resident in the European sectors of the Roman Empire could *not* have been of Palestinian origin. It is primarily these Jews who were to form the nucleus of all subsequent European Jewries. In the early Christian era the demographic profile rapidly shifted in favor of the diaspora population, since the latter could grow unaffected by the devastations of the Jewish Wars of 66–70 and 132–5 in Palestine, which led to the radical depopulation of Jewish Palestine by the 3rd century A.D. In the opinion of some historians, the Jewish population of Judea (and the north as well?) was radically depleted during the Bar Koxba revolt in 135 A.D. (Kedourie 1979c:71).

6.2 The major venues of conversion in the diasporas

A major goal of Jewish history is to determine the ethnic origins of the non-Jewish cast of characters involved in the genesis of the diaspora

Jews. The linguistic and non-linguistic evidence, presented in chapters 4 and 5 above, allowed me to identify possible ancestors of the speakers of Judeo-Sorbian/Yiddish in the Balkans and other Hellenic areas, such as Greece itself, the Black and Caspian Sea littoral and the Asia Minor hinterland. Closer to the mixed Germano-Slavic lands, Yiddish speakers also seemed to have had contacts with Hungary and Bohemia. In Asia Minor and southern Europe, the first proselytes would have been of Greek, Illyrian, Iranian, Phrygian, Roman, South Slavic, Turkic and West Semitic stock. Once ensconced in the Germano-Sorbian and Pannonian (Hungarian, northern Croatian and Serbian) lands, the north European Jews would have attracted newcomers from among Germanic, Magyar, Turkic and primarily West and South Slavic groups. The widespread conversion to Judaism in Europe terminated in approximately the 11th–12th centuries as Christianity became institutionalized in the Slavic lands and the Jews' status worsened after the First Crusade of 1096; after the 12th century, proselytism was much reduced in scope and limited to Slavic and Hungarian territories.

There is little way to rank the relative contribution of most centers of proselytism to the transformation of the diaspora Jews, though historical sources sometimes suggest clues, e.g., conversions to Judaism were apparently more numerous in Greece than in Rome. Eloquent testimony to the importance of the Greek ethnic component is the change of the Greek word *prosēlytos* from 'foreigner, visitor' to 'convert (usually to Judaism)' (the borrowed English *proselyte* has lost a unique Jewish connotation). Pagan intellectuals who opposed Christianity tended to be somewhat more receptive to Judaism, see, e.g., Celsus (2nd century, author of *Sermo vermus*), Porphyry (also known as Malchus, c.234 Tyre or Palestine–c.305 Rome) and Flavius Claudius Julianus (331 Constantinople–363 Maranga on the Tigris). This may be because pagans saw a political threat in Christianity that Judaism could not pose. The chronology of conversion to Judaism needs to be ascertained. M.Goodman proposes the 2nd–3rd centuries as the period of most active Jewish interest in converts (1992:74). He also suggests that the impetus for conversion came primarily from non-Jews; this might explain the paucity of references to conversion in Jewish writings from all historical periods.[4]

Apart from individual conversions, there are records that the rulers of one European and one Asian kingdom converted to Judaism—those of Adiabene, Parthia (Iraq) in the early 1st century A.D. and the Turkic Khazar state, which, at its heyday in the 8th century, stretched from

Kiev in the west up to Khwārizm in the east and from Bulġar on the Volga in the north to the Crimea and the Caucasus in the south. My hypothesis that pagan Slavs in the bilingual Germano-Sorbian and Germano-Polabian lands or in the Balkans at the close of the first and early second millennium were drawn to Judaism is harder to substantiate, given the paucity of documentation; paganism as an official religion was short-lived in many areas after the development of writing, and hence left few traces. For the German area, I shall have to supplement the actual historical records, both Christian and Jewish, with the facts of Yiddish and Ashkenazic religion and folklore.

Christian sources provide most of the direct corroboration of the conversion hypothesis. This should not surprise us, given that there are no Jewish records originating in Slavic or Germanic Europe, or in Hungary, in any language, from before the 12th century, and given that church councils and secular rulers since the 4th century repeatedly forbad conversion to Judaism, threatening dire punishments for converted as well as converter; under these conditions, the topic could not enjoy a free airing in either the Jewish or the Christian literature. The very frequency with which the Christian prohibitions were reiterated—almost once every 15–20 years between the 4th and 13th centuries—shows the alarm with which ecclesiastical and secular authorities in Asia Minor and all over the European continent viewed the phenomenon of conversion to Judaism.

While it is customary to speak of the conversion of the "Turkic Khazars", the latter controlled a number of non-Turkic peoples, some of whom also converted to Judaism, such as the Alans (among the ancestors of the modern-day Iranian-speaking Ossetes, who reside in the central Caucasus, mainly in Russia and Georgia) and Eastern Slavs. The large-scale conversions to Judaism in the Balkans and the West Slavic lands are hardly ever cited in the scholarly literature on the history of the Jews, though documentation has been available for about a century (see Aronius 1902).

We can indirectly reconstruct the major venues of conversion to Judaism by following the spread of Christianity (frequently through the intercession of indigenous Jews) and by examining the status of institutionalized Christianity (the weaker the local church, the more easily the conversion to Judaism and other non-Christian religions). Since the initial successes of Christianity were in areas with a sizable Jewish population, we may assume that ethnic Jews were one of the chief reserves for Christianity. The "conversion" (or "re-calibration") of most of the Jews to Christianity would account for the initial drop in the European population practicing some form of Judaism immediately after the collapse of the independent Jewish state in Judea.

In Europe, extensive conversion to Judaism was possible where strong Christian or Muslim ecclesiastical control was lacking, e.g., where Catholicism competed with paganism, with other Christian sects such as Arianism, the Bogomil heresy (see chapter 5, fn 2 above) and Orthodoxy, or with Islam. For example, in 4th-century southeastern Europe, in Roman Illyria and south Pannonia (at Osijek, Croatia and Sremska-Mitrovica and Belgrade in Serbia), the brief Arian presence impeded the establishment of strong Catholic control. Jews enjoyed relatively more freedom in areas under Arian Christian control, such as Visigothic Spain and Italy until the 7th and 8th centuries, respectively (on Arianism, see Caro 1:1908:51, M.Gaster 1915:45, Blumenkranz 1949–50:6, Baron 3:1957:7, 32, Egger 1963:11–2, Thomas 1986:519, 528). The relative tolerance of the Arians may have been the reason that Catholics accused the former of being a "Jewish" movement (Baron 3:1957:7), unless Arians showed a marked tendency to convert to Judaism; though, a comparison of Visigothic Arian and Catholic rulers would not cast the former in the role of tolerant democrats (see Juster 1976). The competition among religions meant that some areas underwent Christianization more than once, as, e.g., coastal Illyria (now Slovenia and Croatia) and Dacia (Rumania) in the 9th century. Conversion to Judaism may also have been facilitated by the presence of a heterogeneous population, as, e.g., in Hungary (Kniezsa 1933, Sós 1973), where a German and Romance population—ensconced primarily in the west, in Transdanubia—coexisted with Turks and Slavs (on Islam in Eastern Europe, see Lewicki 1937, 1964a, 2/2:1977:293–4, Balić 1964).

Even in territories which officially had accepted Christianity, conversion was still possible as long as pagan rites persisted with some vigor. For instance, Islam (in both Shiite and Suni variants), which was practiced mainly by Turkic groups, coexisted with paganism in Hungary between the 11th–14th centuries long after the official conversion of the ruling classes to Christianity in the 10th century. Persecution of Christianity could occasionally even result in the conversion of Christians to Judaism, e.g., in Rome in 202–3 (Blondheim 1925:xviii) or during the Persian occupation of Asia Minor, Syria and Palestine in the early 7th century (Baron 7:1958:256, fn 29). Repeated pagan uprisings against Christianity in European, mainly Slavic, territories may also have created a climate conducive to conversions to Judaism.

Moravia is a good example of the "battleground" for Christianity: Prince Mojmír I (d.846) favored German Catholicism, while his nephew Rastislav (ruled 846–70) favored Byzantine Christianity with the new Church Slavic liturgy (written in a language based on the Slavic of Macedonia). The Church Slavic liturgy was ultimately eliminated in Moravia in 885, and Latin liturgy triumphed (was the spread of Christianity decelerated by the imposition on the Slavs of an incomprehensible liturgical language like Latin?). The Byzantine Orthodox ritual was also briefly used in Hungary. Archeological evidence shows that throughout the 9th century adherents of Christianity in Moravia were concentrated in the major settlements and at court while paganism persisted in the countryside. Similarly, while Christianity had officially arrived in Bulgaria in 864 (in the face of strong pagan opposition), the Arab traveller-historian Abū l-Ḥasan ʿAlī al-Masʿūdī (Baghdad c.895–Cairo c.956) could still encounter pagan practices there.

In many Slavic and Baltic areas, elements of paganism persisted as late as the 15th century, with isolated practices appearing even three centuries later (see, e.g., the custom of leaving food and drink at the gravesite: Lewicki 1952–3:133). Below, I have culled representative examples from West and South Slavic areas; a comprehensive collection of the historical facts needs to be made. For example, the consecration of a church in Nitra (Slovakia) by the Archbishop of Salzburg c.833 was probably intended for a Frankish colony there, since the local prince Pribina was still pagan. The Christianization-cum-Hellenization of the Slavs in Epirus, Macedonia, Thrace and possibly the Peloponnesus began in the 9th century but there were still many pagans there in the 10th century. Mention of pagan survivals comes both from Wolin (Poland) in the mid–11th century, and from the German lands: on Rügen Island in the 12th century, at Havelberg 1127, Wagria (Holstein) and Mecklenburg in 1171; Christianized Slavic paganism was also attested in Bamberg in the 11th century. As soon as Břetislav II assumed the throne in 1092, he found it necessary to issue an edict to suppress pagan survivals in the Czech lands. The early antagonism to Christianity among many Western Slavs is vividly reflected in the fact that Latin *castellum* 'fortress' is the basis for Czech *kostel*, Polish *kościół* 'church'; this is a hint that early churches in these areas had to be fortified against attack (Old High German also designated the church by this Latinism, see *kastel*: on the Christianization of the Slavs, see Dvornik 1959, Kowalenko 1961, Burszta 1967, Hilczer-Kurnatowska 1986b).

Syncretism and sectarianism have long been a characteristic feature of South Slavic religious life. For example, in the Balkans, some people still profess two religions simultaneously, one public and one secret, see, e.g., among the Orthodox Albanians, and until recently, Orthodox Serbs. Membership in two religions often arose on the border between two religions and not from forced conversion. Hungary also witnessed the rise of a syncretic religion consisting of elements of Christianity, Islam and paganism, see, e.g., the Slavic-Polovtsian (Turkic) symbiosis in Siebenbürgenland (Rumania) after the Hungarian occupation in 1066. All these facts point to an environment in which Judaism too might have easily gained adherents and undergone syncretism with local religions. Kraabel posited such a syncretism in the early Roman diaspora, but there is no question that a similar development could well have characterized the later Balkan and probably also the north European Jewish diasporas as well:

> "Diaspora Judaism will never come fully into focus as long as it is seen chiefly as an extension of the religion of the 'Old Testament', the Hebrew Bible, or an aspect of the rabbinic Judaism whose literature is available in such abundance. It is both of these of course, but it is also a religion of the Roman Empire, not mindlessly mixing with Cybele [the Phrygian goddess worshipped in Rome] or Dionysus [the Thracian deity worshipped in Rome as the god of wine] or Christianity, but not sealed off from them either, not oblivious to the values they contained and the aid they offered. Isis [the Egyptian goddess venerated in the Greco-Roman world], Mithras [the Aryan god worshipped in Italy and in the German lands in the 2nd century A.D.], Christianity, Judaism—all of these changed as they expanded beyond their respective homelands and 'holy lands' and moved into the Roman world. As this 'gentile' context is taken more fully into account, Diaspora Judaism begins to fit together; it is only within that context that the Diaspora synagogue—in its many shapes and locations and with its several purposes—will finally be understood" (1979:502–3).

Religious syncretism was often accompanied by racial mixing, as we can see from graveyard artifacts as early as the 7th century: Christian and non-Christian symbols, artifacts and skeletons of diverse racial types coexist in the same grave sites. Mixed Slavo-Avar (Turkic) graves exist, *inter alia*, in Slovakia, Moravia and Austria. An Avar-Slav culture, in which Avars came to be dominated by the Slavic majority, took shape in Bohemia, Moravia, Slovakia, Lower Austria, northeast Croatia, Hungary, south Silesia, Albania and Bulgaria and possibly even parts of central Germany; Avars had contacts with Slavs on the Baltic coast as well.

Shevelov proposes that many innovations in the Common Slavic language may even be of Avar origin (1965). Sixth-century mixed Avar-Slav-Langobard graves (the latter were a Germanic tribe) have been found in central Istria (Slovenia). There are also pagan-Christian graves in southwest Bulgaria and mixed Germano-Avar settlements in Bavaria. Biritual cemeteries continue even after the collapse of Avar hegemony in the early 9th century. Highly significant is the discovery of the mixed Avar-Jewish necropolis in Čelarevo, Vojvodina, thought to date from the 8th century (see chapter 1 above and discussion below). Al-Bakrī (d.1094) writes that the Khazars were mixed with Slavs and spoke Slavic (see Adrianova-Peretc 2:1950:223).

Research into conversion of European ethnic groups to Judaism is complicated by our ignorance not only of early European Jewish history, but also of the fate of the two major Turkic (or Turkic-dominated) groups which played a role on the center stage of the European arena during the first millennium: the Avars and Khazars. Following the collapse of their Empires in the 9th and 10th centuries, respectively, both groups disappeared abruptly from world view. Consciousness of the historical role of the Khazars and the Avars today is probably not much greater today than in earlier periods; the Historiska Museet (Museum of National Antiquities) in Stockholm may be the only major museum with a Khazar exhibition while the Janus Pannonius Museum in Pécs, Hungary is probably unique for its possession of a Khazar Jewish artifact.

On the fate of the Khazars:

> "Given the importance and longevity of the Khazar state (approximately three hundred years...), one is surprised that more is not known about them... In geographic terms, the Khazar state was one of the largest political units of the day... Itil, the Khazar capital on the Volga, was one of the important trade emporiums of its day. In spite of this, it has vanished without a trace, as indeed has much of urban Khazaria itself" (Golden 1:1980:14–6).

On the fate of the Avars:

> "Charlemagne (771–814) and his son Pepin disposed of the Avars forever. After several expeditions the last and decisive blow was delivered against them by Pepin in 796... They were allotted territories in southern Pannonia [southern Hungary, northern Croatia, Serbia], but their defeat was so decisive that they never rose again. They have disappeared completely from history and we do not even know how the remnants were absorbed by other populations" (Dvornik 1959:68).[5]

Might the historical oblivion into which Khazars and Avars have sunk be connected, in part, to the fact that many of the former and some of the latter had become Jews? The church would clearly not have been enthusiastic about trumpeting aloud widespread acts of conversion to Judaism. Even in Medieval Jewish writings the Khazar Jews warranted surpisingly little discussion—due to church pressures, the reluctance of certain elements of the Jewish population to readily accept converts (in general, or specifically those of Turkic origin?), or the creation of a unique Khazar form of Judaism that did not meet with approval from non-Khazar Jews? It would be useful to explore Jewish attitudes to "deviant Jewish" practices, e.g., 11th–12th-century Navarran Jews like Binjamin of Tudela and Avraham ibn Ezra (also from Tudela) were both critical of the "Cyprians"—a group of Cypriote Jews who celebrated their Sabbath on Sunday rather than Saturday (see Hill 2:1948:4–5).

While the conversion of the Khazars to Judaism in the 8th century enjoys careful scholarly coverage (see most recently Golden 1980, Golb and Pritsak 1982), the connection of the Avars with Jews has only recently—and at that, very gingerly—emerged in the historical literature. The impact of Judaism among the Khazars is difficult to assess due to the lack of physical remains and the difficulty of identifying the fate of the Khazar population after the collapse of their empire. In recent excavations, Soviet archeologists have found no structures that they could identify unambiguously as synagogues (or mosques for that matter: Magomedov 1983:173–4, 190), though some toponyms in the Daghestan Autonomous Republic of Russia contain the element "Jew" and some scholars think that the local Tat-speaking Jews (Tat is an Iranian language spoken by Jews and Muslims) may be the descendants of Alans who converted to Judaism along with the Khazars (Baron 3:1957:208; see also above). According to al-Masʿūdī (10th century), a Judaized group called the Sabaeans (= the contemporary Mandaeans in southern Iraq?) were neighbors of the Slavs (see Kawerau 1967:13).

Two important archeological finds of the 1970s strongly suggest the existence of widespread conversion to Judaism and the syncretic nature of Judaism in Asia Minor and the northwest Balkans: they are the Greek Jewish inscription at Aphrodisias, Anatolia, and the Jewish artifacts from the Avar necropolis at Čelarevo, in the southern Pannonian plain.[6]

The Greek inscription found at Aphrodisias in 1976 describes a population of *θeosebīs* 'God-Fearers' associated with the Jewish community. The inscription dates from about the 3rd century A.D., though specialists have also considered an alternative dating in the late 4th–5th centuries. The God-Fearers were pagans who had assimilated some aspects of Judaism. The Greek term "God-Fearer" is also found in Latin as *theuseues* (Venosa, Italy, 6th century A.D.). Jews and God-Fearers were part of the same community, but maintained separate status and nomenclature. Almost half of the contributors to the synagogue in Aphrodisias were God-Fearers. The latter could, but did not necessarily, also worship pagan gods. The Aphrodisias inscription allows us to posit three types of membership in the Jewish communities of the diaspora: ethnic Jews, formal proselytes to Judaism and God-Fearers (see also the classifications proposed in chapter 6.1 above).

Aside from Anatolia and Rome, groups of God-Fearers have also been mentioned on inscriptions from the Crimea, Egypt, the Balkans and in the New Testament between the 1st–5th centuries, see, e.g., possibly the so-called Hypsistarians of Cappadocia (Anatolia, an area now bounded by Kızılırmak, Yeşilırmak, Seyhan) and possibly Macedonia in the 4th century; the Sabbatists of Cilicia (southeastern Anatolia); the Sambatha followers at Thyateira (now Akhisar, western Anatolia). The dedication to the "Most High God" in Serbia among a brotherhood consecrated to Sabazios, the Phrygian deity, may also be cited (on Sabazios, see discussion in chapter 5.1 above). Condurachi also speaks of "Judaizers" at Sarmizegetusa, Dacia (near modern Grădiştea Muncelului, Rumania: 1937:91). I wonder whether the Greek and Latin inscriptions (in Greek characters) found in southwest and southeast Roman Germany which scholars do not attribute to Jews (see Frey 1975: ##673–4 and Lifshitz 1975:59) may have been made by and for proselytes.

The only known mixed Avar-Jewish necropolis, at Čelarevo, Vojvodina (Serbia), is thought to date from the 8th century, and contains numerous brick fragments with Jewish motifs and one Hebrew inscription. The late chief rabbi of Hungary, Alexander Scheiber, steadfastly rejected the suggestion that Avars and Jews (of undetermined ethnic origin) had intermarried (1982). He thought the bricks with the Jewish motifs were most likely brought by Avars from an earlier abandoned Roman Jewish cemetery. I cannot see why Avars would pillage brick fragments from a neighboring cemetery which had no structural significance. I suspect that the rabbi's conclusion reflected his reluctance to admit intimate Avar-Jewish contacts. Aside from the brief remark by Scheiber, no historian of the Jews has mentioned the Čelarevo find (so far discussed almost uniquely in Croatian, Serbian, Slovenian and Hungarian archeological literature). The archeologists Živanović (1975) and Bunardžić (1978–9:52) are of the opinion that the skeletons belong to a north Mongolian population which had become Judaized prior to arriving in the northern Balkans.

It is not surprising to find Jews buried together with non-Jews, e.g., Palestinian Jewish cemeteries included pagans. Jews have even been buried in non-Jewish cemeteries; an example is the Christian catacomb of Praetextat in Rome c.250 A.D. which contains the tomb of Vincentius, a believer jointly in the Phrygian deity Sabazios (whose worship incorporated Judaic elements), Christianity and possibly also Judaism; his wife was evidently Jewish. Mixed Jewish-Christian cemeteries are also attested in North Africa (Blondheim 1925:xxi, fn 8). The case of Vincentius is not unique. In his monumental collection of Jewish inscriptions, Frey mentions an inscription from the Campanie district of Italy which he believed combined two originally separate inscriptions since it began with a cross and ended with a Hebrew phrase (1:1975, no. 88); Balász subsequently proposed (correctly, I suspect, given the existence of religious syncretism at this time) that the inscription was originally single (1947:7–8). An open question is when and where the Jews came to prefer separate burial. Historians should check whether Jews and/or non-Jews advocated the disappearance of cemeteries comprising mixed ethnic and/or religious groups.

Another possible link between Avars and Jews comes from the term "giant" in a number of Slavic languages, Greek and Rumanian. Adversaries are commonly transformed into giants or powerful warriors, e.g., Ukrainian *kozarljuha* 'strong, courageous warrior' < *kozar* 'Khazar (Jew)' (but note cognate Hungarian *kazár* 'kike'), German *Hüne* 'giant' (attested since the 13th century) is probably related to *Hunne* 'Hun' (or 'Hungarian' in Old High German). In a single South Slavic language, Slovenian, as well as in West Slavic languages and Greek, a term for giant appears to have been derived from the tribal name Avar, e.g., Slovenian *óber*, Czech *obr*, Old Polish *obrzym* (Polish *olbrzym*), Upper Sorbian *hober*, Greek *ovrimos* (though Machek 1956, 1971 doubts this etymology). Kronsteiner observes that these languages are spoken in territories once controlled by Avars (1978:143, fn 28). Curiously, in parts of the South and East Slavic territory and in Rumania, the term for Jew has assumed the meaning of legendary giant, e.g., north Bulgarian *žid*, east Serbian *žìd*, Bulgarian *(d)židovec*, Russian *Židovin*, the name of a mighty giant in the Russian folk epics known as *byliny* (attested since the 11th century); Rumanian *Jidov* 'Jew'/ *jidov* 'giant'. In some of these languages the standard term for Jew may have a related form, see, e.g., Bulgarian *žid* (now archaic, except in the northern dialects), *evrein*, Russian *evrej* < Greek *hebraîos* < Hebrew *ʿivrī.* Macedonian *visok* 'tall' has assumed the secondary meaning of Jew. However, in south Bulgarian and Macedonian, the term giant is based on the word for Greek. The only explanation for the shift of 'Jew' > 'giant' is that a bellicose group in the area, the Avars, had become, in part, identified with the Jews. In Siebenbürgen (Rumania) giants or Jews were considered the builders of fortresses, while in Bulgaria, Jews and Tatars performed this function (Winkler 1930–1:1649). Without the Avars, it is unlikely that the European Jews on their own, lacking an army or political structure (apart from the Khazar empire in the Ponto-Caspian area, destroyed in the 10th century), would have become associated with giants in the indigenous folklore. (The epithet 'giant' may also have been applied independently of Jews and Avars, if the West Slavic tribe known as German *Wilzen*, Polish *Wieleci* comes from Common Slavic **vel-* 'large': see the interpretations cited by Rzetelska-Feleszko 1977 and Trillmich 1985:14–5, fn 33.)[7]

I also wonder whether the pejorative terms for Jew that begin with *o* in two languages, e.g., Greek *ovreos* (vs. standard *hebraîos*) and Rumanian *ovrei* (vs. standard *evreu*), were not originally derived from the ethnonym Avar, or resulted from a cross of phonetically similar 'Avar' with 'Hebrew' (see also Greek *ovrimos* 'giant'). In view of the intensive mixing of Avars and Slavs (which led to the ultimate disappearance of an Avar identity: see Skok 1934:59, 74, 76, 81, 110 and Simonyi 1942), the "Avars" with whom the Jews became associated were probably a mixed Slavo-Avar population rather than Avars alone.[8] The Alans, ancestors of the Ossetes, have provided the Karaites with the word for giant, see Karaite *alankasar* (Moskovich and Tukan 1985:90).

Finally, I would note that the association of the Jew with large size is reflected in Romani *biboldo* 'Jew' (literally 'unbaptised'), which is found throughout German slang in this meaning, in addition to Berlin *babold* 'big, strong man' (Schildt and Schmidt 1986:349; Wolf 1956:#450 cites the first attestation of *babolde* from 1812, but only in the meaning of Jew). If the semantic shift of 'Jew' > 'big, strong man' in Romani *biboldo*, etc., is related to the other European data given above, then the Romá may have associated Jews and giants prior to their arrival in Europe some seven centuries ago.

A linguistic link between the Jews and the Turkic groups in the Caucasus, the Khazars, is suggested by two facts. Spoken in the area of the former Khazar kingdom, the Ossete language offers the term *gumīr* 'giant'; if this is derivable from Judeo-Aramaic *kūm(ā)rā*ʾ '(idolotrous) priest', then we may be witnessing an illusion to the Khazar Jews (Abaev's proposal to derive the term from Biblical Hebrew *gomɛr*, a name for the Cimmerians in Ezekiel 38:6, seems less plausible: see 1:1958:530). The Rumanian Jewish linguist Lazar Şăineanu also noted over a century ago that Rumanian used both ethnic terms *Tătar* 'Tatar, Turk' and *Jidov* 'Jew' to denote a giant, a fact which he ascribed to the conversion of the Khazar Turks to Judaism (1888:154, 158, 160).

Future research will need to determine the extent to which there was demographic continuity between the different zones of conversion. For example, was the Jewish community of Greco-Roman origin the primary catalyst for the conversion of Slavs and other Balkan peoples to Judaism? To what extent were Jews of Balkan ethnic origins responsible for the conversion of the Slavs in the mixed Germano-Slavic lands?

Ascertaining the main zones of conversion is tantamount in many cases to ascertaining the ethnic (and linguistic) backgrounds of the proselytes, e.g., the establishment of Judaism in the Khazar kingdom involved not only Turkic Khazars, but also local East Slavs. The West Slavs, especially those living among the Germans, undoubtedly provided the bulk of the proselytes to Judaism in northern Europe. In addition, some Germans and Scandinavians might also have converted in the mixed Germano-Slavic lands (see Oxenstierna 1966:294; on contacts between Viking and Jewish slavers, see ibid.:92–4; on the Viking presence in the northwest Slavic lands, see Vasmer 1932, Hensel 1962: 39, 41 and Żak 1977; on the slave trade between Vikings and Khazars, see Cross and Sherbowitz-Wetzor [1953]:46). By steadfastly rejecting Christianity, the West Slavs living among the Germans provided the German missionaries and colonists with an excuse to expand into their territories. Hence, the West Slavs came to form the bulk of the slave population in a German-dominated society. As I shall relate below, the Jews were also active in the international slave trade, most of which centered in the Slavic lands; Jewish practice called for the conversion of non-Jewish slaves employed by Jewish households. The association of Slavs with slavery is the cause of the common western European practice of coining the term slave from Slav (as in English), a practice which also found its way into some Medieval Hebrew texts, see Hebrew *knaʿan* 'Canaan; the Slav lands', an allusion to the Canaanites in the Bible who were reduced to slavery. The identification of slave and Slav was not usually made by the Slavs or Slavic-speaking Jews. Though the rare

Judeo-Polish family name *Chanaan* (attested in two Christian sources from 14th-century Świdnica and Kraków 1495: M.Mieses 1934:253) may indicate the pagan (rather than Christian?) origins of the bearer. See other proselyte-slave names cited below.

The Hungarian lands also provided slaves for the international slave market. See the mention to this effect in the writings of Ibrāhīm ibn Ja'qūb, the Catalan Jewish slave dealer who traveled widely in the Germano-Slavic lands in the second half of the 10th century in the service of the Caliph of Córdoba, and Thietmar of Merseburg (cited by Hensel 1962:49 and Brankačk 1964:179 and fn 238, respectively). A possible indication for this is the Medieval Hebrew name *hāgār* for Hungary, assuming that it was chosen not just on phonetic grounds (note Serbo-Croatian *ùgar*, Czech *uher* 'Hungarian', from an earlier 12th-century *ug-*), but because the biblical figure Hagar was an Egyptian handmaid of Sarah. Alternatively, since Sarah was the mother of Ishmael, traditionally the scion of the Arabs according to Jewish tradition, *hāgār* may also have been linked to Hungary due to the presence there of large numbers of Turkic Muslims who had arrived with the Magyars; in Medieval Hebrew literature, *hāgār* also denotes Arabs. The Turkic (including Khazar) tribes that accompanied the Magyars in their westward migrations appear to have settled in what is now primarily south Slovak territory (if we accept Kniezsa's analysis of the topographic evidence: 1933:14–5).

There is no way to reconstruct even the approximate numbers of non-Jews who may have become Jews, but I would not rule out the possibility that in northern Europe at the beginning of the second millennium their numbers vastly exceeded the population of "genuine Palestinian" Jews and their descendants. In contrast, the ratio of born Jews to converts to Judaism in the Iberian Peninsula or in the Muslim world may have been in favor of the former; this topic awaits further research (see my ms c).

Various opinions have been expressed in the literature as to how long the conversion of substantial numbers of north European non-Jews to Judaism continued. Giese places the *terminus ad quem* at the Black Plague in 1348/9 (1968:413), but Goldmann prefers 1000 (1927: 1149) and Blumenkranz the First Crusade of 1096 (1961, 1966a). As I shall demonstrate below, the earlier dates are probably correct for western Europe, while Giese's is a more likely terminal point for Slavic Europe and Hungary. An Italian traveller to the Cuman lands along the Black and Caspian Seas reported meeting Jewish missionaries called

"Brutaxi" in the 13th century (Sevortjan 1967:101–2), but I am unable to identify these people further.

A major desideratum of Jewish historians should be to ascertain as precisely as possible the specific tribal or regional origins of the Slavic populations from whose ranks converts to Judaism might have been drawn. The most likely candidates between the 9th and 12th centuries can be reconstructed from German missionary sources on slave trading as well as from the itinerary of the Catalan Jewish slaver, Ibrāhīm ibn Jaʿqūb.

From the German sources we learn that since the 8th century the Franks took hostages from the Slavic Obodrites, Wilzi, Sorbs and others, all of whom were allegedly brought up as Christians, and that Slavic tribes from a number of areas were required to pay the German conquerors a slave tithe in the 10th century: the Milzeni (in the Bautzen region), Lusizi (near Cottbus), Daleminzi (near Dresden and Meissen) and Nisani (east of the Daleminzi: see the map in J.Herrmann 1985:55). The north German Slavic lands were particularly favored as sources for slaves, as a result of the Saxon-Obodrite battles in the 9th century. Slavs themselves traded in Slavic slaves in the late 8th–early 9th century. Obodrite slaves (from Mecklenburg, near Wismar) were sold by the Pomoranians to the Poles, Czechs and Sorbs. In the north Danish slaves were also sold, e.g., in Mecklenburg in 1168.

Ibrāhīm ibn Jaʿqūb writes of visiting a number of locales which had slave markets, presumably one of the reasons for his visits there: e.g., Haithabu (the southern-most Viking trading center, south of modern-day Schleswig, Germany, known as Hedeby in Danish), Magdeburg, Mecklenburg, Merseburg, Prague, Schwerin and Wurzen (east of Leipzig). For accounts of Slavic slaves in Arabic writings, see, e.g., al-Jāḥiẓ and Ibn Xordādhbeh (9th century) and al-Masʿūdī and Ibn Ḥawkal (10th century: reprinted by Harkavi 1870 and Lewicki 1:1956; for additional sources, see E.Herrmann 1965:189, fn 225). Other clues to the major venues of the slave trade are the location of the longest centers of Slavic pagan practice (see Düvel 1970), the staggered chronology and geography of prohibitions against the public use of Sorbian (see Páta 1934:10 and Frinta 1955), the centers of Christian missionary activities among the Slavs (see details in Brüske 1955, Frinta 1955:15) and the existence of an atmosphere of relative religious tolerance, as, e.g., in the Khazar Kingdom or pagan Lithuania (on the latter, see Urban 1987).

As I noted in chapter 3 above, the first Jewish settlers in the mixed Germano-Slavic lands were probably speakers of South Slavic; thus, they had little difficulty in acquiring Sorbian, the only Slavic language to survive to the present in Germany. Indeed, the similarity between the ethnic names "Sorb" in Germany and "Serb", a major Slavic ethnic group in the Balkans, may not be coincidental; Serbs and Sorbs may be descended from a common Slavic tribal group in Eastern Europe that split into two groups during the westward migrations of the Slavs in the 6th century, one migrating to the northwest into Germany and the other to the southwest into the Balkans (Kunstmann 1987). In the 9th–12th centuries the differences among the Slavic languages were marginal, but since Sorbian is the only surviving Slavic language in Germany today, I take the liberty of defining the Judeo-West Slavic speech as (Judeo-)Sorbian. My choice of the latter term does not mean that the Jews were settled in, or that Slavic slaves converted to Judaism uniquely or predominantly from, Lausitz (the area with the highest concentration of Sorbs today), since the primeval Slavic settlements in Germany were far more extensive a millennium ago.

Finally, I should note that some scholars who have sought to identify areas of conversion to Judaism on the basis of racial criteria have operated with two assumptions: that (a) it is possible in principle to distinguish between "more" and "less" genuine Jewish roots among the contemporary Jews, and (b) since the majority of the contemporary Jews are members of the Caucasian race, "genuine" Jews should look like Europeans. Non-European Jews who do not meet the requirement of race-type have usually been labeled "the descendants of converts to Judaism"; the latter group includes the Yemenite, Ethiopian, Indian and Chinese Jews, who are alleged to be for the most part indistinguishable from the coterritorial non-Jews (see J.Jacobs 1885 above, though the recent study by Livshits, Sokal and Kobyliansky reveals that genetically the Yemenite Jews are distinct both from most other Jews as well as from the coterritorial Yemeni Arabs: 1991:137).

Non-European Jewish communities are stigmatized as being descended from converts for two other reasons: they are relatively small in numbers and isolated from most other Jews. Consider again the Chinese Jews, who probably never numbered more than a few thousand at any historical period, and whose last organized community in Kaifeng-fu, Henan province, was dissolved in the mid 19th-century, or the Ethiopian Jews who, until very recently, were ignorant of relatively late Jewish holidays, such as Hannukah (which commemorates an event that took place in the 2nd century B.C.). Some observors take this fact to mean that the Ethiopian form of Judaism came to Ethiopia before the rise of this holiday. An Israel government advertisement in the *New York Times* of 1 September 1991 read:

> "A child in Ethiopia whose forefathers left the Land of Israel 2500 years ago and did not know about Hannukah, returns home to Israel..." (Savir 1991).

It is also possible that Judaism reached Ethiopia after the rise of Hannukah, but without the latter. In Ethiopia, the indigenous Jews are not the only Judaized population, see also the Qemant (Gamst 1969; for a more factual account of the Ethiopian Jews than Savir gave, see Ullendorff 1956). However, the factor of "isolation" can sometimes work in favor of the alleged "purity" of a Jewish community, especially in matters of culture. Isolated Jewish groups, especially those in the Caucasus, have often been identified as the descendants of the "Ten Lost Tribes" (see J.Samuel 1841). Consider the following characterization of the Yemenite Jews by the Israeli musicologist, Gerson-Kiwi:

> "Their great age as an ethnic group, their exclusion from the European sphere of influence, as well as their strong musical talents have elevated them [Yemenite Jews] to be the prototype of the purest old Hebrew folk traditions. Their legends of origins take us back to the time of the Babylonian exile (587 B.C.)" (1981:157).

On the alleged racial pedigree of the Yemenite Jews, see P.Johnson (1987:182; on arguments for and against the view that the Jews in the Moroccan Berber lands were descended from Berber converts, see Hiršberg 2:1965:36). The heterogeneity of the Jews in many areas may hold important clues to the chronology of the Judaization process. For example, Jews living in the southern regions of Yemen reveal a higher frequency of African marker genes than those living in the north of the country (see Mourant et al. 1978:31; Patai and Patai-Wing 1989:331). Goitein provided a linguistic parallel, i.e., that Jews in Ṣanʿāʾ, central Yemen, spoke the Arabic of the coterritorial Muslims, while the speech of Jews in the south of the country differed from that of their neighbors (1930:357, 361, fn 2).

In contrast to Gerson-Kiwi, who saw original Jewish roots in at least one non-European Jewish group, Richard Andree, the 19th-century German sociologist-anthropologist, characterized four non-European Jewish communities as of non-Jewish origin on the grounds of alleged similarities (racial and/or cultural) with the coterritorial non-Jews; not unexpectedly, it did not occur to him to doubt the "Jewish" pedigree of European Jews:

(a) On the Jews of Gharyān, western Libya: "They totally assumed there the customs and practices of the native mountaineers, from whom they are sharply distinguished in their external features" (1881:205).

(b) On the Jews of Kurdistan: "In general the customs of these Jews deviate markedly from those of the European Jews, so that they are probably of a different [i.e., "non-Jewish"] origin" (ibid.:219).

(c) On the Jews of Cochin, India: "The men observe circumcision but they took funeral celebrations and polygamy from the Hindus, a hairlock over each ear being their only distinction" (ibid.:242).

(d) On the Jews of Kaifeng-fu, Henan Province, China: "...the Chinese Jews have some customs that are particularly distinctive of them; for example, they read the Law through a veil, construct a throne for Moses and others... Aside from their circumcision and religion they are genuine Chinese in language, dress, customs and practices, and bear Chinese names" (ibid.:245, 247).

Theoretically, Jewish groups could differ in the extent to which they retained a Palestinian Jewish ethnic component. But given the extreme racial heterogeneity of the contemporary Jews, it is more likely that no Jewish community is racially "pure"—including the European Jews, who often resemble coterritorial or contiguous non-Jewish groups no less than the tiny Afro-Asian Jewish groups mentioned above. I fail to see how the nationalist Belorussian Jewish historian, Simon Dubnow (1860–1941), could have regarded the Jews as the relatively purest of all existing ethnic groups, especially since much work on discontinuities among the Jews had been done by his time (see Ginsberg 1963:41–2; on relative purity, see also Mourant 1959:171). A geographically Euro- or racially Caucaso-centered view is hardly convincing, as non-European Jews themselves were quick to point out when they first encountered European visitors who claimed to be Jews. For example, the Yemenites were so sceptical that light-skinned people could be Jews that they coined the label "Christian Jew" for visiting European Jews. See the Judeo-Arabic term *yehudi nasrani* (in Godbey's spelling 1930:186 and fn 20, citing Landberg 1906:273). The Black Jews of Cochin, Kerala State (India), also call the white Jews "Christians" (Malayalam *meholah*[?]: Godbey 1930:356, who calls them under the old British administrative term "Madras" Jews).

If the non-European Jews can be described as the mixing of migrant Palestinian Jews with indigenous non-Europeans, theoretically European Jews could also be the product of intermarriage between Palestinian Jews and indigenous Indo-European, Altaic and other speakers. This possibility has rarely been explored. The only European Jews whose Palestinian Jewish pedigree has been repeatedly questioned over the last century or so are the pre-Ashkenazic Jews of Poland and the Eastern Slavic lands; from time to time a Turkic Khazar (ultimately non-European!) origin has been postulated for these Jews—only to be rejected by most scholars—who were themselves often of Polish and Eastern Slavic provenience with undisguised Western European prejudices!

6.3 Candidates for conversion to Judaism (with special attention to the Slavs)

There are several reasons why Western Slavs, especially those in the areas being settled by Germanic tribes beginning with the 6th century, might have converted to Judaism.

(a) Association with the Sorbian Jews would have enabled the Slavs to avoid "denationalization" at a time when German settlers were imposing their Christian religion, their German language and culture, and political control on the indigenous Slavs in the German lands. The Sorbs might also have been attracted to Judaism since the Jews were largely a Sorbian-speaking population who were not the immediate object of German missionary activity:

> "Since the time of Charlemagne the apostles of religion and love for our Slavs appeared merely as the advance troops of the enemy army, and for them Christianity was in fact synonymous with slavery" (Beyer 1848:9).

> "The persistence of pagan beliefs, and even of the organized pagan cult in Mazovia, after the Christianization of the country [Poland]...appears to us like a political manifestation... This phenomenon could also have been the proof of a certain Mazovian separatism, perhaps also a protest against the politics of the ruling Piast dynasty or a remembrance of the ancient political independence of this province" (Szafrański 1960:171).

Conversion to Judaism would have protected the Sorbs from German Christian persecution, since the independent status of the Jews was recognized by the Christian authorities. A valuable confirmation of this claim comes from Saint Bernard of Clairvaux (1090–1153), who expressed greater tolerance for Jews than for East European (Slavic) pagans; while the Jews should not be converted by force, he believed the Slavs who did not convert should be wiped out (see Berger 1972:93). Conversion to Judaism as a statement of political independence against a coterritorial or contiguous national threat was the major reason for the conversion of the rulers of the kingdoms of Adiabene in the 1st century and Khazaria in the 8th century (see Neusner 1984:65–6). Around 950, the Khazar Jewish rulers converted to Islam, this time in order to ensure Khwārizmian support against the invading Turks (Cross and Sherbowitz-Wetzor [1953]:227, fn 56; Golden 1:1980:82). On the possibility of slaves bettering their condition by conversion to Judaism, see Kočev (1978:66–7). On the religious debates between Khazar Jews and the Kievan prince Volodymyr in 986, related in the Russian Primary Chronicle *(Povest' vremennyx let),* see Cross and Sherbowitz-Wetzor [1953]:97 and Adrianova-Peretc 1:1950:60, 2:330.

The Sorbian-speaking Jews were one of the few elements of the Slavic population of Germany in the Middle Ages to maintain a separate identity during the Germanization of the territory. I theorize that conversion to Judaism was most likely wherever the Slavs felt that their ethnic identity was in danger, e.g., in the Sorb lands. The Czechs, on the other hand, by becoming Christians under the tutelage of Byzantine Slavic missionaries (in order to counterbalance the influence of German Christian missionaries), robbed the Germans of an excuse to annex their territories, though Germans did eventually settle there in significant numbers.

(b) Jews were active in the slave trade in northern Europe. Slaves who were owned by Jews were obliged to adopt the Jewish religion or else they were sold to non-Jews (in the Talmud, the regulations pertaining to slaves are given in Yevamot 48b, 70b and Pesaxim 96a). Moreover, Jews were not supposed to sell slaves to non-Jews if this resulted in a loss to the Jewish community. As unenslaved Jews, the Slavs might have fared better than as slaves in Christian society.[9] Jews needed pagan Slavic slaves since the church periodically opposed the employ of Christians in Jewish households. Scholars disagree about the numbers of Slavic slaves who converted to Judaism. Swoboda posits a small number (1982:273), but Verlinden and Lewicki are of the opinion that a large number of Slavic converts to Judaism were slaves (1933, 1955–77 and 1964b:342 respectively). The evidence supports the opinion of Verlinden and Lewicki. From northern Europe and the Balkans, Slavic slaves were transshipped to Muslim buyers in the Iberian Peninsula and

North Africa (on Slavic slave trade through Italy, see Lewicki 1958:67–8, 1964a, 1964b, Swoboda 1975).

Evidence of Jewish participation in the slave trade in the Slavic lands comes from both Christian and Jewish sources. Christian sources reveal that the Jews in the Frankish realm were not permitted to own slaves in 599, and that the Jewish slave trade in Gaul/France was denounced in the early 7th and late 9th centuries; Louis the Pious (who ruled the Holy Roman Empire between 814 and 840) allowed the Jews to buy and sell Christian slaves (for a similar allowance in 1090 in the Rhineland, see Battenberg 1990:61); the students of the Saloniki missionary-monk, Methodius (c.815–85), active in Moravia, were redeemed from Jewish slavery in Venice in 886, according to the Life of Saint Naum. The document known as the Raffelstetten toll ordenance from 903–6 (the town is in Upper Austria between Linz and Enns) mentions Jewish merchants, presumably slave dealers;[10] Venice opposed the slave trade in 960; Thietmar, Bishop of Merseburg (975–1018), cites Jewish slavers (see Trillmich 1985:272, 302); Anonymus Gallus, the first Polish chronicler, relates in the early 12th century the redemption of Slavs by Judith, a Czech princess (d.1085) married to the Polish prince Władysław Herman (1079–1102). The eighth panel of the bronze doors of the Gniezno Cathedral, constructed c.1175, shows Saint Wojciech (who lived in the late 10th century) with slaves and a Jewish slaver, condemning the Czech ruler Boleslav II (971/2–999) for selling Christians into slavery (for an illustration, see *DA* 1966, figure 1). In the German lands Jewish slavers are last mentioned at Koblenz in 1100 (from a source of 1209), though as late as 1462 a Jew was arrested in Caltagirone, Sicily for purchasing a Christian slave girl. By the 11th century, the few references to the participation of Jews in the north European slave trade are limited to Poland and the Eastern Ukraine (Friedman 1959:1507–8); in the 15th century, sporadic citations of Jewish slavers emanate from the Western Ukraine, e.g., from Halyč and Hrubešiw. It has been suggested that the Christian belief that Jews stole Christian children in order to have them circumcized stems from the participation of Jews in the north European slave trade (see Peuckert 1931–2:824); this suggestion deserves further study.

Primary Jewish sources are also available, though there are few references to Jews holding or selling slaves in Western Europe from the early 10th century due to the church prohibitions against Jews holding Christian slaves: in his responsa, Mešulam ben Kalonimos of Mainz (c.910–985) called slaves "semi-Jews"; even the Babylonian scholar, Haj Gaon

(Pumbedita, Iraq, 939–1038), mentions "Canaanite" (Slavic) slaves in his *Sefer haštarot;* the Slav *Soimel* (from Kraków) who became a Jew, is mentioned by Jehuda Hakohen (c.980–1050) in his *Sefer hadinim* (see Kupfer and Lewicki 1956:56); the Champagne scholar, Rashi (1028/1040?–1105), has a number of references to slaves owned by Jews and their suitability for participation in Jewish religious practices (see von Mutius 1984–5, 1987:39–43); a Slovenian(?) prelate converted to Judaism in Mainz at the beginning of the 11th century; Jewish slavers are mentioned by the Navarran traveler, Binjamin of Tudela (1160–73), though this is a second-hand report (Lewicki 1961b); Jicxak ben Moše of Vienna (c.1180–c.1260) cites the name of a freed Slavic slave, *Ubriš* ~ *Obriš* (Kupfer and Lewicki 1956:213–4, 226–7);[11] Jewish slaves in 13th-century Bohemia are mentioned in the writings of Mordexaj ben Hilel (see also the Judeo-Czech name *Naamon* given to a slave: I.A.Agus 1:1968:281); Meir of Rothenburg (c.1220–1293) had Christian maids and servants; Barux bar Jicxak of Worms (13th century) speaks of the acquisition, circumcision and ablution of Christian slaves in his *Sefer hatruma* (which Baron regarded as "exceptional": 4:1957:333, fn 48; the mention of Slavs might have been "exceptional", but certainly not the phenomenon); a Jew named Kussiel (or Cussiel) of Wrocław 1434 was punished for actively engaging in the conversion of Christians, including the circumcision of a boy and his transference abroad (see also the discussion of the name *Chanaan* above).[12]

The circumcision of slaves in Spain is also mentioned in the Jewish responsa literature of the 13th–14th centuries. The black woman shown seated at the foot of the Passover table in an illustration from the "Sarajevo Haggada" (thought to have been produced in Aragón around 1350) was probably a slave who, after converting to Judaism, joined her Jewish household as a free person (see Verber 1983:35). A responsum of Šlomo ben Adret of Barcelona (c.1230–c.1310) alludes to the hypersensitivity of some Jews over the slave origins of their parents; according to ben Adret, two Jews accused of being descendants of slaves tried to clear their names at Austerlitz (Slavkov, Moravia).

On the slave trade at Lyons, Verdun, Mainz, Regensburg, Prague and Kiev, see Lewicki 1961b:231.

(c) The existence of similarities between pagan Slavic and Judeo-Slavic religious culture suggests that conversion to Judaism was not a radical step. The examples of overlap between indigenous Jewish and Slavic practices cited below are tentative, since there is always the possibility that some customs were shared as a result of early diffusion between the two groups; a few of the customs have broad attestation outside the area (on possible Jewish influences on the Ukrainians, see Barac 1908, 1924–6; Dombrovsky 1959:1541). For further discussion and examples, see chapter 5.2 above.

Some Slavs had become monotheists before conversion to Christianity (Cabalska 1979:125). Their temples were built near a body of water and facing the east, the source of the sun (Harkavi 1870:171, citing medieval German chronicles; Reiter 1973:183); these two considerations are also observed in the traditional construction of European synagogues, though the requirement that the ark containing the Torah face east is traditionally interpreted in terms of facing Jerusalem rather than the sun. The absence of a Slavic priestly class, except in Pomerania or the Balkans, parallels the modest role of the rabbi in the early Ashkenazic communities: the rabbi did not always attend synagogue services regularly, was often not available in many German towns, and was not needed to conduct a wedding ceremony (traditionally, two witnesses sufficed). The status of the rabbi changed through time, especially when Christian rulers began to invest considerable political power in the hands of the rabbis, as a means of guaranteeing efficient taxation of the Jews (on the role of rabbis in early Ashkenazic society, see Steiman 1963:63, 48, fn 21, 76, I.A.Agus 1:1968:491). For example, by 1530 the Bavarian Jewish convert to Christianity, Anthoni Margaritha, could write that a rabbi was required for the wedding ceremony (cited by J.Mieses 1916:47). The emergence of rabbinical power might have been triggered off by heightened Judaization or by the resulting dislocations in religious practice brought about by Judaization (see Gimbutas 1963:183 for a parallel among the Baltic pagans).

Pagan Slavic priests, unlike the laiety, wore beards and long hair, as Orthodox Jews in general are wont to do (see the account of the Slavs by Saxo Grammaticus 1208, cited by Ellis 1978:3). However, the popularity and chronology of this custom among Eastern European Jews need more study, since in quite a number of medieval etchings of Jews, in both Jewish and Christian sources, Jewish males appear without beards (see, e.g., Margaritha 1530); though, there is some discussion in the Jewish literature that if the Christians grew long hair, the Jews should cut theirs short to maintain their distinctiveness (see Eidelberg 1962:121 and fn 33 and discussion in paragraph 4 of chapter 5.2 above). The growing of sidelocks, now *de rigeur* with many Orthodox Jews, is not universally depicted, though Jews could certainly have differed on this practice in the Middle Ages just as they do at present.

Moreover, it is possible that among the pagan Slavs priestly functions were carried out primarily by the tribal elder within the framework of the clan or family (Cabalska 1979:137); this is reminiscent of the Jewish tradition of classifying males in three groups, defined by the Hebrew names *kohanīm* 'descendants of priests', *ləvi'im* 'descendants of Levites, assistants of the priests' and *jisrā'elīm* 'the common folk' (literally 'Israelites'). While Jewish tradition maintains that these distinctions were passed on from Palestine to the diaspora, generation by generation, I wonder if these "castes" were not introduced rather late in some of the diasporas, including the European diaspora, during the period of Judaization. This would account for the fact that in the Slavic lands, Jews have synonymous family names of the type Hebrew *kohen* = Slavic *kaplan*, literally 'priest'; *kaplan*, not exclusively a Jewish name, may have been the original name, with *kohen* a later replacement that became popular during the period of "Hebrew component dominance" (see the discussion of Judaization in chapter 7 below). It is counterintuitive to believe that a "Palestinian" custom of this sort would be named by non-Hebrew terms that designated Christian religious professions as well. (On the Old Sorbian family name *Knez*, literally 'priest', from the 14th century, see Schlimpert 1978:62.)

The Ashkenazic family name *levin* is usually assumed to be a derivative of Hebrew *levī*; yet it may too have been an originally Slavic name, meaning left-handed, see, e.g., Upper Sorbian names *Lěwa, Lěwać, Lěwiš* < *lěwak* 'left-handed', and/or a derivative of 'lion', e.g., Upper Sorbian *law*, Russian *lev*, which, through formal similarity, was later replaced by Hebrew *levī* (Unbegaun also made the point that "Russian" Jewish names like *Levin* were probably not all of Hebrew origin: 1972:344). Today both Jews and non-Jews tend to regard Russian *Levin* as a quintessential Jewish name; hence, when Tigay finds a Russian character by this name in Tolstoy's *Anna Karenina*, he assumes the figure was descended from Jewish converts to Christianity (1992:36). For Sorbian and Polabian placenames formed from the term left-handed, see Trautmann 1948:92; Schlimpert 1978:59, 76. The name *levin* is not known outside of the Ashkenazic communities. The name *levī* that is popular in non-Ashkenazic communities may be unrelated to Ashkenazic *levin* and may be of Palestinian Jewish origin (see the examples among Arabized Iberian Jews, gathered by Laredo 1978, no. 665). Polish Jews also have names cognate with *lěwak, law*, e.g., *levko* (14th century).

In both Ashkenazic Jewish and Slavic societies marriages were traditionally arranged through a male marriage broker; this may have been an originally Slavic practice, since in Jewish sources, the profession had legal status only from the 12th century on (Abrahams 1896:170, 173–4). It is noteworthy that the institution of the male matchmaker is more common in northern than in southern (non-Ashkenazic) Europe (Baron 12:1967:288, fn 33; see also paragraph 8 of chapter 5.2 above).

The preference for home, as opposed to public ceremonies in a house of worship, is characteristic of both Slavs and Jews, in counterdistinction to the Christians. Heydzianka-Pilatowa (1971:62) cites Thietmar of Merseburg (11th century) to the effect that the Polabians rarely attended temple services but did make offerings to their household gods. The Jews also have quite a number of home ceremonies, e.g., the celebration of the Passover seder and the incoming and outgoing of the Sabbath, lighting the eight-branched candelabrum during the Hannukah holiday, circumcision (accompanied by the bestowal of a liturgical Hebrew name), the secular name-giving ceremony, the building of a *sukkāh* or tent (during the Festival of Tabernacles), *kappārōt* (see paragraph 6 in chapter 5.2 above), the Purim banquet, and optionally, the wedding ceremony. Most of these events are rarely or not at all depicted in Medieval Jewish or Christian art. The preference for home-oriented ceremonies may be motivated by the desire of minority groups to avoid attention from a hostile majority (Čistov also notes the home wedding ceremony among the minority of "Old Believers" in northern Russia: 1987:409).

There is also a large body of superstitions shared by Jews and Slavs. Compare the Slavic practice of smearing the blood of a slaughtered cock on the four corners of the house to appease the house gods (attested up to the 19th c). and the Jewish practice known in Yiddish as *kapores* (< Hebrew *kappārōt*), the slaughtering of a cock at the New Year as a propitiatory offering. The Jewish prohibition against consumption of pork is matched by a pagan Slavic practice of not eating wild boar. The Jewish talisman containing biblical verses attached to the doorpost in a Jewish home, known in Yiddish as *mezuze* (< Hebrew *məzūzāh*), has a pagan Slavic parallel in the placing of a cult figure in the corner of a building (see details on these two Yiddish terms in paragraphs 6 and 3, respectively, in chapter 5.2 above). Finally, there are striking similarities between the architecture of European synagogues constructed by the 15th century and reconstructed pagan Slavic temples (see the example at Pliska, Bulgaria); also Krautheimer's attempt in 1925 to draw parallels between early European synagogues and the plain churches erected by beggars' orders is worth noting.

(d) Slavs may have been attracted to certain aspects of Jewish culture, such as the relatively high status of women among the Jews (see chapter 5.11 above). These considerations were certainly at play in the decision of Anatolians to adopt Judaism in the early Christian period. For example, Feldman notes that the Jews in Aphrodisias were active in local government, supported law and order in a period of general lawlessness, organized philanthropy and excelled in astrology and astronomy (1986, 1989; on Jewish philanthropy, see Glanz 1968:8, 10–12, Goitein 2:1971:310, Reynolds and Tannenbaum 1987:86). Apparently, organized Jewish generosity to non-Jews was such that Saint Jerome (Dalmatia 340?–Bethlehem 420) felt the need to urge Christians to refuse Jewish charity lest it attract them to Judaism (Kimelman 1981: 240).

(e) The Jewish community absorbed Slavic members through means other than the acquisition of slaves. Slavic women could have early on joined the Jewish community through marriage to Jewish merchants, peripatetic or stationery, who had migrated to northern Europe without womenfolk (see, e.g., the 9th-century Slavic-speaking peripatetic Jewish merchants known as "Radhanites", who traveled between southern France and China, known primarily from a description of the Persian geographer ibn Xordādhbeh, c.846–86: Toch 1990:783). Some scholars have suggested that German and Slovenian placenames in Austria dating from the 10th century that contain the word "Jew" were, in fact, way-stations for these peripatetic merchants (though I share the doubts of many scholars about the accuracy of the etymology "Jew" for these toponyms).[13]

Finally, our understanding of conversion to Judaism will be greatly enhanced once the cordial contacts between Jews and Christians in the Middle Ages are systematically investigated. To this end, it would be useful to comb carefully both the Christian and Jewish literature of the Middle Ages. For example, Iserlin permitted Christians to bring cakes to a Jewish wedding in Wiener Neustadt and Jews could send New Year's gifts to Christian friends, including the clergy, provided they did so a day before in order to avoid the appearance of participating in the Christian ritual (Baron 11:1967:186–7, 376, fn 86).

6.4 Christian attitudes towards conversion to Judaism

Conversions to Judaism were recorded in pre-Christian (Roman and Greek), and in Byzantine Christian sources (in reference to Khazars), but usually without any particular expression of alarm. However, in Asia Minor and Western Europe, between the 4th and 13th centuries, the Church repeatedly issued edicts forbidding Jews from holding non-Jewish slaves (though sometimes non-Christian slaves were exempted) and from converting them to Judaism. The incessant preoccupation of church councils with these topics is a good indication of the widespread nature of the phenomenon and of the ability of Judaism to attract new followers. Conversion to Judaism posed a problem for a Church actively seeking the conversion of Jews and others to Christianity, one of the very concerns which fueled the First Crusade in 1096.

Two of the earliest anti-Jewish church edicts come from the Church Council of Sirmium (Sremska Mitrovica, Serbia) in 351–2, which criticized Christians who interpreted the Bible in the "Jewish manner", and the first Byzantine codification of Roman law, the Theodosian Codex 438 (Istanbul), which opposed mixed marriages and the conversion of slaves to Judaism. Saint John Chrysostom (Antioch 345?–407) admonished Christians about frequenting synagogues no less than fifteen times in his *Homilies against the Jews* (Harkins 1979; Kimelman 1981:240). The materials collected by Aronius in 1902 comprise 35 documents between 425 and c.1275 prohibiting the employment of Christian servants by Jews, 2 documents between 1159 and c.1261 prohibiting the employment of Christian nursemaids by Jews, 40 documents between 583 and 1267 against owning Christian slaves, 8 documents between c.500 and 1241 against mixed marriages, and 2 documents between 581 and 828 against Jews and Christians living together.[14] For example, as late as 1233, Pope Gregory IX was berating the German episcopate for allegedly allowing Christian servants employed by the Jews to be circumcised. The topic of the conversion of slaves surfaces in the Mainz Provinzialkonzil of 1259 (canon #8), and the employment of Christian servants in Jewish homes is the subject of the Mainz Council of 1310; similarly, the Wiener Provinzialsynode in 1267 prohibited conversion, the hiring of Christian maids, and even Jews discussing religion with ordinary folk. The Prague Synod of 1346 ruled against the employment of Christian midwives, nurses and servants of both sexes. A late document from Basle 1434 prohibited Christian nurses for Jewish children, social contacts and Christian participation in Jewish holidays, weddings or joint bathing. Numerous laws also emanated from the Hungarian territories, e.g., King Koloman (who ruled between 1095–1116) opposed the trading of Christian slaves, Archbishop Robert of Esztergom 1229 complained to the Pope about Jews converting Christian women and slaves, and King Béla IV (who ruled between 1235–1270) publically opposed conversion.

That Jews fared better in non- or partly Christianized areas is clear from the Christian literature. Church councils particularly feared the impact of Judaism in Slavic areas that had only recently been converted to Christianity: in Bulgaria, the first Christian monarch, Boris-Mixail, wrote in 866 to Pope Nicholas I that Christians and pagans were becoming Jews and converting others to Judaism. This is a unique reference to the practice of proselytes converting other proselytes. The Breslau Synod of 1267 complained that Gniezno Province, only recently converted to Christianity, would be an easy prey for alleged Jewish missionary activity:

> "Since the Polish country still is a young plant in the body of Christendom, the Christian people might the more easily be infected by the superstitions and the depraved mores of the Jews living with them. In order that the Christian faith be more easily and quickly implanted in the heart of the faithful in these regions, we strictly prescribe that the Jews...of Gniezno should not indiscriminately dwell among the Christians..." (Aronius 1902, #724; I follow here the translation of the original Latin text by Baron 9:1965:32–3).

A similar fear was voiced for Hungary before 1200 and for Lithuania in the late 15th century. The preoccupation with Jewish conversion of slaves also surfaces in Romance countries. Edicts prohibiting Christian participation in Jewish religious ceremonies are known from France (8th century) and Provence (13th century). See the Bull of Pope Honorius IV to the Archbishop of Evreux 1286 against Christians converting to Judaism, as well as the edicts of Pope Nicholas IV in 1288 and King Philippe le Bel of France in 1299. Jews who circumcised Moorish slaves were being admonished by Juan I of Castile as late as 1380. Finally, the Ordenance of Fernando I in Barcelona 1413 inveighed against proselytism.

What is the significance of these numerous ecclesiastical edicts? Caro, in commenting on Pope Gregory IX's letter in 1233 to the German clergy calling for prohibiting conversion of slaves, argued that conversion was largely empty rhetoric, except perhaps in the east German lands, though he does not say why these areas should be an exception (1:1908:408). Vetulani is more cautious when he submits that the definitive interpretation of the edicts cannot yet be given:

> "Fear of Jewish proselytism is easily discernible in the anti-Jewish law, especially with regard to Christian servants in Jewish households. To what extent such fears were reflected in actual cases of conversion to

> Judaism (...such cases were known in Central Europe from the tenth century) and to what extent they were supposed to motivate the anti-Jewish discriminatory provisions...is impossible to say" (1962:288).

Most recently, Lotter saw no reason to doubt the appeal of Judaism to Christians in medieval Europe (1991:163–4). A few of these myriad church edits could conceivably have been motivated more by ideological concerns and internal politics than by immediate realities. However, a host of linguistic and non-linguistic evidence (besides the actual recorded cases of conversion and slave trading) encourages me in the belief that widespread conversion of pagan and Christian slaves to Judaism was indeed commonplace.

6.5 Jewish attitudes towards conversion to Judaism

The Jewish records make scant mention of conversion to Judaism, since acceptance of converts by the organized Jewish community would have resulted in severe punishment by the Christian authorities of both the Jewish converters and Christian converts. The dramatic conversion of the Khazars to Judaism in the 8th century may have inspired the European Jews to engage in proselytism (see Löwe 1988:168), which in turn provoked strong official Christian opposition. Indeed, it was after the Khazar conversion that Archbishop Agobard of Lyon (816–40) expressed concern over the appeal of Jewish preachers to Christian audiences (ibid.:162–3; Battenberg 1990:54–5). Fear of persecution in their country of origin forced many European Christian converts to Judaism between the 11th and 14th centuries to take up residence in the Jewish communities in Muslim countries, primarily in Egypt. Of course, not all converts emigrated; occasionally graves of converts can be identified in European Jewish cemeteries by the epithet *ger* 'proselyte' written after the name of the deceased or by the patronymic name 'son of Abraham' on a tombstone (Abraham was a name popularly assumed by converts; see also fn 11 above). The grave of an aristocratic Polish convert to Judaism who died in 1749 attracted vast pilgrimages of Jews to a Vilna Jewish cemetery prior to World War II (see Cohen 1953:150 and photograph facing 161).

The attitudes of Jews to converts varies widely from writer to writer, and from area to area, but it may be permissable to venture the generalization that Ashkenazic Jews were by and large more receptive to converts than their Iberian coreligionists. For example, the religious Iberian writer, Jehuda Halevi (c.1075–1141), ranked proselytes lower than real

Jews, and some Iberian rabbis regarded Marranos, forced Jewish converts to Catholicism in the Iberian Peninsula in the late 14th–15th centuries, as gentiles (this ruling presented a problem for Marranos who later sought to rejoin the Jewish community). The complaint voiced by some Iberian rabbis in the 15th century that Jews were acquiring Muslim slavegirls as concubines may be motivated both by fear of Christian prohibitions of Jewish slave owning, and the general Iberian Jewish disdain for non-Jewish accretions to the Jewish community, especially the mixed offspring of non-Jewish concubines (on the notion of "Sephardic racial purity" among 16th–17th-century Portuguese Marranos in northern Europe, see Salomon 1982). The Iberian Jewish attitudes may reflect recognition of major ethnic differences between Jews and non-Jews in the Iberian Peninsula (due to the rarity of intermarriage and/or a desire to insulate the Jews from assimilation to the non-Jewish culture), but in northern Europe the notion may have developed as a defense against the much more numerous Ashkenazic Jews. In contrast, German rabbis, despite the problems inherent in conversion, displayed tolerance for proselytes in their midst. For example, the *Sefer xasidim*, attributed to Jehudah Hexasid of Regensburg (d.1217) states that it was better to marry a good Christian than a bad Jewess. Jomtov Lipman of Mühlhausen (end 14th century-early 15th century), rabbi in Lindau, Kraków and Prague, praised Christian converts in his *Sefer nicaxon* (finished by 1410). The Rhineland rabbi, Ja'akov ben Moše Halevi Mölln (c.1360–1427), declared it a misdemeanor to have relations with a Christian girl while pretending to be uncircumcised; I wonder if he was objecting to a Jew personifying a non-Jew, or to a Jew having intercourse with a non-Jewess. The attitudes of Ashkenazic and non-Ashkenazic rabbis towards the status of proselytes require a comprehensive comparative study.

6.6 *Implications for Jewish historiography*

The conversion hypothesis can provide a smoother explanation than any given heretofore for a number of heterogeneous phenomena in Jewish history:

(a) Conversion as the major cause of Jewish population growth up to the 12th century solves the problem of explaining the phenomenal growth of the Jewish settlements in Slavic Europe. The suggestions of an exaggerated natural rate of increase and/or significant migrations from other areas cannot be documented.

(b) Conversion could explain the use of Christianized Hebrew names in Yiddish, e.g., *zalmen* (discussed in chapter 5.12 above); some of these names became exceedingly popular. In addition, Ashkenazic Jews used Christian names frequently.

(c) A large body of converts, largely ignorant of Judaism and Jewish learning, could account for the relatively low level of Hebrew grammar and Talmud studies recorded in early medieval Germany (Güdemann 1880:119, 178–227, Abrahams 1896:358, Zimmels 1958:64, 66, 274, fn 3, Schatzmiller 1982:590–1) and in the Slavic lands (Kupfer and Lewicki 1956:160, Vetulani 1962:283). The German rabbi, Ašer ben Jexiel (c.1250–1327), declares that his Hebrew was too poor to teach Spanish Jews the language when he migrated to Toledo. In the 13th century Provençal and Iberian Jews regarded Ashkenazic Jews as "backward". Eliezer ben Joel Halevi (c.1140–c.1225, active in Cologne) wrote that there were no Torah scholars in most locales of Poland, Russia and Hungary due to the poverty of the local Jews (see also the correspondence of a Bohemian rabbi to Jehuda Hexasid in the early 13th century noted by Kupfer and Lewicki 1956:160). Even in the 16th century, the Bavarian Hebraist, Elia Baxur (c.1468–1549), blamed his fellow Jews for grammatical errors and cumbersome expressions in Hebrew (1541, under the discussion of Hebrew *dāraš, qrōvaz, māḥah, māzag, pāṭar, tiqqen*). Baxur may have had in mind the way Hebrew words were used in spoken Yiddish, but this is no indication of a low knowledge of Hebrew in the community, since Yiddish could have inherited features of old colloquial Hebrew which differ from the written Hebrew of liturgical writings (see Wexler 1990a). Baxur's contemporary, the author of the Hebrew-Yiddish dictionary known as *Mirkeves hamišne* (Kraków, circa 1534), also bemoaned the low level of Hebrew scholarship among young Jews:

> "...for young people...have learned nothing and understand nothing of [Hebrew] grammar. They make masculine into feminine, and vice versa, second person into third person and vice versa, singular into plural and vice versa. That all stems from the fact that the young folks did not become accustomed to grammatical categories in their youth..." (quoted by Timm 1991b:60).

The alleged migration of Judeo-Aramaic-speaking Babylonian (Iraqi) Jewish scholars to Europe by the 9th–10th centuries, which many scholars have posited, might have led to a "Judaizing" movement among the Ashkenazic Jews if the new emigrés comprised a larger percentage of ethnic Jews, and/or a larger proportion of scholars well versed in normative Judaism and Hebrew/Judeo-Aramaic letters. It was presumably these Iraqi Jewish scholars who brought the study of the Talmud to Europe, first to southern Italy and the Iberian Peninsula and subsequently to the Germano-Slavic lands (Clemen 1931:42, M.Weinreich 1:1973:352, 3:377–9). The recognized impact on German Jewish scholarship of French Jewish scholars and their descendants in the Rhineland, might also be accounted for by the hypothesis that some of the northern French Jews were of Provençal origin, and hence more likely to be of Palestinian origin, assuming that conversion played a less dominant role in the ethnogenesis of the Franco-Provençal Jews.

(d) The conversion theory enables us to propose a new interpretation of the recurrent traditions that (i) the Jews had settled in a number of European cities, e.g., Augsburg, Halle, Regensburg, Ulm, Worms before the crucifixion of Christ, and thus could not be held responsible for that event, (ii) that the south German Jews were descended from a Germanic tribe, the Vangions (Latin *Vangiones*, a tribe related to the Swabians that settled in the Worms area around 71 B.C.: Brüll 1879), (iii) that the Jews first arrived in Poland a century before the conversion of the Polish ruling class to Christianity (Weinryb 1962b:454–5). Weinryb dismissed such traditions (as well as similar claims among the Jews of Aden, Bukhara, the Caucasus, China, Cochin, the Crimea, France, Iran, North Africa and Yemen) as unsubstantiated since European Jews preserved only post-exilic forms of Judaism and talmudic traditions (ibid.:449, 451). I would suggest, alternatively, that traditions of this type may have been attempts by proselytes, or the descendants of proselytes, to defend their historically justified claims to a local origin. Weinryb's argument of post-exilic forms of Judaism and Talmudism is unconvincing, since these could have been superimposed at a much later date (the Talmud makes its appearance in Europe only by the close of the first millennium!). His claim that the myths were a reflection of a minority group in a difficult situation looking for justification of its rights (ibid.:452) could remain, however, relevant for the period after proselytizing had ended.[15]

In addition to the German Jewish traditions about a primeval settlement in the German lands, there is also a Czech Christian account in the Dalimil text (the oldest Czech rhymed chronicle of local history, covering events up to 1310, which was compiled in the early 14th century), that relates how Czech Jews joined with Czech Christians in defense of their common homeland against German attacks in the 10th century (for the text, see Havránek et al. 1958, Graus 1981:23–4). Despite factual inaccuracies, it is significant that the Dalimil text attempts to establish a Jewish presence in the earliest period of Czech national history, and particularly in the retelling of the Slavic struggle against German colonization. There is also a Jewish legend that Charlemagne, the first emperor of the Holy Roman Empire, invited the Jews to settle in his realms in the late 8th century (the legend is considerably more recent than the 8th century; see Baron 4:1957:64, Grabois 1966).

(e) Conversion could explain why the German Jewish mystics and pietists were so attracted to pagan and Christian forms of magic and superstition, a fact which scandalized the Iberian Sephardic Jews (see Güdemann 1880:222, fn 1, Berliner 1900:102 and Trachtenberg 1939: 24). In Zimmels' words:

> "While [the Ashkenazic Jews] were susceptible to any kind of superstition prevalent among their non-Jewish neighbors, [the Sephardic Jews] adopted only those practices which were regarded as being 'scientifically' well founded or approved of in the Talmud" (1958:249).

I would assume from this that either Judaization processes among the Iberian Jews began before those of the Ashkenazic Jews (assuming that the former were also descended from non-Jewish converts in North Africa or the Iberian Peninsula), or that Judaization was not necessary in the Peninsula since the impact of the local Christians and Muslims on the Jews was minimal.

(f) Conversions would not only account for the preoccupation with "Judaization" that characterizes medieval Ashkenazic intellectual circles (see chapter 7 below), but also for the widescale disinterest among Jewish scholars in the Middle Ages and Renaissance in recording the history of the "Jews" after the destruction of the Second Temple, or for that matter in studying post-Mishnaic non-Palestinian Hebrew (the neglect of the latter also characterizes contemporary scholars: see Horvath and Wexler ms).

(g) A substantial convert population among the Jews jibes with the claim that the first Jewish settlers in the mixed Germano-Sorbian lands spoke Sorbian (which was subsequently to become re-lexified to High German). Additional evidence is the Slavic vocabulary in Yiddish pertaining to aspects of the Jewish religion (see chapter 5.11 above).

(h) It is difficult to determine the significance of the absence of castes such as *kohen* 'priest' and *levī* 'levite' (indications of hereditary office) in some diasporas, for example the Caucasus (see also chapter 6.3 above). My guess is that such Jewish communities were largely of proselyte origin; the absence of a substantial Iraqi Jewish immigration to the Caucasus may account for the weak Judaization process in that region which would have been capable of introducing the caste names. The Ashkenazic Jews, who are prime candidates for a proseleyte origin, do have this caste tradition, possibly as a result of subsequent Judaization. It is imperative to determine how old these caste distinctions are in each Jewish group.

(i) Largescale conversion movements in the German lands might explain the need for a relatively tolerant attitude towards converts there, in contrast to the disapproving stance on proselytes of many Iberian rabbis.

(j) Conversion might explain why so many synagogues were recorded in 13th-century Poland (the evidence comes from two Christian sources). A separate synagogue might have been necessary for each group of Jews (as in Imperial Rome!), e.g., recent converts of German, Khazar or Slavic origin, "old Jews", etc. Some scholars have, in fact, suggested that Polish Jewry consisted of two ethnic components: the German Jews (a community, which, in my view, would have included both converts and some ethnic Jews) and Turkic Khazars (almost exclusively converts: see Poljak 1951 and Koestler 1976). Polish anthropologists have suggested that an ethnic dichotomy may have persisted into the 20th century, with the descendants of the Turkic Khazars represented in the main by the poorer segments of the Polish Jewish urban population (see Czekanowski 1960, citing pre-World War II anthropological studies of Jews in Lvov, the Western Ukraine). Earlier Czekanowski had also proposed that Polish Christians in urban environments were racially different from rural Poles by having a significant admixture of "Armenoid" features, due to intermingling with Jews who were primarily urban dwellers: "there is no doubt that this contact more significantly remodeled the structure of the Jewish population, as the minority group" (1957:368, citing Krzywicki 1912). A unique study of skeletal remains from a late 14th-century Jewish cemetery in Basle also postulated that the medieval Swiss Jews may have comprised two racially distinct types (Kollmann and Kahnt 1885:653–4).

(k) Conversion could explain the findings of geneticists that Iraqi, Iranian, Georgian and German Jews reveal striking similarities in their genetic profile, as opposed to Yemenite and some North African Jews

(Livshits et al 1991), or that wide segments of Polish Jewry showed considerable similarities with Poles in genetic and physical features (Krzywicki 1912). The common genetic features could be explained by a similar mix of Slavic and Turkic converts: Turkic Khazars and Eastern Slavs in the case of the Iranian, Iraqi and Georgian Jews, and Turkic Avars and Khazars, Southern and Western Slavs in the case of the Ashkenazic Jews.

7

THE JUDAIZATION OF THE GERMANO-SLAVIC JEWS

I have assumed that the defining hallmark of Germano-Slavic Judaism in the first millennium was its gradual paganization and Christianization, as ever larger numbers of converts joined the Jewish fold. During this period, but with increasing intensity in the early second millennium, the pagan-Christian elements of Judaism underwent Judaization. The latter phenomenon is relevant to the study of early Christianity, the final stages of paganism in Europe and diaspora Judaism.

Without Judaization the unchecked paganization and Christianization of diaspora Judaism would have ultimately resulted in the total disappearance of the Jewish entity in Europe, as the differences between the "Jews" and their coterritorial non-Jewish neighbors would have become virtually nonexistent. Indeed, most ethnic Palestinian Jews in Europe did blend into the newly emerging Christian communities. It is possible that even at this early time some Jews (of ethnic and convert origin both) from time to time may have sought to accentuate the differences between their culture and that of the coterritorial non-Jews, by espousing lapsed Palestinian Jewish practices anew and by reinterpreting current practices in terms of Old Palestinian Jewish norms still known in Europe or newly reintroduced by Palestinian Jewish immigrants. I call this compound process "Judaization". A separate Jewish identity could also have been reenforced by the failure of the Jews to eliminate pagan elements to the same extent as the coterritorial Christians.

I cannot at present measure the extent of Judaization of European Jewish culture in the first millennium. Presumably, as long as the Ashkenazic descendants of the Jews and proselytes remained in close contact with the German and Slavic communities, the impact of Judaization was likely to be minimal. The 12th century marked the beginning of new social forms that accelerated the Judaization process and served to protect the tiny European Jewish entities from oblivion. This was the first century after the First and Second Crusades of 1096 and 1146 which brought about the destruction of many Jewish communities in the German and Bohemian lands and marked the beginning of the institutionalized exclusion of the Jews from Christian society. The 12th century also witnessed a marked change in the representation of the Jew in Christian religious art, from a neutral unmarked European to a marked foreigner, often depicted as an "Oriental". The status of the Jew in northern European society continued to deterioriate progressively through the early 16th century, as witnessed by the expulsion of the Jews from the major German cities, beginning with Basle in 1397 and culminating with Regensburg in 1519.

The Judaization process assumed both an active and a passive form. Active Judaization involved the deliberate acceptance of pagan and Christian practices and the fusing of these practices with inherited Palestinian Jewish practices. Passive Judaization (or "Judaization by default") involved the retention by the Jews of pagan and Christian practices which had become obsolete in the original donor communities; as such practices became exclusively associated with the Jews, they could be recalibrated as "uniquely Jewish", both by Jews and non-Jews. After the onset of segregation, the Jews refrained from accepting new Christian practices, either because of accelerating Judaization or because of diminishing familiarity with Christian customs.

Judaization by default contributed to the widespread notion, shared by many contemporary Jews and non-Jews alike, that Jewish language, culture and religion are "archaic", i.e., that they retain practices that have disappeared from Christian and Muslim use. The label archaic is inappropriate, since living Jewish practices can hardly be called "archaic" and there is no reason to judge Jewish practices by the yardstick of Christian norms. Obsolescence of a custom among the Christians made a custom potentially more attractive to the Jews, though the need for finding a talmudic or biblical precedent persisted. For example, the Jews today define the Orthodox Christian and Roman Catholic practice of lighting a candle on the anniversary of a relative's death as a "unique Jewish" concept; even the German name of the practice, *jorcajt*, is regarded as a unique Jewish term. Among the Germans the concept became archaic in some areas about the 1200s, and the word itself has since undergone changes in form and meaning, to *Jahreszeit* 'season of the year' in standard German. While Yiddish *jorcajt* became Judaized by default, other originally non-Jewish concepts and terms had to be subjected to a conscious process of Judaization. For example, the glass-breaking ceremony at the wedding required active Judaization since glass- (or plate-)breaking persisted among Christians in one form or another.

If it is inaccurate to label the Jewish culture more *archaic* than Christian culture, it may be appropriate to suggest that Jewish society tended to be more *archaicizing* in specific ways than the coterritorial Christian societies. For example, the practice of the Ashkenazic Jews to name children after deceased grandparents meant that names obsolete among Christians could continue in use among Jews (see M.Simon 1992:172). The emulation of Old Palestinian practices inherent in Judaization also represents a marked archaicizing trend.

The anti-Jewish riots and communal expulsions that were set off by the First Crusade in 1096 and the Black Plague in 1348/9 brought about a diminution in Jewish-Christian contacts. Paradoxically, while these events led to the death of numerous Jews, the ensuing segregation of the Jews in Christian society also enhanced their group security. Though Jewish culture, religion and language enjoyed some degree of "protection" from Christian influences after these events, active Judaization appears, nevertheless, to have continued unchecked after 1100:

> "...Christian anti-Semitism...forc[ed]...[the Jews] to turn inward and shut themselves in isolated communities, thus maintaining, reinforcing and even creating many of their religious traditions..." (Friedmann 1967:236).

This echoes Trachtenberg's recognition, that the phenomenon of Judaization (the term itself is rarely used) gained force precisely when "Jewish life had turned more and more inward, as relations with the Christian world grew more difficult" (1939:17). While the rank and file of the Jews had good reason to deplore their diminished status and relative isolation within northern European society, there were Jews, especially among the rabbis, who joined the church in sanctioning the new conditions, since segregation not only offered some physical protection to a persecuted minority, but also facilitated the relatively unhampered Judaization of Jewish religious expression and folk culture and the Yiddish language that would have been more difficult, and perhaps even impossible, in a more open, pluralistic society. Segregation also enhanced the status of the rabbis within the Jewish community, as collectors of tax revenues and unquestioned representatives of the Jews at the Christian courts. Blumenkranz raises the possibility that the Jews may actually have been receptive to Christian measures which institutionalized differences in dress between Jews and Christians (1966b:140, fn 18). While historians have long been aware that a "Jewish golden age" in Hebrew letters and religious scholarship opened up in the 13th century in the German lands, few dwell on the significance of the timing. The interrelationship of this "cause-and-effect" process requires further study. The role of Christianized Jews, such as the crypto-Jews or Marranos in the Iberian Peninsula, in introducing non-Jewish practices into European Judaism, also needs further study.[1]

It would also be particularly useful to compare the Ashkenazic experience with that of the Jewries in those European societies that did not enact laws to isolate Jews. However, a brief perusal of the literature suffices to reveal disagreement even over the venues where the Jews enjoyed the most penetrating contacts with their non-Jewish neighbors:

> "[Contacts were] especially [close] in Germany—and nowhere else notably than in the folk beliefs that constitute the commonest denominator between peoples" (Trachtenberg 1939:x).

> "Without doubt...the reciprocal influence between Jews and Christians,..was much more significant in Spain than in any other country" (Beinart 1987:11).

There is also no little disagreement among scholars over whether Babylonia, Greece or (non-Jewish) Palestine exercised the greatest impact on Jewish superstitions (see chapter 5.2 above).

By approximately 1100, Judaized proselytes and/or ethnic Jews had created unique languages in Europe, primarily through the idiosyncratic merging of heterogeneous dialectal elements. Such a superdialectal quality was not typical of the speech of most Christians. In this way Judeo-Sorbian could become distinct from all forms of Sorbian spoken by pagans and Christians. Subsequently, in the partial language shift from Judeo-Sorbian to High German vocabulary, the German component of Yiddish came to differ from that of any single German dialect through a similar receptivity to and merger of a wide variety of German lexical materials. After 1100 we begin to note an acceleration in the Judaization of Eastern Yiddish (in contrast to the Yiddish spoken in the monolingual German lands) that took the form of increased use of Hebraisms, but the paucity of texts makes it impossible to judge the extent to which Jewish languages were already widely receptive to Hebraisms before this date.

Judaization often resulted in unique Jewish cultural, religious and linguistic creations, see, e.g., the reshaping of pagan and Christian practices, or the fusion of Slavic and Germanic customs with original Old Palestinian Jewish elements. Max Weinreich was right to stress that Jews constituted an independent cultural group and as such did not need to look around in the neighboring cultures for something to imitate. But I do not agree with him that

> "...in the final analysis, the question of where the single elements of a configuration came from is subordinate to the one of what the configuration has come to be and to mean" (1967:244).

Whatever the originality of Ashkenazic Jewish religion and folk culture, we still need to search for the origins of the components. I wonder whether Weinreich did not stress the originality of the Jews in order to soften the "shock [of] find[ing] the pagan *Holle* so firmly installed in a pious Jewish setting" (ibid.:246). I had occasion to cite a number of other original Jewish features in chapter 5.11 above, e.g., the maintenance by German Jews of the Slavo-Greek term for werewolf (though the coterritorial Germans used a different vocabulary for this concept), or the original meanings ascribed to Yiddish Hebrew *qwpwlṭ* /kopold ~ kobold/ and *trejbern.*

Despite the inroads of Judaization, the Jews may be the last repository of many European pagan customs that have died out elsewhere. But the old Slavic and Germanic customs do not always remain in a pure form. Many practices assume original forms among the Jews due to idiosyncratic mergers inspired by Judaization (a consideration internal to the Jewish community) and due to the reciprocal Slavicization and Germanization of Germanic and Slavic practices (considerations external to the Jewish community). Jewish religion and folklore thus provide us with a fascinating non-linguistic correlate to the original dialect *mergers* in Judeo-Sorbian/Yiddish that I postulated above. For example, some of the Balkan Jewish immigrants who arrived in the mixed Germano-Sorbian lands were probably speakers of South Slavic and carriers of a Judaized South Slavic culture and religion. In the Germano-Slavic lands, West Slavic linguistic and ethnographic elements were added to the South Slavic base. When the Ashkenazic Jews began to migrate eastwards into the monolingual Slavic territories, further Slavic adstrata were added—this time from Polish, Belorussian, Ukrainian, and lastly, from Russian. The custom of *jorcajt* is a confirming instance of such component merger.

The existence of active Judaization presupposes that the Jews were aware of the non-Jewish origins of many of their terms and practices; it is also conceivable that some non-Jewish practices were tolerated or not recognized as such, even though they had not become obsolete among the Christians. The heterogeneous mechanisms of Judaization need a thorough study; so far, the topic has hardly ever been treated comprehensively in the scholarly literature, though the phenomenon is vividly described in the writings of the medieval participants themselves. Another open question is the nature of the Jewish identity that prevailed among the Germano-Slavic Jews, both the common folk and the intelligentsia, before and after the Judaization processes.

In language active Judaization involved the replacement of non-Jewish terms by Hebrew words that bore a similarity in form and meaning to the latter. For example, German Jews today believe that *barxes* 'Sabbath, festive bread' comes from Ashkenazic Hebrew *birkes* 'blessing of' (the age of this contemporary interpretation is unknown to me). But it is hard to see why a bread would be named after the awkward expression 'blessing of', presumably the first word of the benediction; furthermore, *barxes* and *birkes* are not close in form (e.g., *a...x* for *i...k* (see also my discussion of Yiddish *tašlex/tešlex* in chapter 5.2 above). The hypothesis that *barxes* is derived from a Germanic goddess' name makes more sense, particularly since the expression 'Frau Holle's bread', another name for the bread prepared for the Sabbath and festive occasions, was apparently replaced by the similar-sounding Biblical Hebraism *xale*, which originally denoted the part of the dough offered to the priests in the temple (more examples and a detailed description of the Hebraization of the Yiddish language are given in my 1991b).

In the Eastern Yiddish dialects spoken in the Slavic lands, the intensified Judaization processes led to the replacement of many non-Hebrew words of various origins that designated aspects of the Jewish religion and culture. The following Greek, Romance, Arabic and Slavic terms have become obsolete everywhere in Eastern Yiddish and survive only in peripheral Western Yiddish (originally Judaized German?) dialects: e.g., Greek *tolme* 'bier' (in Judeo-Romance languages 'marriage canopy'), Romance *antšpojzn* 'get engaged, married', *memern* 'commemorate the death of martyrs', *memōrbūx* 'book commemorating the death of martyrs'; *poršn* 'porge the meat for ritual purposes', *prājen* 'ask' (now only with the direct object 'forgiveness'). Arabic *ʾalmemer* 'synagogue reading desk' has become *balemer* in Eastern Yiddish, presumably by crossing with the Hebraisms *bal* 'owner of' or *bime* (the latter is ultimately of Greek origin). Slavic *trejbern* 'porge the meat for ritual purposes' is alive throughout Eastern Yiddish territory, but competes regionally with Hebraisms like *menakern, menaker zajn*, etc. Some Romance words remain in Yiddish but without religious connotations, e.g., Romance *fačejle* 'kerchief' (formerly 'wedding veil') and *lejenen* 'read' (formerly 'read Hebrew books'?).

Linguistic Judaization by default takes place whenever Jews preserve Slavisms or Germanisms no longer retained by non-Jewish speakers of these two languages. Examples of unique Yiddish Slavisms are *litvak* 'Jew from the Baltic region or Belorussia', *nudnik* 'pest, bore', *pral'nik* 'laundry beetle'; in Polish or Eastern Slavic, these terms are now either archaic or narrowly dialectal (for details, see Wexler 1987b:172, 174–5 and 186–8, respectively; ms a).

In the domain of ritual, Judaization involved reinterpretations based on linking up non-Jewish practices and artifacts with references in the Bible or Talmud. Thus, as we saw in chapter 5.2 above, the pagan practice of breaking a glass at the wedding ceremony which was intended to ward off the devil coming from the north came to symbolize mourning over the destructions of the two temples in Jerusalem in 586 B.C. and 70 A.D. It would be interesting to know whether contemporaneous Christians also felt this custom was of pagan origin, and whether Jews knew how Christians categorized the practice. Occasionally, old arguments for Judaization came to be replaced by purely pragmatic considerations, as when ritual food laws are said to be worthy of preservation on hygienic grounds (Hobsbawm 1983:4); future studies should seek to determine the chronology of such waves of de-Judaization.

Contemporary scholars do not agree over the motivation and implications of Judaization. *My findings stand in opposition to the traditional conception of Judaization as a process of adjusting foreign elements to a predominantly Jewish framework.* For example, in Heler's view, the Judaization of non-Jewish customs protected the latter from rejection among the Jews:

> "In spite of its strong conservative character, the traditional Jewish way of life always accepted elements from the surrounding foreign cultures. Thus, it made such changes in them, and bound them so firmly to the whole old inherited system of Jewish laws and commandments, that the originally foreign elements assumed a new meaning. The main point was that everything in the foreign customs had to be erased that had some connection with another, non-Jewish faith, with the "Gentile laws". Only in that way did they become "koshered" and recognized as suitable for the Jewish way of life" (1939:605; see also 608).

For Jacob Katz, Judaization was a defense against the loss of original Old Palestinian Jewish customs and assimilation to Christianity (1961: 46, also cited in chapter 5.2 above). Finally, a few scholars even deny the existence of Judaization altogether (see Ta-Šma's critique of the views of Lauterbach and Freehof in 1992:98, fn 143).

For over a century now, a few scholars have recognized that biblical and talmudic citations were provided for non-Jewish customs (see, e.g., Güdemann 1880:166, 218; Schauss 1938:160–1), but other than characterizing the Judaization (and Hebraization) process in culture, religion and language as a "relatively late" phenomenon, even fewer scholars have sought to establish precise chronologies:

> "...not everything that we have taken over from the Middle Ages and that circulates for genuine and old Jewish, is rightly so; rather, many customs and views, taken as holy,..are a foreign admixture and totally opposed to the spirit of Judaism" (Güdemann 1880:227).

> "In fact the entire act [the *holekrāš* naming-ceremony], if one filters out the uttering of Bible verses, which could have been added in a later time, in order to impart a religious holiness, has nothing Jewish in it, so that the suspicion arises that one is dealing with an old German custom that may reach back to the pagan period. Such a custom could have been preserved more easily among the Jews, since...there was still room for a home name-giving alongside the ritual name-giving, whereas a second name-giving ceremony could not hold its own alongside the church act of baptism" (Landau 1899b:72–3).

In other words, Christianity may have been less tolerant of pagan practices than European diaspora Judaism.[2] We urgently need to determine both the relative chronology of each Judaizing citation and each non-Jewish practice. One of the problems confronting Jewish linguistics is that we cannot always be sure whether the Hebrew or non-Hebrew term for a single practice was original, e.g., compare the standard Eastern Yiddish Romanism *čolnt* and the rare Ashkenazic Hebrew (and colloquial Yiddish?) *ṭāmūn* 'Sabbath food prepared on Friday' (14th century). *Ṭāmūn* might have been a later unsuccessful attempt at Judaization or the original term (it does have semantic parallels in most Afro-Asian Jewish languages) which was supplanted in Europe (possibly under proselyte influence) by a Romance translation of Hebrew/Judeo-Aramaic *ḥammīn* 'hot (food)'. Many Hebrew male names were clearly coined later than the non-Hebrew translation equivalents used by Jews (see, e.g., Hebrew *ḥaim* ~ Romance, e.g., French *vital*, literally 'life', Hebrew *šem ṭōv* ~ Romance, e.g., Latin *bonum nomen*, literally 'good name', etc.: see Zunz 1837). Despite the obvious linguistic problems, a pressing desideratum of Jewish history is to separate genuine Jewish practices of biblical and mishnaic origin from later biblical and mishnaic pedigrees that were attached to Jewish practices of non-Jewish origin in the wake of Judaization.

The process of Judaizing shows signs of staggered implementation. For example, the practice of salting food as an antidote against the devil was widespread in German Christian circles in the early Middle Ages (see Ta-Šma 1992:257–8); the abandonment of this practice manifests itself first in the non-salting of *maccāh*, the unleavened bread eaten at Passover, possibly because the Passover Seder ritual itself was viewed as sufficient protection against satanic designs. In other words, the Judaization process may have first been applied to the celebration of Jewish holidays.

The Judaization process seems to have accelerated in northern Europe at the beginning of the second millennium, though some scholars have proposed even an earlier date, e.g., von Mutius dates the process of "rabbinizing" diaspora Judaism to the 8th century (1990:783), but such an early date seems to me valid, if at all, only for southern Europe. (The suggestion that rabbinic Judaism became the standard form of Judaism in the diaspora after the 4th century A.D. [see, e.g., Trebilco 1991:189] has no basis—given the Jewish iconographic evidence discussed in chapter 5.2 above and the evidence of proselytism presented throughout this book. Which diaspora does Trebilco have in mind?) Future studies will also need to ascertain the chronology of both types of Judaization (active and passive) in each European and non-European Jewish community; comparative studies will no doubt open up many new avenues of research. Also the search for correlations between intensified Judaization processes and other developments (e.g., widespread conversion to Judaism, or the cessation of conversion to Judaism under Christian pressure, segregation, etc.) will lead to sharper relative chronologies.

Future research should also explore the possibility that Judaization was motivated by movements of national consolidation among coterritorial Slavic ethnic groups. For example, Graus suggests that "Slavic unity" is not attested among the Czechs or Poles until the 13th century (1980:130—motivated perhaps by hostility to German eastward expansion?). This would mean that Jewish ethnic and national consolidation may be among the earliest such movements in Europe.

As I indicated in chapter 5.2 above, the chronology of Judaization can be reconstructed, at least *grosso modo*, by establishing when rabbis complained about Jews practicing what they regarded as non-Jewish customs. Another clue to chronology is when the rabbis complained that the European Jews were lax in their religious observances. For example, in early 13th-century Spain, rabbis complained that Jews neglected to wear the *tallīt* 'prayer shawl' or affix the *məzūzāh* 'amulet' to their doorposts (Freehof 1962:215); Meir of Rothenburg also rebuked German Jews who ignored the use of the *məzūzāh*. These exhortations suggest that the rabbis, alarmed at the close resemblances between many Jews and their non-Jewish neighbors, were actively attempting to return to Old Palestinian concepts and practices, or to eliminate (via Judaization) widespread non-Jewish practices and interpretations that had become mingled with Old Palestinian practices, such as the *məzūzāh*. Also instructive are attempts to "rewrite" superstitions. For example, rabbi Ptaxya of Regensburg described superstitious practices he observed among various Jewish communities during his journeys abroad in the late 12th century; an overzealous contemporary editor attempted to delete many of these passages (see Nachama and Sievernich 1991:124, #6/41). It is imperative to collect Christian practices preserved among the Jews stage by stage. For example, in art, some Christian themes were retained in Jewish illuminated manuscripts (e.g., zodiac signs, the Bestiary), but other Christian symbols were removed (e.g., symbols of Christ: Metzger and Metzger 1982:16, 32–3, 39). Particularly surprising is the fact that the Christian symbolization of the synagogue in medieval art and sculpture as a blindfolded maiden with a broken or deposed crown (see examples in Blumenkranz 1966b:64–6) emerges in a mid–14th-century south German Hebrew illuminated manuscript, only this time not blindfolded and with a crown on her head (see Narkis 1984:53, #49).

A major problem is to determine how the European Jews acquired knowledge of the Jewish written tradition that was a prerequisite for the intensified Judaization processes of the early second millennium. Some scholars have assumed that Aramaic-speaking Babylonian and Palestinian Jews who migrated to Europe after the Islamization of their homelands in the 8th and 9th centuries brought a Hebrew and Judeo-Aramaic tradition with them. Jewish scholars in the 10th century who came to Spain from Iraq include Moše ben Xanox, founder of the rabbinical academy in Córdoba, and the Hebrew grammarian Dunaš ben Labrat; the names of Iraqi or Palestinian immigrants to northern Europe are not known to us, but the existence of Arabic names among West European Jews, including graffiti on the 14th-century Gothic synagogue walls in Sopron, west Hungary, supports the case for an east-to-west migration.

Until the close of the first millennium, there was little use of Hebrew in northern Europe: the first German Hebrew literary documents date only from the late 11th–12th century (Elbogen 1916:22; Ta-Šma 1992: 19), though in southern Europe, the interest in Hebrew letters began earlier, e.g., in Byzantium, southern Italy and Muslim Spain in about the 10th century, to judge from the south Italian work *Josippon* and the Hebrew correspondence of the Iberian Jewish diplomat Ḥasdaj ibn Šaprūṭ from Jaén (see Colorni 1964:21ff; M.Weinreich 1973; Simonsohn 1974:831).

The appearance in Europe of the Babylonian Talmud (mainly in Judeo-Aramaic and codified in Babylonia and Palestine by the 5th century) and the Passover Haggadah (containing some materials from the 2nd–3rd centuries A.D. but codified in Babylonia in the 8th century) is also to be dated in the late first millennium (see Ta-Šma 1992:9). It is conceivable that the Hebrew/Judeo-Aramaic Bible was also introduced into Europe at this late date. As additional support for the claim that Hebrew was not always used by the Germano-Slavic Jews, I could cite the gradual acquisition of new functions by Hebrew among the Germano-Slavic Jews. For example, there is evidence that Yiddish was once widely used as the medium of prayer among the Ashkenazic Jews, but by the 16th century Hebrew dominated this domain, except marginally among women who were not usually fluent in Hebrew (see Fišman 1991). Despite the fact that Max Müller, the well-known 19th-century philologist, had pointed out the striking discontinuities between Old Hebrew (of the Bible and Mishna) and written Medieval Hebrew (1863: 233), many contemporary Hebrew scholars still continue to assume (without any justification) that all Jewish diaspora communities had an uninterrupted knowledge of Hebrew (see Rabin 1985:32).

In addition to Near Eastern sources, the Old Jewish literary tradition could have come to the Germano-Slavic lands from neighboring Romance Jews among whom proselytes possibly formed a smaller component and who thus preserved more of the original Palestinian Jewish culture, or who absorbed a larger Near Eastern immigration. The two Romance sources for Judaization that immediately come to mind are Provence and Italy. France, often cited as the homeland of much of German Jewish religious thought (see Ta-Šma 1992:95), is a possible source if some of its population could be shown not to have comprised settlers from Germany. Finally, it is conceivable that the Palestinian Jewish written tradition was actually brought by Balkan Jews to the Germano-Sorb lands in the 9th century but remained the property of a very small circle of scholars—hence the absence of extant original Hebrew literature and Hebrew inscriptions on Balkan Jewish tombstones. More research is needed on these pivotal questions.

The partial language shift, or re-lexification, of Judeo-Sorbian to High German lexicon, intended as a barrier against galloping Germanization, could also have served as a stimulus for increased Judaization, by favoring Hebraisms as replacements for some original Slavic vocabulary. The receptivity of Yiddish (and, to a lesser extent, other Jewish languages) to Hebraisms in turn stimulated the rise of a Hebrew literary tradition in northern Europe. *It is hardly a coincidence that the rise of written Hebrew in northern Europe and the Judaization (i.e., Hebraization) of Judeo-Sorbian both took place around the beginning of the second millennium—precisely when proselytism to Judaism was becoming more and more difficult due to the institutionalization of Christianity among the Slavs and Magyars.* There is little way to date the partial language shift from Judeo-Sorbian to High German lexicon, but the fact that no German Jews are recorded as speaking Sorbian in the Polish lands suggests that the partial language shift had been completed at the latest by the 13th century, when the first wave of German Jews appeared in the east.

Scholars have tended to ascribe the absence of European Hebrew documentation until the early second millennium to the ravages of a turbulent European history. I would interpret the break in the Hebrew tradition between 3rd-century Palestine and the European diasporas six-seven centuries later as a reflection of the rise of a massive convert community which was generally ignorant of Hebrew and had no need for the language. With mounting Judaization in the early Middle Ages Hebrew acquired the functions of a Jewish liturgical language and *lingua franca*, parallel to Latin or Church Slavic among the Christians. The use of written Hebrew—codified in Palestine and Babylonia by Jewish scholars between the 8th and 10th centuries (along with the fixation of reading norms of the Hebrew Bible)—curiously follows by a century or two the Christian efforts to codify the pronunciation of Latin in the Carolingian Holy Roman Empire (see Wright 1982); the rise of a Church Slavic liturgical language in the 9th century may also have provided a model for the Jews. Future studies should explore the possibility of a Christian influence on the Jews' choice of Hebrew as their literary and liturgical language.

It is unlikely that the alleged international trade carried on between Jewish communities throughout the world could have played a role in fostering Hebrew as a *lingua franca* among Jews, or encouraged the borrowing of Hebraisms in Jewish languages, as Abrahams proposed, since the Jewish role in international trade diminished by the 9th century (with the Radhanites), i.e., just prior to the intensification of the Judaization processes:

> "Jewish jargons arose in the middle of the fifteenth century *[sic!]*, and the phenomenon was due less to ignorance than to too much knowledge. The Jews were always bilingual, but in the fifteenth century there was hardly a congregation in which a large foreign element had not been forced to settle by continued expulsions from their native land. A jargon was inevitable, for as the only linguistic element common to all the Jews was the Hebrew, it came that many Hebrew words were introduced into the vernacular" (1896:359).

This argument fails to recognize that, of all the Jewish languages, only Yiddish is relatively rich in Hebraisms, partly as a result of the partial language shift from Judeo-Sorbian to German vocabulary (see chapter 4 above), and only a tiny educated élite could have availed itself of an artificial "spoken Hebrew". Though the Ashkenazic Jews, as speakers of the Jewish language with the most significant Hebrew component, would have been the major supporters of a Hebrew lingua franca (just as they were to be the prime movers in the Hebrew language "revival" at the close of the 19th century). Abrahams does, however, make one valuable point: inter-Jewish contacts could have contributed to the rise of a common written Hebrew lexical norm, as literary works tended to spread beyond their original borders. We must remember also that the unspoken Hebrew of each Jewish speech community was a dialect of the indigenous native language, e.g., French "Hebrew", Belorussian "Hebrew", etc., were lexically peculiar dialects of French and Belorussian, respectively. Thus, it is not surprising to find that the differences among the "Hebrew" recensions were particularly pronounced in syntax and phonology. Hence, Abrahams errs when he speaks of Hebrew as "the only linguistic element common to all the Jews". He is right, of course, that the Jews themselves thought that this was indeed the case.

It seems reasonable to assume that the Hebrew (and Judeo-Aramaic) tradition was abandoned in Europe in the early Christian era since most of its carriers, the Palestinian Jews and their immediate European descendants, had ceased to exist. The surviving Jews, and their Judaized descendants, in different historical periods, may have felt the need to speak a different language, or at least a different dialect, from the surrounding non-Jewish populations. This goal could best be achieved by incorporating some elements of Hebrew and Judeo-Aramaic, which still survived to some extent as liturgical, and maybe even limited spoken, languages, into the newly developing non-Jewish languages. But the motivation for borrowing Hebrew and Judeo-Aramaic might have been not only to preserve a separate ethno-religious profile (see chapter 3 above); the experience of the Romá (Gypsies) in Europe suggests that the Jews may also have had a need for a secret language. For example, those Romá who abandoned their native Indic language, Romani, often developed a variant of many coterritorial non-Romani languages based on non-Romani grammar and phonology and a small vestigial Romani lexical corpus. (The result was a mixed language similar in component structure to that of Yiddish—a Judeo-Sorbian grammar with a major German and a small inherited Hebrew lexical component.) Bakker and van der Voort have called these mixed Romani languages "Para-Romani" variants of European and Central Asian languages and have identified examples among Romá in the Armenian, Basque, Danish, English, French, Greek, Spanish, Norwegian, Swedish, Tadjik and Uzbek speech communities (1991:16; on language secrecy among the Romá, see Hancock 1976:87–8, 90).

The Para-Romani languages are both similar and dissimilar to the Jewish languages. The Jews and Romá alike developed Judaized and Para-Romani languages by means of common linguistic processes in most areas; both the Jewish and Para-Romani languages are used as *intragroup* languages. But unlike the Jewish languages, which are acquired at birth, Romá children were apparently exposed to Para-Romani languages only at the age of 8 or 9 when they began to accompany their parents outside of the Romá community. This is the reason that observors of the Romá conclude that a primary purpose of the Para-Romani language was to be unintelligible to non-Romá (Kenrick 1979: 115, 119 and Bakker and van der Voort 1991:40); children could not be taught the language until their "initiation" into Romani adult society. Note also that Romá in many parts of the world are loathe to teach their language to non-Romá. Secrecy may also explain why some Para-Romani languages prefer some elaborate original terms for new concepts, rather than immediately recognizable international loans, see, e.g., Angloromani *dikin-mokta*, literally 'looking box', instead of English *television*. The use of Hebrew, Judeo-Aramaic, and other Judaized substratal elements is also likely to render Judaized languages unintelligible to speakers of the non-Judaized cognates. The desire for separation and group solidarity, as well as secrecy, undoubtedly also explains the phenomenon of widespread lexical bifurcation that I observed in Jewish languages in chapter 5.11 above (lexical bifurcation has not been systematically explored in the Romani linguistic literature, to the best of my knowledge).

Now, if a major purpose of Judaized and Para-Romani languages was to insulate the group from the non-initiated, why then did the Jews and Romá not preserve their imported Asian languages in Europe as the optimal means of insulating the two communities from external influences? I can think of three possible answers:

(a) The original languages of the Jews and Romá were lost due to the inroads of linguistic assimilation that affected the original members and to the accretion of large numbers of Europeans who either converted to Judaism or assumed the non-sedentary life style of the Romá. (Future studies should explore possible contacts between Jews and Romá, since both shared a [semi-]nomadic way of life—the Jews usually by force of circumstances, the Romá by choice. If the amount of reciprocal linguistic interference so far seems to have been minimal, cultural contacts loom large, see, e.g., the adoption of Jewish symbols and practices in contemporary forms of Romani Christianity and the common preoccupation of both groups with ritual cleanliness.) Para-Romani languages are often spoken by originally non-Romani populations, e.g., see the so-called *Kaskarotak*, a group of non-Romá jugglers and acrobats who speak Basque Romani (Bakker 1991:71). Some elements of Yiddish, especially the Hebrew component, were borrowed by German Christians who fancied them for their own slang lexicons (e.g., German *Rotwelsch* is rich in both Yiddish and Romani elements, in different mixes, depending on the time and place of creation).

(b) The original languages of the Jews and Romá may also have been deliberately abandoned because they drew unwelcome attention to their immigrant speakers. Just prior to becoming bilingual in the local European languages and discarding their native tongue, the Jews and the Romá could have transferred sizeable amounts of vocabulary from their native linguistic baggage to the newly acquired European languages (curiously, a Greek component is embedded in all the Judaized and "Romanized" languages of Europe—though the actual vocabularies differ almost entirely). By using the local language, with varying amounts of a Jewish or Romani lexicon, the Jews and Romá could give the impression that they spoke dialects related to the speech of the surrounding Christian populations (on the Romá, see Hancock 1976:90; Bakker and van der Voort 1991:41). On occasion, the local authorities banned the use of both Judaized and Romized languages (e.g., Romani was illegal in Spain between 1633 and 1783: ibid.:39). This scenario is predicated on open channels of communication between the Jews and non-Jews, Romá and non-Romá. Later, in the period of segregation, the Jews and Romá could pursue the creation of unique languages independently of Christian linguistic norms.

(c) Non-natives who joined the Jewish and Romani communities might have found the indigenous languages obstacles to membership. In time, the percentage of speakers of the Jewish languages and Romani in these originally mixed communities would have become very small.

As the Jews retained two written liturgical languages, they alone were in a position to create, in addition to their Jewish vernaculars, a sort of "Para-Hebrew" *written* language—consisting in the main of the syntactic and phonological norms of their native Judaized European languages and Biblical and Mishnaic Hebrew vocabulary. As I indicated in chapter 3 and just above, Para-Hebrew in all countries of use should be defined as a special written dialect of the local spoken Jewish language, thus Ashkenazic Hebrew, like Yiddish, is a dialect of West Slavic; Sephardic Hebrew, like spoken Judezmo, is a dialect of Judeo-Ibero-Romance, etc. (Similarly, original "Medieval Latin" texts should also be regarded not as forms of Latin, but as dialects of the spoken languages of the users, thus, Latin written by a native speaker of French is a dialect of French, etc., since it follows the syntactic norms of French rather than of Latin: see Wright 1982; Horvath and Wexler ms.)

It is puzzling that so few scholars have noted the existence of the Judaization phenomenon, though suspicious facts have long been available. The phenomenon may have been eclipsed since the last century by the rise of Jewish nationalism in Europe and Palestine/Israel. Sympathy with Zionist ideology would also explain why almost all native speakers of Israeli Hebrew and non-native observors persist in the illusion that Israeli Hebrew is a "revived" form of the earlier Semitic Hebrew in which most of the Bible and Mishnah were composed. The fallacy of this claim is easy to demonstrate, but objective discussion of the Hebrew language "revival" is impeded by the fact that the topic has become somewhat of a tabu issue in Israeli linguistic and educational circles.

The unwarranted assumption by Jewish nationalists of the allegedly uninterrupted identity of the Jewish religion and peoplehood from the Palestinian period to the present sorely impedes the systematic study of Judaization. Hence, one could hardly expect the Belorussian-born Jewish nationalist (but non-Zionist) historian, Simon Dubnow, who accepted the non-interruption of the Jewish entity as a *fait accompli*, to take an interest in a phenomenon like Judaization which implied radical fissures and discontinuities in the Jewish tradition:

> "Jewish history presents by its sweep, or, more correctly, by its duration, a unique phenomenon. It includes the longest series of events ever recorded in the annals of one and the same people. Put briefly, it encompasses a period of time of more than three and a half millennia. And along this immeasurable expanse it was never interrupted..." (1921:6).

Most recently, the American historian, Paul Johnson, has added an imaginary "homogeneity" to the claim of an uninterrupted identity of the Jews:

> "From the time of Abraham up to the present covers the best part of four millennia... The Jews created a specific identity earlier than almost any other people which still survives. They have maintained it, amid appalling adversities, right up to the present... What was the particular strength of the all-consuming idea which made the Jews different and kept them *homogeneous*?" (1987:1—italics mine).

A major point of disagreement in the literature is the domains in which Judaization could or did operate. Many scholars believe that the non-Jewish impact on Jewish life affected only non-religious domains. The following quotations represent but a fraction of the existing literature:

> "The Jew has never changed this religion of his despite his two-thousand-year dispersal, but always and everywhere he has become acclimatized to the culture of the land in which he resided. So the Jew of the 19th century is still a Jew, just as the one of the 9th and 1st century... Now among Germans he is a German, among Frenchmen a Frenchman" (Steinthal 1901:64).

> "The Hellenistic and Roman period Jewish movements, which may have continued during six or seven hundred or more years, must have brought scores of thousands, perhaps some hundreds of thousands, of Palestinian-Mesopotamian non-Hebrew-speaking Jews into the Balkan countries and onto the northern shore of the Black Sea. Wherever they went they adopted languages and culture traits, always retaining only one inventory of distinctive traits—religious-ceremonial—from their historic past... ...culturally and linguistically, in all respects save religious and ceremonial, the Balkan-Roman Jewish communities became much the same as the peoples among whom they were living" (M.Jacobs 1942:43–5).

> "During the High Middle Ages...the core of Jewish life and thought still was the traditional law... Under its reign, the people weathered all sectarian onslaughts and maintained its unity and solidarity amidst diverse civilizations... On the whole, Judaism remained...the same monolithic entity it had become in the talmudic age, and its law served as both the most effective reflection of contemporary, socioreligious realities, and the main vehicle of historic continuity" (Baron 6:1958:148–9).

Future research into Judaization will need to pay much closer attention not only to the details of chronology, but also to cause-and-effect relationships and to the ranking of the different factors. For example, many scholars have claimed that the separate religion of the Jews and Christian discrimination were the main factors that assured the survival of the Jews in the diaspora (see Fishberg 1911:555). Such a statement blurs the relative chronologies and cause-and-affect relationships. In my view, entirely different factors encouraged the consolidation of a Jewish entity in the Germano-Slavic diaspora before and after the 12th–13th centuries. In the early first millennium, the tiny ethnic Palestinian Jewish enclaves in Europe were in large measure protected from oblivion by the accretion of massive numbers of Slavic and other converts to Judaism. It was the ensuing paganization of the north European Jews that ensured their uniqueness vis-à-vis the Christians, among whom pagan culture and religious practices were being gradually eradicated by Christianity. The process of Judaizing pagan culture further widened the gap between Jews and Christians. It was only after the 12th–13th centuries that Christian discrimination against the Jews could become a primary factor in the consolidation of a separate Ashkenazic Jewish religion. By advocating the physical separation of Jews and Christians, the latter inadvertantly unleashed an intensified process of Judaization which produced an unbridgeable chasm between Ashkenazic Judaism and Christianity.

The intensification of Judaization was accompanied by a change in the depiction of Jews in Christian religious art. Blumenkranz has noted that prior to the 12th century Jews enjoyed little if any stereotyping in Christian art; but after that date, they appear with a typical hat and costume, and with sidelocks and beards (though sidelocks and a beard are not universal in contemporaneous Jewish illuminated manuscripts: see Metzger and Metzger 1982:118, #168; 138, #43; 145, ##201–2; 210, #306; 225, #336 for examples of Jewish hats from the 13th–15th centuries). Jews begin to appear also in "Oriental" (Muslim) attire (see Blumenkranz 1966b:20, 24, 36–8, 103 for Christian examples; Metzger and

Metzger 1982:145 for Jewish examples). The preference for "Oriental" attire suggests that the Christians were reclassifying the Jews as a foreign element in the Christian body politic instead of as a marginal, yet "autochthonous" element (on the identification of Jews with Muslims in Christian eyes, see Cutler and Cutler 1986). The latter propose that the early medieval Jews identified themselves closely with the Muslims since most resided in Islamic lands and because of the overlap in Jewish and Muslim religion. This argument might be appropriate for southern Europe, but hardly applies to the Balkan and north European Jewries who are not of Islamic origin. Blumenkranz raises the possibility that Jews may have been prompted to accept the sidelocks and beard as symbols of Jewish orthodoxy from the Christian stereotypes (1966b:140, fn 18). On the other hand, the tendency of Christian artists to depict the Jews in their midst as "Oriental foreigners" may have been a reaction to the Judaization processes that were already gaining ground among the Jewish communities. Significantly, illustrations in Jewish books imitated the Oriental garb ascribed to the Jews by Christians; it is immaterial if the artists of illustrations in Jewish books should prove to be largely Christian, since the Jews could have demanded different depiction.

Evidence that the "Orientalization" of the Jews in medieval art has Christian rather than Jewish roots comes from medieval synagogue architecture, which until the 12th century did not differ strikingly from Gothic secular architecture; at this time, as I noted in chapter 5.11 above, the women's section, a distinctive feature of the contemporary synagogue, appeared in the German and Slavic lands. By emphasizing the Jews' preference for non-ecclesiastical architecture, Künzl loses sight of the fact that medieval synagogue architecture was, nevertheless, motivated by indigenous styles:

> "[Early European synagogue architecture] shows clearly the attempt of the medieval Jews to avoid any imitation of the church. This was also clear in the external construction, which with its vaulted architecture resembled a Gothic secular edifice, perhaps a city hall" (Künzl 1988a: 64).

The preference for Gothic secular rather than ecclesiastical architecture emphasizes the Jews' conception of themselves as part of the indigenous culture. Künzl also ignores the suggestion voiced by Krautheimer (1925) that medieval synagogue architecture may have been patterned on the plain churches preferred by the beggars' orders, which raises the possibility that the Jews constituted a "social" class with close affinities to other disenfranchised segments of the population, such as the indigent. By contrast, many European Jews in the 19th century sought a synagogue architecture which could highlight their uniqueness within the European body fabric. It is interesting that they espoused non-indigenous architectural styles that linked them with the Near East:

> "It was, after all, Christian synagogue architects of the nineteenth century who introduced the Egyptian, Islamic, and Byzantine styles that made Jews seem most alien from European and western Christian culture" (Krinsky 1985:71).

8

SUMMATION AND RESEARCH AGENDA

The purpose of this book was to account for the discontinuity of the Jewish people through time and space and to try to identify the probable forebears of the Ashkenazic Jews. Eleven important conclusions emerge from my investigations:

(1) The primary goal of Jewish linguistics is to uncover the common properties of component structure and evolution of the approximately two dozen Jewish languages that have been created in Asia, Africa and Europe over the last 2500 years. An ancillary goal of Jewish linguistics is to help to clarify major topics in early diaspora Jewish history and historiography, by posing new hypotheses and by assisting historians in choosing between competing hypotheses. For example, historians differ broadly among themselves over the extent of conversion to Judaism in the first millennium; the linguistic data (supplemented by ethnography) suggest that those scholars who see in conversion a powerful factor in the preservation of the early diaspora Jewish communities may be right. At the same time, we must never lose sight of the importance of corroborating linguistic hypotheses with non-linguistic evidence.

An analysis of the Yiddish language and Ashkenazic religion and folklore provides data which refute three traditional claims made about the origins of the Ashkenazic Jews, Yiddish and Modern Hebrew:

(i) The original Ashkenazic Jews in the German lands are *not* of French and Italian Jewish origin, as is commonly maintained. Rather they are descended primarily from non-Jewish, specifically Slavic and Turkic, proselytes of Balkan origin, who migrated to the Germano-Sorbian lands, where the Jewish community continued to grow in number mainly through proselytism.

(ii) Yiddish is *not* a variant of High German, as is commonly maintained. Rather it is a Slavic language, specifically a form of Sorbian.

(iii) Modern Israeli Hebrew is *not* a "revived" form of Old Hebrew, as is commonly maintained. Rather it is a derivative of Yiddish, and thus is also a Slavic language.

(2) The Jewish migration to northern Europe occurred at a time when the eastern reaches of present-day Germany and southern Austria were thickly populated by Slavs. The first Balkan Jews in the mixed Germano-Slavic lands were probably speakers of Balkan Slavic, though Greek and Balkan Romance may have also been spoken. These Jewish pioneers in northern Europe became speakers of the local Slavic language which they Judaized into what I called, for want of a better name, Judeo-Sorbian. Judeo-Sorbian exchanged most of its Slavic lexicon for High German at different places and at different times, but in no case later than the 13th century, since German Jews apparently emigrated into the Polish lands exclusively as speakers of Yiddish, a language with an overwhelmingly German vocabulary. In addition to a Slavic language, the ethnic origins, folkways and religion of the Ashkenazic Jews are also largely of Slavic origin.

The linguistic and ethnographic evidence compelled me to reject the traditional view that the Ashkenazic Jews were conceived in the Franco-German lands in the 9th–10th centuries. Instead, I saw reason to opt for the eastern Germano-Sorbian lands as the venue for Yiddish and the Ashkenazic Jews. While the term *ʾaškenaz* for the last several centuries has referred exclusively to Germany and the German Jews, this is not the original meaning of the ethno-toponym. From the biblical period to the end of the second millennium A.D., the term "Ashkenaz" has designated first Iranian, then Slavic and German territories; this fact gives a clue to the European "homeland" and migratory patterns of the people now known as the Ashkenazim, the largest of today's "Jewish" groups. The basic components of what we understand by Ashkenazim include Palestinian Jews, Slavs and Turks, and, marginally, others (e.g., Germans, Balkan peoples, and possibly also Greeks and Romans). Since the unique constellation of Slavs, Turks and Jews is found in the Balkans several centuries before the arrival of the first Jews on Slavo-German soil, the birthplace of the Ashkenazic diaspora should be placed in the Balkans in approximately the 6th century A.D. The Balkan Jewish communities themselves may have been colonial offshoots of Jews and proselytes from Greece and Asia Minor, but this earlier ethnic mix never called itself "Ashkenazic"; we might define it as "pre-Ashkenazic".

An important factor that motivated my hypothesis of a proselyte origin for the Ashkenazic Jews was the body of terms in Yiddish of

Greek, Romance, Slavic, Arabic, Turkic and Iranian origin that denote aspects of the Jewish religion and folk culture. The extent and intricacy of detail in the non-Jewish customs and religious practices of the Ashkenazic Jews convince me that Ashkenazic culture was largely "inherited", rather than "borrowed" from non-Jewish cultures. Two pieces of historical evidence offer further corroboration for this hypothesis: (a) the massive drop in the ethnic Palestinian Jewish population, both in Palestine and in the diasporas, due to the Roman conquest of Judea and the espousal by most Jews of Christianity (originally a recension of Judaism); (b) evidence of widespread conversion to Judaism in Asia Minor and Europe, especially in the Balkans and in the mixed Germano-Slavic lands up to the onset of the second millennium. Three arguments that motivate my claim that a major component of the Ashkenazic Jews was specifically Slavic are (a) that the first Jews in northern Europe, coming from the Balkans, chose to settle among Slavic peoples in the mixed Germano-Sorb lands, (b) that Yiddish is a Slavic language and (c) that the bulk of the non-Jewish terms and customs appear to be of Slavic or Slavicized Balkan and German origin.

(3) It is significant that a Balkan impact can be identified both in Yiddish and in Ashkenazic religious and folk practices. Some Ashkenazic folk practices turn out to be shared at one time by Germans, West and Balkan Slavs, but the *linguistic Balkanisms* in Yiddish are unknown in the German dialects. This is not surprising, since only the Jews were speakers of the three Balkan languages: Slavic, Romance and Greek. As some Jewish practices of putative Balkan origin were also shared by Germanic tribes, the offspring of the Judaized proselytes born in the German lands could have acquired indigenous German names for some of their Balkan non-Jewish practices, see, e.g., the Yiddish terms *jorcajt*, *hole-(xale)* and *barxes/berxes*.[1]

(4) Assuming that the Balkan Jewish immigrants to the Germano-Sorb lands were predominantly South Slavic-speaking, they could relatively easily have become speakers of the very similar West Slavic language, Sorbian. The language shift might also have been partial, involving the replacement of South by West Slavic lexicon, while the grammar and phonology for the most part remained unchanged. Presumably, differences among Slavic languages (dialects?) in those days would have been minimal. If a model of partial language shift could be ascertained from Balkan to West Slavic, then Yiddish would be the end result of double re-lexification: first Judeo-Balkan Slavic was re-lexified to Judeo-Sorbian and then the latter was re-lexified to High German.

(5) The vestigial Palestinian Jewish community that took root in southern Europe after the destruction of the Second Temple in Jerusalem in 70 A.D. succeeded in maintaining its group identity largely through the incorporation of considerably larger numbers of converts to Judaism in Asia Minor and Europe which lasted until approximately the early second millennium. During the period of proselytism, the Palestinian Jews exchanged their languages, religions and folk cultures for the languages, religions and folk cultures of the coterritorial European pagans, Christians and, to a minor extent, Muslims. All scholars agree that the approximately two dozen Judaized languages created in Europe, Africa and Asia during the course of the last two and a half millennia (perhaps by proselytes primarily or exclusively?) were based on coterritorial non-Jewish linguistic material. In this book I proposed for the first time that Ashkenazic Jewish religious practice and folk customs, *as well as the very "Jewish" practitioners themselves*, were also of largely non-Jewish, specifically Slavic, origin. This would mean that Ashkenazic Judaism offers a key to reconstructing European paganism and early Christianity, especially among the Slavs.

Hence, it is incorrect to view the contemporary Jews as descendants of the ancient Palestinian Jews or contemporary Jewish religious expression and folkways as uninterrupted evolutions of Palestinian talmudic Judaism and folkways. My thesis prompts a reassessment of the widely held view that the contemporary Jews enjoy an unbroken evolution of close to four millennia. *In my estimation, the Ashkenazic Jews have a history of approximately 1400 years, which overlaps briefly, in its inception, with the closing days of the Old Palestinian Jews. The extent to which the latter played a role in the rise of the Ashkenazic Jews must be clarified in future studies.*

(6) I have entertained the possibility that at least some of the early Jewish languages of Bible translation may have been created by converts to Judaism and not by ethnic Palestinian Jews.

(7) By about 1200 at the latest, the European "Jews" in the Germano-Slavic lands underwent an intensification of the Judaization processes in all aspects of language, religion and folk culture. The phenomenon of Judaization has never been satisfactorily described in the literature before. The onset of Judaization follows in the wake of the First and Second Crusades in 1096 and 1146. Judaization was made possible (or at least facilitated) by the immigration to northern Europe of Iraqi, Palestinian (and perhaps Romance-speaking) Jews with a smaller

proselyte component, who could have brought with them knowledge of the Talmud and Hebrew/Judeo-Aramaic letters (the latter was the native language of the Iraqi and many Palestinian Jews). Two of the results of Judaization which I alluded to above were the gradual change in the architecture of the synagogue (see the addition of a separate women's section) and a more prominent status of the rabbi. Discussions over some of the customs incorporated in the Jewish tradition are found in the rabbinical literature of the Middle Ages.

The present study shows that it is imperative to distinguish between the origins of a Jewish population and the origins of its religious practices and folklore. Sorting out the origins of Jewish communities and their religious and folkloristic practices respectively is complicated by the repeated mergers (both partial and complete) of originally disparate communities.

(8) The widely used term "Franco-German Jewry", allegedly representing the kernel of Ashkenazic Jewry, is unjustified. As far as the relations between the French and German Jews are concerned, the evidence shows linguistic elements being diffused from north to south (from Germany to northern France). Moreover, the most significant spiritual movement of Medieval German Jewry, the pietist movement known as Hassidism, developed in the 12th–13th centuries in the Rhineland and from there spread to northern France and south central Germany (Scholem 1966:39). Hence, a more felicitous label for any common Jewish culture shared by the French and German lands might be "Germano-French Jewry". This Jewry postdates the genesis of the Ashkenazic Jews.

(9) Scholars have been discouraged from positing a Slavo-Turkic origin for the Ashkenazic Jews since the latter have historically spoken Yiddish, both in the Slavic and German lands. The erroneous perception of Yiddish as a form of High German led scholars to assume that the Jews must have migrated from the German to the Slavic lands. Scholars repeatedly argued that the spread of German Jewish culture and language to the indigenous Slavic (and Khazar) Jews was due to the greater numbers, greater wealth and higher cultural level of the German Jews (see Baron 16:1976:7). A west European origin for the Ashkenazic Jews is unnecessary if we recognize that Yiddish was a Slavic language which underwent re-lexification to High German vocabulary in the wake of the eastward expansion of German colonialism; re-lexification was not at first accompanied by the eastward expansion of the Jews. The

homeland of Yiddish is to be sought in the mixed Germano-Slavic east, where we have a compelling argument for the espousal of "German" (lexicon only!) by Slavic-speaking Jews. From the Germano-Sorb lands, the new Jewish ethnic amalgam migrated westward into the monolingual west German lands and France for the first time, and southward into northern Italy and back east into the Sorb lands for the second time.

(10) The manifestations of the intense Judaization process in language that I noted in the Judeo-Sorbian/Yiddish-speaking communities were three:

(i) The massive use of Hebraisms in Yiddish.

(ii) The phenomenon of Hebrew component dominance in Yiddish (whereby non-Hebrew components of uncertain etymology were Hebraized or replaced by similar-sounding Hebraisms).

(iii) The large number of new "Hebraisms" that were coined by Yiddish speakers for Yiddish and written Hebrew.

No other Jewish language borrows Hebrew vocabulary to the extent that Yiddish does. Indeed, Hebrew ordinarily plays a very minor role in the formation of a Jewish language—in contrast to the idiosyncratic selection of dialectally heterogeneous non-Jewish linguistic material. Further studies should explore why Hebraization of a Jewish language and the scope of use of Hebrew was limited in some Jewish communities, e.g., in the Iberian Peninsula (where written Hebrew was used almost exclusively in the genre of poetry while Judeo-Arabic filled all other written functions). Note the comment (in chapter 2 above) that Iberian Jewish philologists in the 12th century sought Arabic and Aramaic etyma for Hebrew words rather than Hebrew etyma for non-Hebrew words.

A distinguishing feature of the Ashkenazic Jews is that they actively sought Hebrew words that had semantic and formal similarities with the non-Jewish terms earmarked for replacement in the Judaization process. Yiddish examples were pseudo-Hebrew *mogen dovid, -(e)n, gojlem, nadn, xale*—all possibly stimulated by similar-sounding Slavic and German terms. Future research should explore the extent that this phenomenon existed in other Jewish speech communities. Among the latter I am acquainted with this principle only in Jewish Bible translations (see Blondheim 1925:cviii; Banitt 1985:79–94).

(11) It is interesting to note that the largest Jewish diaspora communities are those which appear to have experienced periods of considerable proselytism before the second millennium A.D. For example, there is evidence that the Iberian Jews, who may have numbered as many as 250,000 at the time of their expulsions in 1492–8 (in addition to what must have been a sizeable Marrano population), comprised a significant proselyte population (acquired first in North Africa and later in Spain) and their Judaized descendants. The Italian Jewish community, on the other hand, despite the central role of Italy as point of entry of Palestinian Jews into Europe, never reached large numbers, perhaps because proselytism was banned in Italy as early as the 5th century (Stobbe 1866:171ff; Battenberg 1990:42).

In support of my claims, I presented a variety of linguistic and non-linguistic evidence, some of it discussed in the literature for the first time. The originality of the present work lay in the harnessing of diverse linguistic and non-linguistic data together. These data enabled me to refute the unsubstantiated thesis expounded by Arthur Koestler in his *The thirteenth tribe* (London 1976), that the Ashkenazic Jews descended largely from a Turkic tribe, the Khazars, who had converted to Judaism in the 8th century in the area between the Black and Caspian Seas. While Koestler proved to be right about a Turkic component in the Ashkenazic ethnogenesis, he erronenously overemphasized this component (which appears to have been far less significant than the Slavic), located the Turkic (I would have said Slavo-Turkic) ancestors of the Ashkenazic Jews in the Caucasus (whereas the evidence points to the Balkans and the mixed Germano-Slavic lands as the major venues of conversion to Judaism), and ignored the tradition of conversion to Judaism that began in Asia Minor and Greece at about the time of Christ, which contributed (significantly?) to the Ashkenazic ethnogenesis in the Balkans.

The present study has created a new agenda for research. Of the numerous research topics enumerated below, most have never been formulated, let alone explored before:

(1) What is the significance of the fact that during the revolt of the Palestinian Jews against the Romans in the 1st century A.D., the much larger Jewish communities in the Mediterranean and Near Eastern diasporas apparently offered the Palestinian Jews little support? Godbey assumes that this was because the diaspora Jews were largely not of Jewish (Judean) origin (1930:706–7). This apparent lack of solidarity

stands in sharp contrast to the solidarity most contemporary diaspora Jews express on behalf of Israel. See also paragraph (5) below.

(2) We need a clearer picture of the nature of Judaism in the diaspora communities at the beginning of the Christian era, especially of the differences between communities—those that were under pharisaic (tannaitic) influence and those that were not (the latter included, e.g., Arbela, Dura-Europos and Edessa [Syria] in the Euphrates Valley: see Neusner 1984:175, 183). It is not yet clear in which locales European diaspora Judaism deviated drastically from normative Palestinian Judaism; in this regard, it would be useful to explore when and where, for example, circumcision was abandoned (see Kohler 1903:94 and Schiffman 1985:25).

Moreover, the attitudes of Palestinian and diaspora Jews towards Christianity varied: ethnic Jews tended to regard Jewish Christians as fellow Jews as late as the 1st century A.D., perhaps because in Palestine most Christians were originally Jews, in contrast to the Christian populations outside of Palestine which consisted of non-Jewish majorities (Schiffman 1985:67).

The development of European Judaism illustrates vividly that Palestinian rabbinic Judaism was not the only type of Judaism practised in the Greco-Roman world. Unfortunately, we know little of these non-normative types, except for the evidence preserved by Christianity. Though often neglected by historians of the Jews, archeological discoveries, e.g., amulets, papyri, inscriptions, mosaics and architectural styles, can make important contributions to our understanding of the variety that characterized Palestinian and early diaspora Jewish cultures. There is, unfortunately, a large measure of truth in Godbey's statement, that Jewish history has too often been reconstructed exclusively from talmudic sources:

> "Efforts to write Hebrew history have generally been dominated by the apologetic pretensions and special claims which Judaism set up for itself more than two thousand years ago... rabbinism or Talmudism represents an effort to arrest the process of appropriating non-Israelite customs and traditions" (1930:686, 697).

(3) Both Judaism and Christianity absorbed masses of converts in Europe, Africa and Asia, but the impact of the proselytes on each differed considerably. The considerable numbers of pagans who converted to Judaism accepted some sort of Jewish ethnic identification, while profoundly reshaping the Jewish religion and folk culture. On the other

hand, the mass conversions of pagans to Christianity eventually resulted in the dilution of the original Jewish roots of the religion and in the break between Christianity and its Judaic parent. Future research will need to explore why a Jewish ethno-religious identity was successfully maintained in one context but not in the other.

Moreover, while Christians appear to have made no secret of the incorportion of pagan customs into European Christianity, some Slavo-Turkic Jews in medieval Europe objected to the retention of pagan and Christian customs, and contemporary Jewish scholars often rebel against the notion that any major Jewish practices might be of European pagan origin. The reasons for this difference in attitude to a shared cultural heritage need to be clarified. Specifically, we want to know (a) how the Christianization of paganism differed from the Judaization of paganism (and Christianity) in Germanic and Slavic Europe, and (b) to what extent Ashkenazic Judaism can enable us to reconstruct pre-Christian Slavic (and other) religious and folk practices. To the best of my knowledge, neither of these intriguing questions has ever been posed.

(4) The reciprocal influences between Jews and non-Jews in medieval Europe need further study. A mirror image to the Christianization of the diaspora Jews was the spread of Jewish features, e.g., talmudic motifs, to the pagan and Christian population (see M.Weinreich 1967:253, fn 36; Schwarzbaum 1968:441). On a possible Jewish (Khazar) impact on Slavic literature and culture, see Meščerskij 1956, 1958:119, 133ff, 152, Mathiesen 1983:195, 198, Flier 1985, Alekseev 1987 and Wexler 1987b; on a possible Khazar contribution to the East Slavic pantheon (in the form of the Russian sun-/fire-god *Xors*), see Haase 1939: 43 (as well as the cautions of Vasmer 1953–8).

A prerequisite to assessing the reciprocal relations between Jews and Christians is a better understanding of the synthetic forms of Judaism that may have developed in early Medieval Europe. It is unjustified to take the presence of Christian motifs and folk practices in a medieval text as clear proof of a Christian authorship. For example, Meščerskij ruled out a Jewish source for the 11th-century Eastern Slavic translation of Josephus Flavius' *History of the Jewish War* on the grounds that the text contained numerous passages that were reminiscent of "Christian" phraseology (1958:119). Such phraseology may indeed have been quite appropriate for some forms of Judaism at the time.

(5) Does Judaization occur in the absence of widespread proselytism? A full answer to this question requires a comparison of various

Jewish groups. It is curious that the volume of Hebrew in a colloquial Jewish language reaches its peak in Yiddish—precisely in the language of a society suspected of originating from a massive convert population.

Moreover, when did the notions of a single "Jewish people" or common Jewish historical consciousness come into existence? The chronology and geography of these notions are presently shrouded in uncertainty. The concomitant motif of the Jews as a "chosen people" (which is reflected in Jewish liturgy) is unlikely to have been current at a time when manumission of slaves and proselytism were resulting in sizeable accretions to the "Jewish" community. I cannot accept the claims of scholars like Dubnow (1921) or J.Katz (1961:6–7), that the concept of a Jewish peoplehood dates from the Palestinian period and was nurtured by a common historical consciousness, common religion and messianic hope. Friedmann has a valid point that

> "if Jews had had the feeling they constituted a nation, they would not have waited for [Theodore] Herzl [the founder of political Zionism at the end of the nineteenth century]...to call for the creation of a Jewish state" (1967:238).

It is astounding that tens of thousands of Iberian Jewish refugees expelled from the Peninsula between 1492–8 settled in Turkey and Turkish-dominated Europe and North Africa, but hardly ever in Palestine—an area occupied by the Turks between 1517 and 1917.

Nowadays, the notion of a Jewish peoplehood has few detractors: there is a tiny movement of Israeli Jews, known as "Canaanites", who stress the uniquely Semitic Near Eastern roots of the Jews (did they know that this very term denoted the Slavs in medieval Ashkenazic Hebrew!) and reject the cultivation of special ties between Israel and the Jewish diaspora (see Šavit 1984 for details); conversely, a few anti-Zion ist Jews, mainly in the diaspora, regard Judaism as a religion with no elements of nationhood.

It would be useful to collect information relating to contacts between all diaspora Jews and Palestine, see, e.g., alleged contacts of early medieval German Jews with the Holy Land (Büchler 1902:243; Freimann 1929:166). Two of the major European Jewish communities, the Sephardim and the Ashkenazim, do not appear to have had substantial contacts with one another before the expulsions of the Jews from the Iberian Peninsula beginning in 1492 (Baron 4:1957:80; I.A. Agus 1961: 242–4). Ta-Šma also points to an array of customs dividing early Ashkenazic communities (1992:22ff, 104). Many coterritorial Jewish groups coexist in a state of hostility even to this day. While the reasons could be social and economic, I wonder about the commitment of these "warring" Jews to the notion of a Jewish peoplehood. For example, the Castilian rabbi Moše de Arragel (of Guadalajara) described his early 15th-century coreligionists as members of a nobler "lineage" than non-Castilian Jews (1920–2:3), a view echoed by the Portuguese Jews in northern Europe in the 17th–18th centuries who regarded themselves as descended from a unique source, i.e., the "Portuguese nation" (Hertzberg 1968:270). The strained relations between Portuguese and Ashkenazic Jews in Hamburg and Holland in the 19th century, manifested in prohibitions against intermarriage with non-Portuguese Jews, suggest the term "Portuguese nation" was not viewed only as a statement of geographical provenience (see Wexler 1981a; on conflicts between Iraqi and indigeneous Jews in India, see ibid.:1983c).

Jewish speech communities also differ markedly in their Hebrew vocabulary, especially in the fields of Jewish religion and ritual. For example, 'evening prayer' and 'day of atonement' are *majrev* and *jom kiper* among Ashkenazic Jews vs. *arvit* and *kipur* among Sephardic Jews; 'prayer book' is *sider* among Ashkenazic Jews vs. *tixlal* among Yemenite Jews. The metal decorations on the staves of the Torah scroll are called by a different Hebrew name in the three major diasporas, see, e.g., Iberian (Sephardic) *tapuxim* (literally 'apples'), north European (Ashkenazic) *ace xaim* (literally 'trees of life') and Arabic *rimonim* (literally 'pomegranates'). These facts suggest both disparate origins and geographically separate processes of Judaization. The desire of the different diasporas to maintain separate profiles also contributed to the cultivation of different Hebrew terminologies. (On factors stimulating a common Hebrew norm, see paragraph ii below.) The relative age of all Hebraisms in each Jewish language requires immediate study.

The factors which contributed to the formulation of the notion of a single Jewish people are heterogeneous. Future research should seek to determine which factors played a major role at each period and in each diaspora. The following relevant points have been raised to explain the "unification" of the Jewish people:

(i) The anti-Jewish policies of the Church were motivated by the need for the existence of a Jewish people in order to justify the message of Christ (see the comments of Saint Bernard of Clairvaux, cited by Berger 1972:91, and of King Alfonso X of Spain from 1348, in the *Partidas* VII, xxiv, 1, cited by Baron 11:1967:54, 59). The need to preserve a "Jewish" people would explain Christian attempts to forbid Jews exposure to anti-Jewish literature, as, e.g., set forth in the Spanish *Fuero real* IV, ii, 1 of 1255 (see Castro 1971:546). Future studies should evaluate Christian intolerance as a factor in preserving the Jewish diaspora populations, since not all scholars agree on its importance:

> "It is indeed characteristic of the alienated Jew—e.g., Spinoza and Marx—to transfer the impetus for preservation from the Jew to society; the former declaring in his *Theologico-Political Treatise* that the Jews have been preserved in great measure by gentile hatred; the latter in his *On the Jewish question* that 'Judaism has been preserved not in spite of history, but by history'" (Kochan 1977:4).

(ii) The existence of a significant class of peripatetic scholars facilitated the spread of shared religious doctrines (see also the spread of Hebrew in chapter 7 above). For example, Meir of Rothenburg (d.1293) lived and taught in Augsburg, Konstanz, Mainz, Nürnberg, Worms and Würzburg, while Jicxak ben Moše (c.1180–c.1260), the author of *Or zarua*, worked in such distant locales as Meissen, Paris, Regensburg, Speyer, Vienna and Würzburg. We lack a comprehensive study of the correspondence between Jews around the world in different historical periods. For example, Ḥasdaj ibn Šaprūṭ (c.915–c.970), a physician-statesman at the court of Córdoba, maintained a correspondence with some of the most famous Jews of his epoch, including the Khazar Jewish king (Swoboda 1961:239; Lewicki 1964b). How typical was this? Baron notes that rabbinical decisions made by rabbis in Egypt and France were often cited as precedents for judgements released in Iran or Spain (6:1958:148). Expulsions and migrations also brought heterogeneous Jewish communities into contact, see, e.g., the mixing of indigenous, Greek, Arabic, Spanish, Portuguese and Ashkenazic Jews on Italian soil—a phenomenon which certainly could have encouraged the development of a common written Hebrew norm, if not of a common Jewish people.

(iii) Judaization is a powerful factor in crystalizing belief in a unified Jewish people. Both Jews and Christians favored the social segregation of the Jews. For example, Aŝer ben Jexiel (1250–1327), the illustrious pupil of Meir of Rothenburg, who migrated to Spain in 1303, opposed sexual intercourse between Jews and Christians because it would lead to the birth of offspring by non-Jewish maids (Zimmels 1958:257). Similar views obtained in non-Ashkenazic Jewish communities, e.g., Jehuda ibn Verga (d. Lisbon 1497) gave sexual intercourse between Jews and Christians as one of seven reasons for the catastrophic expulsion of the Jews from Spain in 1492. On the attempt by Ashkenazic Jews in France in 1789 to retain the right to a Jewish communal organization alongside their newly gained full citizenship, see Hertzberg 1968:344.

Economic transformations in Christian and Jewish society undoubtedly encouraged the rise of Judaization and Jewish nationhood. For example, Zamoyski tied the rise of Polish Jewish autonomy (a royal charter in 1264 first envisioned the Jews as a "nation within a nation": 1988:25) to rampant poverty between 1500 and 1700:

> "The most pauperized segment of the population were the Jews... The Jewish communities found it difficult to revive their economic position in a climate of mercantile stagnation which also exacerbated conflicts with Christian merchants. They underwent the same slide into parochialism as the rest of Polish society, which permitted the Rabbinate to re-establish a medieval grip over their lives..." (ibid:214).

(iv) The rise of separate unified Christian and Islamic worlds could also have encouraged the notion of a unified Jewish people—first in the framework of the *pax christiana* or *pax islamica,* and later in a larger universal framework. The origin and geography of the two Hebrew terms *gālūt* 'exile' and *gōlāh* 'diaspora', implying links between European and Old Palestinian Jewish communities, need to be ascertained in detail. For example, only the former word is used in Yiddish (*goles* has both meanings); it also appeared in the Judeo-Aramaic title *rēš gālūtā*ʾ 'exilarch (of the Jewish community)' used in Iraq up to the 11th century. The second term was used as an epithet for distinguished European rabbis in the form *məʾōr haggōlāh* 'light of the diaspora', I believe first attached to the name of rabbi Geršom ben Jehuda (born in Metz c.965–1028, and active in Mainz).

(v) The ability to initiate Judaization processes and to fuse bonds among diverse Jewish communities with varying proselyte inputs depends on the existence of unique Jewish liturgical writings, e.g., the Old Testament (even though this was shared by Christians and Muslims as well, though not subjected to the same interpretations) and the Talmud. For example, the absence of a unique literary tradition to serve as the basis of ethnic redefinition accounts for the failure of many related groups to become rebonded anew into a single people (see, e.g., the Celts, the Romá and paragraph 9 below).

Judaization should also be compared with the endeavors of numerous non-Jewish groups to link themselves with earlier civilizations. For example, the present-day Greeks, who are to some extent descended from the substantial Avar and Slavic invaders who settled in Greece between the 6th–8th centuries, also choose to ignore the non-Greek ethnic strains in favor of an ancient Greek pedigree (see Fallmerayer 1:1830, chapters 3–5 and Vasmer 1970). The Greek-speaking Cypriotes' claim to be of Greek origin seems to be predicated on ties of language and religion only (see Information Department 1964:1). On the elements of artificial archaicization in the Welsh national "renascence", see Morgan 1983. Many Western Slavs have long entertained the theory (unsubstantiated) that their ancestors resided along the Vistula, the Oder and the Elbe rivers at the time of the birth of Christ. Here again we note a "longing for 'roots' and for genealogical parity with their West European neighbors" (Schenker 1985:370).

I believe that the Jewish experience with Judaization provides phenomena which have been overlooked in the literature on "archaicizing societies" (on the latter, see Hobsbawm 1983:4; Kern 1983; D.Lowenthal 1985). For example, suggestions that a preoccupation with a prehistoric natural heritage is typical of new countries (D.Lowenthal 1985:54; one could add peoples without a unique territorial base), that interest in the past first developed in the Renaissance (ibid.:75) or that one cannot return to an abandoned traditional faith (Kedourie 1971:66; D.Lowenthal 1985:371) need qualification in view of the Jewish experience.

(6) The detailed history of the differential impact of ethnic Palestinian Jews on each diaspora community and the sources of the unique features of the different Jewish "communities" remain to be written. For example, how can we account for the existence of Jewish communities with radically different beliefs and customs, e.g., the Sephardic Jews in the Iberian Peninsula vs. the Ashkenazic Jews in northern Europe? Zimmels notes in his classic comparative study of the two communities that there was hardly a prayer in which the two groups did not differ (1958: 99); moreover, 13th-century testimony relates that while the Ashkenazic Jews tended to cover their heads during prayer, the Sephardic Jews did not (ibid.:102). Curiously, Zimmels (1958) skirted the factors which led to the mergers and (later) reciprocal influences between the two originally different groups (see also Baron 4:1957:80; I.A.Agus 1961:242).

It is significant that in the 13th century, it was primarily Ashkenazic Jews who migrated to Spain for purposes of studies and not the other way around (Marmorstein 1927:41). A less significant proselyte component in the ethnogenesis of the Iberian Jews may explain why these Jews excelled in the study of Hebrew grammar (Abrahams 1896:358; Zimmels 1958:66, 274) and traditional Jewish civil law (ibid.:6, 15). Iberian Jews may have also been less attracted to coterritorial non-Jewish superstitions, frequently ridiculing the Ashkenazic Jews for their espousal of "German" superstitious practices (Abrahams 1896:290).

Up till now, many scholars have attempted to explain the break between the Ashkenazic and Sephardic Jews in terms of different cultural orientations and geographical origins, e.g., the former were allegedly influenced by Palestinian Judaism, the latter by Babylonian Judaism (Blondheim 1925:cxxxi; Baron 4:1957:4; R.M.Goodman 1979:4–5; Goldstein 1985:8ff, 38; Ta-Šma 1992:10, 86, 229), or in terms of late differential coterritorial influences which led to a fissure in what was originally a single people, e.g., the Sephardic Jews were "Mediterraneanized" while the Ashkenazic Jews were "Germanized and Slavicized". On the other hand, Kahn represents the minority view that the Sephardic and Ashkenazic Jews descend from "two completely distinct peoples" (1927:1245).

A better understanding of the role of proselytes in the ethnogenesis of the Jews might enable us eventually to classify all Jewish communities according to the approximate mix of ethnic Palestinian Jews and proselytes. The possibility of quantifying the Palestinian Jewish element in Jewish diasporas through time has not been discussed in the scholarly literature. A rare appreciation of the fact that the relative mix of Jews and proselytes may have differed in different Jewish diasporas comes from Battenberg:

> "While one can establish an *astounding continuity from the late antique period* with regard to the Spanish *[sic!]* and Italian Jewish settlements, which in particular was passed on through the Babylonian and Palestinian schools of learning and was accompanied by a living surviving consciousness of the talmudic tradition, with regard to the Frankish [i.e., Germano-Slavic] Jewry we rather have to assume a new beginning, which in only a few lines of tradition reached back to the time of the Roman Empire. The question of a continuous development for the time being can hardly be answered, since there is practically no internal Jewish evidence in this area and even the external expanse of Jewish history can only be reconstructed with difficulty from legal texts of ecclesiastical or royal origin. The consciousness of the common root in ancient Ju-

daism seems to have been only later transmitted through the Talmud and talmudic commentaries" (1990:45).

The extent of the Palestinian roots of the various Jewish diaspora communities cannot yet be determined with any precision (this is the major challenge for the future), but Jewish languages can be classified roughly by the nature of their links to colloquial Palestinian Hebrew and Judeo-Aramaic. For example, speakers of Judeo-Greek and Judeo-Latin, through their direct contacts with Hebrew and Judeo-Aramaic, could encorporate a significant substratum from the latter languages; Judeo-Latin, in turn, probably fragmented into Judeo-Italian, Judeo-Provençal and Judeo-Catalan. However, Judeo-French, Judeo-Spanish and Judeo-Portuguese appear to be much later results of linguistic Judaization after the first millennium—of French, Spanish and Portuguese, respectively. I suspect that Judeo-Slavic speech was also the heir of *non*-Judaized Latin and Greek spoken in the Balkans, and thus cannot be placed on an uninterrupted chain of language shift leading back to Palestinian Hebrew and Judeo-Aramaic. It remains to be seen to what extent these two distinct linguistic "pedigrees" (with or without an unbroken link to Palestine) can be correlated with proselyte activities.

(7) We need to expand our knowledge of the racial and anthropological features of Jews in earlier periods. Unfortunately, the present information is spotty and difficult to assess:

"We cannot, at present, except in a few cases, correlate the varying blood group frequencies shown by local surveys, with the detailed history of the communities concerned... While the study of the blood groups and other genetical characteristics of the Jews has so far solved comparatively few problems, it can nevertheless be said that the results obtained are sufficient to show that this approach to problems of Jewish classification and origins is of great value" (Mourant 1959:172).

The earliest European Jewish remains appear to be the skulls found in the Roman catacomb of Saint Calixtus dating from the 2nd century A.D. According to Fishberg (1911:47), they show no evidence of racial admixtures in the community. In the 13th–14th centuries, we have skulls taken from a Jewish cemetery in Basle, which displayed two distinct anthropomorphic types (Kollmann and Kahnt 1885; Fishberg 1911:48).

Genetic studies can become a valuable tool for tracing the migrations of Jews and reconstructing racial contacts provided they compare

Ashkenazic Jews with the peoples who inhabit the areas in which large numbers of proselytes are suspected of converting to the Jewish fold. With one exception: comparison of Ashkenazic Jews with Western Slavs would probably be of little value, since the Sorbs themselves are too mixed with German stock. Hence, I can readily agree with Wijsman that "it is possible that a more complicated set of relationships may be necessary to adequately describe the ancestry of the Ashkenazic Jews" (1984: 446).

(8) The continuity of Palestinian Jewish culture in the diaspora requires more detailed study. Of particular interest to us is to determine which aspects of Old Palestinian culture survived longest in the diaspora. There are many striking examples of discontinuity. On the one hand, the Jewish religious art of the Roman and Byzantine periods differs in many regards from that of the Gothic and Renaissance periods in Europe (K.Katz 1968:156, but see Roth 1953 for an example of continuity). On the other hand, a small core of colloquial Hebraisms and Judeo-Aramaisms appears to have survived in most Jewish languages spoken in Europe, Africa and Asia, e.g., Judeo-Aramaic *rībbī* 'rabbi', Hebrew *gallāḥ* 'priest' (from the root 'cut hair'), etc. (see Wexler 1990e). However, Yiddish shows little or no trace of a number of expressions found in Judeo-Greek and Judeo-Latin, and in some of the later Judeo-Romance languages: e.g., 'prayer' used in the meaning of synagogue (see Judeo-Greek *proseuxē*), or 'hidden' used in the meaning of Sabbath food. (See also examples of distinctive Hebrew terminology in the Jewish languages mentioned above.)

The comparative study of the non-Hebrew component in the religious terminology of all Jewish languages also needs to be accelerated. It is interesting to note that the massive Greek influence on Mishnaic Hebrew is not matched by an equivalent volume of Grecisms in any colloquial Jewish language, though a Greek substratum is found in all European Jewish languages (see my 1985b). A comparative study should note in particular the semantic fields in which the non-Hebraisms cluster. For example, the concept of porging meat in order to render it ritually fit for consumption, or kosher, is expressed by semantically diverse non-Hebrew terms in *all* Jewish languages (dialectally, Yiddish also has Hebraisms).

It would be useful to determine whether religious expression was more subject to Judaization than other aspects of the culture; here a comparison of original diaspora rituals would be imperative. For example, the notion of a neutral type of food, such as vegetables, that can be cooked in either meat or milk pots and consumed with either type of meal is typical of Iberian, but not Ashkenazic Judaism (see the discussion of Yiddish *par[e]ve* in category II, Slavic 3 in chapter 5.11 above).

I have assumed that the relative loss of Palestinian Jewish practices would probably depend in large part on the practices of the proselytes absorbed in different locales in Asia Minor, the Balkans and northern Europe. But each practice needs to be studied in detail. Presumably, in the period of intense proselytism, Palestinian customs which enjoyed no support in Asia Minor and Europe might be among the first to be discarded; conversely, Palestinian customs could be retained by the Jews as long as they were also being practised by proselytes and non-Jews. In the case of a partial overlap in customs, I would expect to see partial restructuring of the Palestinian customs in the direction of the similar non-Jewish practices, see, e.g., the annual commemorative ceremony for the dead. There is also considerable evidence that Jews voluntarily abandoned customs which the non-Jews found threatening, e.g., the custom of throwing crumbs into the river during the performance of the *tašlīx* ceremony was abandoned by Jews in some locales since Christians thought they were poisoning the water sources; the custom of clapping upon hearing mention of the name of Haman, the anti-Semitic figure, during the recitation of the Purim tale, also had to be dropped whenever it exposed the Jews to ridicule (Güdemann 1880:156, fn 6). However, after the period of proselytism, it is Jewish customs which differed from non-Jewish practice which stood the best chance of retention by the Jews.

It would also be useful to compare the phenomenon of Judaization with that of de-Judaization, e.g., when Iberian Jews who were obliged to embrace Catholicism in the 15th–16th centuries clandestinely retained elements of Judaism, while at the same time creating innovative "Jewish" features, or when many late 18th-century German Jews began giving up Yiddish (for standard German: see my 1981a) and orthodoxy (for reform or liberal Judaism).

(9) European Jews should be compared with other European populations that lacked a single territorial base, and which also failed to submerge fully into the surrounding host populations, such as the Romá (Gypsies). While the latter seem to have parallels to the linguistic and cultural Judaization of the Jews (see chapter 6 above and my 1986a), they have lacked, until recently, a sense of Romani peoplehood and certainly entertain little or no connection to their ancestral northwest Indian homeland (see paragraph 6 above). The Jewish experience should

also be compared specifically with nomadic and semi-nomadic groups, since in certain periods, Jews were obliged to migrate frequently; here the Romá again offer a useful comparison, as well as the Avars, who had no fixed domicile until the late 6th century (Kollautz 1954:133).

I suspect that Battenberg is justified in defining the European Jews as primarily a "social" rather than ethnic or religious group:

> "...the history of the Jews in Europe cannot be understood from the standpoint of the history of a minority. Nor should their history be reduced to that of anti-Semitism, which only concentrates on negatively cast mentalities in relation to the Jews and the ruling majority populations. Rather it should be a matter of the interface of two competing social groups, which, even though their religious tradition has a common origin in the Old Testament, face each other as strangers. Self-maintenance and verification, types of reaction and mentalities have to be in like manner objects of the analyses, if one wants to understand the history of the Jews in Europe in its totality" (1990:23–4).

The definition of the Jews in the Germano-Slavic lands as a social group needs to be put in clearer focus. For example, there is some evidence that in certain historical periods significant numbers of converts to Judaism may have been drawn from the indigent sectors of the non-Jewish population, but the extant written references, which are mainly to non-Slavs, first date only from the 15th century. For example, according to the blood libel case from Endigen (in Breisgau, Baden) in 1470, a Christian beggar family asked shelter from a Jew, but the latter murdered them for their blood (which was necessary in the baking of *maccāh*, the unleavened bread eaten at Passover, according to Christian accounts). The Bavarian Jewish convert to Christianity, Anthoni Margaritha, relates the existence in 1530 of two Hungarian beggars converted to Judaism. Scheiber mentions such cases (the same?) from Trnava and Bratislava (Slovakia) and from Esztergom, Pest, Székesfehérvár and Tata (Hungary: 1970:564). In the Middle Ages, beggars, vagabonds, foreigners, the unemployed, criminals, the incurably ill, prostitutes and the Jews all constituted peripheral elements of the society. A comparative study of such stigmatized people would be in order. My belief that some marginal Christians may have drifted into (or were propelled to join) the Jewish communities is based on the fact that heretics, sinners, the religious unfaithful, criminals and opponents of the church are all portrayed in medieval Christian art since the mid-12th century with stereotypical Jewish features (see Blumenkranz 1966b:33, 42, 44, 77, 135, 141, fn 30).

Contacts between Christian thieves and Jews (also thieves?) clearly existed in the late 15th-early 16th century, since contemporary German slang lexicons (known as Rotwelsch, *inter alia*) had a significant Hebrew component (there are also distorted Hebraisms in many Christian ritual murder accounts from this period: see J.Mieses 1916:29–31, 55, Hsia 1988:50, 63, 80, Wexler 1988:chapter 3, 1993b). However, it is unclear to what extent Jews formed a contingent in Christian robber bands. In the 19th century we find increasing testimony of Christian beggars pretending to be converted Jews (Schwenken 1820, #571, Thiele 1:1840:10, Glanz 1968:13, 307, fn 19, 308), and of Christian thieves practicing aspects of Jewish ritual (Christensen 1814, Schwenken 1820, Thiele 1: 1840, Avé-Lallemant 2:1858:32, Andree 1881:111–2, Güdemann 1888: 173–5, Glanz 1968:307–8).

At different periods in history, membership in the Rom or Gypsy community has also been contingent on social factors, e.g. by learning the Romani language, by adhering to Romani customs and ethnics, by having family and clan connections; conversely, Romá who lost knowledge of their ancestral language and customs might be considered by Romá to be outsiders (though not necessarily identical to non-Romá: see Hancock 1976:86–7).

By conceiving the Palestinian Jews in northern Europe during the first millennium A.D. as primarily a social group, we can better understand how large numbers of Slavo-Turkic and other proselytes might have joined the tiny Jewish comunities; in this period, it may be appropriate to define the Jews as a subgroup of the Christian population. It was only at the beginning of the second millennium, under the impact of mounting Christian discrimination and the reception of the Talmud from Iraqi and other Jewish emigrés in the Germano-Slavic lands, that this "subgroup of Christian society" was propelled or enabled to forge its own, more independent, identity.

The fact that mention of Jews in early Christian documents is spotty might reflect the Christian conception of the Jews as essentially a socially, rather than an ethnically or religiously, defined subgroup in early medieval Christian societies. The Jews could have been included in the mention of ethnic or religious labels like "Slavs", "Avars" or "Christians", since a common ethnic origin of Jews and non-Jews might have rendered a special mention of "Jews" unnecessary.

(10) The process of Judaization in the diaspora invites comparison with the process of "Hebraization", whereby various Semitic and non-Semitic groups living in Palestine were brought into the Jewish fold in the biblical period and numerous non-Jewish practices were acquired by the Palestinian Jews (see Lieberman 1942:97, 106).

The study of the Germano-Slavic Jews suggests that Judaization intensified as a reaction to preceding periods of widespread conversion to Judaism. Other Jewish groups need to be studied before I can speak of a cyclical rise and fall in the intensity of Judaization through time and space. The motivations behind and means for Judaization need to be studied in each Jewish community. Here it is imperative to establish with precision the ethnic origins of each Jewish community and the nature of inter-Jewish contacts. For example, might the high achievements in Jewish religious scholarship in the Rhineland and Champagne between the 11th and 13th centuries reflect a higher percentage of ethnic Jews there than in the Germano-Sorbian lands? Or an earlier reception of the Judeo-Iraqi religious tradition.

(11) In the preceding chapters I have emphasized the commonality of customs among north European Jews and Slavs. But there are also important differences between the two groups both in inventory and distribution of practices. For example, while Jews and Slavs both utilized the cock or hen in expiatory sacrifices, the use of the cock seems to be greater in Slavic pre-Christian circles than among the Jews. Also, the absence of widespread (common?) Slavic customs among the Jews requires explanation, see, e.g., the preference for white as the color of mourning among early Slavs or the burial of an unmarried woman in bridal garb (discussed by Schneeweiss 1931:47, 95, 99, 113; 1933:368–70).

(12) The possibility that Balkan Jews migrated north into the mixed Germano-Slavic lands together with Southern Slavs has never been raised before in the literature and opens up numerous new topics for research.

It would be useful to try to determine the relative chronology of three events: (i) Balkan immigration (of Jews and non-Jews both) to the Germano-Slavic lands, (ii) the process of partial language shift from Judeo-Sorbian to High German lexicon, and (iii) the various forms of Judaization (it would be interesting to know if all forms were simultaneous). For example, could the partial language shift from Judeo-Sorbian to German vocabulary have taken place while Balkan Jews were still migrating into the Germano-Sorb lands?

Also to be explored is the question of whether the proselytes and their descendants who formed the basis of the Asia Minor Jewish diasporas played a role in the ethnogenesis of the Balkan Jews, or whether the latter were first constituted *in situ* from local converts. One revealing indication of the northward Jewish migration from Greece to the Germano-Slavic lands might be the distribution of Judeo-Greek *sambata* 'Sabbath' (< Hebrew *šabbāt*) in Christian languages which I mentioned in chapter 4 above. The dissimilation of *bb* to *mb* looks like an attempt by Judeo-Greek speakers to imitate the original long consonant in Hebrew, which was ungrammatical in Greek (note the simplification of *bb* to *b* in non-Judaized Greek and Latin). Reflexes of the nasal consonant resulting from dissimilation (either in the form of a consonant or a nasalized vowel) run throughout the Balkan Peninsula, see, e.g., Old Church Slavic (= Old Macedonian) *sõbota*, Rumanian *sâmbătă*, Hungarian *szombat*, German *sam(stag)* and French *samedi* (from German). Non-Balkan languages have reflexes of the Hebraism without *m* which reflect the non-Judaized Latin or Greek Christian form, e.g., Spanish *sábado*, Italian *sabato*. I wonder whether the spread of the loans with Judeo-Greek *mb* can serve as a faithful mirror of the gradual northward migration of Jews (see Wexler 1987b:25–7).

(13) The traditional disinterest among Jewish scholars prior to the 19th century in recording and writing Jewish diaspora history (see details in Lewis 1975:21–8; Kochan 1977) stands in contrast to their interest in biblical and Hellenistic Jewish history. Could this be a reaction to the Jewish diaspora experience of accepting large numbers of proselytes into the community? Also, I wonder whether the Jewish attitudes were in any way shaped by the coterritorial Christian preoccupation with biblical topics in the framework of their theological studies (see H.Simon 1992:155–7). Alternatively, periodic disinterest in Jewish diaspora history might have been caused by a belief in the unity of the Jewish people and their links with Palestine. Yerushalmi has suggested that the long-term Jewish disinterest in post-biblical history may have been motivated by the belief that the biblical interpretation of history sufficed and required no discussion of new events (1982:22ff). Kern believes that the absence of surviving landmarks (in contrast to the Christians) obliged the European Jews to internalize their landmarks in memory and oral form (1983:51).

As further evidence for the disregard for diaspora Jewish culture, I would note the traditional disdain of the Jews for their own diaspora languages in contrast to their high regard for Biblical and Mishnaic (but less so medieval) Hebrew, and the fact that no major universal Jewish holidays are connected with historical events that postdate the Maccabean revolt in 165 B.C. (the basis for the holiday of Hannukah). In fact, some Jewish liturgical works, such as the Books of the Maccabees, were preserved only among Christians (Yerushalmi 1982:15–6).

(14) Native German religion and folk culture apparently played a relatively minor role in the formation of early Ashkenazic religion and folk culture, even though, significantly, the Sorbian-speaking Jews did undergo a partial language shift to High German vocabulary. This topic invites further study.

(15) The traditional view holds that Medieval Latin was a direct continuation of the written Latin of Imperial Rome. In 1982 Roger Wright broke with this convention by proposing that Medieval Latin was "invented" by Carolingian scholars in approximately the early 9th century in order to standardize the pronunciation of the liturgy. If Wright's hypothesis is correct, then the "revived" Latin of 9th-century Europe offers a parallel with written Hebrew, which, in my view, also developed in northern Europe at the end of the first millennium. Unlike the Old Semitic Hebrew which had become extinct as a spoken language by the 3rd century A.D., and possibly as a written and liturgical language in most of Europe until the 10th–11th century, written Medieval Hebrew was "revived" by superimposing a Biblical and Mishnaic Hebrew lexicon onto a Yiddish (Slavic) syntax. The possiblity that the "revival" of Latin served as a model for the "revival" of Medieval Hebrew by the Jews merits study; the chronological parallels are suspicious (see Horvath and Wexler ms).

A related topic that also awaits clarification is the extent to which Modern Hebrew language planning of the late 19th and early 20th century was influenced by the ideologies of coterritorial Belorussian and Ukrainian language planners. The three Slavic language revivals show striking parallels. In all three speech communities planners (their stated ideologies notwithstanding) were preoccupied with "nativizing" (i.e., Hebraizing, Belorussifying, etc.) their lexicon; in the case of the Jews, the syntax of Hebrew remained entirely Yiddish, while most Belorussians continued to graft a Belorussian lexicon onto a Russian or Polish syntax and phonology (see Wexler 1990f on Modern Hebrew and 1974b and 1992a on Belorussian and Ukrainian).

Interruptions in the transmission of Hebrew in other Jewish communities need to be collected; for an Egyptian Jewish example from the first millennium A.D., see Golb 1965:269–70.

(16) The syncretic processes which I have identified in the Ashkenazic Jewish community can be defined as both "progressive" and "regressive". When the original Palestinian Jewish culture and religion in the Balkans and northern Europe were becoming radically submerged in the surrounding non-Jewish culture and religion up until the beginning of the second millennium, we may speak of progressive syncretism. Subsequently, after about 1200, when the process of radical Judaization set in, the retroactive attempts to recalibrate Ashkenazic Jewish norms according to Old Palestinian Jewish models constitute what may be called regressive syncretism. Future studies should compare the progressive/regressive processes in the Ashkenazic experience with similar merged types elsewhere. For example, the adaptation of the African slave diaspora to Portuguese Catholic culture and religion in colonial Brazil may be called progressive syncretism; in the 19th century, contacts with the West African homeland led to a recalibration along African norms—i.e., regressive syncretism (see details in Verger 1981).

I have had occasion to note that anachronistic interpretations of earlier historical events and subjective biases are, unfortunately, all too common in the field of Jewish history (see also Kraabel 1979:479). For example, Kedourie expresses surprise that a 14th-century Spanish Haggadah illustration shows men and women together in the synagogue, when they should be segregrated according to contemporary orthodox practice (1979c:76); he does not entertain the possibility that the role of women in the Iberian syngogue service may well have differed from the diminished role of women in contemporary orthodox Ashkenazic practice. Moreover, Kedourie assumes that since the Jews were allegedly proficient in Hebrew in the Middle Ages, errors in Hebrew grammar or spelling in Medieval Jewish illuminated manuscripts must reflect the work of non-Jewish artists not sufficiently familiar with Jewish requirements (1979a:132; see also Reider 1929:158–9 and Metzger and Metzger 1982:67). This is a simplistic argument. Note also the surprise of Metzger and Metzger that a prayer shawl should be depicted with red, rather than blue, stripes that I mentioned in chapter 5.2 above.

Subjective judgements, all too frequently embedded in scholarly investigations, must be extirpated. Consider the two following comments expressing disdain for Germanic and Slavic customs:

> "The "Star of David", which developed out of the protective blessing against the Drud, may now have rid itself of its misunderstood meaning in the realm of superstition and kabbalistic mysticism; but scholarship cannot be satisfied with the fact that Judaism has hauled out a symbol or mark for itself from the lumber-room of superstition, which it must share with cow stalls and the maternity room" (Güdemann 1916:139).

> "And what is perhaps more regrettable is the fact that Slavonic and Teutonic pagan superstitions and customs also forced their way into the folklore of the Jews and are now being styled Jewish survivals of primitive Judaism" (Rappoport 1937:4).

At least, the awareness of Slavic pagan origins of Jewish cultural patterns in Rappoport's statement is unusual among Jewish ethnographers.

While it is our obligation to avoid interpreting the past through the eyes of the present, the lessons of the present can sometimes give guidance in interpreting the past. There are two ways in which this is true for the proselyte hypothesis:

(a) Some readers may balk at the proposition that large numbers of non-Jews might have chosen to become Jews. Contemporary Jews do not actively proselytize (possibly this is the heritage of centuries of segregation in societies where conversion to Judaism was illegal); conversion today occurs almost only in the context of marriage. Yet, present developments offer a compelling parallel to the conversion model that I have proposed for the first millennium in Europe. Statistics show that at least fifty percent of the marriages contracted by Jews today in North America, Western Europe and the European regions of the former Soviet Union are with a non-Jewish spouse, few of whom convert formally to Judaism. Though there are no statistics on the ethno-religious affiliation of the offspring of mixed marriages, clearly some of them are raised as Jews. There is hardly a synagogue of the reform, liberal or conservative, and even orthodox, rite today in Western Europe or North America which does not count among its members converts to Judaism and non-Jewish "frequenters", or to use the old term, "God-Fearers". If the current rate of intermarriage continues unchecked for several generations, then the gene pool of the Jewish community will be considerably altered. This is precisely the development I have proposed for the creation of the first Ashkenazic Jews in the Balkans and Germano-Sorb lands.

(b) During the first millennium Judaism assumed a variety of forms in the diasporas of Asia Minor, Africa and Europe, in part due to internal innovations stemming from the lack of communication with Palestinian normative Judaism, and in part due to the impact of local pagan cults (see, e.g., the fusion of the Phrygian Sabazios cult with Judaism, and its spread from Asia Minor to Rome in the early centuries of the Christian era, cited in chapter 6 above). There is no clearer testimony to the variety of Jewish expression in the early Christian centuries than the art of the synagogue ruins unearthed in Western Asia, southern Europe and North Africa, and early Christian art itself. It was in such vibrant and intellectually variegated atmospheres that numerous non-Jews became attached to the Jewish community in one form or other. The rise of the reform or liberal movement within German Judaism in the 19th century and the "Jews for Jesus Movement" in America in the 20th century have restored a variety of religious expression to the Jewish diaspora communities that had not been tolerated for many centuries and is still not tolerated by the state-sponsored Judaism in Israel. Arguments that these movements in Judaism were influenced by Christianity and are thus counter to the "spirit of Judaism" miss an important point: many of the "innovations" that these movements introduced, e.g., the absence of a segregated women's section in the synagogue and the ordination of women cantors and rabbis, could be found in early diaspora forms of Judaism, i.e., they were authentic aspects of earlier Judaism which had been lost for many centuries in normative Judaism and thus had ceased to be regarded as "Jewish".

In chapter 2 above I mentioned three unique features often attributed to the contemporary Jews: (a) they are in the main the direct descendants of the Palestinian Jews of biblical and talmudic times; (b) modern Judaism has evolved from Palestinian Judaism and (c) Modern Hebrew is a revived version of the Old Hebrew that had died out in Palestine around the 3rd century A.D. If these "unique" features proved to be chimeric, two genuinely unique features of the Jews have been revealed: (a) an original symbiosis created by Palestinian Jews, Slavs, Turks and other pagans, and (b) the nearly total denial of the non-Jewish roots of this symbiosis by contemporary Jews, stemming from a long and successful process of Judaization.

I hope to have succeeded in demonstrating the reasons for the penetrating Slavicization of the Palestinian Jews, as well as the espousal by

Slavs and other non-Jews of a syncretic diaspora Judaism in the Balkans and northern Europe. No other group has had such an impact on the "Jews" as the Slavs have. Yet, of the European nations that have left a major imprint on the Palestinian and diaspora Jews, historians have singled out for special comment only the Greek impact on the Jews that began in earnest in the 3rd century B.C. and died out (in non-Hellenic Europe) by the 4th–5th centuries A.D. or the "Arab" contribution to the reshaping of the Near Eastern Jews.

After the creation of the State of Israel in 1948, most of the Jewish communities of Africa and Asia were liquidated when hundreds of thousands of their members immigrated to Israel. There they gradually became "assimilated" to Ashkenazic religious, cultural and linguistic patterns. The assimilation of the non-Ashkenazic Jews to Ashkenazic culture is certainly one of the most grandiose instances of Slavicization in modern history. To be sure, the Slavicizing of the Jews was more modest in numerical scope than the massive, state-sponsored Russification of language and culture that affected Belorussians, Ukrainians and well over a hundred non-Slavic ethnic groups in the defunct Russian Empire and defunct Soviet Union, but it was the only instance of Slavicization detached from the Slavic land mass. Moreover, it involved a population of close to a million people who were, *mirabile dictu*, like the "Slavicizers" themselves, barely aware of the on-going Slavicization process (in contrast to the non-Russians in the Czarist and Soviet Empires).

This study took its initial stimulus from linguistics. It is thus appropriate to conclude with linguistics. While the Slavo-Turkic origins of so many of the linguistic and ethnographic features of the north European Jews have become obscured, a single Biblical Hebrew word reminds us of the peoples who contributed most to the maintenance of a Jewish entity in Europe between the 6th and 11th centuries: that is the ethnonym *ʾaškenazī* which over more than a millennium designated variously non-Jewish Iranians, Slavs and Germans, before settling finally on the indigenous "Jews" of the Germano-Slavic lands.

ENDNOTES

Chapter 1

1 The Jewish Bible is believed to have been composed between 1000 and 200 B.C. The Talmud, which contains the records of academic discussion and judicial administration of Jewish law, was composed in two versions in Palestine and Babylonia (the more voluminous variant) between the 3rd and the mid 8th centuries A.D. The Talmud consists of two parts: the text is known as the Mishnah, while the commentaries are known as the Gemarah.

2 The Sorbs formerly occupied wide regions of present-day eastern Germany and western Poland (see Popowska-Taborska 1965). Today, they are a small population of some 70,000 bilinguals in Upper and Lower Lausitz (in Saxony and Brandenburg respectively). The Polabians historically occupied approximately the northern regions of present-day Germany; a major Polabian center in the late first millennium which also had a known Jewish settlement was Magdeburg. The last speakers of Polabian died out in the late 18th-early 19th century in the Lüneburg region, some 30 miles southeast of Hamburg. For the distribution of other Slavic groups on the territory of Germany in the early Middle Ages, see J.Herrmann 1985.

Chapter 2

1 On the history of Yiddish, see M.Mieses 1924, Bin-Nun 1973, M.Weinreich 1973, S.A.Birnbaum 1979, Faber and King 1984, King 1987, Marchand 1987, Wexler 1987b, 1988, 1991b, 1992b; on Judeo-Slavic linguistics, see M.Weinreich 1956b, Jakobson 1957, Jakobson and Halle 1964, Wexler 1987b.

2 For a recent exposé of the non-historical roots of contemporary orthodox Judaism, see J.Katz 1992.

Chapter 3

1 Most contemporary Yiddishists define Western Yiddish broadly as the dialects spoken west of the pre–1939 German-Polish frontier, including the Yiddish of western Czechoslovakia and Hungary; Eastern Yiddish dialects are spoken to the east of this line. An exception is Kurland Yiddish in the Baltic lands which appears to be a derivation of German Yiddish. This classification needs to be revised in view of the Slavic origin of the Yiddish language. In my view, Eastern, and most Western Yiddish dialects are of Slavic, i.e., Judeo-Sorbian, origin, while a few "Western Yiddish" dialects were originally Judaized forms of German, created by an original French-speaking Jewish community (see my 1991b).

2 The Marranos disappeared as a separate entity in most areas of the Iberian Peninsula, except for rural areas in north central Portugal, and on the island of Mallorca; they tend to marry mainly among themselves and retain minimal Jewish identity or cultural patterns. Recently, there has been a reawakening of Marrano/

Jewish consciousness among some Hispanics living in the southwestern United States. See also chapter 7, footnote 1.

3 On the term "Ashkenaz(ic)", see Zunz 1919:66, Zobel 1929, Krojs 1932, Mann 1933, Huntingford 1935:788, Rieger 1936, Wallach 1939, Rosenthal 1943:60, Baron 4:1967:4, Weinryb 1974:964, fn 36, Wexler 1987b:3, 160, 1991b:21, 105–6, 1992b: chapter 1, fn 21.

Chapter 5

1 Ladino consists mainly of Castilian Spanish material. The Ladino translation language was also used—in a slightly different form from the Ladino of the Balkan Sephardic Jews—by the Jewish descendants of Portuguese Marranos in Italy, Holland, England, Germany and the New World, who were Portuguese-speaking until the early 19th century (see Wexler 1982a). No Ladino translations survive from the Iberian Peninsula, but it is fair to assume that the translation language existed there. On the rejection of *ara* by early Christian writers (and its eventual reacceptance), see Mohrmann 2:1961:20, 102; 3:1965:241.

2 Manicheism was a Persian religious philosophy of the 3rd–7th centuries A.D. which comprised Zoroastrian, Gnostic Christian and pagan elements. The Bogomil heresy was a Christian sect popular in Bulgaria and Bosnia between the 10th and mid-15th centuries named after a sectarian leader, which espoused the Manichaean doctrine and rejected the Mass, the Sacraments, all images (including the cross), and the Old Testament (except for the Psalms).

3 The Karaite *ḥāxām* ('rabbi') in Troki, Lithuania said he removed the star of David from the cupola of the Karaite synagogue because it smacked too much of orthodox Judaism (Cohen 1953:155, describing a visit before World War II). The limited spread of the star to the iconography of Spanish, Portuguese, Italian and Greek Jews requires study. In Van Praag's study of Jewish exlibris designs in Holland (1988), the star motif is conspicuously absent among Dutch Jews of Portuguese descent.

4 The Jewish musicologists seem to be oblivious to the difficulties of ascertaining the origin of a given song; as Downey wrote, "one cannot definitively establish that the melody [of a particular Hungarian song] is of Hungarian, Rumanian or Ukrainian origin. All that is certain is that the very music of this Hungarian song belongs equally to the folklore of the neighboring peoples" (1966:176).

5 See also the detailed discussion in category I, Germanic 6 in chapter 5.11 above. M.Samuel, on the other hand, recognized the non-Jewish origin of the practice (1971:48).

6 On German folklore, see Grimm 1876–8, 1883–1900, Wuttke 1900, *HDA* 1–10:1927–42. On Jewish folklore, see Brück 1837, Joel 1881–3, Abrahams 1896, Rappoport 1937, Schauss 1938, Steiman 1963, Freehof 1967, Pollack 1971, T.H. Gaster 1980. On Slavic folklore, see Grohmann 1864, Dmitriev 1867, von Schulenburg 1880, 1892, Krauss 1885, Tetzner 1902, Dovnar-Zapol'skij 1909, Piprek 1914, Bystroń 1916, Vovk 1928, Bogatyrev 1929, Biegeleisen 1930, Wienecke 1940, Schneeweis 1953, Kowalczyk 1968. On pagan customs, see Kostrzewski 1964a,

Seweryn 1964:516, Urbańczyk 1964, Russocki 1967:159, Swoboda 1970b:489, Łosiński 1975:643. On the persistence of paganism among the Christianized Slavs, see Lewicki 1937, 1958:71, 77, 1964a, 1975:35, Dvornik 1959:45, 78, 117, 186, Kappesowa 1961, Kowalenko 1961:263, Labuda 1961b, 1964a:71, 1964b:352, Balić 1964, Swoboda 1970a:54, Wypych 1973:88, J.Herrmann 1985:38.

7 On the Christian practice in Silesia of putting out a pot of food on the grave, see Jahn 1886:28 and Peuckert 1931–2:830; on the Jewish practice of leaving food out, see category I, Germanic 1 in chapter 5.11 above. The "Lausitz culture" designates a West Slavic (?) agrarian culture of the late Bronze Age, named after the earliest finds from the Niederlausitz (southeast Germany). The typical feature of the finds is the ceramic work, found mainly in grave urns.

Chapter 6

1 The recent book by Will and Orrieux 1992 is a superficial and tendentious denial of proselytism among the Jews.

2 For anthropological and genetic studies of the Jews, see Kollmann and Kahnt 1885, Fishberg 1905, 1911, Ruppin 1:1930, Mourant 1959, Mourant et al. 1978, Carmelli and Cavalli-Sforza 1979, Karlin et al. 1979, Kobylianski, Micle, et al. 1982, Kobyliansky and Livshits 1983, 1985, Wijsman 1984, Patai and Wing-Patai 1989, Livshits et al. 1991.

3 The first group is also known as "*Rassenjuden*" 'Jews by race' (Kahn 1921: 156), and the second group alternatively as "pseudo-Jews" (Andree 1881:81, 89–91, 247), "*Fremdstämme* 'foreign tribes' (Kahn 1927:1245) or "semi-Jews, half-Jews" (Ruppin 1:1930:38ff; Patai and Patai-Wing 1989:205, 227, 292, 330). Contemporary Near Eastern Karaites tend to identify themselves as Jews, but those in Europe insist they are descended from the Turkic Khazars (see the views of the late Polish Karaite scholar, Ananiasz Zajączkowski 1961:12–23). Faber and King write approvingly that "it is common sense that the Karaites are in general the only Jewish descendants of the Khazars" (1984:412), but I see no reason to accept Zajączkowski's thesis. The Karaites are thus the only members of the "Jewish people" in the diaspora to deny historic links with the ethnic Palestinian Jews. It would be interesting to explore the attitudes of Karaites to proselytizing among Slavs. Karaite attitudes to de-Judaization are discussed in detail by Freund 1991. Even Jewish groups which formally converted to Christianity or Islam but still maintained a separate group identity, e.g., the Marranos in Portugal and Mallorca in the 15th–16th centuries or the Dönmes in Turkey in the 17th century, respectively, do not deny their "Jewish" origins.

4 On early proselytism and the origins of Jewish diaspora communities, see Graetz 1884, Cumont 1897, Aronius 1902, Kahn 1921, Goldmann 1927, Godbey 1930:354, 378, Grayzel 1933, Condurachi 1937:87, Wacholder 1956, Leon 1960:226, Kraabel 1969:86, Smallwood 1976:523, Solin 1980:303, Meeks 1983:207, fn 175, 208, Feldman 1986, 1989, Lasker 1990.

5 As early as the 12th century, the *Russian Primary Chronicle* (*Povest' vremennyx let*) could write that "God destroyed [the Avars]. They all perished and not one Avar survived. There is to this day a proverb in Rus' which runs, 'they

perished like the Avars'. Neither race nor heir of them remains" (cited by Dvornik 1959:69).

6 On Aphrodisias and other "God-Fearers", see Goodenough 1957, Struve et al. 1965, Feldman 1986, 1989, Tannenbaum 1986, Reynolds and Tannenbaum 1987 (with bibliography 231); on Čelarevo, see Petricioli 1960 (describing similar artifacts from Vojvodina), Živanović 1972–3, 1974–8, 1975, Bunardžić 1978–9, 1980, Nagy 1979, Scheiber 1982.

7 The use of "Avar" and "Jew" in the secondary meaning of giant is discussed by Mladenov 1941, Vasmer 1953–8, Matl 1956:294, 306, Weinryb 1962b:487–8, Pritsak 1963:930, Swoboda 1967:443, Georgiev et al. 7:1969:543–4, Machek 1971, Mollova 1973:101–2, Wexler 1987b:142.

Curiously, Polish, Belorussian and Ukrainian *haman* 'giant' appear to be derived from Hebrew *hāmān*, the name of the main anti-Jewish figure in the Scroll of Esther, read on the holiday of Purim (see Wexler 1987b:204). See also discussion of the Ukrainian cognate in chapter 5.13 above. On the use of the term 'pagan' for 'Jew' and vice versa in Russian and Polish, see ibid.:142, fn 196 and 149.

8 On Avar-Slav contacts, see Preidel 1952, Shevelov 1965:13, 225, 347, 382, 622, Hilczer-Kurnatowska 1986a. Almost all Turkic groups that settled in central and southern Europe merged with the coterritorial Slavs or Hungarians (see, e.g., the fate of the Bulġars). The only Turkic groups to maintain a separate profile in northern Europe were the Crimean Tatars and Karaites who settled in the Grand Duchy of Lithuania in the late 14th century (though the former assimilated linguistically to Slavic by the 1600s: see Wexler 1983b). In Lvov Polish, *karaim* (ordinarily 'Karaite') has the meaning of Ukrainian (Kurzowa 1985:181).

9 On Jewish attitudes to conversion, see Abrahams 1896:20, Täubler 1916:382, Wacholder 1956:98, Steiman 1963:51, fn 37, 135, #39; Scheiber 1967:377, W.P. Eckert 1968:253, Goitein 2:1971:204, 208, Lasker 1990. On Jewish laws regarding the holding of slaves, see Abrahams 1896:99, Wacholder 1956:90–1, Baron 4:1957:187, I.A.Agus 2:1968:797–8. On the Jewish slave trade in Europe, see Aronius 1902, Hoffmann 1910:16–9, 22–6, Šiper 1926:25, 35, 129, fn 84, 183–4, Zimmels 1926:9–10, 1952:156, Steinherz 1930:49, fn 85, Bretholz 1934:100, Blumenkranz 1948–9:63–4, ##84, 86, 1949–50, 1954, 1955:80, Kisch 1949:200, 459, fn 89, Verlinden 1955–77, Baron 4:1957:187–96, 333, 336, fn 57, 9:1965:251, fn 25, Lewicki 1959:98, 1961a, Vetulani 1962, Golb 1964, Labuda 1964a:69–70, I.A.Agus 1:1968:280–3, 2:567.

10 On the ordenance, see Raffelstetten 1897, Bretholz 1934:54–5, Ganshof 1966 and Strzelczyk 1970. The oldest manuscript of the toll ordenance dates from 1254–65. The text relates the coming of slaves from "Rugii", a Slavic name probably taken over from a Germanic tribe in the area of Thunau, north of the Danube, which had converted to Arianism by the late 5th century (Thompson 1963:76; J.Herrmann 1985:46).

11 Kahan 1938:54, 86, fn 76; see also 54–5. Kahan thinks the name is a Slavicized form of Hebrew *ʾāvraham* 'Abraham', a name frequently assumed by converts to Judaism, but I wonder if it is not related to the term for Avar (see the discussion above). According to Kronsteiner, *ʾāvraham* was a common "Christian" name

among European Avars (1978:144, fn 32); we should entertain the possibility that some Avars with this name might have been converts to Judaism. On the other hand, M.Mieses notes that the name (also as a family name) was retained by numerous Jewish converts to Christianity and their Christian descendants (1991: 27–8).

12 Jews who converted to Christianity often adopted names that commemorated the act of conversion. For example, Clemen mentions the case of a Ukrainian Jew who, upon converting to Christianity in 1697, changed his name to *Ivan Perekrestev* (1931:156). The surname resembles Ukrainian *perexrest, perexryst* 'converted Jew; turncoat; neophyte'. On possible proselyte names, see Šiper 1926:129, fn 84, Wexler 1987b:5 *(Chanaan)*, ibid., 1991b:20–1 (*Hāgār*) and Labuda 1961a, 1977 (*Obriš*). On the Hebrew name *kna*ʿ*an (Chanaan)* for Slavs, see Jakobson and Halle 1964, Lewicki 1964c, Wexler 1987b:5, 88, 160, 1991b:21.

13 For a discussion of Austrian place names possibly based on the word "Jew", see Babad 1945:17–9, Kranzmayer 2:1958 (under Judenburg, Seidolach and Völkermarkt) and Swoboda 1975:564. Khazar toponyms have been identified in Poland and Hungary, but these etymologies are unconvincing; for discussion, see Šiper 1926:37–44, Brutzkus 1929:56, Poljak 1951:304, Wiesenberg 1955:76, Balić 1964:33, Altbauer 1968, Koestler 1976 and Wexler 1987b:211–2.

14 The Church councils are discussed by Loeb 1880, 1893:8, fn 4, 19, Robert 1881:220, 223, Morel-Fatio 1882:41, Aronius 1902, Grazyel 1933:22–6, Baron 5: 1957:113, 1962:43, fn 1, 9:1965:32–5, 10:1965:319, fn 47, Vetulani 1962:286, Scheiber 1966:314, Giese 1968, Lewicki 2/2:1977:293, Feldman 1989:298. Mixed marriages are cited rarely in Christian sources, see, e.g., the mention of a Christian man and his Jewish wife from Cologne c. 1161 (Aronius 1902:#288).

15 On traditions of ancient Jewish settlement in Europe, see Freimann 1929:165 and Graus 1981:14–6. Blumenkranz (1955:86) quotes a German writer, Heriger de Lobbes (d.1007) to the effect that the Huns, chased out of Rome by Claudius (see Acts 11:28), were said to be proud of their Jewish origin. On alleged Hun-Jewish ties, see also Godbey 1930:296.

Chapter 7

1 The Marranos who have survived as a separate group in parts of central Portugal and Mallorca up to the present are an excellent laboratory in which to study the development of a unique syncretic religion and folklore, consisting of Jewish and Catholic elements (see da Costa Fontes 1990–3). See also chapter 3, footnote 2.

2 On Christian rejection of pagan Latin terms, see Mohrmann 1961–5. A comparative study of the Christianization and Judaization of pagan terms and practices needs to be carried out. Curiously, one aspect of Judaization—the attempt to find biblical antecedents—also appears among the Eastern Slavs (see the description of the pre-Christian god Perun in medieval texts, described by Haase 1939:52).

Chapter 8

1 Dietrich proposed that Hellenized Balkan Jews carried the Greek expression *tōu pouliōu to gala* 'unimaginable wealth, something fantastic, very rare' (literally 'bird's milk') to Slavic languages and Yiddish (1931:337, fn 3); see Yiddish *fojglmilx*, Bulgarian *ptiče mleko*, etc. As far as I can tell, the expression is found in all Slavic languages today except Sorbian (where the expression exists but in the meaning of a constellation); for details of the geography of the expression in Jewish and non-Jewish languages, see M.Weinreich 1956b:629, 3:1973:72, 4:261; Wexler 1987b:42–3; Theodoridis 1990–3.

BIBLIOGRAPHY

Abbreviations used in the bibliography

AECO — *Archivum Europae Centro-Orientalis*

AEJ — *Algemejne encikopedje. Jidn* 1–3. Paris-New York 1939–42

AHB — *Annals of human biology*

AHK — I.Kríza, ed., *A hagyomány kötelékében. Tanulmányok a magyarországi zsidó folklór köréből.* Budapest 1990

AJHG — *American journal of human genetics*

ANRW — W.Haase, ed., *Aufstieg und Niedergang der römischen Welt* 1–2. Berlin-New York 1979

AR — *Alba Regia. Annales musei Stephani regis.* Székesfehérvár

ARW — *Archiv für Religionswissenschaft*

AS — H.-P.Schwarz, ed., *Die Architektur der Synagoge.* Stuttgart 1988

AUA — *Annals of the Ukrainian Academy of Arts and Sciences in the U.S.*

BAR — *Biblical archaeology review*

CJ — J.Neusner, ed., *Christianity, Judaism and other Greco-Roman cults. Studies for Norton Smith at sixty* 1–4. Leiden 1975

DA — C.Roth and I.H.Levine, eds., *The Dark Ages, Jews and Christian Europe 711–1096.* [New Brunswick, NJ] 1966

EJ/B — *Encyclopaedia judaica* 1–10. Berlin 1929–34

EJ/J — *Encyclopaedia judaica* 1–16. Jerusalem 1971.

EP — *Encyclopedya polska* 1–22. Kraków 1912–39

EY — *Eranos yearbook*

FRCS — *Folklore Research Center Studies.* Jerusalem

FSMP — *Festschrift zum siebzigsten Geburtstage Martin Philippsons.* Leipzig 1916

FSRMR — S.H.Hooke, ed., *The labyrinth. Further studies in the relation between myth and ritual in the ancient world.* London 1935

GDAJ — R.M.Goodman and A.G.Motulsky, eds., *Genetic diseases among Ashkenazic Jews.* New York 1979

GJ — M.Brann, I.Elbogen, A.Freimann and H.Tykocinski, eds., *Germania judaica* 1. Wrocław 1934; 2nd edition, Tübingen 1963 (with notes by Z.Avneri); 2/1–2/2, ed. Z.Avneri. Tübingen 1968

HCS — F.Zagiba, ed., *Das heidnische und christliche Slaventum* II/1–2. Wiesbaden 1969–70

HDA — E.Hoffmann-Krayer and H.Bächtold-Stäubli, eds., *Handwörterbuch des deutschen Aberglaubens* 1–10. Berlin-Leipzig 1927–42

HJ — *Historia judaica*

HTR — *Harvard theological review*

HUCA — Hebrew Union College Annual

IGK — Akten des VIII. Internationalen Germanisten-Kongresses, Tokyo 1990 11. Munich

IJSL — International journal of the sociology of language

IJSLP — International journal of Slavic linguistics and poetics

IT — E.Hobsbawm and T.Ranger, eds., *The invention of tradition.* Cambridge 1983

JA — Jewish art

JE — Jewish encyclopaedia 1–12. New York 1901–6

JF — Jidiše filologje

JGGJČR — Jahrbuch der Gesellschaft für Geschichte der Juden in der Čechoslowakischen Republik

JGW — I.Graeber and S.H.Britt, eds., *Jews in a Gentile world. The problem of anti-Semitism.* New York 1942

JJGL — Jahrbuch für jüdische Geschichte und Literatur

JJS — Jewish journal of sociology

JJSt — Journal of Jewish studies

JL — Jüdisches Lexikon 1–4/2. Berlin 1927–30

JM — P.Wilpert, ed. (assisted by W.P.Eckert), *Judentum im Mittelalter. Beiträge zum christlich-jüdischen Gespräch (= Miscellanea mediaevalia* 4). Berlin 1966

JPC — J.Lieu, J.North and T.Rajak, eds., *The Jews among pagans and Christians in the Roman Empire.* London-New York 1992

JQR — Jewish quarterly review

JW — E.Kedourie, ed., *The Jewish world. History and culture of the Jewish people.* New York 1979

KS — K.H.Rengstorf and S.von Kortzfleisch, eds., *Kirche und Synagoge. Handbuch zur Geschichte von Christen und Juden. Darstellungen mit Quellen* 1–2. Stuttgart 1968–70

LM — Lexikon des Mittelalters. Munich-Zurich 1980ff

MedLR — Mediterranean language review

MGJV — Mitteilungen der Gesellschaft für jüdische Volkskunde

MGWJ — Monatsschrift für Geschichte und Wissenschaft des Judentums

MQ — Mankind quarterly

MR — P.Bakker and M.Cortiade, eds., *In the margin of Romani. Gypsy languages in contact.* (Instituut voor Algemene Taalwetenschap, Universiteit van Amsterdam). Amsterdam 1991

NJ — Nordisk judaistik

OO — B.Schindler and A.Marmorstein, eds., *Occident and Orient... In honour of Haham Dr.M.Gaster's 80th birthday.* London 1936

OYL — D.Katz, ed., *Origins of the Yiddish language.* Oxford 1987

ÖZV — Österreichische Zeitschrift für Volkskunde

PWCJS — Proceedings of the 9th World Congress of Jewish Studies. Jerusalem 1986

REJ — Revue des études juives

RFE — *Revista de filología española*
RS — *Rocznik slawistyczny*
RSJL — J.A.Fishman, ed., *Readings in the sociology of Jewish languages* 1. Leiden 1985
SAV — *Schweizerisches Archiv für Volkskunde*
SEER — *Slavonic and East European review*
SEHAAN — M.Ben-Horin, B.D.Weinryb and S.Zeitlin, eds., *Studies and essays in honor of Abraham A.Neuman.* Leiden 1962
SH — *Slavica hierosolymitana*
SJLCF — J.Z.Lauterbach, *Studies in Jewish law, custom and folklore,* ed. B.J.Bamberger. New York 1970
SO — *Slavia occidentalis*
SOF — *Südost-Forschungen*
SSS — *Słownik starożytności słowiańskich* 1ff. Wrocław-Warsaw Kraków 1961ff
ST — M.Gaster, *Studies and texts. In folklore, magic, mediaeval Romance, Hebrew apocrypha and Samaritan archaeology* 2. New York 1971
SWBJV — *Salo Wittmayer Baron. Jubilee volume* 2. Jerusalem 1974
SYL — P.Wexler, ed., *Studies in Yiddish linguistics.* Tübingen 1990
WJ — J.Carlebach, ed., *Wissenschaft des Judentums.* Darmstadt 1992
WS — *Welt der Slaven*
YB — *YIVO bleter*
YBCCAR — *Yearbook. Central Conference of American Rabbis*
YS — *Yidishe shprakh*
ZDMG — *Zeitschrift der Deutschen Morgenländischen Gesellschaft*
ZDMS — *Zeitschrift für deutsche Mythologie und Sittenkunde*
ZGJD — *Zeitschrift für die Geschichte der Juden in Deutschland.* Braunschweig 1887–92; Berlin 1928–34
ZOG — *Zeitschrift für osteuropäische Geschichte*
ZS — *Zeitschrift für Slawistik*
ZSPh — *Zeitschrift für slavische Philologie*
ZVV — *Zeitschrift des Vereins für Volkskunde*

ABAEV, V.I. (1958). *Istoriko-ėtimologičeskij slovar' osetinskogo jazyka* 1. Moscow-St. Petersburg.

ABRAHAMS, I. (1896). *Jewish life in the Middle Ages.* London; New York-Philadelphia. 2nd edition 1958.

ADRIANOVA-PERETC, V.P. (1950). *Povest' vremennyx let* 1–2. Moscow-St.Petersburg.

AGUS, I.A. (1961). Preconceptions and stereotypes in Jewish historiography. *JQR* 51:242–53.

— (1962). The oral traditions of pre-Crusade Ashkenazic Jewry. *SEHAAN,* 1–16.

— (1968). *Urban civilization in pre-Crusade Europe* 1–2. New York.

AGUS, J.B. (1963). *The meaning of Jewish history* 1–2. New York-London-Toronto.

AL-BAKRĪ (11th c). See Kunik and Rozen.

ALBRIGHT, W.F. and T.O.LAMBDIN (1966). *The evidence of language*. Cambridge.

ALEKSEEV, A.A. (1987). Perevody s drevneevrejskix originalov v drevnej Rusi. *Russian linguistics* 11:1–20.

ALTBAUER, M. (1954). W sprawie *kirkutu*. *Język polski* 34:202–4.

— (1968). Jeszcze o rzekomych "chazarskich" nazwach miejścowych na ziemiach polskich. *Onomastica* 13:120–8.

ALY, W. (1927). Brief. *HDA*, 1:columns 1574–6.

ʿAMARA, M. (1967). *ʾIsrāʾīl. Hal hiya šāmiya?* Cairo.

AMIR, Y. (1982). The term *Ιουδαϊσμος (Ioudaismos)*: a study in Jewish-Hellenic self-identification. *Immanuel* 14:34–41.

ANDREE, R. (1874). *Wendische Wanderstudien. Zur Kunde der Lausitz und der Sorbenwenden*. Stuttgart.

— (1878). *Ethnographische Parallelen und Vergleiche* 1. Leipzig.

— (1881). *Zur Volkskunde der Juden*. Bielefeld-Leipzig.

— (1903–5). Trudensteine. *ZVV* 13:295–8; 15:92–3.

ANHORN, B. (1674). *Magiologia; christliche Warnung für dem Aberglauben und Zauberey*. Basle.

ANKORI, Z. (1979). Origins and history of Ashkenazi Jewry (8th to 18th century). *GDAJ*, 19–46.

APTOWITZER, V. (1910). Les noms de Dieu et des anges dans la mezouza. *REJ* 60: 39–52.

ARMISTEAD, S.G. and J.H.SILVERMAN (1982), *En torno al romancero sefardí. (Hispanismo y balcanismo de la tradición judeo-española.)* Madrid.

ARONIUS, J. (with the assistance of A.DRESDNER and L.LEWINSKI) (1902). *Regesten zur Geschichte der Juden im Fränkischen und Deutschen Reiche bis zum Jahre 1273*. Berlin.

ARRAGEL, M. (1422–33). [Judeo-Castilian Bible translation]. See *Biblia...traducida... por Rabi Mosé Arragel...publicada por el Duque de Berwick y Alba*. Madrid 1920–2.

ASARIA, Z. (ed.) (1959). *Die Juden in Köln von den ältesten Zeiten bis zur Gegenwart*. Cologne.

AVÉ-LALLEMANT, F.C.B. (1858–62). *Das deutsche Gaunerthum in seiner social-politischen, literarischen und linguistischen Ausbildung zu seinem heutigen Bestande* 1–4. Leipzig.

AVIDA, J. (1951). Prakim beinjane ha ʾazkeret (jorcajt). *Sinai* 28:45–58.

BABAD, J. (1945). The Jews in medieval Carinthia. *HJ* 7:13–28, 193–204.

BAER, F. (1936). *Die Juden im christlichen Spanien* 1/2. Berlin.

BAKKER, P. (1991). Basque Romani—a preliminary grammatical sketch of a mixed language. *MR*, 56–77.

— and H. VAN DER VOORT (1991). Para-Romani languages: an overview and some speculations on their genesis. *MR*, 16–44.

BALÁSZ, GY. (1947). Mavo lexakirat ikvoteha haxadašim šel hitjašvut hajehudim bepanonja. *Semitic studies in memory of Immanuel Löw*, ed. A.Scheiber, 5–14 (Hebrew section). Budapest.

BALIĆ, S. (1964). Der Islam im mittelalterlichen Ungarn. *SOF* 23:19–35.
BANITT, M. (1985). *Rashi. Interpreter of the biblical letter.* Tel-Aviv.
BANK, L. (1894). Etudes talmudiques. *REJ* 29:91–9.
BARAC, G.M. (1908). *Biblejsko-Agadičeskie paralleli k letopisnym skazanijam o Vladimire Svjatom.* Kiev.
— (1924–6). *Sobranie trudov po voprosu o evrejskom ėlemente v pamjatnikax drevnerusskoj pis'mennosti* 1. Paris; 2. Berlin.
BAR-AŠER, M. (1978). Al hajesodot haivri'im ba'aravit šel jehude maroko. *Lešonenu* 42:163–89.
BAR-EL, J. (1992). *Sefer pitronot raš"i.* Tel-Aviv.
BARON, S.W. (1952–80). *A social and religious history of the Jews* 1–17. Philadelphia. 2nd edition.
— (1964). *History and Jewish historians,* eds. A.Hertzberg and L.A.Feldman. Philadelphia.
— (1971). Population. *EJ/J,* 13:columns 866–903.
BATTENBERG, F. (1990). *Das europäische Zeitalter der Juden* 1. *Von den Anfängen bis 1650.* Darmstadt.
BAUMGARTNER, W. (1946). Das Nachleben der Adonisgärten auf Sardinien und im übrigen Mittelmeergebiet. *SAV* 43:122–48.
BAXUR, E. (1541). *Sefer hatišbi.* Isny.
BEINART, H. (1987). Introducción. In J. Luis Lacave, ed., *Sefarad, Sefarad, la España judía,* 9–12. Barcelona-Madrid.
BELLMANN, G. (1971). *Slavoteutonica. Lexikalische Untersuchungen zum slawisch-deutschen Sprachkontakt im Ostmitteldeutschen.* Berlin-New York.
BENVENISTE, E. (1956). Etudes sur la phonétique et l'étymologie de l'ossète. *Bulletin de la Société Linguistique de Paris* 52:6–59.
BERANEK, F.J. (1961). Die fränkische Landschaft des Jiddischen. *Jahrbuch für fränkische Landesforschung* 21:267–303.
— (1965). *Westjiddischer Sprachatlas.* Marburg.
BERGER, D. (1972). The attitudes of St.Bernard of Clairvaux toward the Jews. *American Academy for Jewish Research. Proceedings* 40:89–108.
BERGSTRÄSSER, G. (1928). *Einführung in die semitischen Sprachen.* Munich.
BERLINER, A. (1900). *Aus dem Leben der deutschen Juden im Mittelalter.* Berlin.
BERNSTEIN, I. (1908). *Jüdische Sprichwörter und Redensarten.* Warsaw.
BEYER, W.G. (1848). König Kruto und sein Geschlecht. *Jahrbücher des Vereins für mecklenburgische Geschichte und Altertumskunde* 13.1–55.
BICKERMAN, E.J. (1986). Symbolism in the Dura synagogue. In his *Studies in Jewish and Christian history,* 225–44. Leiden; originally in *HTR* 58:1965.
BIEGELEISEN, H. (1930). *Śmierć w obrzędach, zwyczajach i wierzeniach ludu polskiego.* Warsaw.
BIN-NUN, J. (1973). *Jiddisch und die deutschen Mundarten; unter besonderer Berücksichtigung des ostgalizischen Jiddisch.* Tübingen.
BIRNBAUM, H. (1985). Some problems with the etymology and the semantics of Slavic *žid* "Jew". *SH* 7:1–11.
BIRNBAUM, S.A. (1931). Aschkenasische Handschriften. Woher stammen die deutschen Juden? *ZGJD* 3:275–7.

— (1954–7). *The Hebrew scripts* 2. London.
— (1979). *Yiddish. A survey and a grammar.* Toronto.
BLAU, L. (1898). *Das altjüdische Zauberwesen.* Budapest.
— (1904). Magen Dawid. *JE,* 8:251–2.
— (1924). Early Christian epigraphy considered from the Jewish point of view. *HUCA* 1:221–37.
— (1926). Early Christian archaeology from the Jewish point of view. *HUCA* 3:157–214.
BLONDHEIM, D.S. (1925). *Les parlers judéo-romans et la Vetus latina.* Paris.
BLUMENKRANZ, B. (1948–55). Les auteurs chrétiens latins du Moyen Age sur les Juifs et le Judaïsme. *REJ* 109:3–67; 110:5–61; 113:5–36; 114:37–90.
— (1961). Die christlich-jüdische Missionkonkurrenz (3. bis 6. Jahrhundert). *Klio* 39:227–33.
— (1965). *Juden und Judentum in der mittelalterlichen Kunst.* Stuttgart.
— (1966a). Jüdische und christliche Konvertiten im jüdisch-christlichen Religionsgespräch des Mittelalters. *JM,* 264–82.
— (1966b). *Le juif médiéval au miroir de l'art chrétien.* Paris.
BOBA, I. (1967). *Nomads, Northmen and Slavs. Eastern Europe in the ninth century.* The Hague-Wiesbaden.
BÖCHER, O. (1959). Die alte Synagoge zu Worms. In Róth, 11–154.
BOGATYREV, P. (1929). *Actes magiques, rites et croyances en Russie subcarpathique.* Paris.
BOGUSŁAWSKI, W. (1900). Pogaństwo. In his *Dzieje Słowiańszczyzny połnocno-zachodniej do polowiny XIII w.* 2, section 2, chapter 27, 710–862. Poznań.
BONNÉ, B. (1966). Are there Hebrews left? *American journal of physical anthropology* 24:135–45.
— [BONNÉ-TAMIR] (1980). The Samaritans: a living ancient isolate. *Population structure and genetic disorders,* eds. A.W.Eriksson, et al., 27–41. New York.
BRANKAČK, J. (1964). *Studien zur Wirtschaft und Sozialstruktur der Westslawen zwischen Elbe-Saale und Oder aus der Zeit vom 9. bis zum 12. Jahrhundert.* Bautzen.
BRETHOLZ, B. (1934). *Geschichte der Juden in Mähren im Mittelalter* 1. Brno-Prague-Leipzig-Vienna.
BRILING, D. (1953). Ve'ele šmot bne jisrael. *Yeda am* 1(2):13–5.
BROOTEN, B.J. (1982). *Women leaders in the ancient synagogue; inscriptional evidence and background issues.* Chico, CA 1982. (I follow the pagination of the PhD, Inscriptional evidence for women as leaders in the ancient synagogue. Brown University. Providence 1982.)
BRÜCK, M. (1837). *Rabbinische Ceremonialgebräuche in ihrer Entstehung und geistlichen Entwicklung.* Wrocław.
BRÜCKNER, A. (1912). Wierzenia religijne i stosunki rodzinne. *EP,* 4, part 2:149–87.
BRÜLL, N. (1879). Stammen die Juden in den südlichen Rheinlanden von den Vangionen ab? *Jahrbücher für jüdische Geschichte und Literatur* 4:34–40.
BRUNNER, K. (1925). *Ostdeutsche Volkskunde.* Leipzig.
BRÜSKE, W. (1955). *Untersuchungen zur Geschichte des Lutizenbundes.* Münster-Cologne.

BRUTZKUS, J. (1929). Di eršte jedies vegn jidn in pojln (in 10tn un 11tn jorhundert). *Historiše šriftn* 1:columns 55–72.

BÜCHLER, A. (1902). Relation d'Isaac B.Dorbelo sur une consultation envoyée par les Juifs du Rhin en l'an 960 aux communautés de Palestine. *REJ* 44:237–43.

BUDZISZEWSKA, W. (1991). *Zapożyczenia słowiańskie w dialektach nowogreckich.* Warsaw.

BUNARDŽIĆ, R. (1978–9). Izveštaj sa zaštitnog arxeološkog iskopavanja ranosrednjovekovne nekropole na lokalitetu "Ciglana" kod Čelareva. *Grańia za proučavanje spomenika kulture Vojvodine* 8–9:33–67. Novi Sad.

— (1980). *Menore iz Čelareva.* Belgrade.

BURCKHARDT, J. (1910). *Weltgeschichtliche Betrachtungen.* Berlin-Stuttgart. 2nd edition.

BURSZTA, J. (1967). Zwyczaje i obrzędy pogrzebowe. *Kultura ludowa Wielkopolski,* 3:177–95. Poznań.

BYSTROŃ, J.S. (1916). *Słowiańskie obrzędy rodzinne.* Kraków.

CABALSKA, M. (1979). Aus den Studien über die Religion der heidnischen Slawen. *Rapports du IIIe Congrès International d'Archéologie slave* 1:125–40. Bratislava.

CARMELLI, D. and L.L.CAVALLI-SFORZA (1979). The genetic origin of the Jews: a multivariate approach. *Human biology* 51:41–61.

CARO, G. (1908-[1918]). *Sozial- und Wirtschaftsgeschichte der Juden im Mittelalter und der Neuzeit* 1–2. Leipzig; Frankfurt.

CASSUTO, U. [U.C.] (1929). Aquila. *EJ/B,* 3:columns 27–35.

CASTRO, A. (1971). *The Spaniards. An introduction to their history.* Berkeley-Los-Angeles-London.

ČAXČIR, N.N.L. (1905). *Sefer šir haširim vetargumo ma'atak ivrit bilšon tatar hame-duberet befinu anaxnu bne hakrimčakim haj"o.* Petrykaw.

ČERIKOVER, A. (1939). Jidiše historiografje. *AEJ,* 1:columns 284–304.

CHRISTENSEN, C.D. (1814). *Alphabetisches Verzeichnis einer Anzahl von Räubern, Dieben und Vagabonden...* Hamburg.

ČISTOV, K.V. (1987). Semejnye obrjady i obrjadovyj fol'klor. In his ed., *Ėtnografija vostočnyx slavjan. Očerki tradicionnoj kul'tury,* 396–416. Moscow.

CLEMEN, C. (1931). *Religionsgeschichte Europas* 2. Heidelberg.

COBERN, C.M. (1917). *The new archeological discoveries and their bearing upon the New Testament and upon the life and times of the primitive church.* New York-London.

COHEN, I. (1953). *Travels in Jewry.* New York.

COLORNI, V. (1964). L'Uso del greco nella liturgia del giudaismo e la Novella 146 di Giustiniano. *Annali di storia del diritto* 8:19–87.

CONDURACHI, E. (1937). Les Juifs en Illyricum. *REJ* 101:87–93.

COON, C.S. (1942). Have the Jews a racial identity? *JGW,* 20–37.

ČORNI, J.J.B.J.H. (1884). *Sefer hamasaot be'erec hakavkaz uvimdinot ašer me'ever lekavkaz.* St.Petersburg.

COSTA FONTES, M. DA (1990–3). Portuguese Crypto-Jewish prayers and their 'Inquisitorial' counterparts. *MedLR* 6–7:67–104.

CROSS, S.H. and O.P. SHERBOWITZ-WETZOR (1953). *The Russian Primary Chronicle. Laurentian text.* Cambridge, MA.

CUMONT, F. (1897). *Hypsistos.* Brussels. Supplement to *Revue de l'Instruction publique en Belgique.*

— (1906). Les mystères de Sabazius et le judaïsme. *Académie des Inscriptions et Belles-Lettres. Comptes-rendus* 4th series 63–79. Paris.

CUTLER, A.H. and H.E. (1986). *The Jew as ally of the Muslim. Medieval roots of anti-Semitism.* Notre Dame, IN.

CZEKANOWSKI, J. (1957). *Wstęp do historii Słowian. Perspektywy antropologiczne, etnograficzne, archeologiczne i językowe.* Poznań.

— (1960). Anthropological structure of the Jewish people in the light of Polish analyses. *JJS* 2:236–43.

DENMAN, H. (1991). Die Bedeutung des Rätoromanischen für die Entstehung der jiddischen Sprache. *IGK,* 11:520–9.

DIETRICH, K. (1931). Zur Kulturgeographie und Kulturgeschichte des byzantinischen Balkanländer. *Byzantinische Zeitschrift* 31:37–57, 334–50.

DILLARD, J.E. (1972). *Black English. Its history and usage in the United States.* New York.

DIRINGER, D. (1950). Early Hebrew script *versus* square Hebrew script. *Essays and studies presented to Stanley Arthur Cook,* ed. D.W.Thomas, 35–49. London.

DMITRIEV, M.A. (1869). *Sobranie pesen, skazok, obrjadov i obyčaev krest'jan severo-zapadnogo kraja.* Vilna.

DOMBROVSKY, A. (1959). A few examples of analogy in the ancient Ukrainian and Judaic cultures. *AUA* 7:1531–41.

DOROSZEWSKI, W. (1958–69). *Słownik języka polskiego* 1–11. Warsaw.

DOVNAR-ZAPOL'SKIJ, M.V. (1909). *Issledovanija i stat'i* 1, ed. A.P.Sapunov. Kiev.

DOWNEY, J.W. (1966). *La musique populaire dans l'oeuvre de Béla Bartok.* Paris.

DRALLE, L. (1991). *Die Deutschen in Ostmittel- und Osteuropa.* Darmstadt.

DRECHSLER, P. (1903). *Sitte, Brauch und Volksglaube in Schlesien* 1. Leizpig.

DUBNOW, S.M. (1921). *Die jüdische Geschichte. Ein geschichts-philosophischer Versuch.* Frankfurt.

DÜVEL, K. (1970). Germanische Opfer und Opferriten im Spiegel altgermanischer Kultworte. *Vorgeschichtliche Heiligtümer und Opferplätze in Mittel- und Nordeuropa,* ed. H.Jankuhn, 219–39. Göttingen.

DVORNIK, F. (1956). *The Slavs. Their early history and civilization.* Boston; 2nd edition, 1959.

ECKERT, R. (1977). Zu den Namen für weibliche mythologische Wesen auf *-yn'i* im Slawischen. *ZS* 22:44–52.

ECKERT, W.P. (1968). Hoch- und Spätmittelalter. Katholischer Humanismus. *KS,* 1:210–306.

ECKSTEIN, F. (1927). Brot. *HDA,* 1:columns 1590–1659.

— (1936–7). Speise. *HDA,* 8:columns 156–234.

— (1938–41). Zopfgebäck. *HDA,* 9:columns 945–54.

EDELMANN, R. (1966). Das "Buch der Frommen" als Ausdruck des volkstümlichen Geisteslebens der deutschen Juden im Mittelalter. Zur Entstehung des aschkenasischen Judentums. *JM*, 55–71.

EGGER, R. (1963). Die Christianisierung der pannonischen Provinzen. *SOF* 22:9–13.

EICHLER, E. (1985). *Beiträge zur deutsch-slawischen Namenforschung (1955–1981)*. Leipzig.

EIDELBERG, S. (1962). *Jewish life in Austria in the XVth century. As reflected in the legal writings of Rabbi Israel Isserlein and his contemporaries.* Philadelphia.

EISENSTEIN, J.D. (1904). Jahrzeit. *JE*, 7:63–4.

ELBOGEN, I. (1916). Zu den hebräischen Berichten über die Judenverfolgungen im Jahre 1096. *FSMP*, 6–24.

— (1930). Deutschland. *EJ/B*, 5:columns 971–1006.

ELLIS, L. (1978). Reinterpretations of the West Slavic cult site of Arkona. *Journal of Indo-European studies* 6:1–16.

ELWORTHY, F.T. (1895). *The evil eye. The origins and practices of superstition.* London; reprinted New York 1958, 1970.

EPPENSTEIN, S. (1919). Zur Frühgeschichte der Juden in Deutschland, besonders in literarischer und kultureller Hinsicht. *MGWJ* 63:165–86.

ESCHWEGE, H. (1980). *Die Synagoge in der deutschen Geschichte.* Dresden.

EVELYN, J. (1901). *The diary of John Evelyn* 1–2, ed. W.Bray. Washington-London.

FABER, A. and R.D.KING (1984). Yiddish and the settlement history of the Ashkenazic Jews. *MQ* 24: 393–425.

FALLMERAYER, J.P. (1830). *Geschichte der Halbinsel Morea während des Mittelalters* 1. Stuttgart-Tübingen.

FEIFALIK, J. (1859). Perahta bei den Slaven. *ZDMG* 4:387–9.

FELDMAN, L.H. (1986). The omnipresence of the God-Fearers. *BAR* 12(5):58–69.

— (1989). Proselytes and "sympathizers" in the light of the new inscriptions from Aphrodisias. *REJ* 148:265–305.

FELLMAN, J. (1973). *The revival of a classical tongue: Eliezer ben Yehuda and the Modern Hebrew language.* The Hague.

FETTKE, D. (1986). *Juden und Nichtjuden im 16. und 17. Jahrhundert in Polen: soziale und ökonomische Beziehungen in Responsen polnischer Rabbinen.* Frankfurt-Berne-New York.

FEUCHTWANGER, N. (1986). Interrelations between the Jewish and Christian wedding in medieval Ashkenaz. *PWCJS*, D2:31–6.

FILIPOVIĆ, M.S. (1960). Volksglauben auf dem Balkan. *SOF* 19:239–62.

FINKELSTEIN, L. (1938). The persistence of rejected customs in Palestine. *JQR* n.s. 29:179–86.

FISCHER, A. (1932). *Etnografja słowiańska* 1. *Połabianie.* Lvov-Warsaw.

FISHBERG, M. (1905). *Materials for the physical anthropology of the Eastern European Jews.* Lancaster, PA.

— (1911). *The Jews. A study of race and environment.* London-New York.

FISHMAN, J.A. (1991). How does Yiddish differ? In his *Turning to Life*, 313–23. Amsterdam-Philadelphia.

FISHOF, I. (1986–8). The origin of the *sîddûr* of the Rabbi of Ruzhin. *JA* 12–3:73–82.

FIŠMAN, D.-E. (1991). Mikojex davnen af jidiš: a bintl metodologiše bamerkungen un naje mekojrim. *YB* n.s. 1:69–92.

FLATTAU, D. (1931). Jahrzeit. *EJ/B*, 8:columns 779–81.

FLEURY, ABBÉ C. (1683). *Les moeurs des Israëlites.* Paris.

FLIER, M. (1985). The non-Christian provenience of Slavic *nedelja. IJSLP* 31–2:151–65.

FOX, N. (1927). *Saarländische Volkskunde.* Bonn.

FRANKL, P.F. (1884). Über die Stellung der deutschen Juden innerhalb der gesamten Judenheit. *MGWJ* 33:1–22.

FRANZ, A. (1909). *Die kirchlichen Benediktionen im Mittelalter* 1. Freiburg/Br.; 2nd edition, Graz 1960.

FREEHOF, S.B. (1962). Home rituals and the Spanish synagogue. *SEHAAN*, 215–27.

— (1963). The Huppah. *In time of harvest: essays in honor of Abba Hillel Silver*, ed. D.J.Silver, 187–93. New York; reprinted in P. and H.Goodman 1965:93–9.

— (1967). Ceremonial creativity among the Ashkenazim. *The seventy-fifth anniversary volume of the Jewish Quarterly Review*, eds. A.A.Neuman and S.Zeitlin, 210–24. Philadelphia.

FREIMANN, A. (1929). Verbindungen von Juden in Deutschland mit denen in Babylonien und Palästina während des Mittelalters bis zum ersten Kreuzzuge. *ZGJD* 1:165–7.

FREUND, R. (1991). *Karaites and dejudaization. A historical review of an endogenous and exogenous paradigm.* (Stockholm studies in comparative religion, 30.) Stockholm.

FREY, J.B. (1975). *Corpus inscriptionum iudaicarum* 1–2. New York; 2nd edition; originally Città del Vaticano 1936–52.

FRIEDMAN, P. (1959). The first millennium of Jewish settlement in the Ukraine and in the adjacent areas. *AUA* 7:1483–1516.

FRIEDMANN, G. (1967). *The end of the Jewish people.* Garden City, NY.

FRINTA, A. (1955). *Lužičtí srbové a jejich písemnictví.* Prague.

FRÖHLICH, É. (1990). Két démonelhárító szöveg a budapesti Zsidó Múzeumból. *AHK*, 131–5.

FUCHS, H. [H.F.] (1927). Aquila. *JL*, 1:columns 407–8.

FUKS, L. (1987). The Romance elements in Old Yiddish. *OYL*, 23–5.

GAMST, F.C. (1969). *The Qemant. A pagan-Hebraic peasantry of Ethiopia.* New York.

GANDER, C. (1890). Sagen, Brauch und Glaube I. Die wichtigsten Momente des Lebens. *Niederlausitzer Mitteilungen. Zeitschrift der Niederlausitzer Gesellschaft für Anthropologie und Urgeschichte* 1:450–65.

GANSHOF, F.L. (1966). Note sur l'"Inquisitio de theloneis Raffelstettensis". *Le moyen âge* 4th series 21:197–224.

GASPARINI, E. (1965). Sul paganesimo degli antichi slavi. *Annali, Istituto orientale. Sezione slava.* 8:135–67.

GASTER, M. (1880). Beiträge zur vergleichenden Sagen- und Märchenkunde. *MGWJ* 29:549–65.

— (1915). *Rumanian bird and beast stories.* London.

— (1971a). Popular Judaism at the time of the Second Temple in the light of Samaritan traditions. *ST*, 724–9.

— (1971b). Two thousand years of a charm against the child-stealing witch. *ST*, 1005–38.

GASTER, T.H. (1980). *The holy and the profane. Evolution of Jewish folkways.* New York.

GEORGIEV, V. et al. (eds.) (1969). *Bəlgarski etimologičen rečnik* 7. Sofia.

GERSON-KIWI, E. (1981). Die Musik der jüdischen Volksstämme. *Begegnungen mit dem Judentum*, ed. B.Rübenach, 155–66. Berlin.

GIESE, W. (1968). In Judaismum lapsus est. Jüdische Proselytenmacherei im frühen und hohen Mittelalter (600–1300). *Historisches Jahrbuch* 88:407–18.

GIMBUTAS, M. (1963). *The Balts.* London.

GINSBERG, M. (1963). On Dubnow's concept of Jewish history. *Simon Dubnov. L'homme et son ouevre*, ed. A.Steinberg, 41–56. Paris.

GINZEL, J.A. (1861). *Geschichte der Slavenapostel Cyrill und Method.* Vienna; 2nd edition.

GLANZ, R. (1968). *Geschichte des niederen jüdischen Volkes in Deutschland. Eine Studie über historisches Gaunertum, Bettelwesen und Vagantentum.* New York.

GLAPA, A. (1970). Postrzyżyny. *SSS*, 4:249–50.

GODBEY, A.H. (1930). *The lost tribes, a myth. Suggestions towards rewriting Hebrew history.* Durham, NC.

GOITEIN, S.D. (1930). Hajesodot haivri'im bisfat hadibur šel jehude teman. *Lešonenu* 3:356–80.

— (1971). *A Mediterranean society* 2. Berkeley-Los Angeles-London.

GOLB, N. (1964). Ger cedek šebarax lemicraim berešita šel hamea haj"'. *Sfunot* 8:87–104.

— (1965). The topography of the Jews in Medieval Egypt. *Journal of Near Eastern studies* 24:251–70.

— and O.PRITSAK (1982). *Khazarian Hebrew documents of the tenth century.* Ithaca-London.

GOLDBERG, J. (1928). Di jidiše miš-špraxike un fremdšpraxike folklider. *Cajtšrift* 2–3:columns 589–606.

GOLDEN, P.B. (1980). *Khazar studies. An historico-philological inquiry into the origins of the Khazars* 1–2. Budapest.

GOLDMANN, F. (1927). Proselyt. *JL*, 4(1):columns 1146–51.

GOLDSTEIN, H. (1985). *Hebrew manuscript painting.* London.

GOLOMB, G.E. (1910). *Milim bilšoni. Hebreiš-idišes enciklopedišes verter-bux ojx talmudiše folks-šprixverter unter dem nomen pitgame orajta.* Vilna.

GOODENOUGH, E.R. (1953–68). *Jewish symbols in the Graeco-Roman period* 1–13. New York.

— (1957). The Bosporus inscriptions to the Most High God. *JQR* 47: 221–44.

GOODMAN, M. (1989). Proselytizing in Rabbinic Judaism. *JJSt* 38:175–85.

— (1992). Jewish proselytizing in the first century. *JPC*, 53–78.

GOODMAN, P. and H. (eds.) (1965). *The Jewish marriage anthology.* Philadelphia.

GOODMAN, R.M. (1979). A perspective on genetic diseases among the Jewish people. *GDAJ*, 1–17.

GOULD, S.J. (1991). Eight (or fewer) little piggies. *Natural history* 1:22–9.

GRABOIS, A. (1966). Le souvenir de la légende de Charlemagne dans les textes hébraïques médiévaux. *Le moyen âge* 4th series 21:5–41.

GRAETZ, H.H. (1884). *Die jüdischen Proselyten im Römerreiche unter den Kaisern Domitian, Nerva, Trajan und Hadrian.* Wrocław.

— (1897–1911). *Geschichte der Juden von den ältesten Zeiten bis auf die Gegenwart* 1–11. Leipzig.

GRANT, R.M. (1980). Dietary laws among Pythagoreans, Jews and Christians. *HTR* 73:299–310.

GRAUS, FR. (1980). *Die Nationenbildung der Westslawen im Mittelalter.* Sigmaringen.

— (1981). Historische Traditionen über Juden im Spätmittelalter (Mitteleuropa). *Zur Geschichte der Juden in Deutschland des späten Mittelalters und der frühen Neuzeit,* ed. A.Haverkamp, 1–26. Stuttgart.

GRAYZEL, S. (1933). *The Church and the Jews in the XIIIth century.* Philadelphia; revised 2nd edition, New York 1966.

— (1947). *A history of the Jews.* Philadelphia.

GRESSMANN, H. (1920). Die Haartracht der Israeliten. *Beiträge zur alttestamentlichen Wissenschaft. Karl Budde zum siebzigsten Geburtstag,* ed. K.Marti, 61–8. Giessen.

— (1927). Jewish life in ancient Rome. *Jewish Studies in Memory of Israel Abrahams,* 170–91. New York.

GRIMM, J. (1876–8). *Deutsche Mythologie* 1–3. Berlin. 4th edition.

— (1883–1900). *Teutonic mythology* 1–2, 4, with notes by J.S. Stallybass. London.

GROHMANN, J.W. (1864). *Aberglauben und Gebräuche aus Böhmen und Mähren.* Prague-Leipzig.

GROSSER, S. (1714). *Lausitzische Merckwürdigkeiten* 1–2. Leipzig-Bautzen.

GROTTE, A. (1922). Eine neue Hypothese über den Ursprung des Magén David. *MGWJ* 66:1–9.

GRÜNBAUM, M. (1877). Beiträge zur vergleichenden Mythologie aus der Hagada. *ZDMG* 31:183–359.

— (1882). *Jüdischdeutsche Chrestomathie. Zugleich ein Beitrag zur Kunde der hebräischen Literatur.* Leipzig.

GRUNWALD, M. (1900). Aus Hausapotheke und Hexenküche. *MGJV* 5:1–87.

— (1901). Ein altes Symbol in neuer Beleuchtung. *JJGL* 4:110–31.

— (1927). Magen David. *JL,* 3:columns 1281–2.

— (1936). Beitraege zur Volkskunde und Kunstgeschichte. *OO,* 184–204.

— (1947). The Magen David. *HJ* 9:178–88.

GÜDEMANN, M. (1866). *Zur Geschichte der Juden in Magdeburg.* Wrocław.

— (1880). *Geschichte des Erziehungswesens und der Cultur der Juden in Frankreich und Deutschland...(X-XIV. Jahrhundert).* Vienna.

— (1884). *Geschichte des Erziehungswesens und der Cultur der Juden in Italien während des Mittelalters.* Vienna.

— (1888). *Geschichte des Erziehungswesens und der Cultur der Juden in Deutschland während des XIV. und XV. Jahrhunderts.* Vienna; Amsterdam 1966.

— (1916). Der "Magen David" oder Davidsschild. *MGWJ* 60:135–9.

GÜNTERT, H. (1930–1). Hahn. *HDA,* 3:columns 1325–36.

— (1931–2). Huhn. *HDA*, 4:columns 448–58.

HAASE, F. (1939). *Volksglaube und Brauchtum der Ostslaven.* Wrocław; Hildesheim-New York 1980.

HADAS, M. (1966). Review of Goodenough 1953–68 [12:1966]. *Midstream* March, 75–7.

HADAS-LEBEL, M. (1979). Le paganisme à travers les sources rabbiniques des IIe et IIIe siècles. Contribution à l'étude du syncrétisme dans l'empire romain. *ANRW*, 2, 19/2:397–485.

HAJLE, Š. (1990). Ibern onhejb fun aškenaz un jidiš. *Oksforder jidiš* 1:107–14. Chur.

HAMMER-SCHENK, H. (1988). Die Architektur der Synagoge von 1780 bis 1933. *AS*, 157–285; 426–30.

HAMP, E. (1987). The pig in ancient northern Europe. In S.N.Skomal and E.C.Polomé, eds., *Proto-Indo-European. The archaeology of a linguistic problem. Studies in honor of Marija Gimbutas*, 185–90. Washington.

HAMPE, T. (1902). *Die fahrenden Leute in der deutschen Vergangenheit.* Leipzig.

HANCOCK, I.F. (1976). Patterns of English lexical adoption in an American dialect of Řomanés. *Orbis* 25:83–104.

HANGI, A. (1907). *Die Moslim's in Bosnien-Hercegovina. Ihre Lebensweise, Sitten und Gebräuche.* Sarajevo.

HANUSH, J.J. (1859). Die Wer-Wölfe oder Vlko-dlaci. *ZDMS* 4:193–8.

HARKAVI, A.A. [A.JA.GARKAVI] (1865). *Ob jazyke evreev živšix v drevnee vremja na Rusi i o slavjanskix slovax vstrečaemyx u evrejskix pisatelej.* St.Petersburg.

— (1870). *Skazanija musul'manskix pisatelej o slavjanax i russkix.* St.Petersburg.

HARKINS, P.W. (1979). *Saint John Chrysostom. Discourses against Judaizing Christians.* Washington.

HAVRÁNEK, B., J.DAŇHELKA and ZD.KRISTEN (1958). *Nejstarší česká rýmovaná kronika t.ř. Dalimila.* Prague.

HELER, J. (1939). Jidišer Lebensštejger. *AEJ*, 1:columns 603–56.

HENSEL, W. (1962). *Méthodes et perspectives de recherches sur les centres ruraux et urbains chez les slaves (VIIe–XIIIe s).* Warsaw.

HERRMANN, E. (1965). *Slawisch-germanische Beziehungen im südostdeutschen Raum von der Spätantike bis zum Ungarnsturm. Ein Quellenbuch mit Erläuterungen.* Vienna.

HERRMANN, J. (ed.) (1985). *Die Slawen in Deutschland.* Berlin.

HERTZBERG, A. (1968). *The French enlightenment and the Jews.* New York-London-Philadelphia.

— (1971). Jewish identity. *EJ/J*, 10:columns 53–65.

HERZOG, M.I. (1965). *The Yiddish language in Northern Poland: its geography and history.* Bloomington.

— (1979). Origins and evolution of the Yiddish language. *GDAJ*, 47–57.

HEYDZIANKA-PILATOWA, J. (1971). Z wierzeń Drzewian połabskich. *SO* 28–9:53–73.

HIGOUNET, C. (1989). *Les allemands en Europe centrale et orientale au Moyen Age.* Paris.

HILCZER-KURNATOWSKA, Z. (1986a). Awaro-słowiańska kultura. *SSS* 7/2:386–7.

— (1986b). Chrystianizacja Słowian. *SSS*, 7/2:590–3.

HILL, G. (1948). *A history of Cyprus* 2. London.

HIRŠBERG, H.Z. (1965). *Toldot hajehudim beafrika hacfonit* 2. Jerusalem.

HOBSBAWM, E. (1983). Introduction: inventing traditions. *IT*, 1–14.

HOERNING, R. (1889). *British Museum Karaite manuscripts. Descriptions and collation of six Karaite manuscripts of portions of the Hebrew Bible in Arabic characters...* London.

HOFFMANN, M. (1910). *Der Geldhandel der deutschen Juden während des Mittelalters bis zum Jahre 1350.* Leipzig.

HOFFMANN-KRAYER, E. (1927). Breve. *HDA*, 1:columns 1573–4.

HÖFLER, M. (1906). Das Haaropfer in Teigform. *Archiv für Anthropologie* n.F. 4: 130–48.

HOLZER, I. (1934). Aus dem Leben der alten Judengemeinde zu Worms. *ZGJD* 5: 169–81; reprinted in Róth 202–13.

HOPE, T.E. (1971). *Lexical borrowing in the Romance languages. A critical study of Italianisms in French and Gallicisms in Italian from 1100 to 1900* 1–2. Oxford.

HORVAT, R. (1896). Koprivnica u Hrvatskoj. *Zbornik za narodni život i običaje južnih slavena* 1:206–7.

HORVATH, J. and P.WEXLER (ms). Unspoken "languages" and the issue of genetic classification. (With special reference to Hebrew).

HOVORKA, O. VON and A.KRONFELD (1908–9). *Vergleichende Volksmedizin* 1–2. Stuttgart.

HSIA, R.P-C. (1988). *The myth of ritual murder. Jews and magic in Reformation Germany.* New Haven-London.

HUNTINGFORD, G.W.B. (1935). Who were the Scythians? *Anthropos* 30:785–95.

IBN BARUN, Y.B.Y. (c.1100). *Kitāb almuwāzana bayn alluġa al'ibrāniyya wal-'arabiyya.* See Wechter.

IBN JA'QŪB, I. (10th c). See Jakimowicz; Kowalski; Lewicki 1971.

IDELSOHN, A.Z. (1922). *Gesänge der babylonischen Juden* 2. Jerusalem-Berlin-Warsaw.

— (1923). *Gesänge der orientalischen Sefardim* 4. Jerusalem-Berlin-Warsaw.

— (1967). *Jewish music in its historical development.* New York. Originally published in 1929.

INFORMATION DEPARTMENT OF THE ROYAL INSTITUTE OF INTERNATIONAL AFFAIRS (1964). *Cyprus: the dispute and the settlement.* Oxford.

ITHEN, A. (1897). Volkstümliches aus dem Kanton Zug. *SAV* 1:115–26.

IXILOV, M.I. (1950). Bol'šaja sem'ja i patronimija u gorskix evreev. *Sovetskaja ėtnografija* 1:188–92.

JACOBS, J. (1885). On the racial characteristics of modern Jews. *Journal of the Royal Anthropological Institute* 15:23–56.

JACOBS, M. (1942). Jewish blood and culture. *JGW* 38–55.

JACOBY, A. (1931–2). Homunculus. *HDA*, 4:columns 286–9.

JAHN, U. (1886). *Hexenwesen und Zauberei in Pommern.* Wrocław.

JAKIMOWICZ, R. (1949). Kilka uwag nad relacją o Słowianach Ibrahima ibn Jakuba. *Slavia antiqua* 1:439–56.

JAKOBSON, R. (1953). Der jidišer klangen-baštand in farglajx mit slavišn arum. *YS* 13:70–83; reprinted in J.Mark, ed., *Juda A.Jofe-bux*. New York 1958:207–220; an abridged Russian version appears in Jakobson, *Selected writings*, ed. I. Matejka. The Hague 1962:402–12.

— (1957). Řeč a písemnictví českých židů v době přemyslovské. *Kulturní sborník ROK*, ed. L.Matějka, 35–46. New York.

— and M.HALLE (1964). The term *Canaan* in Medieval Hebrew. *For Max Weinreich on his seventieth birthday. Studies in Jewish languages, literature and society*, eds. L.Dawidowicz, et al., 147–72. The Hague.

JAMIESON, J.W. (1982). The Samaritans. *MQ* 23:141–8.

JÄNICHEN, A. (1938). *Die Wikinger im Weichsel- und Odergebiet*. Leipzig.

JASNOSZ, S. and L.LECIEJEWICZ (1964). Haithabu. *SSS*, 2:183.

JOEL, D. (1881–3). *Der Aberglaube und die Stellung des Judentums zu demselben* 1–2. Wrocław.

JOHNSON, P. (1987). *A history of the Jews*. New York.

JOHNSON, S.E. (1975). Asia Minor and early Christianity. *CJ*, 2:77–145.

JOSIPPON (10th c). *Sefer josippon*, ed. D.Flusser 1–2. Jerusalem, 1978–80.

JUNGBAUER, G. (1931–2a). Hut. *HDA*, 4:columns 513–43.

— (1931–2b). Jahrtag. *HDA*, 4:columns 617–20.

JUSTER, J. (1976). The legal condition of the Jews under the Visigothic kings. II. *Israel law review* 11:391–411.

KAHAN, J. (1938). Or Sarua als Geschichtsquelle. *JGGJČR* 9:43–99.

KAHLE, P. (1950). Zur Aussprache des Hebräischen bei den Samaritanern. *Festschrift Alfred Bertholet zum 80. Geburtstage*, eds. W. Baumgartner, et al., 281–6. Tübingen; reprinted in his *Opera minora*. Leiden 1956:180–5.

KAHN, F. (1921). *Die Juden als Rasse und Kulturvolk*. Berlin. 2nd edition.

— (1927). Rasse, Jüdische. *JL*, 4(1):columns 1243–7.

KAPPESOWA, H. (1961). Borys-Michał. *SSS*, 1:151.

KARLIN, S., R.KENETT and B.BONNÉ-TAMIR (1979). Analysis of biochemical data on Jewish populations. Results and interpretations of heterogeneity indices and distance measures with respect to standards. *AJHG* 31:341–65.

KARŁOWICZ, J. (1894–1905). *Słownik wyrazów obcego a mniej jasnego pochodzenia używanych w języku polskim* 1–3. Kraków.

— [KARLOWICZ]. (1900). Germanische Elemente im slavischen Mythus und Brauch. *ARW* 3:184–93.

KATZ, J. (1961). *Exclusiveness and tolerance. Studies in Jewish-Gentile relations in Medieval and modern times*. Oxford.

— (1992). *Hahalaxa bemecar*. Jerusalem.

KATZ, K. (1968). Jewish tradition in art. *From the beginning. Archaeology and art in the Israel Museum, Jerusalem*, eds. K. Katz, P.P.Kahane and M.Broshi, 148–215. New York.

KAUDER, V. (1923). *Die deutsche Sprachinsel Bielitz-Biała*. Plauen.

KAWERAU, P. (1967). *Arabische Quellen zur Christianisierung Russlands*. Wiesbaden.

KEDOURIE, E. (1971). Introduction. In his *Nationalism in Asia and Africa*, 1–152. London.
— (1979a). Diaspora: Jews under Christianity and Islam. *JW*, 128–60.
— (1979b). Introduction. *JW*, 7–11.
— (1979c). The making of Jewry. *JW*, 68–88.
KENRICK, D. (1979). Romani English. *IJSL* 19:111–20.
KERN, S. (1983). *The culture of time and space 1880–1918*. Cambridge, MA.
KESSLER, G. (1916). Das festliche Jahr in Wil (St.Gallen). *SAV* 20:191–203.
KHAN, G. (1992). The medieval Karaite transcriptions of Hebrew into Arabic script. *Israel Oriental studies* 12:157–76.
KIMELMAN, R. (1981). *Birkat ha-minim* and the lack of evidence for an anti-Christian Jewish prayer in late antiquity. *Jewish and Christian self-definition*, eds. E.P.Sanders, et al., 2:228–44. Philadelphia.
KING, R.A. (1987). Proto Yiddish morphology. *OYL*, 73–81.
KIPARSKY, V. (1936). *Fremdes im Baltendeutsch*. Helsinki.
KIRCHNER, P.C. (1726). *Jüdisches Ceremoniel*. Nürnberg; Hildesheim-New York 1974.
KISCH, G. (1949). *The Jews in medieval Germany*. Chicago.
KNIESZA, I. (1933). Ungarn zur Zeit der Landnahme. *RS* 11:1–25.
— (1938). Ungarns Völkerschaften im XI. Jahrhundert. *AECO* 4:241–412.
KNOBLOCH, J. (1986). *Sprache und Religion* 3. Heidelberg.
KOBYLIANSKY, E. and G.LIVSHITS (1983). Genetic composition of Jewish populations: diversity and inbreeding. *AHB* 10:453–64.
— (1985). A morphological approach to the problem of the biological similarity of Jewish and non-Jewish populations. *AHB* 12:203–12.
KOBYLIANSKY, E., S.MICLE, M.GOLDSCHMIDT-NATHAN, B.ARENSBURG and H.NATHAN (1982). Jewish populations of the world: genetic likeness and differences. *AHB* 9:1–34.
KOČEV, N. (1978). The question of Jews and the so-called Judaizers in the Balkans from the 9th to the 14th century. *Bulgarian historical review* 6:60–79.
KOCHAN, L. (1977). *The Jew and his history*. London-Basingstoke.
KOESTLER, A. (1976). *The thirteenth tribe. The Khazar empire and its heritage*. London.
KOHLBACH, B. (1914). Das Zopfgebäck im jüdischen Ritus. *ZVV* 24:265–71.
KOHLER, K. (1903). Circumcision. *JE*, 4:92–6.
KOLLAUTZ, A. (1954). Die Awaren. Die Schichtung in einer Nomadenherrschaft. *Saeculum* 5:129–78.
KOLLMANN, J. and [?].KAHNT (1885). Schädel und Skeletreste aus einem Judenfriedhof des 13. und 14. Jahrhunderts zu Basel. *Naturforschende Gesellschaft in Basel. Verhandlungen* 7:648–56. Basle.
KOPCZYŃSKA-JAWORSKA, B. (1986). Annual Jewish festivals in the eyes of the Polish people. *PWCJS*, D2:87–94.
KORN, S. (1988). Synagogen und Betstuben in Frankfurt am Main. *AS*, 347–95; 432–4.
KOSTRZEWSKI, B. (1961). Awarskie importy i wpływy w kulturze słowiańskiej. *SSS*, 1:59–61.

— (1964a). Kaptorgi. *SSS*, 2:371–2.
— (1964b). Kult zwierząt. *SSS*, 2:558–9.
KOVALYK, I.I. (1967). Slovotvorčyj rozrjad prostorovyx nazv u sučasnij verxn'olužyc'kij movi. *Struktura i rozvytok slov'jans'kyx mov*, 86–92. Kiev.
KOWALCZYK, M. (1968). *Wierzenia pogańskie za pierwszych Piastów*. Łódź.
KOWALENKO, Wł. (1961). Chrzescijaństwa, przyjęcie przez Słowian. *SSS*, 1:262–4.
KOWALSKI, T. (1946). *Relacja Ibrāhīma ibn Ja' ḳūba z podroży do krajów słowiańskich w przekazie al-Bekrīego*. Kraków.
KRAABEL, A.T. (1969). *Hypsistos* and the synagogue at Sardis. *Greek, Roman and Byzantine studies* 10:81–93.
— (1979). The Diaspora synagogue: archaeological and epigraphic evidence since Sukenik. *ANRW*, 2, 19/1:477–510.
— (1981). The disappearance of the 'God-Fearers'. *Numen* 28:113–26.
— (1982). The Roman diaspora: six questionable assumptions. *JJSt* 33:445–64.
KRAEMER, R.S. (1985). A new inscription from Malta and the question of women elders in the diaspora Jewish communities. *HTR* 78:431–8.
— (1989). On the meaning of the term "Jew" in Greco-Roman inscriptions. *HTR* 82:35–53.
KRANZMAYER, E. (1956–8). *Ortsnamenbuch von Kärnten* 1–2. Klagenfurt; 1984[2].
KRAUSS, F.S. (1885). *Slavische Volksforschungen. Abhandlungen über Glauben, Gewohnheitrechte, Sitten, Bräuche und die Guslarenlieder der Südslaven*. Leipzig.
— (1892). Der Tod in Sitte, Brauch und Glauben der Südslaven. *ZVV* 2:177–89.
— (1897). Beiträge zur Geschichte der Volkskunde. *Am Ur-Quell* n.F. 1:284–5.
— (1908). *Sitte und Brauch der Südslaven*. Vienna.
KRAUTHEIMER, R. (1925). *Die Kirchen der Bettelorden in Deutschland*. Bonn.
— (1927). *Mittelalterliche Synagogen*. Berlin.
KRESSEL, G.M. (1992). *Descent through males*. Wiesbaden.
KRETZENBACHER, L. (1987). "Der Norden ist böse!" Zu einem Symbolik-Vorurteil des abendländischen Mittelalters und seiner Nachfolge. *ÖZV* n.S. 41:301–29.
KRINSKY, C.H. (1985). *Synagogues in Europe*. Cambridge, MA-London.
KROJS, Š. (1932). Hašemot aškenaz usfarad. *Tarbic* 3:423–35.
KRONSTEINER, O. (1978). Gab es unter den Alpenslawen eine kroatische ethnische Gruppe? *Wiener slawistisches Jahrbuch* 24:137–57.
KRÜGER, R. (1968). *Die Kunst der Synagoge. Eine Einführung in die Probleme von Kunst und Kult des Judentums*. Leipzig.
KRZYWICKI, L. (1912). Obszar etnograficzny Polski pod względem antropologicznym rozważany w zestawieniu z krajami ościennymi. *EP*, 1(1–2):465–654.
KUNIK, A. and V.ROZEN (1878–1903). *Izvestija al-Bekri i drugix avtorov o Rusi i slavjanax*. St.Petersburg.
KUNSTMANN, H. (1987). *Beiträge zur Geschichte der Besiedlung Nord- und Mitteldeutschlands mit Balkanslaven*. Munich.
KÜNZL, H. (1988a). Der Synagogenbau im Mittelalter. *AS*, 61–87, 424.
— (1988b). Europäischer Synagogenbau vom 16. bis zum 18. Jahrhundert. *AS*, 89–114, 425.

KUPFER, FR. and T.LEWICKI (1956). *Żródła hebrajskie do dziejów słowian i niektórych innych ludów środkowej i wschodniej Europy.* Wrocław-Warsaw.

KURZOWA, Z. (1985). *Polszczyzna Lwowa i kresów południowo-wschodnich do roku 1939.* Warsaw-Kraków.

KUTSCHERA, H.F.VON (1910). *Die Chasaren. Historische Studie.* Vienna. 2nd edition.

LABUDA, G. (1961a). Abraham. *SSS*, 1:1.

— (1961b). Brzetysław. *SSS*, 1:168.

— (1964a). Frankonia, Frankowie, Stosunki ze Słowianami. *SSS*, 2:67–72.

— (1964b). Kakacjusz. *SSS*, 2:351–2.

— (1977). Teodor. *SSS*, 6:49.

LANDAU, A. (1898). IV. Sitte und Brauch. *MGJV* 1:81–110.

— (1899a). Fragekasten. Holekreisch. Eine Umfrage. *MGJV* 4:146–7.

— (1899b). Holekreisch. *ZVV* 9:72–7.

— [LANDOY] (1924). Hesofes un bamerkungen cu der "Jidišer filologje" heftn 1–3. *JF*, 323–37.

LANDBERG, COMTE DE (1906). *Etudes sur les dialects de l'arabe mériodionale* 1. Leiden.

LAREDO, A.I. (1978). *Les noms des Juifs du Maroc. Essai d'onomastique judéo-marocaine.* Madrid.

LASKER, D.J. (1990). Proselyte Judaism, Christianity, and Islam in the thought of Judah Halevi. *JQR* 81:75–92.

LASKOWSKI, R. (1966). Słowiańskie **bachorъ : *bachorь: *bachurъ. RS* 26:51–7.

LAUTERBACH, J.Z. (1925). The ceremony of breaking a glass at weddings. *HUCA* 2:351–80; reprinted in *SJLCF*, 1–29A.

— (1928). Should one cover the head when participating in divine worship? *YBCCAR* 38:589–603; reprinted in *SJLCF*, 225–39.

— (1932). The naming of children in Jewish folklore, ritual and practice. *YBCCAR* 42:316–60; reprinted in *SJLCF*, 30–74.

— (1935). The ritual for the Kapparot-ceremony. *Jewish studies in memory of G.A.Kohut...*, 413–22. New York; reprinted in *SJLCF*, 133–42.

— (1936). Tashlik̲: a study in Jewish ceremonies. *HUCA* 11:207–340; reprinted in his *Rabbinic essays.* Cincinnati 1951, 299–433.

LAWSON, E.D. (1991). Most common Jewish first names in Israel. *Names. Journal of the American Name Society* 39:103–24.

LAZAR, Š.M. (1913). Meajin—moca hajehudim bimdinat polin. *Haeškol* 7:50–7. Kraków.

LEIBMAN, R. (1972). Wedding customs in the Ohrid village of Pešteni. *Makedonski folklor* 9–10:125–40.

LEON, H.J. (1960). *The Jews of ancient Rome.* Philadelphia.

LÉVI, I. (1911). Les jardins d'Adonis. Les Kapparot et Rosch Haschana. *REJ* 61:206–12.

LEVY, I. (1963). *The synagogue. Its history and function.* London.

LEWICKI, T. (1937). Węgry i muzułmanie węgierścy w świetle relacji podróżnika arabskiego z XII w. Abu-Hāmid al-Andalusī al-Garnātī'ego. *Rocznik orientalistyczny* 13:106–22.

— (1952–3). Obrzędy pogrzebowe pogańskich Słowian w opisach podróżników i pisarzy arabskich głównie z IX-X w. *Archeologia* 5:122–54, 438.
— (1956–77). *Źródła arabskie do dziejów słowiańszczyzny* 1–2/2. Wrocław-Warsaw-Kraków-Gdańsk.
— (1958). Źródła arabskie i hebrajskie do dziejów Słowian w okresie wczesnego średniowiecza. *Studia źródłoznawcze* 3:61–100.
— (1961a). Chasdaj ben Szaprut. *SSS*, 1:238.
— (1961b). Les sources hébraïques consacrées à l'histoire de l'Europe centrale et orientale et particulièrement à celle des pays slaves de la fin du IXe au milieu du XIIIe siècle. *Cahiers du monde russe et soviétique* 2:228–41.
— (1963). Les rites funéraires païens des slaves occidentaux et des anciens russes d'après les relations des voyageurs et des écrivains arabes. *Folia orientalistyczny* 5:1–74.
— (1964a). Islam w Europie wschodniej. *SSS*, 2:293–4.
— (1964b). Judaizm w Europie wschodniej. *SSS*, 2:341–2.
— (1964c). Kana'an. *SSS*, 2:364–5.
— (1971). Ibn ʿAbd al-Munʿim al-Ḥimyarī. *The Encyclopaedia of Islam*, new edition, eds. B.Lewis, et al., 3:675–6. Leiden-London.
— (1975). Samanidzi. *SSS*, 5:34–6.
LEWIS, B. (1975). *History—remembered, recovered, invented.* Princeton.
LEWY, H. (1927). Zur Vorstellung vom Neide der Götter. *ARW* 25:194–7.
— (1930). Zum Dämonenglauben. *ARW* 28:241–52.
LEWY, W. (1927). Jahrzeit. *JL*, 3:columns 128–9.
LEXER, M. (1862). *Kärntisches Wörterbuch.* Leipzig.
LIBERMAN, X. (1960). Vegn a "šabes" vos iz ajngehilt in a sod. *YS* 20(2):50–5.
— (1967). Raboniše etimologjes fun jidiše verter. *YS* 27:38–9.
LIEBE, G. (1903). *Das Judentum in der deutschen Vergangenheit.* Leipzig.
LIEBERMAN, S. (1942). *Greek in Jewish Palestine.* New York.
LIEWEHR, F. (1954). Zur Ausdrucksverstärkung im Slavischen. *ZSPh* 23:89–115.
LIFSHITZ, B. (1975). Prolegomenon. In Frey 1:21–107.
LILJENTAL, R. (1924). Ejn hore. *JF*, 245–71.
LIVSHITS, G., R.R.SOKAL and E.KOBYLIANSKY (1991). Genetic affinities of Jewish populations. *AJHG* 49:131–46.
LOEB, I. (1880). Bulles inédites des Papes. *REJ* 1:293–8.
— (1884). Deux livres de commerce du commencement du XIVe siècle. *REJ* 8:163–96.
— (1885). Review of J.Jacobs 1885. *REJ* 11:283.
— (1889). Polémistes chrétiens et juifs en France et en Espagne. *REJ* 18:219–42.
— (1893). Réflexions sur les Juifs. *REJ* 27:1–29.
ŁOSIŃSKI, WŁ. (1975). Wustrow. *SSS*, 5:642–3.
LOTTER, F. (1991). Die Juden im Kirchenrecht des Mittelalters. *Aschkenas* 1:161–72. Vienna-Cologne.
LÖWE, H. (1988). Die Apostasie des Pfalzdiakons Bodo (838) und das Judentum der Chasaren. *Person und Gemeinschaft im Mittelalter. Karl Schmid zum fünfundsechzigsten*, eds. G.Althof et al., 157–69. Sigmaringen.

LOWENSTEIN, S. (1969). Results of Atlas investigations among Jews of Germany. *Field of Yiddish* 3:16–35.
LOWENTHAL, D. (1985). *The past is a foreign country.* Cambridge.
LOWENTHAL, M. (1936). *The Jews of Germany.* Philadelphia.
LUKÁCS, L. (1985). Hahnenschlagen in Westungarn. *ÖZV* n.S. 39:1–24.

MACHEK, V. (1956). Expressive Vokaldehnung in einigen slavischen Nomina. *ZS* 1(4):33–40.
— (1971). *Etymologický slovník jazyka českého.* Prague.
MACLENNAN, R.S. and A.T.KRAABEL (1986). The God-Fearers—a literary and theological invention. *BAR* 12(5):46–53.
MAGOMEDOV, M.G. (1983). *Obrazovanie xazarskogo kaganata.* Moscow.
MALER, B. (1979). Western Yiddish *berkhes* or *barkhes*, its origin and offshoots in Scandinavian languages. *NJ* 2:1–5.
MANGA, J. (1956). Morena a jej maďarské obmeny. *Slovenský národopis* 4:421–52.
MANN, J. (1927). Changes in the divine service of the synagogue due to religious persecutions. *HUCA* 4:241–310.
— [J.MAN] (1933). "Ha'aškenazim" hem hakuzarim! *Tarbic* 4:391–4.
MARCHAND, J.W. (1987). Proto Yiddish and the glosses: Can we reconstruct Proto Yiddish? *OYL*, 83–94.
MARGARITHA, A. (1530). *Der ganz jüdisch Glaub.* Augsburg.
MARGOLIS, M.L. and A.MARX (1927). *A history of the Jewish people.* Philadelphia.
MARKEY, T.L. (1988). Ladin and other relic language forms in the eastern Alpine region. *Historical dialectology: regional and social*, ed. J.Fisiak, 357–75. Berlin.
MARMORSTEIN, A. (1927). David ben Jehuda Hasid. *MGWJ* 71:39–48.
— (1928). L'Acte de se couvrir la tête chez les Juifs. *REJ* 85:66–9.
— (1936). Comparison between Greek and Jewish religious customs and popular usages. *OO*, 409–23.
MARX, A. (1924). Glimpses of the life of an Italian rabbi of the sixteenth century. *HUCA* 1:605–24.
MASSER, A. (1966). *Die Bezeichnungen für das christliche Gotteshaus in der deutschen Sprache des Mittelalters.* Berlin.
MATHIESEN, R. (1983). The typology of Cyrillic manuscripts. (East Slavic vs. South Slavic Old Testament manuscripts.) *American contributions to the ninth International Congress of Slavists* 1. *Linguistics*, ed. M.S.Flier, 193–202. Columbus, OH.
MATL, J. (1956). Zur Bezeichnung und Wertung fremder Völker bei den Slaven. *Festschrift für Max Vasmer zum 70. Geburtstag*, eds., M.Woltner and H.Bräuer, 293–306. Wiesbaden.
MATRAS, Y. (1991). Zur Rekonstruktion des jüdischdeutschen Wortschatzes in den Mundarten ehemaliger "Judendörfer" in Südwestdeutschland. *Zeitschrift für Dialektologie und Linguistik* 58:267–93.
MAYER, R. (1967). Israel, Jude, Hebräer. *Theologisches Begriffslexikon zum Neuen Testament*, eds. L.Coenen, et al., 2/1:742–52. Wuppertal.
MEARS, A. (1738). *The book of religion, ceremonies, and prayers of the Jews.* London.

MEEKS, W.A. (1975). "Am I a Jew?" Johannine Christianity and Judaism. *CJ*, 1:163–86.

— (1983). *The first urban Christians. The social world of the Apostle Paul.* New Haven.

MELLINKOPF, R. (1982). Judas's red hair and the Jews. *Journal of Jewish art* 9:31–46.

MENGIS, C. (1935–6). Rot. *HDA*, 7:columns 792–834.

MERXAV, R. (1992). Hajom, kešehaxoma hasinit nifrecet. *Jediot axaronot* 23 January, p.19. Tel-Aviv.

MEŠČERSKIJ, N.A. (1956). Otryvok iz knigi "Iosippon" v "Povesti vremennyx let". *Palestinskij sbornik* 2:56–68.

— (1958). *Istorija iudejskoj vojny Iosifa Flavija v drevnerusskom perevode.* Moscow-St.Petersburg.

METZGER, T. and M. (1982). *Jewish life in the Middle Ages. Illuminated Hebrew manuscripts of the thirteenth to the sixteenth centuries.* Secaucus, NJ.

MIELKE, R. (1927). *Siedlungskunde des deutschen Volkes und ihre Bedeutung zu Menschen und Landschaft.* Munich.

MIESES, J. (1916). *Die älteste gedruckte deutsche Uebersetzung des jüdischen Gebetbuches a.d. Jahre 1530 und ihr Autor Anthonius Margaritha.* Vienna.

MIESES, M. (1924). *Die jiddische Sprache.* Berlin-Vienna.

— (1934). Judaizańci we Wschodniej Europie. *Miesięcznik żydowski* 4:241–60.

— (1991). *Z rodu żydowskiego. Zasłużone rodziny polskie krwi niegdyś żydowskiej.* Warsaw. A revised version of his *Polacy-chrześcijanie pochodzenia żydowskiego.* Warsaw 1938.

MLADENOV, ST. (1941). *Etimologičeski i pravopisen rečnik na bəlgarskija knižoven ezik.* Sofia.

MOHRMANN, C. (1961–5). *Etudes sur le latin des chrétiens* 1–3. Rome.

MOLLOVA, M. (1973). Quelques lexèmes turcs septentrioneux *ǧ ~ č ~ j*...dans les langues slaves méridionales. *Zeitschrift für Balkanologie* 9:89–127.

MORAG, S. (1971). Pronunciations of Hebrew. *EJ/J*, 13:columns 1120–45.

MOREL-FATIO, A. (1882). Notes et documents pour servir à l'histoire des Juifs des Baléares sous la domination aragonaise. *REJ* 4:31–56.

MORGAN, P. (1983). From a death to a view: the hunt for the Welsh past in the Romantic period. *IT*, 43–100.

MORGENSTERN, J. (1973). *Rites of birth, marriage, death and kindred occasions among the Semites.* New York.

MOSER, H. (1964). *Sprache und Religion.* Düsseldorf.

MOSKOVICH, W. and B.TUKAN (1985). Caraimica. The problems of the origin and history of East European Khazars in the light of linguistic evidence. *SH* 7:87–106.

MOURANT, A.E. (1959). The blood groups of the Jews. *JJS* 1(2):155–76.

—, A.C.KOPEĆ and K.DOMANIEWSKA-SOBCZAK (1978). *The genetics of the Jews.* Oxford.

MULCAHY, F.D. (1979). Studies in Gitano social ecology: linguistic performance and ethnicity. *IJSL* 19:11–28.

MÜLLER, M. (1863). *Vorlesungen über die Wissenschaft der Sprache.* Leipzig.

MUTIUS, H.-G. VON (1984–5). *Rechtsentscheide rheinischer Rabbinen vor dem ersten Kreuzzug* 1–2. Frankfurt-Berne-New York.
— (1987). *Rechtsentscheide Raschis aus Troyes (1040–1105)* 2. Frankfurt-Berne-New York-Paris.
— (1990). Juden, -tum. *LM*, 5(4):columns 783–6.

NACHAMA, A., J.H.SCHOEPES and E. VAN VOOLEN (eds.) (1992). *Jüdische Lebenswelten. Essays.* Berlin.
NACHAMA, A. and G.SIEVERNICH (1991). *Jüdische Lebenswelten. Katalog.* Berlin.
NADEL, B. (1960). *Jidn in mizrex-ejrope. Fun di eltste cajtn biz der mongolišer invazje (1240).* Warsaw.
NAGY, S. (1979). Parallelen des Steines von Aracs in der Wojwodina. *AR* 17:95–7.
NARKIS, B. (1984). *Kitve-jad ivri'im mecujarim.* Jerusalem.
NEDOMAČKI, V. and S.GOLDSTEIN (1988). Arheološki nalazi. *Židovi na tlu Jugoslavije*, 17–25, 216–8. Zagreb.
NEMOY, L. (1974). The attitude of the early Karaites towards Christianity. *SWBJV* 1:697–715.
NEUSNER, J. (1984). *A history of the Jews in Babylonia* 1. *The Parthian period.* Chico, CA.
NÍ CHATHÁIN, P. (1979–80). Swineherds, seers, and Druids. *Studia celtica* 14–5:200–11.
NICHOLS, J. (1987). Russian *vurdalak* 'werewolf' and its cognates. *Language, literature, linguistics. In honor of Francis J.Whitfield on his seventieth birthday, March 25, 1986*, eds. M.S.Flier and S.Karlinsky, 165–77. Berkeley.
NIEDERLE, L.(1953). *Rukověť slovanských starožitností.* Prague.
NIESIOŁOWSKA-WĘDZKA, A. (1975). Štúrovo. *SSS*, 5:552–3.
NIKIFOROVSKIJ, N.JA. (1897). *Prostanarodnye primety i pover'ja, suevernye obrjady i obyčai, legendarnye skazanija o licax i mestax.* Vicebsk.
NUSENBLAT, T. (1939). Mogen dovid. *YB* 13:460–76

OESTERLEY, W.O.E. (1935). The cult of Sabazios. *FSRMR*, 113–58.
OSSOWSKI, L. (1968). *Kabán* 'kogut' w dorzeczu Cny. Ślady wierzeń pogańskich w słownictwie Polesia. *SO* 27:167–71.
OXENSTIERNA, E. (1966). *The Norsemen.* London.

PÁTA, J. (1934). *Les Serbes de Lusace.* Geneva.
PATAI, R. (1944). 'Arisah. *JQR* 35:165–72.
— and PATAI-WING, J. (1975). *The myth of the Jewish race.* New York; revised edition, Detroit 1989.
PAULINY, E. (1964). *Slovesnosť a kultúrny jazyk Veľkej Moravy.* Bratislava.
PECH, V. (1948). *Velký slovník cizích slov.* Prague.
PELTZ, R. (1985). The dehebraization controversy in Soviet Yiddish language planning: standard or symbol? *RSJL*, 125–50.
PERLES, J. (1880). Etymologische Studien zur Kunde der rabbinischen Sprache und Alterthümer. *MGWJ* 19:415–31.
PETRICIOLI, I. (1960). *Pojava romaničke skulpture u Dalmaciji.* Zagreb.

PETRIKOVITS, A. (1922). *Die Wiener Gauner-, Zuhälter- und Dirnensprache.* Vienna.
PEUCKERT, W.-E. (1928). *Schlesische Volkskunde.* Leipzig.
— (1931–2). Jude, Jüdin. *HDA*, 4:columns 808–33.
PFALZ, R. (1929). Arabische Hochzeitsbräuche in Tripolitanien. *Anthropos* 24:221–7.
PIPREK, J. (1914). *Slawische Brautwerbungs- und Hochzeitsgebräuche.* Stuttgart.
PÓCS, É. (1990). "Lilith és kísérete" (Gyermekágyas-démonoktól védő ráolvasások Délkelet-Európában és a Közel-Keleten). *AHK*, 110–30.
POLJAK, A.N. (1943). *Kazarja. Toldot mamlaxa jehudit be'eropa.* Tel-Aviv; revised 3rd edition, 1951.
POLLACK, H. (1971). *Jewish folkways in Germanic lands (1648–1806). Studies in aspects of daily life.* Cambridge, MA-London.
POPOWSKA-TABORSKA, H. (1965). *Dawne pogranicze językowe polsko-dolnołużyckie (w świetle dannych toponomastycznych).* Wrocław-Warsaw-Kraków.
POTKAŃSKI, K. (1895). *Postrzyżyny u Słowian i Germanów.* Kraków.
POVEST' VREMENNYX LET (11th–12th cc). See Adrianova-Peretc; Cross and Sherbowitz-Wetzor.
PREIDEL, H. (1952). Awaren und Slawen. *SOF* 11:33–45.
PREUSS, J. (1910). Biblische und talmudische Bezeichnungen der Gesichtsfarbe. *Festschrift zum vierzigjährigen Amtsjubiläum des Herrn Rabbiners Dr.Salomon Carlebach in Lübeck*, ed. M.Stern, 225–31. Berlin.
PRILUCKI, N. (1923). *Dos gevet. Dialogn vegn šprax un kultur.* Warsaw.
— (1924). Purimdiks. *JF*, 89–90.
PRITSAK, O. (1963). Altaic elements. *Ukraine. A concise encyclopaedia*, ed. V.Kubijovyč, 1:928–31. Toronto.

R. (1850). Judenschule. *Allgemeine Encyklopädie der Wisssenschaften und Künste*, eds. J.S.Ersch and J.G.Gruber, section 2, part 27: 322. Leipzig.
RABIN, X. (1985). Tkufoteha šel halašon haivrit. *Mexkarim balašon* 1, ed. M.Bar-Ašer, 27–35. Jerusalem.
RACHABI, J. (1982). Lešonot besifrut še'elot učuvot. *Lešonenu la'am* 33:99–113.
RADDATZ, A. (1990). Judendarstellung. *LM*, 5(4):columns 788–9.
RAFFELSTETTEN (1897). [Toll ordenance 903–6; extant ms from 1254–65.] *Monumenta Germaniae Historica. Legum*, section 2, part 2, eds. A.Boretius and V.Krause, 249–52. Hannover.
RAJAK, T. (1992). The Jewish community and its boundaries. *JPC*, 9–28.
RANKE, R. (1936–7). Trude (Trute). *HDA*, 8:columns 1173–4.
RANKIN, O.S. (1935). The festival of Hanukkah. *FSRMR*, 159–209.
RAPHAEL, F. (1974). Le mariage juif dans la campagne alsacienne dans la deuxième moitié du XIXe siècle. *FRCS* 4:181–98.
RAPPOPORT, A.S. (1937). *The folklore of the Jews.* London.
REIDER, J. (1929). Non-Jewish motives in the ornament of early Hebrew books. *Studies in Jewish bibliography and related subjects in memory of Abraham Solomon Freidus (1867–1923)*, 150–9. New York.
REITER, N. (1973). Mythologie der alten Slaven. *Wörterbuch der Mythologie*, part 1, section 6, ed. H.W.Haussig, 163–208. Stuttgart.

RENAN, E. (1883). *Le judaïsme comme race et comme religion.* Paris.
REUSCH, W. (ed.) (1965). *Frühchristliche Zeugnisse im Einzugsgebiet von Rhein und Mosel.* Trier.
REYNOLDS, J. and R.TANNENBAUM (1987). *Jews and God-Fearers at Aphrodisias. Greek inscriptions with commentary.* Cambridge.
RIEGER, P. (1936). אשכנז = *Deutschland. MGWJ* 80:455–9.
ROBERT, U. (1881). Catalogue d'actes relatifs aux Juifs pendant le moyen âge. *REJ* 3:211–24.
ROMANO, S. (1933). Dictionnaire judéo-espagnol parlé-français-allemand, avec une introduction sur la phonétique et sur la formation des mots dans le judéo-espagnol. Unpublished PhD, University of Zagreb.
ROSENTHAL, J. (1943). Ashkenaz, Sefarad, and Zarefat. *HJ* 5:58–62.
ROTH, C. (1953). Jewish antecedents of Christian art. *Journal of the Warburg and Courtauld Institutes* 16:24–44.
— (1966a). Introduction. *DA*, 3–11.
— (1966b). The early Jewish settlements in Central and Eastern Europe 1. General setting. *DA*, 302–4.
RÓTH, E. (ed.) (1959). *Festschrift für Wiedereinweihung der alten Synagoge zu Worms.* Frankfurt.
ROTTLEUTHNER, W. (1985). Bäuerliches Hochzeitsbrauchtum in Südmähren zur Jahrhundertwende (Prittlach 1895). *ÖZV* n.S. 39:25–44.
ROWE, C. (1972). Conceptions of colour—colour symbolism in the ancient world. *EY* 41:327–64.
RUDNYC'KYJ, J.B. (1967). *An etymological dictionary of the Ukrainian language* 6. Winnipeg-Ottawa.
— [RUDNYĆKYJ]. (1969). Pre-Christian anthroponyms among Slavs. *HCS*, II/1:34–7.
RUPPIN, A. (1930). *Soziologie der Juden* 1. Berlin.
RUSEK, J. (1983). Bułgarskie *golěmъ* 'wielki, magnus'. *RS* 43:21–8.
RUSSOCKI, S. (1967). Małżenstwo. *SSS*, 3:159–61.
RZETELSKA-FELESZKO, E. (1977). Wieleci. *SSS*, 6:430–1.

SADAN, D. (1952). Marat hole (gilgulo šel motiv). *Jeda am* 9:15–7.
— (1960). Tašlix. *Maxanaim* 49:64–8.
SADEK, V. (1991). David's Star (Magen David) on the tombstones of the old Jewish cemetery in Prague. *Judaica Bohemiae* 27:79–81.
SADNIK, L. and R.AITZETMÜLLER (1963–4). *Vergleichendes Wörterbuch der slavischen Sprachen.* Wiesbaden.
ŞĂINEANU, L. (1888). Jidovii saŭ Tătarii saŭ uraisii. *Anuar pentru Israeliţi* 11:153–60.
ŠAKI, ʾA.R. (1981). *Dawlat alxazar aljadīda aw isrāʾīl.* Beirut.
SALFELD, S. and A.BEIN (1934). Mainz. *GJ*, 1:174–223.
SALOMON, H.P. (1982). *Portrait of a New Christian. Fernão Alvares Melo (1569–1632).* Paris.
SALZMANN, Z. and V.SCHEUFLER (1974). *Komárov. A Czech farming village.* New York.

SAMUEL, J. (1841). *The remnant found; or...the Jews of Daghistan on the Caspian Sea are the remnant of the ten tribes.* London.
SAMUEL, M. (1971). *In praise of Yiddish.* Chicago.
SARTORI, P. (1935–6). Rumpelmette. *HDA*, 7:columns 851–2.
SAVIR, U. (1991). [Advertisement by the Government of Israel]. *New York Times. Book review* 1 September. New York.
ŠAVIT, J. (1984). *Meivri ad knaʿani.* Tel-Aviv.
SCHATZMILLER, J. (1982). Doctors and medical practice in Germany around the year 1200: the evidence of *Sefer Hasidim. JJSt* 33:583–93.
SCHAUSS, H. (1938). *The Jewish festivals. From their beginnings to our own day.* New York; 1958[8].
SCHEFTELOWITZ, I. (1911). Das Fischsymbol im Judentum und Christentum. *ARW* 14:1–53, 321–92.
— (1912). *Das Schlingen- und Netzmotiv im Glauben und Brauch der Völker.* Giessen.
— (1914a). *Das Stellvertretende Huhnopfer. Mit besonderer Berücksichtigung des jüdischen Volksglaubens.* Giessen.
— (1914b). Sündentilgung. *ARW* 17:353–412.
— (1925). *Alt-Palästinensischer Bauernglaube in religionsvergleichender Beleuchtung.* Hannover.
SCHEIBER, A. (1966). Hungary. *DA*, 313–8.
— (1967). A proselyte's letter to the congregations in Fostat. *Essays presented to Chief Rabbi Israel Brodie on the occasion of his seventieth birthday*, eds. H.J.Zimmels et al., 377–80. London.
— (1970). Juden und Christen in Ungarn bis 1526. *KS*, 2:559–68.
— (1972). Šne minhage am jehudiʾim. *FRCS* 3:205–7; reprinted in his *Essays on Jewish folklore and comparative literature*, Budapest 1985:35–7 (Hebrew pagination).
— (1982). Further traces of Jewish settlement in Pannonia. *JJSt* 33:495–7.
SCHENKER, A. (1985). Were there Slavs in Central Europe before the Great Migrations? *IJSLP* 31–2:359–73.
SCHIFFMAN, L.H. (1985). *Who was a Jew? Rabbinic and halakhic perspectives on the Jewish-Christian schism.* Hoboken, NJ.
SCHILDT, J. and H.SCHMIDT (eds.) (1986). *Berlinisch. Geschichtliche Einführung in die Sprache einer Stadt.* Berlin.
SCHLIMPERT, G. (1978). *Slawische Personennamen in mittelalterlichen Quellen zur deutschen Geschichte.* Berlin.
SCHMELLER, J.A. (1872–7). *Bayerisches Wörterbuch* 1–2. Munich; 1985.
SCHNEEWEIS, E. (1931). *Feste und Volksbräuche der Lausitzer Wenden. Vergleichend dargestellt.* Leipzig; reprinted as *Feste und Volksbräuche der Sorben.* Berlin 1953 (with some additional illustrations).
— (1933). Zur wendischen Volkskunde. *ZSPh* 10:368–74.
— (1935). *Grundriss des Volksglaubens und Volksbrauchs der Serbokroaten.* Celje.
SCHOLEM, G. (1949). The curious history of the six-pointed star. *Commentary* 8:243–51.
— (1966). Jüdische Mystik in West-Europa im 12. und 13. Jahrhundert. *JM*, 37–54.

— (1971). Golem. *EJ/J*, 7:columns 753–5.
— (1972). Farben und ihre Symbolik in der jüdischen Überlieferung und Mystik. *EY* 41:1–49.
SCHUDT, J. (1714–18). *Jüdische Merckwürdigkeiten* 1–4. Frankfurt.
SCHULENBURG, W. VON (1880). *Wendisches Volkssagen und Gebräuche aus dem Spreewald.* Leipzig.
— (1892). *Wendisches Volkstum in Sage, Brauch und Sitte.* Berlin; 2nd revised edition, Leipzig 1934.
— (1905). Trudensteine. *ZVV* 15:91–2.
SCHÜRER, E. (1909). *Geschichte des jüdischen Volkes im Zeitalter Jesu Christi* 3. Leipzig. 4th edition.
SCHWAB, M. (1897). *Vocabulaire de l'angélogie d'après les manuscrits hébreux de la Bibliothèque nationale.* Paris.
SCHWARZ, E. (1932–3). Zur Wortgeographie tschechischer Lehnwörter in den deutschen Mundarten. *Germanoslavica* 2:221–37; 327–43.
SCHWARZBAUM, H. (1968). *Studies in Jewish and world folklore.* Berlin.
SCHWARZFUCHS, S. (1980). L'opposition *Tsarfat*-Provence: la formation du judaïsme du nord de la France. *Hommage à Georges Vajda. Etudes d'histoire et de pensée juives*, eds. G.Nahon and C.Touati, 135–50. Louvain.
SCHWENKEN, C.P.T. (1820). *Notizen über die berüchtigsten jüdischen Gauner und Spitzbuben.* Kassel.
SELLIN, E. (1896). *Israelitisch-jüdische Religionsgeschichte.* Leipzig.
SEVORTJAN, E.V. (ed.) (1967). *Dokumenty na poloveckom jazyke XVI v.* Moscow.
SEWERYN, T. (1964). Krew. *SSS*, 2:516–7.
— (1967). Manizm. *SSS*, 3:161.
SHAPIRO, H.L. (1960). *The Jewish people. A biological history.* Paris.
SHEVELOV, G.Y. (1965). *A prehistory of Slavic.* New York.
SIMON, H. (1992). Wissenschaft vom Judentum in der Geschichte der Berliner Universität. *WJ*, 153–64.
SIMON, M. (1992). Zunz als Begründer der Onomastik im Rahmen der Wissenschaft des Judentums. *WJ*, 165–79.
SIMONSOHN, S. (1974). The Hebrew revival among early medieval European Jews. *SWBJV*, 2:831–58.
SIMONYI, D. (1942). Slawische Burgwälle. *AECO* 8:486–503.
ŠIPER, J. (1924). Der onhejb fun "lošn aškenaz" in der balajxtung fun onomatiše kveln. *JF*, 101–12, 272–87.
— (1926). *Di virtšaftsgešixte fun di jidn in pojln besn mitlalter.* Warsaw.
SKOK, P. (1930). La terminologie chrétienne en slave: le parrain, la marraine et le filleul. *Revue des études slaves* 10:186–204.
— (1934). *Dolazak Slovena na Mediteran.* Split.
— (1971–4). *Etimologijski rječnik hrvatskoga ili srpskoga jezika* 1–4. Zagreb.
SMALLWOOD, E.M. (1976). *The Jews under Roman rule. From Pompey to Diocletian.* Leiden.
SOLIN, H. (1980). Juden und Syrer im römischen Reich. *Die Sprachen des römischen Reiches der Kaiserzeit*, eds. G.Neumann and J.Untermann, 301–30. Cologne.

SÓS, Á.CS. (1973). *Die slawische Bevölkerung Westungarns im 9. Jahrhundert.* Munich.

SOSNOVIK, A. (1924). Materialn cu der jidišer folksmedicin in vajsrusland. *JF*, 160–8.

SPIEGEL, S. (1949). On medieval Hebrew poetry. *The Jews. Their history, culture, and religion*, ed. L.Finkelstein, 1:528–66. New York.

SREZNEVSKIJ, I.I. (1893–1903). *Materialy dlja slovarja drevnerusskogo jazyka po pis'mennym pamjatnikam* 1–3. St.Petersburg.

STAERK, W. (1922). Zwei alte jüdische Beschwörungsformeln. *MGWJ* 66:200–3.

STARR, J. (1939). *The Jews in the Byzantine Empire 641–1204.* Athens.

STASIEWSKI, B. (1934). Die ersten Spuren des Christentums in Polen. Ein Beitrag zur Erfassung der ältesten slavischen Zustände. *ZOG* 8:238–60.

STEIMAN, S. (1963). *Custom and survival. A study of the life and work of Rabbi Jacob Molin (Moelln) known as the Maharil (c.1360–1427) and his influence in establishing the Ashkenazic Minhag (customs of German Jewry).* New York.

STEINHERZ, S. (1930). Der Sturz des Vicedominus Jacob (1124). *JGGJČR* 2:17–49.

STEINTHAL, H. (1901). Die Stellung der Semiten in der Weltgeschichte. *JJGL* 4:46–69.

STERN, M. (with the assistance of S.SALFELD) (1894–6). *Die israelitische Bevölkerung der deutschen Städte* 3. *Nürnberg im Mittelalter.* Kiel.

STOBBE, O. (1866). *Die Juden in Deutschland während des Mittelalters in politischer, socialer und rechtlicher Beziehung.* Braunschweig; Amsterdam 1968.

STRUVE, V.V. et al. (eds.) (1965). *Korpus bosporskix nadpisej.* Moscow-St.Petersburg.

STRZELCZYK, J. (1970). Raffelstetten. *SSS*, 4:460–1.

STSCHERBAKIWSKYJ, W. (1952–3). The early Ukrainian social order as reflected in Ukrainian wedding customs. *SEER* 31:325–51.

SWOBODA, W. (1961). Chazarowie. *SSS* 1:238–9.

— (1967). Obrowie. *SSS*, 3:443–5.

— (1970a). Peloponez. Słowianie na Peloponezie. *SSS*, 4:53–4.

— (1970b). Religia Protobulgarów. *SSS* 4:489–90.

— (1975). Völkermarkt. *SSS*, 5:564–5.

— (1982). Żydzi. *SSS*, 7:272–4.

— (1986). Awarowie. *SSS*, 7/2:388–90.

SZAFRAŃSKI, W. (1960). Un lieu du culte païen du haut moyen âge découvert à Plock. *Archeologia Polona* 3:167–71.

SZYFER, A. (1976). Ludowe zwyczaje, obrzędy, wierzenia i wiedza. *Kultura ludowa mazurów i warmiaków*, ed. J.Burszta, 407–40. Wrocław-Warsaw-Kraków-Gdańsk.

TA-ŠMA, J. (1992). *Minhag aškenaz hakadmon.* Jerusalem.

TANNENBAUM, R.F. (1986). Jews and God-Fearers in the holy city of Aphrodite. *BAR* 12(5):54–7.

TÄUBLER, E. (1916). Zur Handelsbedeutung der Juden in Deutschland vor Beginn des Städtewesens I.II. *FSMP*, 370–92.

TAYLOR, A. (1949–50). *Standard dictionary of folklore* 1–2. New York.

TEIMANAS, D.B. (1933). *L'Autonomie des communautés juives en Pologne aux XVIe et XVIIe siècles*. Paris.
TETZNER, F. (1902). *Die Slawen in Deutschland*. Braunschweig.
THEODORIDIS, D. (1990–3). Der Euphemismus *los mižores de mozotros* im Judezmo und seine Parallelen in anderen Sprachen. *MedLR* 6–7:105–112.
THIELE, A.F. (1840). *Die jüdischen Gauner in Deutschland...* 1–2. Berlin.
THIETMAR OF MERSEBURG (11th c). See Trillmich.
THOMAS, E.B. (1986). Spätantike und frühchristliche Charakterköpfe aus Pannonien. *Klio* 68:501–41.
THOMASON, S.G. and T.KAUFMAN (1988). *Language contact, creolization and genetic linguistics*. Berkeley-Los Angeles-London.
THOMPSON, E.A. (1963). Christianity and the Northern Barbarians. *The conflict between paganism and Christianity in the fourth century*, ed. A.Momigliano, 56–78. Oxford.
TIGAY, A.M. (1992). Moscow. *Hadassah magazine* August-September, 36–41.
TIMM, E. (1977). Jiddische Sprachmaterialien aus dem Jahre 1290: Die Glossen des Berner kleinem Aruch—Edition und Kommentar. *Fragen des älteren Jiddisch*, eds. H.-J.Müller and W.Röll, 16–34. Trier.
— (1991a). Das ältere Jiddisch als Gegenstand sprachpragmatischer Forschung. *IGK*, 11:500–13.
— (1991b). Die Bibelübersetzungssprache als Faktor der Auseinanderentwicklung des jiddischen und deutschen Wortschatzes. *Vestigia bibliae* 9/10:59–75.
TOCH, M. (1990). Juden, -tum. *LM*, 5(4):columns 781–3.
TOPOROV, V.N. (1989). Iz slavjanskoj jazyčeskoj terminologii: indoevropejskie istoki i tendencii razvitija. *Ėtimologija 1985–1987*, 3–50. Moscow.
TOYNBEE, A. (1935). *A study of history* 2. London.
TRACHTENBERG, J. (1939). *Jewish magic and superstition. A study in folk religion*. Philadelphia; 2nd edition, New York 1970.
TRAUTMANN, R. (1948). *Die Elb- und Ostseeslavischen Ortsnamen* 1. Berlin.
TREBILCO, P.R. (1991). *Jewish communities in Asia minor*. Cambridge.
TRILLMICH, W. (ed.) (1985). *Thietmar von Merseburg. Chronik*. Darmstadt.
TRUBAČEV, O.N. (1967). Iz slavjano-iranskix leksičeskix otnošenij. *Ėtimologija 1965*, 3–81. Moscow.
TYKOCINSKI, H. (1934). Oesterreich. *GJ*, 1:256–65.

ULLENDORFF, E. (1956). Hebraic-Jewish elements in Abyssinian (Monophysite) Christianity. *Journal of Semitic studies* 1:216–56.
UNBEGAUN, B. (1970). Heidnisches und Christliches in der ostslavischen Namengebung. *HCS*, II/2:94–7.
— (1972). *Russian surnames*. Oxford.
UNVERSAGT, W. (1919). *Terra sigillata mit Rädchenverzierung*. Frankfurt.
URBAN, W. (1987). The conversion of Lithuania 1387. *Lituanus* 33:12–22.
URBAŃCZYK, ST. (1964). Kapłani pogańscy. *SSS*, 2:371.
— (1970). Perepłut. *SSS*, 4:59–60.
— (et al., eds.) (1965–9). *Słownik staropolski* 5. Wrocław-Warsaw-Kraków.

VAN DER VOORT, H. (1991). The Romani dialect(s) of the Finnish Gypsies. *MR*, 132–51.

VAN PRAAG, PH. (1988). *Joodse symboliek op nederlandse exlibris.* Amsterdam-Zutphen.

VASMER, M. (1932). Wikingerspuren bei den Westslaven. *ZOG* 6:1–16.

— (1953–8). *Russisches etymologisches Wörterbuch* 1–3. Heidelberg.

— (1970). *Die Slaven in Griechenland.* Leipzig.

VENY CLAR, J. (1960). Paralelismos léxicos en los dialectos catalanes. *RFE* 43:117–202.

VERBER, E. (1983). [separate notes to the facsimile edition.] *Sarajevska Hagada.* Belgrade-Sarajevo.

VERGER, P.F. (1981). *Orixás. Deuses iorubás na África e no Novo Mundo.* São Paolo.

VERLINDEN, C. (1933). Problèmes d'histoirc économique franque. *Revue belge de philologie et d'histoire* 12:1090–5.

— (1955–77). *L'Esclavage dans l'Europe médiévale* 1. Brugge; 2. Ghent.

VETULANI, A. (1962). The Jews in medieval Poland. *JJS* 4:274–94.

VLACHOS, T. (1971). Geister- und Dämonenvorstellungen im südosteuropäischen Raum griechischer Sprachzugehörigkeit. *ÖZV* n.S. 25:217–48.

VOLLBEDING, J.C. (1804). *Handwörterbuch der jüdisch-deutschen Sprache, nebst Erläuterung jüdischer Sitten, Gebräuche, Kleidungen, Fast- und Festtage, Monate, Zählungsart und dergl.* Leipzig.

VOVK, XV. (1928). *Studiji z ukrajins'koji etnohrafiji ta antropolohiji.* Prague.

WACHOLDER, B.Z. (1956). The Halakah and the proselytizing of slaves during the Gaonic era. *HJ* 18:89–106.

WAGENSEIL, J.CHR. (1699). *Belehrung der jüdisch-teutschen Red- und Schreibart.* Königsberg.

WAGNER, M.L. (1931). Zum Judenspanischen von Marokko. *Volkstum und Kultur der Romanen* 4:221–45.

— (1950). Espigueo judeo-español. *RFE* 34:9–106; reprinted in his *Judenspanisch* 2. Stuttgart 1990:102–99.

WALLACH, L.I. (1939). Zur Etymologie Aschkenaz—Deutschland. *MGWJ* 83:302–4.

WECHTER, P. (1964). *Ibn Barun's Arabic works on Hebrew grammar and lexicography.* Philadelphia.

WĘDZKI, A. (1986). Buzet. *SSS*, 7/2:557.

WEIL, G. (1968). Prolegomenon to S.Frensdorff, *Die Massora Magna* 1 (1876), i–xxxii. New York.

WEINREICH, M. [VAJNRAJX] (1924). Cu der xarakteristik fun undzere folks-glejbenišn. *JF*, 168–76.

— (1956a). The Jewish languages of Romance stock and their relation to earliest Yiddish. *Romance philology* 9:403–28.

— (1956b). Yiddish, Knaanic, Slavic: the basic relationships. *For Roman Jakobson: Essays on the occasion of his sixtieth birthday*, eds. M.Halle, et al., 622–32. The Hague.

— (1967). *Holekrash*: A Jewish rite of passage, a preliminary statement. *Folklore international. Essays in traditional literature, belief and custom in honor of Wayland Debs Hand*, ed. D.K.Wilgus, 243–53. Hatboro, PA.

— [VAJNRAJX] (1973). *Gešixte fun der jidišer šprax* 1–4. New York. Partial English translation, Chicago 1980.

WEINREICH, U. (1958). Yiddish and Colonial German in Eastern Europe: the differential impact of Slavic. *American contributions to the Fourth International Congress of Slavists*, 369–419. The Hague.

— (1968). *A modern Yiddish-English English-Yiddish dictionary*. New York.

WEINRYB, B. (1957). Origins of East European Jewry. *Commentary* 24 (December), 509–18.

— (1962a). *The beginnings of East European Jewry*. Leiden.

— (1962b). The beginnings of East-European Jewry in legend and historiography. *SEHAAN*, 445–502.

— (1974). Reappraisals in Jewish history. *SWBJV*, 2:939–74.

WEISSENBERG, S. (1905). Eine jüdische Hochzeit in Südrussland. *Mitteilungen zur jüdischen Volkskunde* n.R. 1:59–74.

WELLHAUSEN, J. (1894). *Israelitische und jüdische Geschichte*. Berlin.

WELLISCH, S. (1937). Rassendiagnose der Juden und ihrer Vorfahren. *Anthropos* 32:783–94.

WENZEL, W. (1987). *Studien zu sorbischen Personennamen* 1. Bautzen.

WEXLER, P. (1964). Slavic influence in the grammatical functions of three Yiddish verbal prefixes. *Linguistics* 7:83–93.

— (1971). Some observations of structure in language contact. *Symbolae in honorem Georgii Y.Shevelov*, eds. W.E.Harkins, O.Horbatsch, J.P.Hursky, 474–82. Munich.

— (1972). A mirror image comparison of languages in contact: verbal prefixes in Slavicized Yiddish and Germanicized Sorbian. *Linguistics* 82:89–123.

— (1973). Jewish, Tatar and Karaite communal dialects and their importance for Byelorussian historical linguistics. *Journal of Byelorussian studies* 3:41–54.

— (1974a). Explorations in Belorussian historical bilingual dialectology and onomastics. *SEER* 52:481–99.

— (1974b). *Purism and language. A study in Modern Ukrainian and Belorussian nationalism (1840–1967)*. Bloomington.

— (1974c). The cartography of unspoken languages of culture and liturgy. Reflections on the diffusion of Arabic and Hebrew. *Orbis* 23:30–51.

— (1977). Ascertaining the position of Judezmo within Ibero-Romance. *Vox romanica* 36:162–95.

— (1978). The term 'Sabbath food': a challenge for Jewish interlinguistics. *Journal of the American Oriental Society* 98:461–5.

— (1979). Jewish onomastics: achievements and challenges. *Onoma* 23:96–113.

— (1981a). Ashkenazic German: 1760–1895. *IJSL* 30:119–30.

— (1981b). Jewish interlinguistics: facts and conceptual framework. *Language* 57:99–149.

— (1981c). Review of M.Mieses, *Die Entstehungsursache der jüdischen Dialekten*. Vienna 1915; Hamburg 1979. *Language in society* 10:294–9.

— (1981d). Terms for 'synagogue' in Hebrew and Jewish languages. Explorations in historical Jewish interlinguistics. *REJ* 102:101–38.
— (1982a). Marrano Ibero-Romance: classification and research tasks. *Zeitschrift für romanische Philologie* 98:59–108.
— (1982b). Review of S.A.Birnbaum 1979. *Beiträge zur Geschichte der deutschen Sprache und Literatur* 104:291–7.
— (1982c). Slavicization vs. de-Slavicization in Yiddish verb derivation *(linirn, ojslinirn ~ ojslin'even ~ ojslin'[en]jen).* *WS* 27:359–81.
— (1983a). Hebräische und aramäische Elementen in den slavischen Sprachen: Wege, Chronologien und Diffusionsgebiete. *ZSPh* 43(2):229–79.
— (1983b). Is Karaite a Jewish language? *MedLR* 1:27–54.
— (1983c). Notes on the Iraqi Judaeo-Arabic of Eastern Asia. *Journal of Semitic studies* 28:337–54.
— (1983d). Review of *Jewish language review* 1 (Haifa 1981). *Language* 59:420–3.
— (1984). Zihui jesodot lešoniʾim jehudiʾim bisfat džudezmo. *Peamim* 18:38–52.
— (1985a). Jewish languages in Kaifeng, Henan Province, China 1163–1933. *ZDMG* 135:330–47.
— (1985b). Recovering the dialects and sociology of Judeo-Greek in non-Hellenic Europe. *RSJL*, 1:227–40.
— (1985c). The role of Yiddish in the recovery of Slavic linguistic history. *WS* 30:1–23.
— (1986a). Exploring the distinctive features of *Wandersprachen*: the case of European Romani and Jewish languages. *MedLR* 2:7–45.
— (1986b). Review of E.Y.Kutscher, *A history of the Hebrew language* (Jerusalem-Leiden 1982). *Language* 62:687–90.
— (1986c). The reconstruction of pre-Ashkenazic Jewish settlements in the Slavic lands in the light of linguistic sources. *Polin* 1:3–18. Oxford.
— (1987a). De-Judaicization and incipient re-Judaicization in 18th-century Portuguese Ladino. *Iberoromania* n.F. 25:23–37.
— (1987b). *Explorations in Judeo-Slavic linguistics.* Leiden.
— (1987c). Interdialectal translation as a reflection of lexical obsolescence and dialect distance. (The West Yiddish Bible translation of 1679 in the *Biblia pentapla* of 1711.) *IJSL* 67:7–26.
— (1987d). Review of Golb and Pritsak. *MedLR* 3:136–9.
— (1988). *Three heirs to a Judeo-Latin legacy: Judeo-Ibero-Romance, Yiddish and Rotwelsch.* Wiesbaden.
— (1989). *Judeo-Romance linguistics. A bibliography (Latin, Italo-, Gallo-, Ibero- and Rhaeto-Romance except Castilian).* New York-London.
— (1990a). Review of R.Jütte, *Abbild und soziale Wirklichkeit des Bettler- und Gaunertums zu Beginn der Neuzeit* (Cologne 1988). *SYL*, 171–5.
— (1990b). Review of J.Matisoff, *Blessings, curses, hopes, and fears. Psycho-ostensive expressions in Yiddish* (Philadelphia 1979). *SYL*, 175–7.
— (1990c). Review of M.Šexter, *Lajtiš mame-lošn* (New York 1986). *SYL*, 178–80.
— (1990d). Review of B.Simon, *Jiddische Sprachgeschichte* (Frankfurt 1987). *SYL*, 181–2.

— (1990e). The role of Yiddish in reconstructing and reviving old colloquial Hebrew. *SYL*, 111–26.

— (1990f). *The schizoid nature of Modern Hebrew: a Slavic language in search of a Semitic past.* Wiesbaden.

— (1990g). Two comments on Yiddish contacts with Indo-Iranian languages. *SYL*, 127–41.

— (1991a). Jiddisch—die fünfzehnte slawische Sprache. *IGK*, 11:530–5. A summary of Wexler 1991b.

— (1991b). *Yiddish—the fifteenth Slavic language. A study of partial language shift from Judeo-Sorbian to German* (= focus article, *IJSL*, #91.) With reviews by B.Comrie, J.R.Dow and T.Stolz, P.Glasser, N.G.Jacobs, D.F.Marshall, G.Schaarschmidt, H.Schuster-Šewc, E.Stankiewicz and a rebuttal essay by P.Wexler. Berlin-New York.

— (1992a). *Diglossia et schizoglossia perpetua*—the fate of the Belorussian language. *Sociolinguistica* 6. *Nationalsprachenentstehung in Osteuropa*, eds. K.J.Mattheier and B.Panzer, 42–51. Tübingen.

— (1992b). *The Balkan substratum of Yiddish. (A reassessment of the unique Romance and Greek components.)* Wiesbaden.

— (1993a). Jewish historical linguistics: 1981–1991–2001. *Proceedings of the Tenth International Conference of Historical Linguistics*, ed. J.van Marle, 1–18. Amsterdam-Philadelphia.

— (1993b). Languages in contact: the case of Rotwelsch and the *two* Yiddishes. *In and out of the Ghetto: Jewish-Gentile relations in late and medieval and early modern Germany*, eds. R.P.Hsia and H.Lehmann. New York.

— (ms a). Judeo-Slavic frontispieces of late–18th–19th-century books and the authentication of "stereotyped" Judeo-Slavic speech. To appear in *WS*.

— (ms b). Review of M.Altbauer, *The five biblical scrolls in a sixteenth-century Jewish translation into Belorussian (Vilnius Codex 262)* (Jerusalem 1992). To appear in *SEER*.

— (ms c). The Sephardim: (Ḥimyarized, Arabized, Berberized, Hispanized) Jews or Judaized (Ḥimyarites, Arabs, Berbers, Europeans)?

WIEHL, I. (1974). *Untersuchungen zum Wortschatz der Freisinger Denkmäler. Christliche Terminologie.* Munich.

WIENECKE, E. (1940). *Untersuchungen zur Religion der Westslaven.* Leipzig.

WIESENBERG, E. (1955). Review of D.M.Dunlop, *The history of the Jewish Khazars.* Princeton 1954. *HJ* 17:74–6.

WIJSMAN, E.M. (1984). Techniques for estimating genetic admixture and applications to the problem of the origin of the Icelanders and the Ashkenazi Jews. *Human genetics* 67:441–8.

WILL, E. and C.ORRIEUX (1992). *"Proselytisme juif"? Histoire d'une erreur.* Paris.

WINKLER, [?]. (1930–1). Heiden. *HDA*, 3:columns 1634–53.

WISCHNITZER, R. (1947). Mutual influences between eastern and western Europe in synagogue architecture from the 12th to the 18th century. *YIVO annual of Jewish social science* 29:25–68.

WOLF, S.A. (1956). *Wörterbuch des Rotwelschen.* Mannheim.

— (1979). Barches. *NJ* 2:4–5.

WRIGHT, R. (1982). *Late Latin and early Romance in Spain and Carolingian France.* Liverpool.
WRÓBLEWSKI, T. (1961). Demony. *SSS*, 1:335–8.
WUTTKE, A. (1900). *Der deutsche Volksaberglaube der Gegenwart.* Berlin. 3rd edition.
WYPYCH, K. (1973). Jahresfeuer in Polen. *Zeitschrift für Ostforschung* 22:86–115.

YERUSHALMI, Y.H. (1982). *Zakhor. Jewish history and Jewish memory.* Seattle-London.

ZAJĄCZKOWSKI, A. (1961). *Karaims in Poland. History. Language. Folklore. Science.* Warsaw-The Hague-Paris.
ŻAK, J. (1977). Wikingowie. *SSS*, 6:458–64.
ZAMOYSKI, A. (1988). *The Polish way. A thousand-year history of the Poles and their culture.* New York-Toronto.
ZARĘBA, A. (1965). Z zapomnianych wyrazów polskich: *(z)golemy. Prace filologiczne* 18(4):199–206.
ZELENIN, J. (1927). *Russische (ostslawische) Volkskunde.* Berlin.
ŻELEXOVS'KYJ, JE. and S.NEDIL'S'KYJ (1882–6). *Malorusko-nimec'kyj slovar'* 1–2. Lvov; 1–3, Munich 1982.
ZIMMELS, H.J. (1926). *Beiträge zur Geschichte der Juden in Deutschland im 13. Jahrhundert.* Vienna.
— (1952). *Magicians, theologians and doctors. Studies in folk-medicine and folk-lore as reflected in the Rabbinical responsa (12th–19th centuries).* London.
— (1958). *Ashkenazim and Sephardim. Their relations, differences and problems as reflected in the Rabbinical responsa.* London.
ZINGERLE, I.V. (1855a). Nachträgliches zu Perahta. *ZDMS* 3:205–6.
— (1855b). Perahta in Tirol. *ZDMS* 3:203–5.
ZIRLIN, Y. (1986–8). The Schocken Italian Haggadah of c.1400 and its origins. *JA* 12–3:55–72.
ŽIVANOVIĆ, S. (1972–3). Prvi rezultati antropološkog proučavanja nekropole u Čelarevu. *Rad Vojvoñanskix muzeja* 21–2:153–65. Novi Sad.
— (1974–8). Apsolutno datovanje skeletnix ostataka iz nekropole u Čelarevu. *AR* 23–4:19–20.
— (1975). Skeletons of the Mongolian population from Čelarevo (Vojvodina). *Folia anatomica Iugoslavica* 4:1–47. Ljubljana.
ZOBEL, M. (1929). Aschkenasim. *EJ/B*, 3:columns 493–8.
ZUNZ, L. (1832). *Die gottesdienstlichen Vorträge der Juden, historisch entwickelt.* Berlin.
— (1837). *Namen der Juden.* Leipzig; revised in his *Gesammelte Schriften* 2:1–82. Berlin 1876; Hildesheim 1967.
— (1865). *Literaturgeschichte der synagogalen Poesie.* Berlin.
— (1919). *Die Ritus des synagogalen Gottesdienstes, geschichtlich entwickelt.* Berlin. 2nd edition.